Ira Thompson.

Ira Thompson.

A FIRST VIEW OF
ENGLISH AND AMERICAN
LITERATURE

SPRING SONG: "SOMER IS ICUMEN IN"
(Thirteenth Century.)

Middle-English and Latin texts, with music, from a manuscript in the British Museum

A FIRST VIEW OF ENGLISH AND AMERICAN LITERATURE

BY

WILLIAM VAUGHN MOODY
ROBERT MORSS LOVETT

AND

PERCY H. BOYNTON

ILLUSTRATED

NEW YORK
CHARLES SCRIBNER'S SONS
1913

PREFACE

THIS volume is based upon the authors' more advanced *History of English Literature.* The aim has been to preserve those features of the previous book which have most commended themselves to high-school and academy teachers, to remove everything which they have found too detailed or too difficult for their students, and to add whatever was suggested by their friendly criticism as likely to increase the value of the book in class-room practice. The literary comment has been simplified, partly by omission, partly by the substitution of explicit statement in the place of what was before only suggested. The number of authors treated has been much reduced, and the attention of the student centred exclusively on a few great representative figures. More space has been given to biography and descriptive sketches, especially in the later periods. Each main epoch has been prefaced by a full historical introduction, and summarized in the form of a review-commentary and questions, together with tabular views. Suggestions concerning the best available texts, and the best biographical and critical aids to study, are given at the close of each chapter. A number of portraits are added, taken in each case from an authentic source. For purposes of fuller reference, some authors not treated in the text are included in the tabular views.

The thanks of the authors are due to the many teachers, in all parts of the country, who have, either personally or by letter, generously aided them in their effort to give a

" first view " of English literature which should be at once a practical manual adapted to the routine work of the class-room, and an unfolding story whose intrinsic interest should claim the student's willing attention. The authors also desire to thank Scott, Foresman, and Company for permission to include in the text two or three paragraphs originally written for their school edition of Coleridge's "Ancient Mariner," and the Macmillan Company for permission to reproduce, from Garnett and Gosse's *English Literature : an Illustrated Record,* the manuscript facsimile which forms the frontispiece of the present volume.

CONTENTS

ENGLISH LITERATURE

Contents

AMERICAN LITERATURE

LIST OF ILLUSTRATIONS

List of Illustrations xi

ENGLISH LITERATURE

CHAPTER I

OLD-ENGLISH PERIOD: ANGLO-SAXON LITER-ATURE ON THE CONTINENT

I. THE EARLIEST HOME OF THE ENGLISH.

The Anglo-Saxon Tribes.—To find the beginnings of English literature we must go back to a time when the ancestors of the English people lived on the continent of Europe, and spoke a tongue which, though related in its roots to modern English, is unintelligible to us without special study. Anglo-Saxon, or Old English, belongs to the Low-German family of languages, of which Dutch is the best modern representative; and the men who spoke it lived, when history first discovers them, along the German ocean from the mouth of the Rhine to the peninsula of Jutland. They were divided into three principal branches: the Saxons, dwelling near the mouth of the Elbe; the Angles, inhabiting the southwest part of Denmark; and the Jutes, whose territory extended north of the Angles into modern Jutland.

Anglo-Saxon War and Seafaring.—How extensive these tribes were, and how far into the interior their territories reached, we do not know. That portion of them which concerns us, dwelt along the sea. Their early poetry gives glimpses of little tribal or family settlements, bounded on one side by wild moors and dense forests, where dwelt monstrous creatures of mist and darkness, and on the other by the stormy northern ocean, filled likewise with shapes of shadowy fear. As soon as spring had unlocked the harbors, their boats would push out in search of booty and adventure: sometimes to wreak blood-feud on a neighboring tribe, sometimes to plunder a monastery on the seaboard of Roman Gaul, or to coast along the white cliffs of England, their future home. This seafaring life, full of danger and change, was the fruitful source of early poetry. Whenever an Anglo-Saxon poet mentions the sea his lines kindle; it is the "swan-road," the "sealbath," the "path of the whales." The ship is the "sea-steed," the "wave-house of warriors"; its keel is "wreathed with foam like the neck of a swan." The darker aspects of the sea are given with the same fervor. It is characteristic of the grim nature of the Anglo-Saxon that he should fill with terror and gloom the element which he most loved to inhabit.

Anglo-Saxon Religion.—The poetry which has come down to us from this early period has been worked over by later hands and given a Christian coloring. But from other sources we know who were the primitive gods of the race: Tiu, a mysterious and dreadful deity of war; Woden, father of the later dynasty of gods, and patron of seers and travellers; Thor, the god of thunder; Frea, mother of the gods and giver of fruitfulness. These are commemorated in our names for the days of the week, Tuesday, Wednesday, Thursday, and Friday. The rites of Eostre, a mysterious goddess of the dawn, survive, though strangely altered, in the Christian festival of Easter. In studying the early poetry, we must put out of our minds, as far as we can, all those ideals of life and conduct which come from Christianity, and remember that we have to do with men whose gods were only magnified images of their own wild natures: men who delighted in bloodshed and in plunder, and were much given to deep drinking in the mead-hall; but who nevertheless were sensitive to blame and praise, were full of rude chivalry and dignity, and were alert to the poetry of life, to its mystery and its pathos.

Anglo-Saxon Love of Fame.—Our Anglo-Saxon ancestors had in an eminent degree also that passion which gives the first impulse to literature among a primitive people

—love of glory. When the first recorded hero of the race, Beowulf, has met his death, and his followers are recalling his noble nature, they say as their last word that "he was of all world-kings the most desirous of praise." It was not enough for such men as he that they should spend their lives in glorious adventures; they desired to see their names and their deeds spread among distant peoples and handed down to unborn generations. Hence the poet, who alone could insure this fame, was held in high esteem.

The Gleeman and the Scôp.—Two classes of singers were recognized, first the *gleeman* (*gleóman*), who did not create his own songs, but merely chanted what he had learned from others; and second the *scôp*, the poet proper, who took the crude material of history and legend which lay about him, and shaped it into song. Sometimes the scôp was permanently attached to the court of an aetheling, or lord, was granted land and treasure, and was raised by virtue of his poet-craft to the same position of honor which the other followers of the aetheling held by virtue of their prowess in battle. Sometimes he wandered from court to court, depending for a hospitable reception upon the curiosity of his host concerning the stories he had to chant. Two very ancient bits of poetry tell of the fortunes of the scôp. One of them deals with the wandering and the other with the stationary singer.

"Widsith."—The first is the fragment known as "Widsith," or "The Far-wanderer." The poem opens,—"Widsith spake, unlocked his word-hoard; he who many a tribe had met on earth, who had travelled through many a folk." Then follows a list of famous princes of the past, an enumeration of the various peoples and countries which the bard has visited, and praises of those princes who have entertained him generously. He declares that he has been "with Cæsar,* who had sway over the joyous cities," and even with the Israelites, the Egyptians, and the Indians. The poem ends with a general description of the wandering singer's life, touched at the close with the melancholy which occurs so often in Anglo-Saxon poetry;—"Thus roving, with song-deices wan-

---

* "Cæsar" was a general name for the Roman emperors; compare the German "Kaiser."

der the gleemen through mány lands. . . . Ever north or south they find one knowing in songs and liberal of gifts, who before his court will exalt his grandeur and show his earl-ship; until all departs, light and life together." This fragment has been held by some scholars to date, in part at least, from the fourth century. If so it is the oldest bit of verse in any modern language, and with it English literature "unlocks its word-hoard."

"Deor's Lament."—The second of these poems dealing with the fortunes of the scôp is probably not nearly so old. It is called "Deor's Lament," and again the poet himself speaks. His skill has been eclipsed by another singer, Heorrenda, and his lord has taken away from him his land-right and his place at court, in order to bestow them upon the successful rival. The poet comforts himself by recalling other misfortunes which men and women in past time have lived to overcome, and ends each rude strophe with the refrain, "That *he* endured, this also may I." The personal nature of the theme, the plaintive sadness of the tone, and above all the refrain, give the poem extraordinary interest. It has been called the first English lyric.

II. BEOWULF, THE ANGLO-SAXON EPIC

Original form of "Beowulf."—*Beowulf*, the most important work which remains to us from the pagan period of Anglo-Saxon poetry, in all likelihood existed at first in the form of short songs, which were sung among the Angles and Jutes, inhabiting what is now Denmark, and among the Goths in southern Sweden. Probably as early as the sixth century these lays had begun to be welded together, but just when the poem took its present form we do not know.* It contains something over three thousand lines. The story of the poem is as follows:—

The Story of Beowulf: Hrothgar and Grendel.—Hrothgar, king of the West-Danes, has built for himself near

---

* In all probability the development of "Beowulf" into a complete poem took place largely on English soil, and was completed by the end of the eighth century.

the sea a great hall, named Heorot, where he may sit with his thanes at the mead-drinking, and listen to the chanting of the gleemen. For a while he lives in happiness, and is known far and wide as a splendid and liberal prince. But one night there comes from the wild marchland, the haunt of all unearthly and malign creatures, a terrible monster named Grendel. Entering the mead-hall he slays thirty of the sleeping Danes, and carries their corpses away to his lair. The next night the same thing is repeated. No mortal power seems able to cope with the gigantic foe. In the winter nights Grendel couches in the splendid hall, defiling all its bright ornaments. For twelve winters this scourge afflicts the West-Danes, until Hrothgar's spirit is broken.

The Coming of Beowulf.—At last the story of Grendel's deeds crosses the sea to Gothland, where young Beowulf dwells at the court of his uncle, King Hygelac. Beowulf determines to go to Hrothgar's assistance. With fifteen companions he embarks. "Departed then over the wavy sea the foamy-necked floater, most like to a bird." At dawn of the second day the voyagers catch sight of the promontories of Hrothgar's land; and soon, from the top of the cliffs, they behold in the vale beneath them the famous hall, "rich and gold-variegated, most glorious of dwellings under the firmament." The young heroes in their "shining war byrnies," * and with their spears like a "grey ashwood above their heads," are ushered into the hall "where old Hrothgar sits amid his band of earls." Beowulf craves permission to cleanse Heorot of its pest, and Hrothgar consents that the Goths shall abide Grendel's coming, in the hall that night. Meanwhile, until darkness draws on, the thanes of Hrothgar and the followers of Beowulf sit drinking mead, "the bright sweet liquor," and listening to the songs of the gleeman. The feast draws to a close when Wealtheow, Hrothgar's queen, after solemnly handing the mead-cup to her lord and to Beowulf, and bidding them "be blithe at the beer-drinking," goes through the hall distributing gifts among the

* Corselets of mail.

thanes. The king, queen, and their followers then with-draw to another building for the night, while Beowulf and his men lie down, each with his armor hung on the nail above his head, to wait for the coming of Grendel. All fall asleep except Beowulf, who "awaits in angry mood the battle-meeting."

Beowulf's Fight with Grendel.—The coming of the monster is described with grewsome force. "Then came from the moors, under the misty hills, Grendel stalking. Straightway he rushed on the door, fast with fire-hardened bands. On the variegated floor the fiend trod; he went wroth of mood, from his eyes stood a horrid light like flame." He seizes one of the warriors, bites his "bone-casings," drinks the blood from his veins, and greedily devours him even to the hands and feet. Next he makes for Beowulf, but the hero seizes the fiend with such a mighty hand-grip that he is terror-stricken and turns to flee. Beowulf keeps his hold, and a fearful struggle begins. At last the monster wrenches his own arm from its socket and flees to his lair to die.

In the morning there is great rejoicing. The king, and the queen, with a company of maidens, come through the meadows to gaze in wonder on the huge arm and claw nailed beneath the gold roof of the hall. When the evening feast begins, Beowulf sits between the two sons of the king, and receives the precious gifts,—jewels, rings, and a golden necklace,—which the queen presents to him. But at nightfall, when the warriors have again lain down to sleep in the hall, Grendel's mother comes to take vengeance for her son. She seizes one of Hrothgar's nobles, Aeschere, and bears him away to her watery den.

Beowulf's Fight beneath the Sea.—Beowulf vows to seek the new foe at the bottom of her fen-pool, and there grapple with her. With Hrothgar and a band of followers he goes along the cliffs and windy promontories which bound the moor on the seaward side, until he comes to Grendel's lair. It is a sea-pool, shut in by precipitous rocks, and overhung by the shaggy trunks and aged boughs of a "joyless wood." Trembling passers-by have seen fire fleeting on the waves at night, and the hart wearied by the hounds will lie down and die on these banks rather than plunge into the unholy waters. The pool is so deep that it is a day's space before Beowulf reaches the bottom. Snakes and beasts of the shining deep make war on him as he descends. At last he finds himself in a submarine cave where the "mere-wife" is lurking, and a ghastly struggle begins. Once the giantess throws Beowulf to the ground, and sitting astride his body draws out her broad short knife to despatch him. But with a superhuman effort he struggles up again, throws away his broken sword and seizes from a heap of arms a magic blade, forged by giants of old time. With it he hews off the head of Grendel's mother, and then that of Grendel, whose dead body he finds lying in the cave. So poisonous is the blood of Grendel that it melts the metal of the blade, leaving only the curved hilt in Beowulf's hand. When he reappears with his trophies at the surface of the water, all have given him up for dead. Great is the jubilation when the hero returns to the mead-hall with his thanes, and throws upon the floor the two gigantic heads, which four men apiece can hardly carry.

Beowulf and the Fire-Dragon.—The second great episode of the poem is Beowulf's fight with the Dragon of the Gold-hoard. Beowulf has been reigning as king for fifty years, and is now an old man, when calamity comes upon him and his people in the shape of a monster of the serpent-kind, which flies by night enveloped in fire; and which, in revenge for the theft of a gold cup from its precious hoard, burns the king's hall. Old as he is, Beowulf fights the dragon single-handed. He slays the monster in its lair, but himself receives his mortal hurt.

The Death of Beowulf.—The death of the old king is picturesque and touching. He bids his thane bring out from the dragon's den "the gold-treasure, the jewels, the curious gems," in order that death may be softer to him, seeing the wealth he has gained for his people. Wiglaf, entering the cave of the "old twilight-flier," sees "dishes standing, vessels of men of yore, footless, their ornaments fallen away; there was many a helm old and rusty

and many armlets cunningly fastened," and over the
hoard droops a magic banner, "all golden, locked by arts
of song," from which a light is shed over the treasure.
Beowulf gazes with dying eyes upon the precious things;
then he asks that his thanes build for him a funeral bar-
row on a promontory of the sea, which the sailors, as
they "drive their foaming barks from afar over the misty
floods, may see and name Beowulf's Mount."

III. OTHER EARLY POETRY: SUMMARY

Besides Beowulf, and the short poems "Widsith" and
"Deor's Lament," mentioned above, two other pieces remain to us from the pagan period of Anglo-Saxon poetry.*
They are both fragments. One, the "Fight at Finnsburg,"
full of savage vigor, throws light upon an obscure story
referred to in *Beowulf;* the other, "Waldhere," is connected with the old German cycle of poems which were
brought together many centuries later as the *Niebelungen
Lied.*

When we look at this early literature as a whole we cannot fail to be struck by its grimness. It has, to be sure,
genial moments, moments even of tenderness, but for the
most part the darker aspect of nature,—storm and hail
and mist, the wintry terror of the sea,—are what the
poet loves to dwell upon; and over the fierce martial life
which he depicts there hangs the shadow of Wyrd, or Fate,
huge and inescapable. The great business of life is war;
from it proceeds all honor and dignity. To be faithful
and liberal to his friends and deadly to his foes, that is
the whole duty of a man. But a time was at hand when
these fierce worshippers of Thor and Woden were to hear
a new gospel. Sweeping southwestward in their viking
ships, they were to conquer a new home for themselves in
Britain; and there to be themselves conquered, not by arms,
but by bands of eager monks who came from the seat of

---

* It must be remembered that "Beowulf" is tinged with Christian coloring,
given to it, no doubt, by the English monks who transcribed the manuscript. Still, in general tone it is pagan, and in origin continental.

the Church in Rome and from Christianized Ireland, preaching peace and good-will.

REVIEW OUTLINE.—This chapter deals with the Anglo-Saxon people in their early home on the continent, before they had come in contact with Christianity. Where was this home? Into what tribes were they divided? Which one of these tribes furnished the names " England " and " English " ? (The earliest form of these words was " Angleland " and "Anglisc.") Sum up for yourself their surroundings, pursuits, and beliefs. In what esteem was the poet held among them? Why? Pick out as many characteristics as possible of their early life, from the account given of Beowulf. What virtues and personal qualities make Beowulf, the young gothic Prince, the typical hero of our race in its early state? Grendel is called " God's denier "; was he so thought of by the original makers of the poem? Explain how such Christian references happen to occur in this pagan epic. When, where, and by whom was the poem, in all probability, put in its present form, and given a Christian coloring? (The full answer must be sought in Chapter II.)

For reading in this period, see close of Chapter II.

Here

CHAPTER II

OLD ENGLISH PERIOD: ANGLO-SAXON LITERATURE IN ENGLAND

I. THE COMING OF THE ANGLO-SAXONS TO ENGLAND

Prehistoric England: the Britons.—The very earliest inhabitants of Britain, the cavemen, and men of the stone age, gave way before the beginning of history to a Celtic people, a branch of the same race which inhabited France and Spain. The Celts of Great Britain were known to the Greeks as early as 300 B.C., when Pytheas, a Greek navigator and geographer, visited them; and a Greek writer of the same date mentions their island, calling it Albion, "the white land," from its gleaming chalk cliffs. The Celts who occupied Ireland and Scotland are known as Gaels; those who occupied England, as Cymri or Britons. They were farmers and herders of cattle, and lived in wattled huts fortified with ditches and mounds. Their religion was in the main a worship of the heavenly bodies; their priests, known as Druids, were astronomers and bards. The circle of huge stones at Stonehenge probably marks the site of their chief temple. In character the Britons were impetuous, imaginative, full of curiosity, and quick to learn. Their early literature, which gathers about the names of legendary poets such as Merlin and Taliesin, shows a delicate fancy, a kind of wild grace and love of beauty for its own sake, strikingly in contrast with the stern poetry of the Anglo-Saxons.

The Roman Occupation of Britain.—In the year 55 B.C. Julius Cæsar crossed the straits from Gaul, and began the conquest of Britain. This was continued a hundred years later by the Emperor Claudius, who planted at Colchester the first Roman colony. Agricola became governor in 78 A.D., and built a great wall and line of forts to keep off the

Gaels of Scotland.   The Roman capital was fixed at York, which, with its walls and towers, temples and public buildings, became "another Rome."   Here, for three hundred years, the Victorious Legion, the flower of the Roman Imperial army, was stationed; and here Constantine was proclaimed ruler of the whole Roman world.

When the Roman legions crossed from Gaul there was a short space of fierce resistance.   Many Britons fled to the fastnesses of Wales and Scotland, and there continued, even to our own day, their Celtic traditions.   But the greater part seem soon to have submitted to the Romans, as if by a kind of fascination, even giving up their language to learn that of their conquerors.   The Romans carried wherever they went their splendid civilization, and by the end of the fourth century England was dotted with towns and villas where, amid pillared porticoes, mosaic pavements, marble baths, forums and hippodromes, a Roman emperor could find himself at home.

Recall of the Roman Legions : the Anglo-Saxon Invasion. —This was the state of England when there began that remarkable series of movements on the part of the wild Germanic tribes, which we know as the "migrations."   About the end of the fourth century, urged by a common impulse, tribe after tribe swept southward; some by sea, to harry the coasts of Gaul and Britain, some over the Alps and the Pyrenees, to batter at the gates of Rome, to plunder the rich islands of the Mediterranean, and to found a kingdom in Africa. "Whelps from the lair of the barbaric lioness" (as an ancient chronicler calls them), the fierce Teutonic warriors, armed with "rough-handled spears and swords of bronze," swept down upon the countries of Southern Europe, carrying terror and death everywhere.   In the year 410 the Roman legions were recalled from Britain to guard the imperial city, and the Celtic inhabitants, weakened by three centuries of civilized life, were left to struggle unaided against the pirate bands of Jutes, Saxons, and Angles, which appeared every spring in increasing numbers upon their coast.   The Celts did not yield to these savage invaders as readily as they had done to the polished Romans.   From the middle of the fifth century, when the

first band of Jutes landed on the Isle of Thanet, to the time
when the invaders had subjugated the island and set up the
Anglo-Saxon kingdoms, a hundred and fifty years of warfare elapsed, during which all the monuments which Rome
had left were ruined if not obliterated. Many Celts fled,
as in the times of the Roman invasion, into Wales and Scotland; many were killed; but a great number were undoubtedly absorbed by the invading race. During these years of
struggle there began to grow up, about the person of an obscure Celtic leader, that cycle of stories which was to prove
so fruitful of poetry both in France and England,—the
legends of Arthur, founder of the Round Table, and de-
fender of the western Britons against the weakening power
of Rome and the growing fury of the barbarians.

Earliest Celtic and Roman Traces in the Language.—
Now, also, began the fusion of other languages with the
Anglo-Saxon, a fusion destined gradually to transform the
primitive speech of our Teutonic ancestors into modern
English. The earliest Celtic words absorbed by the Saxon
speech were such as have been preserved in geographical
names, such as Oxford and Stratford-on-Avon (from Celtic
Avon, and *Ox* or *Esk*, meaning *water*), Holcomb (from *comb*,
meaning *valley*), Ben Nevis (from *ben* or *pen*, meaning *mountain*.) The words *down* and *slough*, describing characteristic
features of the island landscape, belong also to these first
borrowings. We must remember that the Celtic language,
in the remoter parts of the country, was preserved after the
Teutons had established themselves, and that wherever the
two races met, along the disputed borderland, the process of
fusion went on. The amount contributed by the Celts to
our language remained, however, surprisingly small.

Along with the first Celtic borrowings, our speech gathered
up a few words which had been left behind by the Roman
occupation. They are words that suggest an imperial military civilization: *street* (which appears in the name of the old
Roman road, Watling Street, running from Dover to Chester, and is derived from *strata via*, a paved way); *wall, fosse,*
and *port* (from Latin *vallum, fossa*, and *portus*); the endings for place names, *coln*, as in Lincoln (Latin *colonia*,

colony), and *chester* or *caster*, as in Winchester and Doncaster (Latin *castra*, camp). These early borrowings, from Celtic and Latin, were in themselves slight; but they are important as the beginnings of a process by which, gathering successively from many sources, English became the richest of modern languages.

II. THE LITERATURE OF NORTHUMBRIA

The Christianizing of England.—The partial union of the Celtic and the Saxon races which took place in England after the Saxon conquest, was to have a great influence upon English character and English literature. But the greatest immediate influence exerted upon the victorious Saxon tribes was that of the Christian religion, with which they now for the first time came into full contact. The literature of this period shows very little trace of the bright Celtic imagination, but it is nearly all deeply colored by Christianity.

Christianity had gained some obscure foothold in England before the Anglo-Saxon invasion. During the Roman occupation a church or two had been built, and the emperor Diocletian had extended his persecution of the followers of Christ even to this far-off colony. But it was not until after the Saxon conquest that the new religion took a firm hold. The Christian teaching came into England in two different streams, one from Rome, one from Ireland, which country had been won from heathenism several centuries before. The first stream began late in the sixth century, with the coming of Augustine, who converted to the new faith Ethelbert, king of Kent, and his whole people. Little by little, after the advent of this great missionary among the Saxons in the south of England, the new creed drove out the old, winning its way by the authority with which it spoke of man's existence beyond the grave.

This stream of religious influence which came from Rome centred chiefly in south and central England, in the kingdom of Wessex. It produced some schools of learning, but almost no literature. It is to the north and east, to the kingdom of Northumbria, which felt the influence of the Irish monks, that we must look for the first blossomings of Christian poetry in England.

Bede and Caedmon.—Many monasteries sprang up in Northumbria in the train of the Celtic missionaries from Ireland.　Two are famous because of their connection with literature—Jarrow and Whitby.　At Jarrow lived and died Baeda, known as the "Venerable Bede," a gentle, laborious scholar in whom all the learning of Northumbria was summed up.　He translated the gospel of St. John into English, but his version has unfortunately been lost.　He wrote many books, nearly all of them in Latin, the most notable being the *Ecclesiastical History of the English People* (Historia Ecclesiastica Gentis Anglorum).　It is from a passage in this book that we know the story of Caedmon, the first poet of Christian England.　Bede tells us that when the inmates of the monastery were gathered together at the evening feast, and the harp was passed round for each to sing in turn, Caedmon, the cowherd, would rise and depart, for he was an unlettered man and knew nothing of the gleeman's art.　So it was for many years, until he was no longer young.　One night, when he had thus left the cheerful company and gone to the stables to tend the cattle, he fell asleep and had a wonderful dream.　The shining figure of the Lord appeared before him, saying, "Caedmon, sing to me."　Caedmon answered, "Behold, I know not how to sing, and therefore I left the feast to-night."　"Still, sing now to me," the Lord said.　"What then shall I sing?" asked Caedmon.　"Sing the beginning of created things," was the answer.　Then in his dream Caedmon framed some verses of the Creation, which in the morning he wrote down, adding others to them. News of the wonderful gift which had been bestowed upon the unschooled man was carried to Hild, the abbess of the foundation, and she commanded portions of the Scripture to be read to him, that he might paraphrase them into verse. So it was done; and from this time on Caedmon's life was given to his heaven-appointed task of turning the Old Testament narrative into song.

Caedmon's Paraphrases.—The poems which have come down to us under Caedmon's name consist of paraphrases

of Genesis, of Exodus, and a part of Daniel. An interesting
fragment called *Judith* is sometimes included in the work of
the "school of Caedmon." In places, especially in dealing
with a warlike episode, the poet expands his matter freely,
adorning it with his own fancy. In *Exodus*, for instance,
all the interest is centred on the overwhelming of Pharaoh's
host in the Red Sea. The Egyptian and the Israelitish
armies are described with a heathen scôp's delight in war,
and the disaster which overtakes the Egyptian hosts is sung
with savage force and zest. In *Judith* the pagan delight in
battle and in blood-revenge is even more marked. First,
king Holofernes is shown, like a rude viking, boisterous and
wassailing in his mead-hall. When Judith comes to him in
his drunken sleep and hews off his head with a sword, the
poet cannot restrain his exultation; and the flight of the
army of Holofernes before the men of Israel is described
with grewsome vividness.

Cynewulf.—If we know little of Caedmon's life, we know
still less of Cynewulf, the poet who succeeded him, and who
was probably the greatest of the Anglo-Saxon poets, if we
except the unknown bard who gave *Beowulf* its present
form. Out of very insubstantial materials a picturesque
story has been made for him. He is said to have been in his
youth a wandering singer, leading a wild life by sea and
shore, as he plied his gleeman's craft, now in the halls of
lords, now in the huts of shepherds and on the village green,
now on the deck of Northumbrian coasting-ships. In the
midst of this free existence he suddenly underwent some
deep religious experience, which, together with the public
disasters then overtaking Northumbria, completely changed
the temper of his mind. He gave up the half-pagan nature-
poetry which up to this time he had written, and turned
to write religious poems. We have, signed with his name
in strange characters called runes, two lives of saints, *St.
Juliana* and *Elene*, and the *Christ*, an epic dealing with the
Saviour's incarnation and ascension, and with the Day of
Judgment. Other poems have been ascribed to him with
varying degrees of probability: *Andreas*, a very lively and
näive story of a saint's martyrdom and final triumph over

his enemies; the *Phœnix*, a richly colored description of the mythic bird and its dwelling-place, with a religious interpretation; and finally a number of *Riddles*, very curious compositions, some of which are full of fine imagination and fresh observation of nature.

The " Riddles " of Cynewulf.—These last are nothing more nor less than conundrums, in which some object or phenomenon is described suggestively, and the reader is left to guess what is meant. The new moon is a young viking, sailing through the skies in his pirate ship, laden with spoils of battle, to build a burg for himself in highest heaven; but the sun, a greater warrior, drives him away and possesses his land, until the night conquers the sun in turn. The iceberg shouts and laughs as it plunges through the wintry sea, eager to crush the fleet of hostile ships. The sword in its scabbard is a mailed fighter, who goes exultingly into the battle-play, and then is sad because women upbraid him for the slaughter he has done. The swan and the beaver are described with an insight and sympathy which remind us, in a far-off way, of modern nature-poetry. It is pleasant, even if not quite scientific, to think of the *Riddles* as the youthful work of Cynewulf, since his is the only poet's name that has survived from those obscure and troubled times.

The " Phœnix."—The *Phœnix* derives a special interest from the fact that it is the only Anglo-Saxon poem of any length which shows a delight in the soft and radiant moods of Nature, as opposed to her fierce and grim aspects. In the land where the Phœnix dwells "the groves are all behung with blossoms, the boughs upon the trees are ever laden, the fruit is aye renewed through all eternity." The music of the wonderful bird, as it goes aloft "to meet that gladsome gem, God's candle," is "sweeter and more beauteous than any craft of song." When a thousand years of its life are done, it flies far away to a lonely Syrian wood, and builds its own funeral pyre of fragrant herbs, which the sun kindles. Out of the ball of ashes a new Phœnix is born, and flies back to its home in the enchanted land of summer. At the end, the whole poem is made into a Christian allegory of the death and resurrection of Christ, and of his ascent to heaven amid the ministering company of saints. Scholars have pointed out that the description of the bird's dwelling-place is influenced by the old Celtic fancy of the Land of Eternal Youth; and certainly it is not difficult to see, in the bright colors and happy fancy of the poem, the working of the Celtic imagination, as well as the transforming touch of hope which had been brought into men's lives by Christianity.

Anglo-Saxon Love Poems and Elegies.—Besides the poetry attributed to Caedmon and his school, and to Cynewulf and his school, there exist a few short poems of the greatest interest. One of these, called "The Wife's Lament," gives us a glimpse of one of the harsh customs of our ancestors. A wife, accused of faithlessness, has been banished from her native village, and compelled to live alone in the forest; from her place of exile she pours out a moan to the husband who has been estranged from her by false slanderers. "The Lover's Message" is a kind of companion piece to this. The speaker in the little poem is the tablet of wood upon which an absent lover has carved a message to send to his beloved. It tells her that he has now a home for her in the south, and bids her, as soon as she hears the cuckoo chanting of sorrow in the copsewood, to take sail over the ocean pathway to her lord, who waits and longs for her. With these two little pieces begins the love-poetry of England.

" The Wanderer."—The longest and most beautiful of all the Anglo-Saxon elegies or poems of sentiment is "The Wanderer." It is the complaint of one who must "traverse the watery ways, stir with his hands the rime-cold sea, and tread the paths of exile," while he muses upon the joys and glories of a life that has passed away forever. "Often," he says, "it seems to him in fancy as though he clasps and kisses his great lord, and on his knees lays hand and head, even as erewhile"; but he soon wakes friendless, and sees before him only "the fallow ways, sea-birds bathing and spreading their wings, falling hoar-frost and snow mingled with hail." At the close the Wanderer breaks out into a song of lamentation over the departed glories of a better time: "Where is gone the horse? Where is gone the hero? Where is gone the giver of treasure? Where are gone the seats of the feast? Where are the joys of the hall? Ah, thou bright cup! Ah, thou mailed warrior! Ah, the prince's pride! how has the time passed away, as if it had not been!" There is a wistful tenderness and a lyric grace in this poem which suggests once more the Celtic leaven at work in the ruder Anglo-Saxon genius. It suggests, too, a state of society fallen into ruin, a time of decadence and disaster. Probably, before it was written, such a time had come for England, and especially for Northumbria.

III. THE STRUGGLE WITH THE DANES: LITERATURE OF WESSEX

The Danes Destroy Northumbria.—While the Anglo-Saxons had been settling down in England to a life of agriculture, their kinsmen who remained on the Continent had continued to lead their wild freebooting life of the sea. Toward the end of the eighth century bands of Danes began to harass the English coasts. Northumbria bore the main force of their attacks. The very monastery of Jarrow, in which Baeda had written his Ecclesiastical History, was plundered, and its inhabitants put to the sword. The monastery of Whitby, where Caedmon had had his vision, was only temporarily saved by the fierce resistance of the monks. By the middle of the ninth century the Danes had made themselves masters of Northumbria. They were such men as the Angles, Jutes, and Saxons had been three hundred years before— worshippers of the old gods, ruthless uprooters of a religion, literature, and society which they did not understand.

Rise of Wessex: King Alfred.—In Wessex, however, a kingdom had arisen with strength enough to offer a firm resistance to the Danes. King Egbert, of Wessex, after compelling the tribes of Central Britain to acknowledge his headship, had taken, in 828, the proud title of "King of the English," for by this time the Angles had given their name to all divisions of the Anglo-Saxon people in Britain. When the Danes, victorious in Northumbria, began to press southwestward into the kingdom of Wessex, Alfred the Great held the throne. His heroism turned back the tide of barbarian invasion. By the treaty of Wedmore, which he forced upon them in 878, the Danes pledged themselves to remain north of Watling Street, the old Roman road running from Dover to Chester. From this time until the Norman conquest, two centuries later, the only literature which remains to us was produced in Wessex. It is almost entirely a literature of prose. The best of it was the work of King Alfred himself, or produced under his immediate encouragement.

What King Alfred Did for Literature.—As a child King Alfred had seen Rome, and had lived for a time at the great court of Charles the Bald in France; and the spectacle of these older and richer civilizations had filled him with a desire to give to his rude subjects something of the heritage of the past. When, after a desperate struggle, he had won peace from the Danes, he called about him learned monks from the sheltered monasteries of Ireland and Wales, and made welcome at his court all strangers who could bring him a manuscript or sing to him an old song. It was probably during his reign that the poems of Caedmon and Cynewulf, as well as the older pagan poems, were brought southward out of Northumbria and put in the West-Saxon form in which we now have them. He spurred on his priests and bishops to write. He himself learned a little Latin, in order that he might translate certain books, which he deemed would be most useful and interesting to Englishmen, into the West-Saxon tongue; putting down the sense, he says, "sometimes word for word, sometimes meaning for meaning, as I had learned it from Plegmund, my archbishop, and Asser, my bishop, and Grimbald, my mass-priest, and John, my mass-priest." The most important of these pious labors was a rendering of Baeda's Ecclesiastical History, which gave a native English dress to the first great piece of historical writing which had been done in England. Alfred also caused the dry entries of the deaths of kings and the installations of bishops, which the monks were in the habit of making on the Easter rolls, to be expanded into a clear and picturesque narrative, the greatest space, of course, being taken up with the events of his own reign. This, known as the Anglo-Saxon

Chronicle, is the most venerable monument of Old English prose.

Decadence of Anglo-Saxon Literature.—Despite all his efforts, King Alfred did not succeed in creating a vital native literature in Wessex. The language was changing, and the literary spirit of the people was almost dead. The sermons or *Homilies* of the great and devoted Aelfric, however, here and there rise to the rank of literature, by reason of the näive picturesqueness of some religious legend which they treat, or by the fervor of their piety. Aelfric also translated a portion of the Scriptures, adding to the beginning which Bede had made, and carrying one step further the long process by which the great English Bible was brought into being. The Anglo-Saxon Chronicle, also, which continued to grow in the monasteries of Peterborough, Winchester, and Ely, here and there breaks out into stirring verse. One of these poetic episodes, known as the "Battle of Brunanburh," is entered under the year 937. Another, the "Death of Byrhtnoth," also called the "Battle of Maldon," bears date 991; it is the swan-song of Anglo-Saxon poetry.

Latin and Danish Word-Borrowings.—During the period we have just traversed the English tongue was enriched from two sources, Latin and Danish. The Latin words which came in during the period of Christianization nearly all refer to the church and its functions. They are such words as church itself (originally a Greek word, kyriakon), minster (monasterium), bishop (episcopus), monk (monachus), priest (presbyter), martyr (originally a Greek word, meaning "witness"), devil (diabolus), and a host of others. The Danish contribution was confined chiefly to such geographical endings as -by and -thorp, meaning "town," preserved in names such as Somersby and Althorp.

End of the Old English Period.—So far as literature was concerned, England at the end of the tenth century was in need of new blood. The Danes had brought no literature with them, and the Anglo-Saxon genius was exhausted. In fact, in spite of all its rugged grandeur and fine persistence, this genius was at its best lacking in many elements necessary to make a great national life. Anglo-Saxon poetry, looked at in the large, betrays a narrowness of theme, and monotony of tone, out of which a great literature could have evolved, if at all, only slowly and with difficulty. Some new graft was needed, to give elasticity, gayety, and range. This need was met when, in 1066, William the Conqueror landed at Hastings with his army of Norman-French knights, and marched to give battle to the forces of Harold, the last of the Saxon kings.

REVIEW OUTLINE.—Who were the earliest known inhabitants of Britain during historic times? How long a period elapsed between the mention of them in Greek history and the time when Cæsar made them known to the Roman world? Sum up the principal facts of the Roman occupation of Britain. Why and when were the Roman forces withdrawn? When did the Anglo-Saxon sea-robbers begin to conquer the Britons, thus left defenceless by Rome, and weakened by her civilization? How long did the struggle endure? How is King Arthur's name connected with it? Bring together as many particulars as you can from this chapter concerning the character of the Celts, and contrast it with what you know of the Anglo-Saxon character. Note the traces which the Celts and the Roman conquerors left in the new language which the Saxon invaders planted in England.

Give some account of the Christianizing of England. Who was Bede? Who was the first Christian poet? Tell his story, and indicate some traces of the pagan spirit in him. What great English poet, centuries later, treated Caedmon's theme, "the beginning of created things"? From what source do we learn the name of the greatest poet of this time? Relate the traditions concerning his life. Which of the writings attributed to him are entirely Christian and which pagan in feeling? What qualities in the "Phœnix" and the "Wanderer" suggest the influence of the Celtic spirit? Of what large group of English poems is the latter a forerunner? Can you name three later English poems that belong to this class?

All the literature, both prose and poetry, which we consider in the two first sections of this chapter, was produced in Northumbria. When, and by what new invaders, was the literary supremacy of Northumbria destroyed? Why did Wessex now become the centre of learning and of literary activity? What kind of literature was chiefly produced in Wessex? Tell what you can of the Treaty of Wedmore. What were the influences which gave King Alfred his interest in literature, and what means did he take to promote literature among his people? What was the Anglo-Saxon Chronicle? What significance has it had for later generations? Note carefully that while the original literature produced in Wessex was of far less interest than that produced in Northumbria, it is to Wessex monks and scribes that we owe the preservation not only of the Northumbrian poetry but of the earlier poetry produced on the Continent, including " Beowulf." Who continued the great work of translating the Bible, begun by Bede in his lost version of the Gospel of St. John? Give date and title of the poem which is called the " swan-song " of Old English poetry. (Note the meaning of the word " swan-song.") What kinds of words came into our language at this period from Latin and Greek sources? Give examples. Why is it probable that a large literary future was not open to the Anglo-Saxon people without the infusion of some new element? What was this element to be?

READING GUIDE.—Students cannot be expected to do much reading in the literature of the Old English period. The teacher should read to the class or have the student read a portion of " Beowulf " in translation. A good translation for the purpose is that by C. G. Child (Houghton, Mifflin), Number 159 in the Riverside Literature series; or that by J. Earle, " The Deeds of Beowulf " (Clarendon Press). " The Battle of Brunanburh," translated by Tennyson, may also be read with profit. All the minor poems mentioned in the text are translated, wholly or partly, in Stopford Brooke's Early English Literature ; the reading aloud of a few of these, as for instance " The Wanderer " and " The Lover's Message," will greatly vivify the class's understanding of the spirit of the early literature. Liberal extracts from " Beowulf " are also given in Brooke, so that a separate edition of that poem may, if desired, be dispensed with. Good examples of early English poetry may also be found in Longfellow's " Poets and Poetry of Europe."

To give the class some notion of the old Celtic literature, and some conception of what manner of men they were whom the Anglo-Saxons found in England when they first invaded the island, the student may profitably read " The Voyage of Maeldune," by Tennyson, which is founded on an old Celtic romance. Further illustrations of the Celtic spirit may be found in " The Boy's Mabinogion," by Sidney Lanier (Scribner), and in the first volume of Henry Morley's English Writers, where many beautiful Celtic pieces are summarized. The reading of Morley's summary of "The Tale of the Cattle Spoil of Chuailgne," and comparison with the summary of "Beowulf" given in the text, may be made of great interest; The Cattle Spoil is a typical product of an agricultural race in its heroic and semi-mythic period, as Beowulf is a typical product of a seafaring race at a similar stage.

To illustrate the Christian literature of the Old English period, the quotations from "The Phœnix" in Brooke's Early English Literature, or from "Judith," translated in Morley's English Writers, Vol. I, pp. 180–188, may be read to the class.

TABULAR VIEW

OLD ENGLISH PERIOD: FROM THE EARLIEST TIMES TO THE NORMAN CONQUEST

HISTORICAL EVENTS	LITERATURE

HISTORICAL EVENTS

1. PERIOD OF ROMAN OCCUPATION OF BRITAIN.

Cæsar's first invasion, 55 B.C. Permanent occupation by Romans under Claudius, 43 A.D. Roman legions recalled from Britain to defend Rome against the barbarians, 410. End of Roman occupation.

2. PERIOD OF ANGLO-SAXON INVASIONS.

The Jutes, invited by the Britons to aid them against their kindred Gaelic tribes in Scotland and Ireland, seize Kent, 449. Saxons conquer Sussex, 477; Wessex, Essex, and Middlesex settled by Saxon bands before 500. King Arthur (according to tradition) temporarily checks the Saxons, 520. Angles invade Northumbria, about 547.

3. THE CHRISTIANIZING OF ENGLAND.

Pope Gregory sends St. Augustine to England, 597. Augustine converts Ethelbert, King of Kent, and becomes the first bishop of Canterbury. Irish missionaries introduce Christianity into Northumbria, 635. Foundation of Whitby, 657 (?).

4. DANISH INVASIONS: RISE OF WESSEX.

Danes begin to raid Northumbria, 789. Political supremacy passes to Wessex. Egbert, King of Wessex, styles himself King of the English, 828. Alfred the Great, king of Wessex, 871–901. Peace of Wedmore, 878, between King Alfred and the Danes.

5. END OF ANGLO-SAXON PERIOD.

Invasions of Northmen, 980. Cnut the Dane, king, 1017–1035. Saxon line restored in Edward the Confessor, 1042. William of Normandy invades England and defeats the Saxon king Harold, 1066.

LITERATURE

1. PAGAN LITERATURE.

Widsith, Deor's Lament, Beowulf, The Fight at Finnsburg, and Waldhere, of unknown date, probably produced on the Continent, from the fourth or fifth century on.

2. CHRISTIAN LITERATURE.

(a) *Literature of Northumbria* (670 to about 825). Caedmon writes his paraphrase of Genesis, Exodus, and Daniel, at Whitby, 670–680. Bede's Ecclesiastical History of England (in Latin), 731; his English version of St. John's Gospel, 735. Cynewulf, born about 720, writes St. Juliana, Elene, Christ, and perhaps also the Riddles. Northumbrian culture destroyed by the Danes, first quarter of 9th century (800–825).

(b) *Literature of Wessex* (880–1066). Alfred translates into English Bede's Ecclesiastical History, Gregory's Pastoral Care, and Boethius's Consolations of Philosophy, about 880. He causes other works to be translated; the old pagan poetry, Beowulf, etc., and much of the Northumbrian poetry, put into West-Saxon dialect, and preserved only in this form. Aelfric's Homilies and parts of Old Testament, 990–999. Anglo-Saxon Chronicle, revised and elaborated by order of Alfred, continues until 1154. Poetic entries in Chronicle include the Battle of Brunanburh, 937, and the Battle of Maldon, 991.

CHAPTER III

MIDDLE-ENGLISH PERIOD: FROM THE NORMAN CONQUEST TO CHAUCER

I. THE COMING OF THE NORMANS TO ENGLAND: UNION OF THE TWO PEOPLES

Character of the Norman People.—The Normans, or Northmen, were an extraordinary people. A century and a half before their invasion of England, they had appeared off the coast of France; and under their leader, Hrolf the Ganger (the "Walker"), they had pushed up the Seine in their black boats, wasting and burning to the very gates of Paris. The French won peace by giving over to them broad and rich lands in the northwest, known henceforth as Normandy. The Normans were a branch of the same Teutonic race which had sent out the Jutes, Saxons, and Angles to conquer England. But, unlike the other northern peoples, they showed a marvellous power of assimilating the civilization which Rome had spread among the Celts of Western Europe. The Normans married with the French women, adopted French manners and the French tongue. In a little over a century they had grown from a barbarous horde of sea-robbers into the most polished and brilliant people of Europe, whose power was felt in the Mediterranean and the far East. They united in a singular manner impetuous daring and cool practical sense. Without losing anything of their northern bravery in war, they managed to gather up all the southern suppleness and wit, all the southern love of splendor and art. When William advanced to meet King Harold at Senlac, a court minstrel, Taillefer, rode before the invading army, tossing up his sword and catching it like a juggler, while he chanted the *Song of Roland*—the French epic. Taillefer is a symbol of the Norman spirit, of its dash, its buoyancy, its brilliancy. The Normans brought with them to England not only the terror of the sword and the strong hand of conquest, but also the vitalizing breath of song, the fresh and youthful spirit of romance.

First Effects of the Norman Invasion.—The sternness and energy with which King William and his nobles set about planting their own civilization in the island, brought with it much oppression and hardship. The land was taken from its Saxon owners and distributed among Norman nobles. Over the length and breadth of England rose those strong castles whose gray and massive walls still frown over the pleasant English landscape. The strong and gloomy Tower of London, which was to be the scene of so much tragic history, was built to hold the capital city in terror. Less forbidding than these, but no less suggestive of the foreigner, splendid minsters gradually took the place of the gloomy little Saxon churches. Forest laws of terrible harshness preserved the "tall deer" which the king "loved as his life"; but when a man was found murdered, if it could be proved that he was a Saxon, no further notice was taken of the crime. The Saxon language, or "Englisc," as it had begun to be called in King Alfred's time, was the badge of serfdom; and not only in the court and camp and castle, but also in Parliament and on the justice-bench, French alone was spoken.

Persistence of the Native Speech.—If a prophet had arisen to tell the Norman nobility of the eleventh and twelfth centuries, that not French, but English, was destined to be the speech of their descendants, he would have been laughed at. But this incredible thing came to pass, because of the dogged persistency of the Anglo-Saxon nature in clinging to its own. At the Conquest English ceased to be written; with the one exception of the Anglo-Saxon Chronicle, which continued to grow in the sheltered monastery of Peterborough, English literature "dives underground" in 1066, and does not reappear for a century and a half. But though no longer having a literary existence, the old tongue lived on the lips of the subjugated race, from father to son. About 1200 it began to be used again as a language of books, disputing with rude and uncertain accents a place by the side of the polished language of the conquerors. When it reappeared, however, it was a changed tongue. It was no longer Anglo-Saxon, but English. In spite of many words now obsolete, many strange forms and spellings, the English of the thirteenth century is unmistakably the same language which we speak to-day. It had sloughed off its inflections, simplified its grammar, and required only to be enriched by French elements, and made flexible by use, to be ready for the hand of Chaucer.

Fusion of the English and Norman-French Tongues.—But to say that English was "enriched by French elements" is hardly to convey an idea of the extent to which the foreign tongue entered into the composition of the language. What really happened was that English absorbed nearly the whole body of the French speech, or rather that the two languages, like the two peoples that spoke them, gradually melted together and became one. The Saxon, however, formed the foundation of the new language, determined its grammar, and furnished the primary indispensable words. The words of French origin in our vocabulary outnumber the Saxon words three to one; but in ordinary speech, where only the common words of daily life and action are used, the Saxon words are greatly in preponderance. French furnished many of the more stately words, those which apply to matters of abstract thought, to law and theology, to ceremonious intercourse, and to the workings of a polished civilization. The result of this fusion was to increase enormously the power of the language to express thought and feeling. It has made English the most splendid poetic language of the modern world. The fusion was accomplished in a period of about a century and a half. When English first appeared, in 1200, after its long sleep, it contained almost no French ingredients; by the middle of the fourteenth century the process of blending the two tongues was beginning to draw to a close. Chaucer, the poet who was to complete it and fix the language in much the shape that it wears to-day, was then a boy in the streets of London.

Fusion of the Saxon and Norman Peoples.—Hand in hand with the fusion of the Saxon and Norman-French languages, went the social fusion of the two peoples. The conquerors, we must remember, were originally of the same race as the conquered. By intermarriage with the French their character, it is true, had been much altered, but not so much but that a sympathy of nature existed still with their Saxon subjects. The Conquest put an end to warfare between the petty English kingdoms, and gave at once a political unity to the nation by placing supreme power in the hands of a single ruler. The struggle of the Conqueror's son, Henry I (1100–1135) with his turbulent barons, led him to draw nearer to the common people, and grant privileges to the towns; he still further strengthened the growing bond between the English and their foreign masters by taking a Saxon wife, a descendant of King Alfred. Under Henry II (1154–1189) the barons refused to furnish troops to be used outside of England; and the growth of national spirit which this shows was increased by the loss of Normandy, during the reign of John, in 1204. Shut in by the sea with the people they had conquered, the Norman noblemen began not only to look upon England as their home, but to find that they were drawn by common interests and a common enemy, closer and closer to the native population. Under Edward I, in 1265, this new feeling of national unity found expression in the establishment of a Parliament composed of both lords and commons, "a complete image of the nation," for the first time regularly and frequently summoned by the king. During the next hundred years the process of unifying the nation and the language progressed rapidly, aided by intermarriage and by daily intercourse; until, by the middle of the fourteenth century, the very terms "Norman" and "Saxon" had begun to lose their meaning. All were Englishmen, and the long process of fusion was nearly complete.

II. KNIGHTLY LITERATURE OF THE ANGLO-NORMAN PERIOD

The Metrical Romance.—A large proportion of the literature of this century and a half of preparation (1200–1350) consists of efforts in a new and fascinating poetic form introduced into England by the Norman-French, the metrical romance. The typical romance was a rambling tale of adventure, in which evil knights, robbers, giants, and Saracens were overthrown by a wandering chevalier, in the interest of some distressed damsel or of holy church. It dealt in a rather unreal, but highly entertaining way, with the three great interests of the Middle Ages—battle, love, and religion.

Sources of the Metrical Romances.—The *trouvères*, as the poets who composed and recited these romances were called, borrowed the material of their richly variegated tales wherever they could find it. A part of it came from Italy and the East, and out of this they made the Troy cycle and the cycle of Alexander the Great. A part of it they found near at hand, in the adventures of Charlemagne and his twelve peers. But the richest storehouse of romance which they had to draw upon, was in the Celtic parts of England and Brittany, where for centuries there had been growing up a mass of legend connected with King Arthur.* A number of these Arthurian legends were gathered up, before the middle of the twelfth century, in a great Latin work called the *Historia Bretonum*, by Geoffrey of Monmouth, a Welsh writer, who also added stories of his own invention. This chronicle of Geoffrey's was translated into French verse by Wace of Jersey, and through this channel came, about the year 1200, into the hands of Layamon, the first writer of romance in the crude English speech, which was just then awakening from its century and a half of silence. It is a curious fact that the first attempt made by the English in the knightly romance should have come from the hand, not of a worldly singer, but of a monk. It is true that Layamon's work is in the form of a chronicle, and pretends to be history; but the material of which it is made up is legendary, and its tone is that of a pure romance.

* See page 12.

Layamon's "Brut."—All that we know of Layamon, and of how he came to write his *Brut*, he tells himself in the quaint and touching words which prelude the poem:

"There was a priest in the land was named Layamon. He dwelt at Ernley, at a noble church upon Severn bank. It came to him in mind and in his chief thought that he would tell the noble deeds of the English; what the men were named, and whence they came, who first had the English land after the flood. Layamon began to journey wide over this land, and procured the noble books which he took for authority. Layamon laid these books before him and turned over the leaves; lovingly he beheld them—may the Lord be merciful to him! Pen he took with fingers, and wrote on book-skin, and compressed the three books into one."

The poem opens with an account of how Æneas's great-grandson, Brutus, who gives his name to the poem, sets out from Italy with all his people to find a new land in the west. They pass the Pillars of Hercules, "tall posts of strong marble stone," where they find the mermaidens, "beasts of great deceit, and so sweet that many men are not able to quit them." After further adventures in Spain and France, they come at length to the shôres of England, and land "at Dartmouth in Totnes." The remainder of the poem recounts the legendary history of Britain. In treating the Arthur legends, Layamon is not content merely to transcribe his predecessors. His home was near the borders of Wales, where these legends were native; and he either gathered up or freely invented several additions of the utmost importance. The most notable of these are his story of the founding of the Round Table, and his account of the fays who are present at Arthur's birth and who carry him after his last battle to the mystic isle of Avalon.

English Imitations of Norman-French Romances.—After Layamon had shown the way to romance writing in the native tongue, other poets in rapidly increasing numbers followed in his footsteps. Rude at first, their efforts gradually approached, in ease and grace, those of their Norman-French teachers. Almost all the English romances of the thirteenth and fourteenth centuries are free renderings from French originals. But of all the romances in English of this period, such as *King Horn, Havelock the Dane, Sir Tristrem*, and *Morte d'Arthure*, the one which is of most genuine native English workmanship is the best of all, and is one of the most charming romances of the world. This is *Sir Gawayne and the Green Knight*. Its date is about 1320–1330. The summary which follows will serve to convey some idea of the charm of the work, and through a single instance to give some insight into the nature of the metrical romances as a whole.

"Sir Gawayne and the Green Knight."—When the poem opens, King Arthur and his court are gathered in the hall at Camelot to celebrate the feast of the New Year. Suddenly there rushes in at the hall door a gigantic knight, clothed entirely in green, mounted on a green foal, and bearing in his hand a great axe. He rides to the dais, and challenges any knight to give him a blow with his axe, and to abide one in turn. Gawayne, the king's nephew, smites off the head of the Green Knight, who quietly picks it up by the hair, and holds it out toward Gawayne, until the lips speak, commanding him to appear at the Green Chapel on the next New Year's day.

On All-hallow's day, Gawayne sets out upon his horse Gringolet, and journeys through the wilderness until at last on Christmas-eve he comes to a fair castle standing on a hill. Asking shelter, he is courteously received by the lord of the castle and his fair young wife, and is assured that the Green Chapel is near at hand.

After the Christmas festivities are over, his host prepares for a great hunt, to last three days; and a jesting compact is made between them that at the end of each day they shall give each other whatever good thing they have won. While her lord is absent on the hunt, the lady of the castle tries in vain to induce Gawayne to make love to her, and bestows upon him a kiss. Anxious to fulfil his compact, he in turn gives the kiss to her lord each night when the hunt is over, and receives as a counter-gift the spoils of the chase. At their last meeting the lady persuades Gawayne to take as a gift a green lace belt which will protect him from mortal harm.

On New Year's morning he sets out through a storm of snow to find the Green Chapel. It proves to be a grass-covered hollow mound, in a desert valley. The Green Knight appears, and deals a blow with his axe upon Gawayne's bent neck. But he only pierces the skin, and Gawayne, seeing the blood fall on the snow, claps on his helmet, draws his sword, and declares the compact fulfilled. The Green Knight then discloses the fact that he is the lord of the castle where Gawayne has just been entertained, that with him dwells the fairy-temptress Morgain, who, because of her hatred of Guenevere, had sent him to Camelot to frighten the queen with the sight of a severed head talking, and who has been trying to lead Gawayne into bad faith, in order that her husband's axe might have power upon him. By his purity and truth Gawayne has been saved, except for the slight wound as punishment for concealing the gift of the girdle. Gawayne swears to wear the "lovelace" in remembrance of his weakness; and ever afterward each knight of the Round Table, and every lady of Arthur's court, wears a bright green belt for Gawayne's sake.

The picturesque language of the poem, its bright humor and fancy, and the vivid beauty of its descriptions, combine with its moral sweetness to make this the most delightful blossom of all pre-Chaucerian romance. *Sir Gawayne and the Green Knight* contains fair promise not only of Chaucer's *Knight's Tale,* but even of Spenser's *Faerie Queene.*

III. RELIGIOUS LITERATURE OF THE ANGLO-NORMAN PERIOD

The " Cursor Mundi."—While the shimmering tapestry and cloth of gold of these bright romances was being woven to beguile the tedium of castle halls, a more sombre literary fabric grew under the patient hands of monks and religious enthusiasts. The *Cursor Mundi*, the author of which is unknown, is among the most notable of these. The author, in beginning, laments the absorption of the readers of his day in frivolous romance, and proposes to give them in place of these vain tales of earthly love, a tale of divine love which shall be equally thrilling. He then proceeds to tell in flowing verse the story of God's dealings with man, from the Creation to the final redemption, following in general the biblical narrative, but adorning it with popular legends, both sacred and secular, and with all manner of quaint digressions.

Richard of Hampole : the " Prick of Conscience."—Of another religious writer whose work rises to the dignity of literature, the name and story have fortunately been preserved. This is Richard Rolle, the hermit of Hampole in southern Yorkshire, who was born about 1300 and died in 1349. In his youth he went to Oxford, then at the height of its fame as a centre of scholastic learning; but he soon revolted against the dry scholastic teaching. He left college, made him a hermit's shroud out of two of his sister's gowns and his father's hood, and began the life of a religious solitary and mystic. His cell at Hampole, near a Cistercian nunnery, was after his death visited as a miracle-working shrine, and cared for by the nuns. He wrote many canticles of divine love, some of which are of great intensity. His longest work is the *Prick of Conscience*, which deals with the life of man, and the terrors of the Last Judgment.

The " Love-Rune " of Thomas de Hales.—Of all the religious lyrical writings of this period, the most beautiful is the famous "Love Rune" of Thomas de Hales, a monk of the Minor Friars. He tells us in the first stanza that he was besought by a maid of Christ to make her a love-song, in order that she might learn therefrom how to choose a worthy and faithful lover. The monkish poet consents, but goes on to tell her how false and fleeting is all worldly love; how all earthly lovers vanish and are forgotten. "But there is another lover," the poet continues, who is "richer than Henry our King, and whose dwelling is fairer than Solomon's house of jasper and sapphire. Choose Him, and may God bring thee to His bride-chamber in Heaven."

" The Pearl."—Another religious poem, which deserves to be classed with this by reason of its beauty and humanity, is much longer. It is called *The Pearl*. The poet represents himself as falling asleep on the grave of his lost daughter,

Margaret (*i.e.*, "the pearl"). He dreams that he is transported to a wonderful land, through which a musical river flows over pearly sand, and stones that glitter like stars on a winter night. On the other side of the river, at the foot of a gleaming cliff, he sees his daughter sitting, clothed in bright raiment trimmed with pearls, and in the midst of her breast a great pearl. The father begs to be taken to her abiding-place; she tells him that he may see, but cannot enter, "that clean cloister." She bids him go along the river bank until he comes to a hill. Arrived at the top, he sees afar off the city of Heaven, "pitched upon gems," with its walls of jasper and streets of gold. At the wonder of the sight he stands, "still as a dazed quail," and gazing sees, "right as the mighty moon gan rise," the Virgins walking in procession with the Lamb of God. His daughter is one of them.

> Then I saw there my little queen—
> Lord! much of mirth was that she made
> Among her mates.

He strives in transport to cross over and be with her; but it is not pleasing to God that he should come, and the dreamer awakes.

The language of *The Pearl* has the same vigor and picturesqueness which distinguishes that of *Sir Gawayne and the Green Knight*. This, indeed, has come down to us in the same manuscript with *The Pearl*. Many scholars believe that they are the work of the same man. If so, he was the most considerable poet between Cynewulf and Chaucer.

IV. END OF THE PERIOD OF PREPARATION

Early Songs and Ballads.—As early as the middle of the thirteenth century, song writers began to put to beautiful use the new tongue formed by the flowing together of Saxon and Norman-French. We possess several songs written between 1250 and 1350, which have in them the promise of Herrick and of Shelley. They are all songs of love and of spring. The best known is perhaps the "Cuckoo Song," with its refrain of "Loude sing Cuckoo!"; but even more charming is the spring-song "Lent is come with love to town," and the love-song called **"Alysoun,"** with its delightful opening:

> Bitwenë Mersh and Averil
> When spray * begineth to springë,
> The little fowlës † have hyre ‡ will
> On hyrë lud § to singë.

To this period also probably belong the ballads which sprang up about the name of Robin Hood, the popular hero of Old England, the embodiment of its delight in the life of green forest and open sky, in bluff, shrewd manners, and in generous adventure. Rude as many of these early ballads are, they tell their story in a wonderfully fresh and vivid way; and they are full of charming bits of nature-poetry.

> When shaws been sheene, and shrads full fayre,
> And leaves both large and long,
> It is merry walking in the fayre forrést
> To heare the small birde's songe.

Final Result of the Norman Conquest.—The England which finds utterance in these songs and ballads is a very different England from that which had spoken in "The Wanderer," and "The Battle of Brunanburh." It is no longer the fierce and gloomy aspects of nature, but her bright and laughing moods, that are sung. Love and merry adventure have taken the place of war, as the poet's chief theme. The Norman invasion has done its work. The conquerors have ceased to be such, for foreign wars and centuries of domestic intercourse have broken down the distinction between men of Norman and men of Saxon blood. The new language is formed, a new and vigorous national life is everywhere manifest. A new poet is needed, great enough to gather up and make intelligible to itself this shifting, many-colored life; and Chaucer is at hand.

REVIEW OUTLINE.—This chapter treats of England under the rule of the Norman and Angevin kings, beginning with the reign of the

* Foliage.　　† Birds.　　‡ Their.　　§ Voice.

Conqueror, in 1066, and ending with the close of Richard II's reign in 1327. It covers, therefore, something more than two centuries and a half. The first part of this period has no literary history, so far as English is concerned, for no English books were written, except that the English Chronicle was continued at the monastery of Peterborough until 1154. The first part of the chapter deals with the fusion of the Norman and Saxon races. The Normans were not originally a very different people from the Saxons. How were they related, in race and by their original habits of life? What had made them different? State the chief facts in the history of the Norman-French up to the time of the conquest of England. Note the changes which took place in England by reason of the conquest, in architecture, in laws, in speech. Note the steps by which the two peoples drew together, politically, under William I, Henry I, Henry II, John and Edward I. In what manner did the English speech manage to survive? When it reappeared again as a written language, how had it changed in character? How long did it take this new language to absorb the French? In view of the fact that English absorbed a body of French words nearly three times its own bulk, how do you explain the fact that it retained its individuality as a language? The metrical romance, or *chanson de geste* (song of deeds) was transplanted to English soil at the very beginning of the Norman occupation, and was for a long time written only in French. Note the various sources from which these romances were drawn; note also that the use of the King Arthur legends by the trouvères brought into English literature the first large Celtic element, corresponding to the large proportion of Celtic blood in the Normans, and the smaller but still considerable ingredient which the Saxons had absorbed from the Celts of Britain. Give the story of Layamon, and indicate the nature of his "Brut." What elements of the King Arthur legend did he add to what was already given by his predecessors? How was he enabled to make these additions? At what period were the French romances translated into English? Outline the story of Sir Gawayne and the Green Knight, answering the following questions: (a) Why does Gawayne set out to find the Green Chapel? (b) Whose is the castle where he finds shelter? (c) What compact does he make with the lord of the castle? (d) Why does Morgain try to tempt him to deceive the lord? (e) Why did the Knights of the Round Table wear the green belt? Why is "The Pearl" so called? What are the indications in the ballads and songs of the late thirteenth and early fourteenth centuries that a new spirit was coming over English literature? Note the joyousness and outdoor freshness of these poems which herald Chaucer, the freshest and most joyous in temper of all English poets.

READING GUIDE.—The literature of this period is accessible only with difficulty and in expensive form; little or nothing can be required of a student in the way of private reading. If the teacher can secure Ellis's Specimens of Early English Metrical Romances, or H. Morley's Early English Prose Romances (in the Carisbrooke Library series), enough should be read to the class to illustrate the nature of the early romance. Extracts from Layamon's "Brut" and an epitome of the whole poem are given in Morley's English Writers, Vol. III, pp. 212–227. This will serve admirably for illustration, and is more accessible than the above. "The Pearl," text and translation, is edited by Israel Gollanz (Nutt). The lyrics "Alysoun" and "Lent is come with love to town" are given in Morris and Skeat's Specimens of Early English. The "Love Rune" of Thomas de Hales can be found in B. Ten Brink's History of English Literature, Vol. I.

Fiction.—Charles Kingsley's "Hereward the Wake" and Sir Walter Scott's "Ivanhoe" give vivid pictures of society during the Norman and Angevin period. Hereward deals with the times of William I, Ivanhoe with those of Richard Cœur de Lion.

For a tabular view of this period, see close of Chapter IV.

GEOFFREY CHAUCER

From the Occleve manuscript

CHAPTER IV

MIDDLE ENGLISH PERIOD: THE AGE OF CHAUCER

I. INTRODUCTION

Historical Events of Chaucer's Time.—In 1327, thirteen years before the date which scholars have set as the probable year of Chaucer's birth, Edward III came to the throne of England. He reigned for fifty years, and the first part of his reign was one of prosperity at home and victory abroad. Up to this time England had been an agricultural country. Now, taking example from Flanders, the birthplace of Edward's queen, Philippa, Englishmen began to grow wool on a large scale. Flemish weavers were imported to teach them to manufacture this wool into finished products. The wool industry became one of the chief sources of English wealth; and to symbolize this fact, a crimson cushion stuffed with sheep shearings, the Woolsack, was used henceforth as the seat of the lord chancellor in the upper house of Parliament. Early in Edward's reign the French, jealous of England's growing trade, attacked her merchant ships. In retaliation Edward boldly laid claim to the throne of France, to which he had a shadowy title. Gathering together his mounted knights and stout yeomen, armed with pike and long-bow, he invaded France, and in 1346 won the great victory of Crécy. Ten years later his heroic son, the Black Prince, won the still more splendid victory of Poictiers, defeating a French force five times as great as his own, and bringing John, the French king, captive to London. The struggle with France went on for a long time under succeeding kings; so long, indeed, that it is known in history as the Hundred Years' War. Its effect was immensely to strengthen the unity of England. It was the Saxon yeomen with their long-bows who won England's victories at Crécy and Poictiers, and afterwards at Agincourt under Henry V. The last remnants of hatred and suspicion between Norman and Saxon faded away in a common national pride and patriotism.

Edward III's successor, Richard II, came to the throne in 1377. He was so weak a ruler that he won the nickname of Richard the Redeless. The royal power during a large portion of his reign of twenty-two years was in the hands of his uncle, John of Gaunt, brother of the Black Prince, and the patron of Chaucer. In 1399, a year before Chaucer's death, the sceptre was wrested from Richard's feeble hands by Henry of Bolingbroke, duke of Lancaster, son of John of Gaunt, who ascended the throne as Henry IV. As will be seen, almost all these political events had an effect in determining the career of the poet whose writings remain as the chief glory of this epoch of English history.

Society in Chaucer's Time.—The society of the period, the brighter and happier aspects of which Chaucer so brilliantly portrayed, was full of sharp contrasts. Riches and poverty, splendor and squalor, unbounded license and the most crushing servitude, existed side by side. No bounds were set to the luxury which court and nobles displayed in dress, food, hunting equipage and furnishings of war. Rich merchants vied with the aristocratic classes in the splendor of their way of living; and the great guilds, or brotherhoods of trade and handicraft, banqueted in halls which a king might have envied. On the other hand, a large proportion of the population were villeins or serfs, bound to the soil, doomed to pitiless labor and harsh exaction. Nor was the contrast merely one of classes. Lords and ladies, dressed in rare silks and cloth of gold, and loaded with precious gems, ate from golden dishes with their fingers, forks being unknown; and threw fragments of the feast to the dogs who quarrelled and fought among the soiled rushes of the floor. At a time when Edward III was founding Winchester College, the first great English public school, and when Oxford was awakening to a new enthusiasm for learning, many nobles could not read. Printing was unknown; books had to be copied by hand, and were very cumbersome and expensive.

Chivalry had reached its highest point of outward splendor; its tournaments and other ceremonies were miracles of great display: but as a vital creed it was fast losing its hold upon men. Side by side with the corrupt clergy, who in their great abbeys and monasteries lived a life of sensual ease, we find an organization of "poor priests" going up and down the country with bare feet, staff, and russet gown, preaching the pure word of God in all meekness and self-sacrifice.

The London of Chaucer's day was in some respects a stately city. On the north ran a strong feudal wall with tower-guarded gates; on the south flowed the broad river, crowded with shipping, and spanned by a great bridge on which houses and shops clustered thick; the gloomy massive Tower rose at one end of the city, the beautiful abbey of Westminster and the Parliament Hall at the other, and the Gothic spires of old St. Paul's crowned the hill between; noblemen's palaces, guild-halls, monasteries and churches, of rich and pictur-esque design, gave splendor to the narrow, tortuous, and ill-kept streets. Throughout the country the gloomy Norman castles, with their moats and thick-walled donjon-keeps, had given way to castles which, though still fortified, were more friendly and habitable. The cultivated parts of the island were dotted with manor houses where hearty free-holders, like the franklin of the Canterbury Tales, ruled their broad acres and dispensed a bounteous hospitality. Travel was very unsafe, for men in "buckram and Kendal green," the successors of Robin Hood and his merry men, lay in wait for booty, and levied tribute upon merchant, nobleman, and churchman alike. England's navy had al-ready come into being, and her growing sea-trade, with which piracy and smuggling were not seldom combined, filled her seaports with a motley crowd of foreign types. Internal com-merce was carried on largely by means of fairs, where chap-men brought their wares and mountebanks their tricks, as to that fair which Bunyan described, three centuries later, in his Pilgrim's Progress. News was spread chiefly by wander-ing pedlers, or by pilgrims journeying to or from some holy shrine. The sports of the nobility and clergy were hunting, hawking, and jousting at tournaments; the poorer classes

amused themselves with wrestling, single-stick, archery, and
in many crueler ways, such as baiting bulls and bears with
savage dogs.   All classes alike looked on with awed interest
at the miracle-plays, biblical dramas presented by apprentices of the trade guilds, with a movable wagon for stage
and the open street for theatre.

Such was the picturesque and varied society which Chaucer,
the great realist and observer, brings before us.   A part of
the rich heritage he has left us he received from loving acquaintance with nature; a part came to him through books,
of which he was a devoted student; but the greater part came
from the human life about him.   He was at once a dreamer,
a student, and a man of affairs; and it was in this last capacity
that he got his largest training,—from war, the court, travel,
business, and politics.

II. geoffrey chaucer (1340–1400)

Chaucer's Youth.—Geoffrey Chaucer was born about 1340,
of a family of London merchants.   His father, a member of
the Corporation of Vintners, had been purveyor to King Edward III.   When Chaucer was a boy of six the nation was
stirred by the news of Crécy; and as a lad of sixteen he may
have witnessed, after Poictiers, the triumphal entry of the
Black Prince into London, bringing with him as a captive
the French king.   The connection of Chaucer's father with
the court, as purveyor of wines to the royal table, may have
been the circumstance which made it possible for Chaucer,
when about seventeen, to become a page in the household of
the king's daughter-in-law, the Duchess of Clarence.   Two
years later he went with the king's army to France.   Here he
saw unrolled the brilliant pageant of mediæval war, at a time
when chivalry and knighthood, though they had lost something of their inner meaning, still gave occasion for rich
display.   He beheld the unsuccessful siege of the city of
Rheims, was captured by the French, and held as a prisoner
of war until ransomed by his royal master.

Chaucer's French Period.—On his return to England Chaucer was made a Squire of the King's Bedchamber, and proba-

bly spent the next ten years at Edward's court, then the most
brilliant in Europe. The court of Edward was still practically a French court; and Chaucer, although he seems to
have decided very early to use his native tongue, necessarily
turned to France for his literary models. The first period of
his poetic life was spent in learning all that the French
trouvères and ballad-writers had to teach him concerning his
chosen art. The most famous work which the school of
French *trouvères* had produced was the *Roman de la Rose,*
an elaborate allegory of love, the rose, growing in a mystic
garden, warded by symbolic figures from the lover's approach.
The *Roman de la Rose* was Chaucer's first training school,
and he took his training with characteristic thoroughness
by translating the poem into English verse. Less than two
thousand lines of this translation have survived; indeed, the
whole may never have been completed. But the *Roman
de la Rose* left a profound impression upon Chaucer's work,
and for years he thought and wrote in the atmosphere which
it created for him. During these years of French influence
he wrote, for the knights and ladies of King Edward's court,
those "ballades, roundels, virelays," by which his fellow-poet
Gower says "the land fulfilled was over-all." The most
important work which remains to us from his pure French
period, however, is the *Book of the Duchesse,* also known
as "The Death of Blaunche the Duchesse," written in 1369,
to solace the bereavement of her husband, John of Gaunt,
the king's third son.

Chaucer's Middle Life : Italian Period.—In 1370, Chaucer
was sent to the Continent on royal business. This was the
first of many official missions which he executed for the king
during the next ten years, in various parts of Europe, especially
in Italy, where he went twice as the king's emissary. The
opportunity afforded by these journeys for converse with
many types of men, and observation of widely varying manners, was of the utmost importance in his poetic education.

On Chaucer's return to England after his first Italian mission, in 1372, his services were rewarded by the gift of the important post of controller of the customs on wool, skins, and
tanned hides at the port of London; to which was added the

grant of a daily pitcher of wine from the king's cellars. His office as controller was an arduous one, requiring his constant attendance. He was by this time married to Philippa, lady-in-waiting to the queen, and lived in a house over one of the city gates near the Tower. We get from his poems various glimpses of his daily life, especially of his eagerness for study, which, after the day's work was done, would send him home, regardless of rest and "newe thinges," to sit "as domb as any stone" over his book, until his eyes were dazed. But he was more than a student. The great books he had come to know in Italy gave him no peace, until he should equal or surpass them. In 1382, on the betrothal of the boy king, Richard II, to the young princess Anne of Bohemia, Chaucer wrote a wedding poem for the royal pair, the *Parlement of Fowls*. *Troilus and Creseide* and the *House of Fame* belong also to this central or "Italian," period, of Chaucer's literary life. In 1385 he was allowed to discharge his duties as customs officer by deputy. The first result of his new-found leisure was *The Legend of Good Women*, dedicated to the young queen.

Chaucer's Later Life : English Period.—In 1386 Chaucer was sent to Parliament as member from Kent. This Parliament was in opposition to Chaucer's patron, John of Gaunt, and Chaucer was deprived of his office as controller. Three years later John of Gaunt regained influence, and as a renewed sign of favor Chaucer was made clerk of the king's works (supervising architect) at Westminster, the Tower, Windsor Castle, and other places. During these years his masterpiece, the *Canterbury Tales*, was written. Toward the end of Richard II's reign Chaucer fell into poverty, from causes not well known; but in 1399, on the accesssion of Henry IV, a ballad entitled "The Compleint of Chaucer to his Empty Purse" brought him substantial aid. He died in 1400.

Influence of Italy Upon Chaucer.—The most important event in Chaucer's life was his first visit to Italy, on the king's business, in 1372. Italy was then at the zenith of her artistic energy, in the full splendor of that illumination which had followed the intellectual twilight of the Middle Ages, and which we know as the Renaissance, or "New Birth." Each of her little city-states was a centre of marvellous activity, and everywhere were being produced those masterpieces of painting, sculpture, and architecture, which still make Italy a place of pilgrimage for all lovers of art. The literary activity was equally great, at least in Tuscany. The world which lay open to Chaucer's gaze when he crossed the Alps, was one calculated to fascinate and stimulate him in the highest degree. Whether he saw Petrarch or Boccaccio in person is not known, but, from this time on, his work was largely influenced by them, as well as by Dante. Through all three he came into closer contact with the great literature of the past, and acquired a new reverence for the ancient masters.

"Troilus and Creseide."—Both the *Parlement of Fowls* and the *House of Fame* are colored with Italian reminiscence; but the chief fruit of Chaucer's Italian journeys was the long poem adapted from Boccaccio's *Philostrato* (The Love-stricken One), entitled by Chaucer *Troilus and Creseide*. The story of the love of the young Trojan hero for Cressida, and of her desertion of him for the Greek Diomedes, Chaucer pretended only to translate, but he changed the theme radically. In his hands, the lovers' go-between, Pandarus, is transformed from a gilded youth of Troilus's own age and temperament, to a middle-aged man, plausible, good-natured, full of easy worldly wisdom and vulgar ideals—a character as truly alive as if Shakespeare had drawn him. The growth of the love-passion in Cressida's heart is traced through its gradual stages with a truth and insight entirely new in English poetry. The "background" of the poem is painted with the most delightful realism. Though the scene is ancient Troy, and the costumes are those of mediæval knights and ladies, we seem, in many passages of the poem, to be looking at a modern play or reading from a modern novel, so homely and actual does it appear.

"The Legend of Good Women."—*The Legend of Good Women*, which marks the close of Chaucer's Italian period, has for its prologue the most charming of the poet's many passages of personal confession and self-revealment. He

represents himself as wandering in the fields on the May-
day, the only season which can tempt him from his books.
The birds are singing to their mates their song of "blessed
be Seynt Valentyn!", and Zephyrus and Flora, as "god and
goddesse of the flowery mede," have spread the earth with
fragrant blossoms.   But the poet has eyes only for one flower,
the daisy, the "emperice (empress) and flower of floweres
alle."   All day long he leans and pores upon the flower;
and when at last it has folded its leaves at the coming of
night, he goes home to rest, with the thought of rising early
to gaze upon it once more.   He makes his couch out-of-doors,
in a little arbor, and here he has a wonderful dream.   He
dreams that he is again in the fields, kneeling by the daisy,
and sees approaching a procession of bright forms.   First
comes the young god of love, clad in silk embroidered with
red rose-leaves and sprays of green, his "gilt hair" crowned
with light, in his hand two fiery darts, and his wings spread
angel-like.   He leads by the hand a queen, clad in green and
crowned with a fillet of daisies under a band of gold.   She is
Alcestis, who died to save her husband Admetus.   Behind
her comes an endless train of women who have been "true
of love."   They kneel in a circle about the poet, and sing
honor to woman's truth, and to the daisy flower, the emblem
of Alcestis.   The love-god then glowers angrily upon Chaucer, and upbraids him for having done despite to women,
in translating the *Roman de la Rose*, with its satire upon
their foibles; and in writing the story of Cressida, so dishon-
orable to the steadfastness of the sex.   Alcestis comes to his
rescue, and agrees to pardon his misdeeds if he will spend
the rest of his life in making a "glorious Legend of Good
Women," and will send it, on her behalf, to the English
queen.   Chaucer promises solemnly, and as soon as he
wakes, betakes himself to his task.

It is probable that Chaucer did indeed enter upon this
poem with the design of devoting to it many years, and of
making it his masterpiece.   But he left it unfinished, perhaps for the reason that all the stories illustrate the same
theme, and lack, when taken together, that element of surprise and contrast essential to keep up the interest.

who was Thomas sir Becket

The Canterbury Tales.''—The drift of Chaucer's, genius, as he grew older, was more and more toward the portrayal of actual life. He had a wide experience of men, of all ranks and conditions; and he had been storing up for years, with his keenly observant, quiet eyes, the materials for a presentation of contemporary society on a great scale. Moreover, while Chaucer was growing up, England had been growing conscious of herself. The struggle with France had at last unified the people. They were no longer Norman and Saxon, but English; and the brilliancy of Edward III's early reign had given to this new people their first intoxicating draught of national pride. The growing power of parliament tended to foster in the nation the feeling of unity and strength. As a member of parliament and a government officer, Chaucer felt these influences to the full. It must have seemed more and more important to him that the crowning work of his life should in some way represent the varied spectacle of the society in which he moved. With the happy fortune of genius, he hit, in his *Canterbury Tales,* upon a scheme wonderfully conceived for the ends he had in view. Collections of stories, both secular and sacred, had been popular in the Middle Ages, and the Renaissance inherited the taste for them. Boccaccio had set the example of throwing a graceful trellis-work of incident and dialogue about the separate stories of a collection. Chaucer, while adopting a similar framework, made his setting thoroughly national and racy; individualized his characters so as to make of them a gallery of living portraits of his time.

The Pilgrims at the Tabard.—He represents himself as alighting, one spring evening, at the Tabard Inn, in Southwark, a suburb at the southern end of London Bridge, where afterward the famous Elizabethan playhouses, Shakespeare's among them, were to arise. Southwark was the place of departure and arrival for all South-of-England travel, and especially for pilgrimages to the world-renowned shrine of Thomas-à-Becket, at Canterbury. A company bent on such a pilgrimage Chaucer finds gathered at the inn. He makes their acquaintance, and joins himself with them for the journey. Counting the poet, they are thirty in all. There is a

Knight lately from the foreign wars, a man who has fought in Prussia and in Turkey, jousted in Trasimene, and been present at the storming of Alexandria—a high-minded, gentle-mannered, knightly adventurer, type of the chivalry which in Chaucer's time was passing rapidly away. With him is his son, a young squire, curly-haired and gay, his short white-sleeved gown embroidered like a mead with red and white flowers; he is an epitome of the gifts and graces of brilliant youth. It is pleasant to think of the Squire as representing Chaucer himself, as he was when a young man at Edward's court. Their servant is a yeoman, in coat and hood of green, a sheaf of peacock-arrows under his belt, a mighty bow in his hand, and a silver image of St. Christopher upon his breast; he is the type of that sturdy English yeomanry which with its gray-goose shafts humbled the pride of France at Crécy and Agincourt.

There is a whole group of ecclesiastical figures, representing in their numbers and variety the immense growth of the mediæval Church. Most of them are satirical portraits, in their worldliness and gross materialism only too faithful representatives of the corrupt Catholicism against which the reformer Wyclif struggled. First of all there is a monk, who cares only for hunting and good cheer; his bald head shines like glass, his "steep eyes" roll in his head; he rides a sleek brown palfrey, and has "many a dainty horse" in his stables; his sleeves are trimmed with fine fur at the wrists, his hood is fastened under his chin with a gold love knot. As a companion figure to the hunting monk, Chaucer gives us "Madame Eglantyne," the prioress; she is a teacher of young ladies, speaks French with a provincial accent, "after the school of Stratford-atte-bowe"; she is exquisite in her table-manners, counterfeiting as well as she can the stately behavior of the court. Other ecclesiastics are there, hangers-on and caterpillars of the Church: the Summoner, a repulsive person with "fire-red cherubim face"; the Pardoner, with his bag full of pardons, "come from Rome all hot," and of bits of cloth and pig's-bones which he sells as relics of the holy saints. Chaucer's treatment of these evil churchmen is highly good-natured and tolerant; he never takes the tone of moral indignation against them. But he does better; he sets beside them, as a type of the true shepherd of the Church, a "poor parson," such as, under Wyclif's teaching, had begun that great movement for the purification of the Church which was to result, more than a century later, in the Reformation. Chaucer paints the character of the Parson, poor in this world's goods but "rich of holy thought and work," with loving and reverent touch.

The Parson's brother travels with him—a Plowman, a "true swinker and a good," who helps his poor neighbors without hire and loves them as himself; he reminds us of that Piers Plowman of whom Langland, Chaucer's great contemporary, wrote in his "Vision." A crowd of other figures fill the canvas. There is a Shipman from the west-country, a representative of those adventurous seamen, half merchant-sailors, half smugglers and pirates, who had already made England's name a terror on the seas, and paved the way for her future naval supremacy. There is a poor Clerk of Oxford, riding a horse as lean as a rake, and dressed in threadbare cloak, who spends all that he can beg or borrow upon books; he represents that passion for learning which was already astir everywhere in Europe. There is a Merchant, in a Flemish beaver, on a high horse, concealing, with the grave importance of his air, the fact that he is in debt. There is a group of guild-men, in the livery of their guild, all worthy to be aldermen; together with the merchant, they represent the mercantile and manufacturing activity which was lifting England rapidly to the rank of a great commercial power. There is the Wife of Bath, a figure conceived with masterly humor and realism; she has had "husbands five at church-door," and, though "somdel deaf," expects to live to wed several others; she rides on an ambler, with spurs and scarlet hose on her feet, and on her head a hat as broad as a buckler. These, and a dozen others, are all painted in vivid colors, and with wonderful truth to nature. Taken as a whole, they represent the entire range of English society in the fourteenth century, with the exception of the highest aristocracy and the lowest order of serfs.

At supper this goodly company hears from the host of the Tabard a proposition that on their journey to Canterbury, to beguile the tedium of the ride, each of them shall tell two tales, and on the homeward journey two more.* He agrees to travel with them, to act as master-of-ceremonies, and on their return to render judgment as to who has told the best story, the winner to be given a supper at the general expense. So it is agreed.

The Pilgrims on the Road.—The next morning they set out bright and early on their journey southward to the cathedral city. They draw lots to determine who shall tell the first tale. The lot falls to the Knight, who tells the charming chivalric story of "Palamon and Arcite." When it is finished the Host calls upon the Monk to follow. But the Miller, who is already drunk and quarrelsome, insists on being heard, and launches forthwith into a very unedifying tale. The Host rises in his stirrups and calls on the Parson for a story, "by Goddes dignitee!" The Parson reproves him for swearing; whereupon the Host cries that he "smells a Lollard † in the wind," and bids the company prepare for a sermon. This is too much for the Shipman, who breaks in impatiently. When the Host calls upon the Prioress, he changes his bluff manner to correspond with her rank and excessive refinement, speaking with polite circumlocution, "as courteously as it had been a maid." The Prioress responds graciously, and tells the story of "Hugh of Lincoln," the little martyr who, after his throat had been cut by the wicked Jews, and his body thrown into a pit, still sang with clear young voice his *Alma Redemptoris* to the glory of the Virgin.

So the stories continue, interrupted by vivid dialogue and action on the part of the pilgrims. Two of the most charming tales are told by the Clerk and the young Squire. The Clerk, after he has been rallied by the Host upon his

* Counting the Canon's Yeoman (who joins them on the road) the story-tellers are thirty-one in number, making a total of a hundred and twenty-four tales to be told. Less than a fifth of this number were actually written, and several of these were left fragmentary.

† The followers of Wyclif were called Lollards. See p. 53.

still and thoughtful manner of riding, agrees to relate a story which he learned at Padua of "Francis Petrarch, the laureate poet, whose rhetoric sweet enlumined all Italy of poetry." It is the story of Patient Grissel, which Chaucer borrowed from Petrarch's Latin version. The Squire's tale, as befits his years and disposition, is a bright tale of love, adventure, and magic, in which figure a flying horse of brass and other wonders.

Chaucer's Picture of Himself among the Pilgrims.—Chaucer introduces himself into the succession of story-tellers with characteristic modesty and sly humor. Sobered by the miraculous tale of Hugh of Lincoln, the company is riding silently along, when the Host, to break the awe-struck mood, turns to Chaucer, and begins to joke him upon his shy abstracted air and his corpulency:

> "what man artow?" quod he;
> "Thou lokest as thou woldest finde an hare,
> For ever upon the ground I see thee stare.
> Approache neer, and loke up merily.
> Now war yow, sirs, and lat this man have place;
> He in the waist is shape as wel as I   .   .   .
> He semeth elvish by his countenaunce
> For unto no wight dooth he daliaunce."

Chaucer, thus rallied, begins one of those doggerel rhymes of knightly adventure, to which the romances of chivalry had in his day degenerated. The "Rhyme of Sir Thopas" is a capital burlesque of a style of poetry which Chaucer himself had come to supplant. He has not got far before the Host cries out upon the "drasty rhyming," and Chaucer meekly agrees to contribute instead "a little thing in prose," a "moral tale"; and he proceeds with the story of Melibeus and his wife Prudence. It is very dreary tale indeed, matched for tediousness only by the prose sermon put into the mouth of the Parson, with which the Canterbury Tales, in the fragmentary form in which they were left, conclude. It is curious to note how Chaucer's style becomes awkward, involved, and wearisome, as soon as he deserts his natural medium of verse, and attempts to write in prose.

Chaucer's Literary Art.—In the sixteenth century and later, when, owing to the change in the pronunciation of words (especially the loss of the final *e*), the secret of Chaucer's versification was lost, he was regarded as a barbarous writer, ignorant of prosody, and with no ear for the melody of verse. The contrary of this was the case. He was an artist in verse-effects, who paid heed to all the niceties of rhythm and tone-color. In a half-humorous address to his scrivener Adam, he calls down curses upon that unworthy servant, for spoiling good verses by bad copying, and in *Troilus and Creseide* he beseeches his readers not to "mis-metre" his book. From his very earliest poems, his work is in all formal details faultless; and as he progressed in skill, his music became constantly more varied and flexible. His early manner reaches its height in the exquisite rondel, intricate in form but handled with great simplicity of effect, which brings the *Parlement of Fowls* to a melodious close. A good example of his later music may be found in the description of the Temple of Venus in the "Knight's Tale"; or, as a study in a graver key, in the ballad "Flee fro the Press," which marks so impressively the deepening seriousness of Chaucer's mind in his last years.

III. JOHN WYCLIF (1320–1384)

The Peasant Rebellion.—The second half of the fourteenth century was a time of great suffering among the poor people of England. Four terrible plagues, the first in 1349, the last in 1375, swept over the country, carrying death everywhere. Frightful storms destroyed the crops. The exactions of the Church, the extravagances of Edward III, and the heavy cost of his foreign wars, added to the burden borne by the distracted peasantry. In 1381 an immense uprising of the peasants occurred, under the leadership of Wat Tyler and a socialist priest of Kent, named John Balle. They marched on London, sacked the Tower and the Savoy palace, and murdered an archbishop; it seemed for a time as if the throne and the whole social order were about to be overturned.

The Lollard Movement.—During this time of social distress, John Wyclif planned and carried out a great practical
movement, known as the Lollard movement, for combat-
ting the corruptions of the Church, and arousing the common
people to a more vital religious life. He sent out simple
devoted men to preach the gospel in the native tongue,
and to bring home to their hearers the living truths of religion. These "poor priests," dressed in coarse russet robes
and carrying staves, travelled through the length and breadth
of the land, as Wesley's preachers travelled four centuries
later, calling men back to the simple faith of apostolic times.
Wyclif and his Lollard priests began the great Protestant
appeal from the dogmas of the Church to the Bible, which
culminated, in the sixteenth century, in Luther and the
Reformation.

Wyclif's Bible.—In order to make this appeal effective
with the masses, Wyclif undertook to translate the whole
of the Bible into English. Up to Wyclif's time the Bible had
not been translated. The Saxon scholar, Bede, had done
the gospel of St. John into the dialect of Northumbria, and
Aelfric had made a version of some parts of the Old Testament in the dialect of Wessex; but the men of the fourteenth
century could understand Saxon no more than we can to-
day. The Bible was in the hands of the priests, in the
Latin form known as the Vulgate. Wyclif determined to
translate it into simple English, and to put it within reach
of the humblest reader. With the assistance of Nicholas
of Hereford, he completed his great task before his death
in 1384. It is the first great monument of prose style in
English. By virtue of it, and of the sermons and tracts
which he wrote in homely vigorous speech for the understanding of simple people, Wyclif earned the title of "father
of English prose." He may with equal justice be called the
father of the English Reformation; for the seed he sowed did
not perish. His corpse was burned by the Church, we are
told, and his ashes thrown into a brook near his parsonage of
Lutterworth, in order that no trace might remain of the ' arch-
heretic"; but, says a pious old historian, "this brook did
convey his ashes into the Avon, Avon into Severn, Severn into

the narrow sea, and that into the wide ocean.   And so the
ashes of Wyclif are the emblem of his doctrine, which is now
dispersed all the world over."

Chaucer Contrasted with Langland.—The peasant rebellion
and the Lollard agitation give us glimpses of an England
which Chaucer, in spite of the many-sidedness of his work,
did not reveal.   Chaucer wrote for the court and the cultivated
classes, to whom the sufferings of the poor were either unknown, or accepted as a part of the natural order of things.
In his graceful worldliness, his delight in the bright pageantry of life, he shows the Norman-French strain, with its large
infusion of Celtic blood; the other half of the English nature, its mystical, sombre, spiritually earnest side, found
expression in William Langland, author of the *Book Concerning Piers the Plowman*.   He proceeds from the pure Germanic strain in the nation, and is the representative of
those moral and spiritual traits which afterward came to be
known as Puritan.

V. LANGLAND AND THE VISION OF PIERS PLOWMAN

Langland's Life and Character.—William Langland was
born at Colesbury Mortimer, near Malvern in Worcestershire,
not far from the Welsh border.   He tells us that "his father
and friends" put him to school, and made a clerk of him.
For a time he "roamed about robed in russet," in the manner of a mendicant, driven by vague thoughts and desires.
Going up to London, he got him a "chantry for souls," one
of the minor offices of the mediæval Church, his duty being
to chant at stated intervals for the release from purgatory
of the soul of some dead man, who had left a bequest for
that purpose.   His poverty was extreme. With his wife Kitte
and his daughter Calote, he lived in Cornhill, where his
tall, gaunt figure, clothed in a sombre priestly cloak, got
him the nickname of "Long Will."   As he stalked through
the crowded Strand, he would refuse to bow to fine lords
and ladies clad in furs and silver, and to cry "God save you,
sir!" to sergeants of the law.   His conduct toward the rich
and great, so unusual in that day, got him the name of an

eccentric person, somewhat touched in the brain. Hints of mental struggles verging upon insanity occur in his confessions. "My wit waxed and waned," he says, "until I was a fool." His writings reveal a half-ferocious sincerity, a flaming indignation against the pretences and base complacencies of the world, combined with the inward exaltation of the visionary. The last trace we get of him is in Bristol, where, in 1399, he was writing "Richard the Redeless," a poem of protest and warning addressed to King Richard II. Apparently, news reached him of the assassination of the king and of the usurpation of the throne by Henry IV., and he threw the poem by unfinished. The date of his death is unknown.

"The Book of Piers the Plowman."—Langland's life-work was his great poem, "The Vision of William Concerning Piers the Plowman." He worked upon it for at least thirty years, constantly rewriting and expanding it. In these rewritings and recastings it grew from eight cantos to twenty-three; and the conception of the chief character, "Piers the Plowman," grew constantly more exalted. At first he is merely an honest, simple-hearted farmer, full of Christian helpfulness and practical justice. But in the later versions he is raised and glorified, and is conceived of mystically as Jesus Christ, incarnate in the form of a lowly tiller of the fields.

On a May morning, on Malvern Hills, the poet, "weary forwandered," lies down to rest, and dreams. Beneath him, in the great plain, he sees gathered together a vast crowd of people, representing the manifold life of the world. All are busy, but their work is, with few exceptions, evil or futile. Some are sowing or ploughing, but only that idlers may waste the fruit of their toil. Pilgrims are journeying to holy shrines, that they may "lie all their lives after;" minstrels and ribald story-tellers are plying their trade; friars and pardoners are abusing their priestly station for their own low ends. Law-sergeants, tradesmen, and taverners mix with the changing crowd, and contribute each his characteristic abuse. The genius of the crowd, the incarnation of the worldly spirit, is Lady Meed (Bribery), a wonderful allegorical figure, symbol of that dishonesty which Langland everywhere saw poisoning the springs of social and political life.

Next we are shown the "Seven Deadly Sins," and other allegorical figures, painted with so much realism, that they seem like living beings, with whom, indeed, they mingle on equal terms. Among them is Piers, and to him they appeal to show them the way to Truth, i.e., to God the Father. Piers knows Truth well, but refuses to go until he has ploughed his half-acre. All who come asking for guidance he sets to work. Many shirk their tasks, but are driven back by Hunger. This part of the poem preaches, as preparatory to personal salvation, the Gospel of Work—the same gospel which Carlyle, who has many points of resemblance to Langland, was to preach five centuries afterward.

The Vision reaches its highest point of imagination in the account of Piers's triumph over Death and Hell. He comes riding barefoot on an ass, without spurs or spear, to his "joust in Jerusalem." With the news of his triumph and resurrection, the dreamer awakes in ecstasy, the joyous Easter bells pealing in his ears.

Spirit of Langland's Poem.—The name of Piers Plowman was used as a rallying cry in the peasant uprising; and the poem probably had much to do with the arousing of Wyclif's zeal as a reformer. Langland's sense of the equality of all men before God, his hatred of social falsities and hypocrisies, his belief in the dignity of labor, give a modern tone to his poem, in spite of its archaic metrical form, and its mediæval machinery of abstract figures. His deep religious sense and the grandeur of his mystical imaginings are neither ancient nor modern, but of all time.

VI. FROM CHAUCER TO THE RENAISSANCE

The Chaucerian Imitators: Lydgate and Occleve.—After the death of Chaucer and Langland, literature declined. Poets, in the dearth of original inspiration, kept turning back to Chaucer, as to their "fader dere and maister reverent," and imitating him both in matter and manner. One of these disciples was John Lydgate, a monk of Bury St. Edmunds (1370?–1451?). Another, Thomas Occleve or Hoccleve (1370?–1450?) had the benefit of Chaucer's personal acquaintance and instruction, loved and mourned him deeply, and preserved, in the manuscript of his "Governail of Princes" (written for the Prince of Wales, afterward Henry V.), the portrait of Chaucer as a gray-haired old man, hooded and gowned.

James of Scotland: "The King's Quair."—Another poet who continued the master's tradition is the young Stuart prince, afterward James I. of Scotland, who was captured by English sailors in 1405, and spent the next nineteen years in England as a prisoner, in the Tower of London, Windsor Castle, and other strongholds. At the time of his capture he was a child of eleven. As he grew up in solitude, he turned for diversion to poetry and music. One day, from the windows of Windsor Castle, he saw a beautiful young girl walking in the garden below, as Palamon saw the fair Emilie in the "Knight's Tale." The story of his love for Jane Beaufort and its happy outcome, the young prince told with tenderness and fancy in *The King's Quair* (i.e., The King's Little Book). *The King's Quair* is, with all its artificiality of manner, a poem which can still be read with delight by reason of its fresh feeling; and our pleasure in it is increased by the modesty of the royal poet, who speaks of it as his "litel boke, nakit (naked) of eloquence."

Popular Literature: Ballads and Miracle Plays.—While the poetry of the cultivated classes languished, the poetry of the people, not yet written down, but passing from mouth to mouth and generation to generation in the form of ballads, took on a new life. It was probably during the course of the fifteenth century that a great number of those ballads arose, which mirror faithfully the life of the people, and which remain to-day as fresh and moving in their simple beauty, as poignant in their pathos, and as heart-stirring in their rude power, as when they were first sung. "Chevy Chase," "Sir Patrick Spens," "The Nut-Brown Maid," "Young Waters," "Edward, Edward," "The Wife of Usher's Well," "Johnnie Armstrong," "Lord Thomas and Fair Annet," and other poems of the great ballad-making time, are among the most precious possessions of our literature; and they will continue to be more precious the further the race removes itself from the primitive conditions of life under which they arose. The fifteenth century also marks the growth of another form of literature, the miracle play, which sprang almost as directly from the life of the common people as did the ballads.*

Fifteenth Century Prose : Sir Thomas Malory.—In prose the fifteenth century produced one work which has much of the elevation and splendor of great poetry, the *Morte D'Arthur* of Sir Thomas Malory. Malory was a knight, a gentleman of an ancient house, with its seat at Newbold Revell, Warwickshire. As a young man he served in France, in the military retinue of Richard Beauchamp, Earl of Warwick, a warrior in whom lived again the knightly ideal of a former age, and who was known by the romantic title of "Father of Courtesy." Such a lineage and training fitted Malory peculiarly for his task of combining in a great prose-poem the legends of King Arthur and the Round Table, which he gathered from Geoffrey of Monmouth (see Chap. III) and the French *trouvères*. By good fortune he was master of a simple, flowing English style, very flexible and musical. The only example which he had for such a use as he made of the new English prose, was in the famous *Travels of Sir John Mandeville*, compiled in French by Jean de Bourgogne, and translated into English late in the fourteenth century. The translator of these fictitious "Travels" is unknown, but whoever he was, he threw his marvellous tales of giant sheep, human beings with dogs' faces, "anthropaphagi, and men whose heads do grow beneath their shoulders," into a simple, lucid prose, which, while lacking the terseness and energy of Wyclif's popular sermons, was a good instrument for the everyday-work of literature. This instrument Malory took up; but in response to the superior dignity and beauty of his subject, he raised it to a higher power. The *Morte D'Arthur* was finished in 1467, but was not printed until 1485, when Caxton, the first English printer, published it with an interesting preface from his own hand.

* We shall study the Miracle Play later, when we come to discuss the beginnings of the regular drama.

REVIEW OUTLINE.—Make a summary of the chief public events of Chaucer's time. Give the leading events of Chaucer's life. Find as many points of connection as possible between the two. Describe the state of Italy at the time of Chaucer's visits, and the effect upon the poet of what he saw there. England as a whole did not feel the influence of the Italian Renaissance until the sixteenth century, in the reign of Henry VII.; but Chaucer was a man of the Renaissance, in his gaiety, his humanity, his interest in what was known of the literature of classic times, in his delight in the humor and picturesqueness of social life. What evidences do you find of these traits in what is here told of his life and work? What circumstances of Chaucer's life were calculated to give him the wide knowledge of men shown in the " Canterbury Tales " ? Bring together as many hints as you can find in the text (or elsewhere) concerning Chaucer's personal appearance; his habits; his character and tastes. Supplement this with a study of the Occleve portrait here reproduced. Note the chief works belonging to each of his three literary periods. What special aspect of his genius comes out for the first time in "Troilus and Cressida "? Make clear to yourself the meaning of the word " realism " here applied to Chaucer's treatment of the Troilus story. What special aspect of Chaucer as a poet and as a man does the prologue to the " Legend of Good Women " illustrate? This prologue suggested Tennyson's " Legend of Fair Women ": if possible, read the two together, and contrast them.

In what direction did Chaucer's genius develop during his later life? Note some reasons for this development in Chaucer's own life and in the life of the nation. Describe the plan of the " Canterbury Tales." A harmonious relation exists throughout the " Canterbury Tales " between story and story-teller: point out as many instances of this as you can find in what is here told of the Pilgrims on the road. Note the means which Chaucer takes to keep the company vividly before our eyes while they are telling their stories. What sly means does the poet take to ridicule the metrical romances of his day? What can you gather from this episode concerning the state of the metrical romance— once so dignified and entertaining a form of literature—at the end of the fourteenth century? What is here said of Chaucer's prose as contrasted with his verse? Note in this connection that nearly all the literature we have reviewed up to this point has been poetic. Can you see any reasons why poetry should develop earlier than prose?

By what accidental circumstance was the secret of Chaucer's melody and careful verse-structure lost to succeeding generations, and only recently found again?

State the social and political conditions which brought on the uprising known as Tyler's rebellion. What were the motives which prompted Wyclif to originate the Lollard movement? (Illustrate your answer from what Chaucer reveals of the worldliness of the church at this time, in the Prologue to the "Canterbury Tales," and study the Parson as a type of Wyclif's "poor priests.") Wyclif is called the "father of English prose;" this is of course not to be understood to mean that he was the first to write prose which can be understood by modern readers, but that his prose style was the first to have a large and lasting influence. By what works has he gained the title? State in your own words why Wyclif deserves to be called the "father of the Reformation." Contrast Chaucer with his great contemporary Langland, in character, and in the kind of themes they each chose to write about. What is the source of our knowledge concerning Langland's life? Give the chief facts known about him. Note that his last work treats of the same king whose story Shakespeare afterward presented in one of his dramas: which one? Describe briefly the subject of "Piers Plowman." What changes does the character of Piers the Plowman undergo in the course of the poem? In what respects is Langland's book mediæval, and in what respects modern?

How and by whom was Chaucer's portrait preserved to us? Tell the story of "The King's Quair." How was lyric poetry nourished and kept alive during the fifteenth century, when, because of disturbed political conditions, it was apparently neglected among the higher classes? (The simple poetry of this period was destined to have a great influence on the later history of English poetry. Keep it well in mind and be prepared to recognize this influence.) If possible read the ballads named in the text; rephrase in your own language one or two of them, as "Sir Patrick Spens," the "Nut-Brown Maid," etc.; then read the originals again, noting how much is lost by the substitution of modern phrases for the picturesque old ones, and by the substitution of prose for the rude but vigorous ballad rhythms. What is the chief prose work of the fifteenth century? What modern poet has used the same material for an epic poem?

READING GUIDE.—Students should read at least the prologue to the "Canterbury Tales," and "The Knight's Tale." Many school editions exist; two of the most satisfactory are by F. J. Mather, Jr. (Houghton, Mifflin), and by Morris & Skeat (Clarendon Press), both of which contain also "The Nun's Priest's Tale." The class work can be much enlivened by calling for volunteers to read and report to the class upon other poems, as "The Nun's Priest's Tale," "The Clerk's Tale," "The Parlement of Fowls," and the prologue to the "Legend of Good Women." G. L. Kittridge's "Selections from the Canterbury Tales," soon to be published (Ginn) will prove excellent for supplementary work. The best complete single-volume edition of Chaucer is "The Student's Chaucer," edited by W. W. Skeat (Clarendon Press).

Good editions of the early ballads are "The Ballad Book," edited by W. Allingham, in the Golden Treasury series, and "Old English Ballads," by W. D. Armes, in Macmillan's Pocket Series. An excellent brief selection is given in the inexpensive series of Maynard's English Classics. For more advanced study consult F. B. Gummere's "Old English Ballads" (Ginn), or Miss Child's "English and Scottish Popular Ballads " (Houghton, Mifflin).

"The Travels of Sir John Mandeville " is included in Cassell's National Library. Selections from Mandeville, and from Wyclif's Bible, are given in Number 107 of Maynard's English Classics. Malory's "Morte D'Arthur," selected portions, is edited by E. Rhys in the Camelot Series.

Biography and Criticism.—Lowell's delightful appreciation of Chaucer in "My Study Windows," also in the fourth volume of his collected works (Houghton, Mifflin), should, if possible, be put before the class. A. W. Ward's life of Chaucer, in the English Men of Letters series, may with profit be made the basis of additional reports to the class, the work being distributed among several students.

TABULAR VIEW

MIDDLE ENGLISH PERIOD: FROM THE NORMAN CONQUEST TO THE MIDDLE OF THE FIFTEENTH CENTURY

POLITICAL HISTORY

THE NORMAN KINGS, 1066–1154.

William of Normandy invades England, and conquers the Saxon king Harold at Senlac, 1066. He builds the Tower of London and other strong castles: he takes the land from the Saxon owners and distributes it among his own lords. Henry I. (1100–1135) marries a Saxon wife (Maud, a descendant of King Alfred), and grants privileges to the towns.

ANGEVIN or PLANTAGENET KINGS, 1154–1399.

Under Henry II. (1154–1178), the barons refuse to furnish troops to be used outside of England. King John, brother of Richard Cœur de Lion, loses Normandy, 1204. Edward I. establishes a Parliament of two houses, Lords and Commons, 1265, after which the union of the Norman and Saxon population progresses rapidly. Edward III. comes to the throne, 1327. Beginning of the Hundred Years War. Victory of Crécy, 1346. Victory of Poitiers, 1356, and capture of John, the French King, by Edward's eldest son, the Black Prince. Result of the French war is to draw Norman and Saxon still closer together. Richard II. comes to the throne, 1377. Royal power chiefly in the hands of John of Gaunt, Chaucer's patron. Peasant uprising under Wat Tyler, 1381. The Lollard movement under Wyclif: institution of the "poor priests." Richard II. deposed, and crown seized by John of Gaunt's son Bolingbroke, 1399. Bolingbroke, the first of the House of Lancaster, takes the throne as Henry IV.

LANGUAGE AND LITERATURE

1. FUSION OF ENGLISH AND FRENCH TONGUES.

From 1066 to 1200 English is not used as a literary language (except in Anglo-Saxon Chronicle). During this period French is the language of the nation, both spoken and written, except among the common people. When English begins again to be written, about 1200, it is much simplified in grammar, and so near modern English that it can be understood, with little difficulty, by a reader of to-day. Between 1200 and 1350 English absorbs a quantity of French words, nearly three times its own bulk. By this time the two languages are substantially fused; and between 1360 and 1400 the East Midland dialect of London, with still further French ingredients, is given permanent form by Chaucer. In 1362, by decrees of Parliament, English supersedes French in all law courts. About the same time it begins to supplant French in the schools. In 1399, Henry IV. takes his coronation oath in English, swearing by "Fadir, Son, and Holy Gost."

2. DEVELOPMENT OF MIDDLE ENGLISH LITERATURE BEFORE CHAUCER, 1066–1340.

First work in English tongue after the Conquest is Layamon's Brut, about 1205, drawn chiefly from the Latin Historia Bretonum of Geoffrey of Monmouth (1147), and the French Brut d'Angleterre, of Wace (1155). Contains also original matter of Welsh origin, dealing with King Arthur. The metrical romances, introduced in the eleventh and twelfth centuries by the

TABULAR VIEW

MIDDLE ENGLISH PERIOD: FROM THE NORMAN CONQUEST TO THE MIDDLE OF THE FIFTEENTH CENTURY (*Continued*)

LANGUAGE AND LITERATURE

Normans, are translated freely into English in the thirteenth and fourteenth. Sir Gawayne and the Green Knight, about 1320. The Love Rune of Thomas de Hales dates probably from the thirteenth century; other important religious poems, *e.g.*, The Pearl, Cleanness, and Patience, from the fourteenth. The lyrics Lent Is Come, Alysoun, etc., and the early Robin Hood ballads, date probably from the same period.

3. THE AGE OF CHAUCER, 1340–1400.

(a) *Chronology of Chaucer's Work*: Romaunt of the Rose, 1360 to about 1365; Book of the Duchesse, about 1369; Troilus and Creseide, 1380–1383; Parlement of Fowls, 1382; House of Fame, 1383–1384; Legend of Good Women, 1384–1385; Canterbury Tales, begun about 1385, though some of the separate tales were written earlier.

(b) *Other Writings of the Period.* Langland's Vision of Piers Plowman, from about 1362 to about 1399. Sir John Mandeville's Travels, translated before 1371. Wyclif's Bible, about 1380. John Gower's Confessio Amantis (a collection of tales set in a conventional mediæval framework) about 1393; Occleve, 1365?–1450?; notable works, The Gouvernail of Princes, and Lament for Chaucer. Lydgate, 1370?–1460; chief work, The Fall of Princes. James I. of Scotland writes The King's Quair between 1405 and 1424. Sir Thomas Malory writes the Morte d'Arthur about 1470; printed 1485. Ballads written throughout fourteenth and fifteenth centuries.

CHAPTER V

THE RENAISSANCE

I. ENGLAND IN THE FIFTEENTH CENTURY

The century following the death of Chaucer was for England a time of political and social disturbance. The deposition of Richard II. in 1399 left the succession to the throne open to dispute among the other descendants of Edward III. Henry IV., who took the throne from Richard, was a strong ruler; and his son Henry V. was a wonderful soldier who won the famous victory over the French at Agincourt (1415) and captured Paris, where he was crowned King of France. His early death left the throne to his baby son, Henry VI., who grew up to be one of the weakest of English kings. His title to the throne was assailed by a grandson of Edward III., Richard, Duke of York, and thus began the long civil war known as the War of the Roses, between the supporters of the two rival families of Lancaster and York. Not until 1485, when the last of the York kings, Richard III. (who had gained the throne by the murder of his two little nephews), was defeated at Bosworth by Henry Tudor, and the conqueror took the throne as Henry VII., was England finally at peace.

During the weak rule of Henry VI., when England was steadily being defeated by the French, and during the disturbed reigns which followed, the wealth which the country had gained under the Edwards was wasted. The ruin of many of the great feudal families by the civil war deprived literature of their support and patronage. The most interesting literary products of this period are to be found in the narrative songs or ballads composed and sung for the common people, and in the early popular religious dramas. Among the commons, also, the religious revival which Wyclif had begun, continued, though the Lollards, as his followers were called, were persecuted by successive sovereigns of both houses. This popular revival prepared the way for the English Reformation, which we shall treat of shortly. At the same time the intellectual movement of the modern world, known as the Renaissance, was having its effect in England, though its full influence did not appear until after the country had settled down to peaceful pursuits under the strong rule of the Tudor kings.

II. THE RENAISSANCE AND THE REFORMATION

The Renaissance Defined.—The Renaissance, or Rebirth, is the name given to the great awakening which marks the end of the Middle Age. Its chief cause was the partial recovery of classical literature, art, and civilization, and of the idea therein expressed of man's life as belonging to himself, and of the world as a place for his development and satisfaction. This recognition of individual freedom, as opposed to the rigid system of living and thinking prescribed by feudalism and the church, may properly be called a *rebirth* of the human spirit. Signs of the change are found in every direction, but they all point to the development of man's personal energy, accompanied by an intense interest in the present world. Instead of renouncing the world as a temptation, at the command of the church, men began to devote themselves to gaining mastery over it through wealth and political power, to discovering its secrets by exploration and scientific experiment, to setting forth its pleasures and adding to them by art and poetry.

The Renaissance in Italy.—Already in the time of Chaucer the spirit of the Renaissance had taken possession of Italy. The division of that country into small states multiplied the opportunities of the individual to gain personal distinction in government or in war. Its situation on the commercial highway between the East and the West was favorable to the acquisition of wealth. The disposition of the Italians, and their opportunities, led them naturally toward the enjoyment of the world about them. Accordingly, the despots and the merchant princes, when they had gained their power or wealth, made their courts and palaces centres of magnificent and cultivated life, the resort of artists and learned men. The fact that Italy possessed the relics of classical civiliza-tion,—buildings, statues, manuscripts,—constantly reminded its inhabitants of the ideals of the ancient Romans, and furnished examples, in all the arts, of perfection of form on which the new taste for beautiful things was nourished. The capture of Constantinople by the Turks in 1453 drove many Greeks to seek shelter in Italy. They brought with them a knowledge of the language and literature of Greece, and thenceforth more than ever the Italian cities became centres for the study of the classics, and for the spread of the classical spirit of interest in human life and in all its op-portunities—a spirit which gave to this revival of learning the name Humanism.

From Italy the influence of Humanism spread to other nations, which in their turn contributed elements to the new world which was being created. Spain and Portugal, by sending Columbus to America and Vasco da Gama to India, made the world a larger place for men to act in. The Ger-mans, in the invention of printing, supplied the means by which the new knowledge of all kinds could be diffused widely among men. And Germany, as the home of Coper-nicus, gave birth to the astronomical discoveries which taught men that the earth, instead of being the centre of the universe, was but one element in a single solar system.

Signs of Renaissance in England.—In the fourteenth cen-tury, England, the home of Chaucer and Wyclif, seemed quite prepared to take part in this forward movement of the modern world. During the fifteenth century something of the early impulse was lost; but there were abundant signs that the promise of new life was not dead. For one thing, the decline of the old noble families, which were cut off by the civil war, left an opening for "new men," as they were called, to come to the front. The passing away of feudalism made the merchant class of more importance, and tended to replace the aristocracy of birth by that of wealth. Thus in England as in Italy we have one essential condition of the Renaissance, the wider opportunity for individual development. The example of foreign countries was not without influence. In 1476 Caxton set up the first printing press in London. Before this date one of the Oxford colleges had engaged an Italian teacher of Greek, and by the close of the century Englishmen had begun to go freely to Italy to study with the Italian humanists. They returned to make Oxford and Cambridge homes of classical scholarship, and especially of the "new learning," as Greek studies were called. This revival of learning had, in England as in Italy, a marked effect upon literature. It turned men's minds strongly toward the discussion of theories of culture and education, and the relation of the individual to society. Further, it set models for imitation, and standards of literary excellence. It is true, this tendency in time became an impediment to native English literature, and we find in poetry and the drama that writers who wished to express themselves in their own way had to struggle to free themselves from forms prescribed by the authority of the Greeks and the Latins. On the whole, however, the revival of learning furnished the youthful literature of England with a very necessary schooling and discipline.

The Court of Henry VIII.—The centre of Renaissance literature in England, however, was not the university, but the royal court, especially after the accession of Henry VIII. in 1509. The new king was ambitious to take a leading part in the affairs of Europe, and his diplomacy, by bringing England into the family of continental nations, opened many channels for foreign influence, which soon manifested itself in dress, building, art, and letters. Naturally Italy, as the most advanced country of Europe, gave most to this new civilization of England. The king, indeed, in his own character resembled strongly some of the Italian princes of the time, who mingled the enlightenment of the statesman with the suspicious cruelty of the despot. In setting aside the relics of feudalism and allowing men of low birth to rise to the highest distinction by personal service of the sovereign, he set a premium upon individual character and ability. The men who played for power in his service had need of skill in a game where the stakes were the highest, and defeat fatal. Moreover, Henry resembled the typical sovereigns of the Renaissance in his fondness for art, learning, and magnificent display. He was himself a musician, a lover of architecture, and the patron of painters, poets, and learned men.

Sir Thomas More.—The most gracious figure of the court of Henry is that of Sir Thomas More (1478–1535). In his early days More was a student of the new learning at Oxford, and though later thrown into active life as member of Parliament and minister of the king, he never lost interest in the intellectual movement of the time. He was captivated by the dignified conception of human character which appeared in the more serious men of the Italian Renaissance; and in the accounts of his own life, notably that by his son-in-law, William Roper, we catch something of the spirit of a man who sought not only righteousness but beauty of life—who made living a fine art. In his most famous work, *Utopia* (1515–1516), More tried to show how this ideal might be realized for all men, under a properly organized social system. The book is written as the narrative of a sailor, returned to England after a voyage to a mysterious island, Utopia, in which the inhabitants have learned to live by reason. The commonwealth of Utopia is a form of what we should call socialism. By simplicity of life, and the equal sharing of its burdens, the Utopians have reduced the necessary labor of each person to a few hours a day. They have no personal wealth, and hence are free from the evil and crime which spring from its possession. The adjective "utopian" has been used ever since More's time to denote a state of society desirable but impossible. The book is altogether characteristic of the hopefulness and enthusiasm of the early Renaissance, when men dared to dream of the perfection of human beings in a perfect state.

The New Poetry.—In the later years of Henry VIII., the refinement of court life developed the practice among the courtiers of addressing the sovereign, the ladies of the court, or each other, in verse. Among the courtly poets of the time are two who, for their reform of English metrical structure by the use of models imported from Italy, may be called the founders of modern English poetry—Sir Thomas Wyatt (1503–1542), and Henry Howard, Earl of Surrey (1517–1547).

Sir Thomas Wyatt.—The career of Wyatt illustrates particularly the value to English literature of the close connection with foreign countries, which Henry VIII.'s ambition to take part in European affairs did much to restore. Wyatt was frequently abroad on diplomatic missions; like Chaucer he visited Italy, and also Spain and France. His poems are, for the most part, translations and imitations of Italian poetry, especially of Petrarch's sonnets in praise of Laura. With Petrarch's imitators the sonnet had become a mere literary exercise, devoted to the expression of a love which might be entirely imaginary, or directed toward an imaginary person. Wyatt's sonnets, therefore, need not be regarded as having strict biographical truth, though attempts have been made to find in them the history of a personal relation, and some have guessed that they were inspired by Henry's second queen, Anne Boleyne. Wyatt's effort to achieve the regularity and finish of the Italian sonnet was not always successful. Yet in freer lyrical verse such poems as "My Lute, Awake," and "Forget not yet," are eminent examples of his power.

The Earl of Surrey.—Wyatt's companion poet, Surrey, born in 1517, and beheaded in 1547, is, like More, notable for his personal quality. He has all the exuberance of the age, a perpetual charm of youth and promise, as his brilliant figure passes through the sunlight and shadow of Henry's court, moving gracefully and carelessly to the scaffold which awaited him. Surrey, like Wyatt, rendered his chief service to English literature by enriching its resources with foreign forms, and especially by his introduction of blank verse, in his translation of two books of Virgil's *Æneid*. Blank verse had been used in Italy a few years before in a translation of the same work, from which experiment Surrey may have obtained the suggestion, but the happy skill with which he adopted it, and thus gave to English poetry its most powerful and characteristic verse form, is worthy of all praise. To Surrey also is due the English form of the sonnet which Shakespeare used, consisting of three quatrains and a couplet.

" Tottel's Miscellany."—The work of these literary courtiers was intended for private circulation in manuscript. By the middle of the century, however, there had grown up a demand on the part of the reading public which publishers attempted to supply by volumes of miscellaneous verse. The first of these collections, "Tottel's Miscellany," contained the poems of Wyatt, Surrey, and several of their followers. It appeared in 1557, a date which marks the public beginning of modern English verse.

The Reformation.—The fact that both Wyatt and Surrey, the introducers of Renaissance poetry, wrote also religious verse, emphasizes the fact that in England the Renaissance and the Reformation were nearly contemporary. The formal beginning of the Reformation in Europe is dated from 1517, when Martin Luther nailed to the door of the church in Wittenberg his attack upon the power of the Pope. The doctrines of the German and Swiss reformers spread rapidly through England. When in 1534 King Henry VIII. quarrelled with the Pope, who refused to grant him a divorce from his first wife, Catherine of Aragon, he found the people at large ready to support him in his proclamation of himself as Head of the Church, and later in his suppression of the monasteries.

The Reformation was the chief political question in the closing years of the reign of Henry VIII., and indeed throughout the rest of the century. Henry was strong enough to hold a moderate course between the reformers and the adherents of the old faith. After his death in 1547, the former controlled the policy of the boy-king, Edward VI., and pushed their advantage by persecution and bloodshed. When the king died in 1553, they tried to retain power by setting up as queen the Lady Jane Grey, but the mass of the nation accepted the claim of Mary, the daughter of Henry VIII. by his first and Catholic wife. In her five years of rule she did her utmost to restore the old faith, outdoing the reformers in the cruelty of her persecution. At her death in 1558, she was succeeded by Elizabeth, who, though of the reformed faith, was inclined to keep a middle course between the two religious parties. However, the movement in

Europe known as the Catholic Reaction was now in full progress under the leadership of Philip II., of Spain. His efforts to stamp out the Reformation in France and the Netherlands, and his support of the claims of Mary Queen of Scots to the crown of Elizabeth, gradually forced England into open hostility to Spain, which the queen signalized by sending troops to help the Dutch revolt against Philip, and by beheading the Queen of Scots in 1586. Philip's response to this challenge was the Spanish Armada, which he sent against England in 1588.

The Literature of the Reformation.—The Reformation had a very important influence on English life. Coming at the time when the Renaissance was drawing men into ardent love of the present world and stimulating their ambition to master it and to enjoy it, the Reformation brought home the thought of the other world, and checked the spirit of selfishness and self-indulgence by enforcing anew the claim of religion. This influence is reflected in the literature of the time, especially the popular literature. The Reformation was to the common people what the revival of learning was to the upper classes: it set the most important topic for discussion, and called into being a simple native English style which could be understood by all. The best example of this style is to be seen in the translation of the Bible by William Tyndale, of which the New Testament appeared in 1526. This was eagerly circulated by the reformers, in spite of the efforts of the authorities to prevent it. Ten years later, when the king himself had turned against the Pope, Miles Coverdale was authorized to revise Tyndale's translation of the scriptures, and his version, completed in 1538, was placed by royal sanction in the churches all over England, where the great volumes, chained to the pillars, were read to the crowds of unlettered folk. Thus the English Bible came to be the strongest influence on English popular prose, for which it supplied a model in opposition to the artificial styles imitated from foreign or classic literature.

Foxe's " Book of Martyrs."—Next to the Bible the most popular work of the time was the *Book of Martyrs* (1563) of John Foxe. This was a genuine text-book of the Reformation; from it we gain those accounts of the martyrs of Mary's reign, of Hooper and Cranmer, Latimer and Ridley, which are among the best known passages of English history. In its plain, literal style it reflects the strenuous temper of the thorough-going reformers. Its stern realism brought home to Englishmen the cruel struggle by which the new faith survived, and its eloquent accounts of spiritual triumph roused the moral enthusiasm of the nation, and prepared the way for Puritanism.

III. THE AGE OF ELIZABETH

The Spirit of the Time.—The accession of Elizabeth in 1558 changed the entire aspect of the nation. Her moderate policy relaxed the religious tension; the gloomy spirit produced by the persecutions was lightened; the force of the Renaissance manifested itself more widely, as the spirit of individual freedom and of eager response to all the new opportunities of the world. It was an age of romantic adventure, which led men into intellectual speculation and commercial enterprise, which sent them to explore the unknown seas of the north, the mysterious rivers and forests of the new world, or drew them into the scarcely less exciting life of London. But the impulses of the time which made for personal and selfish ends were both directed and kept in check by a corresponding growth of patriotism. Elizabeth's reign united the nation, and her personal presence gave it a visible sign of unity. The championship of the reformed faith, moreover, came to be regarded by a large part of the people as a national duty, and the conquest of lands beyond the seas as a national opportunity. When in course of time the pursuit of these ends brought England into open conflict with Spain, the country passed through an experience as dramatic as that of Athens at Marathon; after a long period of suspense the strain was relieved by the wonderful repulse of the Spanish Armada in 1588. The national feeling, made so intense by danger and victory, shines through the literature of the time. The eager, instinctive patriotism of the people found utterance in the choruses of Shakespeare's

Henry V. and in such noble lyrics as Michael Drayton's "Ballad of Agincourt," the ringing metre of which Tennyson used afterward in "The Charge of the Light Brigade." The more conscious political virtue, which touched with high purpose the lives of Sidney, of Essex, and of Raleigh, is reflected in Spenser's *Faerie Queene.*

Lyly's "Euphues."—The beginning of the great period of Elizabethan literature may be dated from 1579, the year of the publication of the most famous prose work of the time, Lyly's *Euphues* and also of Spenser's decisive appearance as a poet in *The Shepherd's Calendar.* The former, though now little read, deserves mention as the best illustration of the narrowly literary ideals of the age.

John Lyly (1553–1606) was educated at Magdalen College, Oxford, where he seems to have gained the reputation of being a trifler—"the fiddlestick of Oxford," an enemy called him. His superficial cleverness, however, enabled him to write a successful account of the culture of the period, in *Euphues or the Anatomy of Wit* (1579), and its sequel, *Euphues and his England* (1580). Together they form a work of fiction in which an exceedingly slight plot serves to connect a succession of conversations, letters, and essays, treating such subjects as love, education, religion, and manners. The book illustrates the interest of the time in intellectual development, restrained, however, by the feeling, stirred by the Reformation, that "vain is all learning without the taste of divine knowledge."

The artificial language which Euphues and his friends talked, and which became a literary fashion, is the characteristic of the book for which it is remembered to-day. Among Lyly's mannerisms the most remarkable is the arrangement of words in antithesis, the contrast being marked by alliteration, thus: "Although I have *shrined* thee in my heart for a *trusty friend,* I will *shunne* thee hereafter as a *trothless foe.*" Another peculiarity is his lavish use of similes drawn from what passed for natural history, as: "The milk of the Tygresse, that the more salt there is thrown into it the fresher it is." Euphuism was but one form of a widely diffused tendency in Renaissance literature, an attempt to prove the

SIR PHILIP SIDNEY

From the miniature by Isaac Oliver, in the Royal Library at Windsor Castle

artistic value of prose by giving it some of the qualities of poetry. Earlier writers than Lyly had shown traces of it; and English prose did not escape from its influence until well on in the next century.

Sir Philip Sidney.—In Lyly's own generation other forms of this tendency appeared, notably that introduced by the most famous Englishman of the day, Sir Philip Sidney. Sidney was born in 1554, of one of the most distinguished families in England. He was sent to Shrewsbury school and to Oxford; and then spent some time abroad. He was in Paris at the time of the terrible massacre of St. Bartholomew's Day, 1572—an experience which must have strengthened the serious purpose of his life, the defence of the Reformed Faith. Later, in Italy, he felt the attraction of the art of the Renaissance, and was himself painted by the great Venetian painter, Paul Veronese. He returned to England to become the most brilliant figure of Elizabeth's court. His uncle, the Earl of Leicester, was the political chief of the Puritan party, which favored committing England to a definite alliance with the Protestant states of Europe; and in furtherance of this policy Sidney was sent on a mission to Germany in 1577. He was also eagerly interested in the development of English power on the sea. In 1583 he got a grant of land in America, and two years later he made an unsuccessful attempt to escape from court and join Sir Francis Drake in one of his half-piratical expeditions against the Spaniards. This same year he accompanied the English army which was sent to help the Dutch Protestants against Spain; and in 1586 he fell in a skirmish at Zutphen.

" Astrophel and Stella." — Sidney's name, more than any other, stands for the greatness of national and personal ideals which we associate with the age of Elizabeth. It is, therefore, somewhat disappointing to find his writing less eminent than his life. It must be remembered, however, that Sidney, like most men of position in his age, wrote not for the public, but for himself and for a few friends. This is especially the case in regard to his poetry. The courtiers of Elizabeth, like those of Henry VIII., expressed themselves in verse, inspired sometimes by love or by a spirit of courtly compliment, sometimes by meditation and self-study. Sidney's contribution to this court poetry is of unusual interest because of its connection with a fascinating, if shadowy, love story. His collection of songs and sonnets, called *Astrophel and Stella*, first published in a pirated edition after his death, is evidently addressed to one person, Lady Penelope Devereux. Sidney and Lady Penelope had been betrothed when the latter was a child. For some reason the match was broken off, and Lady Penelope married Lord Rich, with whom she lived for a while most unhappily. Whether Sidney actually came to love her, or whether he wrote love sonnets as a literary exercise, addressing them to his old friend out of compliment and sympathy, it is impossible to say. On the one hand there is in his sonnets much of the conventional material of the Italian sonneteers; but on the other there are touches so apt to the situation of a man who loves too late, that one hesitates to ascribe them to mere dramatic skill. In none of the many sonnet cycles of the age, except Shakespeare's and Spenser's, do we find so much that has the stamp of personality upon it; surely in none except these, so much that has the accent of great poetry.

" The Arcadia."—Sidney's chief literary enterprise was the *Arcadia*, which he began in 1580, when, in consequence of a quarrel with the Earl of Oxford, he was in temporary disgrace and banishment from court. The writing of the *Arcadia* was merely a summer pastime, undertaken to please the Countess of Pembroke, Sidney's sister. The form of the work was suggested by romances, popular in Italy and in Spain, of which the scenes are laid in a pastoral country like the ancient Arcadia. The prose tale is interrupted at intervals by passages of verse, or eclogues, in which the shepherds sing of love and the delights of rural life. This form of literature had a great charm for people who were becoming a little weary of the activity of the early Renaissance; and Sidney himself, in his banishment from court, doubtless felt the influence of this mood. It was, however, a passing one, for Sidney was essentially a man of action; and his story, which begins in thoroughly pastoral fashion, quickly changes to a kind of romance of chivalry set in an Arcadian landscape. Throughout its great length Sidney spins his tale with a pure love for it, with the enthusiasm that he might have thrown into a buccaneering expedition to the Indies, if fortune had been kind to him; and this is the real source of such pleasure as we feel to-day in reading the *Arcadia*.

The " Defence of Poesy."—Sidney was not only poet and romancer, but also one of the earliest of English critics.   In 1579 Stephen Gosson published a pamphlet called *The School of Abuse*, in which, as a Puritan, he attacked the art of the age, especially the drama.   Sidney replied, in 1581, with his *Defence of Poesy*, in which he replied to Gosson's strictures and defended English verse, even of the native ballad sort, exclaiming, "I never heard the old song of 'Percy and Douglas' that I found not my heart moved more than with a trumpet."

Sir Walter Raleigh.—A name that, partly by force of contrast, is always associated with Sidney's, is that of Sir Walter Raleigh.   Raleigh was born in Devonshire in 1552.   He was at Oxford for a while, but left to join the French reformers in their resistance to the Catholics.   Following his return to England he was busy for many years with intrigues for power at court, with attempts to win estates in Ireland and to establish colonies in America.   He took a leading part in the events of the war with Spain,—the destruction of the Armada and the attack upon Cadiz.   After the accession of James I. he was charged with conspiracy against the new monarch, and thrown into the Tower.   The king released him to lead an expedition to Guiana, in search of gold, but his return without accomplishing his object was the signal for his execution in 1618.

Raleigh's Character.—Sidney is the best example of perfect balance between the opposed tendencies of the times, the impulses that led men to strive for pleasure, richness of experience, and glory, and the motives of religious and patriotic devotion.   Raleigh is representative of all these tendencies in their most exaggerated form.   The well-known story of the young courtier spreading his rich cloak across a puddle for Elizabeth to walk upon, marks the devotion of men to the person of the queen at its most fantastic moment. And in many other things he went beyond other men. He did more against Spain—both in the battle with the Armada and in the great attack on Cadiz in 1596. In his expeditions to South America he was the most splendid of the buccaneers, and he was also the most indefatigable of colonizers. Eight expeditions at his own cost he sent to the shore of Virginia. He was a poet, and he wrote the history of the world. Courtly chivalry, politics, love, war, art, colonization, piracy—he was at home in all fields. In his versatility, his energy, his daring freedom of will, he typifies that individual spirit of the Renaissance which found expression in the exaggerations of personal desires and the over-weening ambitions of Marlowe's dramas. And if there is much that is inconsistent and even false in his character and life, he had always the distinction that came from the magnificence of his enterprises. When he mentioned to Bacon his plan of seizing the Mexico fleet, the latter cried "But that would be piracy." "Oh, no," said Raleigh. "Did you ever hear of men who are pirates for millions? They who aim at small things are pirates."

Raleigh's Writings.—Raleigh's literary work consists of his poems, political tracts, narratives of adventures in which he was directly or indirectly concerned, such as his *Discovery of Guiana*, and the account of the "Last Fight of the Revenge," and finally his *History of the World*, written during the long years of his imprisonment in the Tower.

Raleigh's poems, like those of other courtly poets of the time, were circulated in manuscript, and many have disappeared, including the greater part of his long poem, *Cynthia*, written in praise of Elizabeth. Those which have survived often have special reference to events in his own life or commemorate particular moods, in a strain which a critic of the time calls "most lofty, insolent, and passionate."

That Raleigh, old and in prison, should have addressed himself to writing a history of the world, is another evidence of the greatness of his visions, the preoccupation of his mind with vast issues. He began his work in 1607, and the first volume was published in 1614, under the direction of Ben Jonson, from whom Raleigh received much assistance. Most of the history is written in the rather loose style of Raleigh's personal narratives, with long formless sentences; but at times he rises to a superb eloquence, which gives passages of an imaginative splendor and solemnity of music that have never been surpassed in English prose. Such is the apostrophe to Death with which Raleigh, himself in the shadow of the scaffold, took leave of his mighty enterprise:

"O eloquent, just, and mighty Death! Whom none could advise, thou hast persuaded; what none hath dared, thou hast done; and whom all the world hath flattered, thou only hast cast out of the world and despised—thou hast drawn together all the far-stretched greatness, all the pride, cruelty, and ambition of man, and covered it all over with these two narrow words, *Hic jacet.*"

IV. EDMUND SPENSER (1552–1599)

Spenser's Life.—Spenser was born in London in 1552. He was sent to the Merchant Tailors' School, and then to Pembroke College, Cambridge, where he took his master's degree in 1576. He then spent some time in the north of England. In 1578, however, he was in London, in attendance on the Earl of Leicester, seeking to establish himself through the influence of his friends at court. After the publication of his *Shepherd's Calendar*, in 1579, he received an appointment in Ireland, as secretary to the deputy, Lord Grey de Wilton. In Ireland Spenser was given office, and was granted, among other estates, the Manor of Kilcolman, whither Sir Walter Raleigh came in 1589 to visit him. Raleigh saw the first three books of *The Faerie Queene;* and under his advice Spenser went to London in the following year, to read them to the Queen and to publish them. The success of the poem was immediate, but the reward from the Queen, in whose honor it was written, was disappointingly small. The circumstances of his journey to London he related, after his return to Ireland, in *Colin Clout's Come Home Again*, in which he resumed the pastoral style of *The Shepherd's Calendar.* In the next few years Spenser commemorated his own courtship and marriage

EDMUND SPENSER
From an original picture in the possession of the Earl of Kinnoull

in the sonnet series, the " Amoretti," and in his wedding song, or "Epithalamion." He went to London again in 1596, to publish the second three books of *The Faerie Queene*. During this visit he wrote the "Hymn in Honour of Heavenly Love," and "Hymn in Honour of Heavenly Beauty," to accompany two earlier "Hymns in Honour of Love and Beauty." He also wrote at this time the most exquisite of his shorter poems, the "Prothalamion." Soon after his return to Kilcolman, there broke out one of those frequent insurrections which marked British rule in Ireland. Spenser's castle, which stood in the path of the storm, was sacked and burned. He fled with his family to London, where, in 1599, he died in poverty.

Spenser's Cambridge Period.—Spenser's life was spent chiefly in three places, each of which left strong marks upon his character and work—Cambridge, London, and Ireland. At Cambridge he found the learning of the Renaissance, especially the philosophy of Plato, which appears clearly in *The Faerie Queene* and in the "Hymns." Here also he learned to know the literature of France and Italy, and here he came into contact with the literary theories of the time; one of which was the idea, put forward by Sidney and his friends, that English verse should be written according to Latin rules of prosody. Spenser was too genuine a poet to be injured by such theories, but the influence of the environment where they were rife is seen in his scrupulous attention to the technical requirements of his art.

Of this Cambridge period the typical product is *The Shepherd's Calendar*, a series of twelve pastoral poems or eclogues. The eclogue in general was a poem of pastoral life, in which shepherds were the speakers, rural nature and love their usual themes. The poet might introduce matter personal to himself or his friends, or might even discuss political affairs, but he kept the conventional framework of the pastoral. In Spenser's fifth eclogue, for example, Archbishop Grindal figures as the good shepherd Algrind. The poems of *The Shepherd's Calendar* show much variety in metre, for Spenser was clearly practising and experimenting. But most remarkable among their literary qualities is the diction, which he elaborated for himself with the design of giving a suggestion of antiquity and rusticity to his writings. This curious fondness for obsolete or coined words is characteristic of the artificial style affected by the age. It is carried so far in *The Faerie Queene* that Ben Jonson could say of Spenser that he "writ no language."

Spenser in London and Ireland.— In London Spenser was at the centre of the thrilling national life of England. Through Leicester and Sidney he was introduced to the two leading political conceptions of the time, England's leadership of the Protestant cause in Europe against Spain and Rome, and her expansion beyond the seas—ideas that were the result partly of fantastic chivalry, and partly of a broad view of world politics. Finally, in Ireland he saw the English race in passionate conflict with opposing forces. The chronically disturbed state of the country was aggravated by the intrigues of Philip of Spain and the Pope with the Irish chieftains, provoking those revolts which Lord Grey, strong in his belief that the Irish were the foes of God and of civilization, put down with savage fury. Naturally, Spenser's residence in Ireland, by bringing him into actual conflict with evil, stimulated his moral enthusiasm. Out of the conception of the greatness of England's mission, which Spenser found in London and struggled to realize in Ireland, and out of his chivalric devotion to this ideal, and to the Queen who typified it, grew *The Faerie Queene*. It is the brightest expression of the ideal morality of the time; and in a sense is the epic of the English race at one of the great moments of its history.

The Faerie Queene.—Spenser and his contemporaries regarded moral purpose as essential to the greatest art; and with Spenser this purpose took the form of dealing with the old problem of the Renaissance—individual character in relation to the state. As he explained in his introductory letter to Raleigh, *The Faerie Queene* was to show forth the character of an ideal knight in twelve books, each devoted to one of the twelve qualities of perfect chivalry. This exposition of private virtue was to be followed by a second poem, which should portray the virtues of the ideal knight as governor. In fact, Spenser wrote only six books, each of twelve cantos, and a fragment of a seventh. The first is given to the Red Cross Knight, who represents Holiness; the second to Sir Guyon, or Temperance; the third to Britomarte, or Chastity; the fourth to Cambel and Triamond, or Friendship; the fifth to Sir Artegall, or Justice; the sixth to Sir Calidore, or Courtesy. These knights, as we learn from Spenser's introductory letter, are despatched on their various quests by Gloriana, Queen of Fairyland. In the course of their adventures appears from time to time the perfect knight, Arthur, who is himself in search of the Faerie Queene. The allegory takes at times a political turn, and the characters, besides representing ideal qualities, refer directly to actual persons. Spenser explained: "In that *Faerie Queene* I mean glory in my generall intention, but in my particular I conceive the most excellent and glorious person of our soveraine the Queene." Belphœbe and Britomarte also represent Elizabeth; Arthur is Leicester; the false lady Duessa is Mary Queen of Scots. In the fifth book the political state of Europe is presented at length, with Lord Grey as Artegall, France as Flourdelis, Henry IV. as Burbon, Holland as Belge, and Philip II. of Spain as Grantorto. This was but natural in an age in which politics were colored by religious feeling, and in which public and private conduct, as typified by Sidney, Raleigh, and Essex, was still touched with something of the glamor of the chivalry which had passed away.

Spenser and Ariosto.—The moral seriousness which underlies the poem marks the great difference between *The Faerie Queene* and its Italian prototype. Spenser, like Wyatt and Surrey, was content to go to school to Italy; and he chose as the model for his great work the *Orlando Furioso* of Ariosto. Both Ariosto and Spenser deal with chivalry; but while Ariosto had merely the delight of the artist in the brilliant color which chivalry gave to life, with the easy contempt of the cynic for its moral elements, Spenser found in its persons and ideals a means of making goodness attractive. In details Spenser learned much from Ariosto; many passages he wrote in avowed imitation. His prevailing difference is in the greater richness and elaboration of his style, of which the "Spenserian stanza" is typical. This stanza consists of two interlinked quatrains, with an added line of six feet, the arrangement thus being *ababbcbcc*. The brilliancy of the invention is shown by the fact that it adapts itself readily to the different demands of narrative, descriptive, and moral poetry; **and** that the poem sustains itself throughout its great length with so much variety of effect.

Spenser's Art.—For the rest, Spenser has the great gift of the poet, the power to create the illusion of a different world, a world of magic where the imagination and the senses are satisfied. *The Faerie Queene* is a long procession of figures, brilliant, fantastic, or terrible, which singly or in groups pass across an ever varying, ever wonderful landscape. And almost as marked as Spenser's feeling for form and color, is his use of sound. His sensitiveness of ear is shown by the melody of his verse, so constant yet so varied; but there are also many passages in which he makes suggestions of the music of nature an element of pleasure in his description. Altogether, Spenser has the resources of the whole world of sensation at command, and he never fails to heighten them with the illusions of his art. Of the color, the savor, the music of life, his poem is full—only the color is brighter, the taste sweeter, the music grander, than any which it is given to mortal senses to know.

And this world of imagined splendor is presented as the background of a steadily growing idea of righteousness, of heroic goodness. The union of the two elements, sensuous and moral, seems at times to involve a naïve inconsistency. But Spenser belonged to an age when it seemed not impossible that there should be some common ground between the spirit of the Reformation and that of Humanism. He was perhaps a Puritan; but more fortunate than Milton, he came before Puritanism had narrowed its view of life to the single issue of salvation. There is indeed in Spenser, as in many of his contemporaries, a note of melancholy, which suggests that the eternal contradiction of the joy of the present life by the threat of its hereafter, was not unheard. The flowers are already lightly touched by the frost. But this reminder that the time of free delight in the outer world was so short, its sunshine so threatened by the clouds of Puritanism, makes its brightest product the more precious.

V. PROFESSIONAL WRITING

Prose.—After the literary awakening marked by the writers already treated, the stream of literary production became at once very copious. Curiosity about the world was a leading instinct among men of the Renaissance; this instinct once aroused led to the rapid growth of the reading public, and the business of ministering to its demands became a recognized profession. Romances, essays on religious or political subjects, histories, voyagers' tales, as well as numerous translations from ancient and foreign literature were turned out in great numbers and greedily absorbed. This work was done by men of miscellaneous interests, who labored indifferently in any field to which the taste of the public led them. One of the most broadly characteristic of these writers is Robert Greene (1560–1592). He began his career by writing romances in the style of Lyly. Later, when the *Arcadia* had begun to circulate in manuscript, he imitated Sidney in a pastoral tale called *Menaphon,* and he published also realistic accounts of life in London, translations of Italian stories, pamphlets, and plays. Greene and his particular associates, George Peele, Thomas Nash, and Christopher Marlowe, were the first professional writers. Unlike Sidney, who followed literature as an amateur, or Spenser, who looked for support to the patronage of the rich or preferment from the queen, they undertook to live directly upon their literary earnings. Moreover, as a class, they showed the intense desire for pleasure, the violence of passion, the impatience of restraint, social or moral, which were characteristic of the Renaissance in Italy rather than in England. The irregularity of their lives has made them heroes of stories famous among the tragedies of literature. Marlowe was stabbed to death in a tavern brawl; Peele died of dissipation; Greene, as the story goes, from over-eating, and Nash of starvation.

Poetry.—As the prose literature of the period was injured by the adoption of the euphuistic style for every purpose, so its poetry suffered from the failure of its authors to separate the proper matter of poetry from that of prose. They gave verse form not only to history, but also to politics, philosophy, geography, and science. It is not of these works that we think, however, when we speak of the glory of Elizabethan verse, but of the lyric element, which in nearly all the writers of the time flows somewhere like a stream of living water, making glad the waste places of their larger works. The romances of the time contain many exquisite songs which are preserved in the anthologies of English verse, while the works which furnished the original setting for them are forgotten. The dramas of Lyly, Peele, and, above all, Shakespeare, abound in lyrical interludes, and Marlowe is as famous for his little song "Come live with me and be my love," as for the most imposing of his plays.

Among the courtiers of Elizabeth, as has been said, verse was a natural language. The lyrics of these courtly writers circulated in manuscript and doubtless many of them have disappeared. A number of them, however, are preserved in the poetical miscellanies which from time to time were issued after the fashion of "Tottel's Miscellany." The popular demand for lyric verse is also attested by the numerous books of songs and airs, in some of which not only the words but the music also have been preserved. Indeed the temperament of the age may be tested by its songs. They reflect its delight in youth and nature, in love, and in the glory of arms, sometimes in the mere pleasure of singing. But besides this exuberant joy in life, which the Renaissance brought to men, there is also a steady tone of seriousness and religious feeling, which reminds us that in England the Reformation and the Renaissance advanced together. In the lyric poetry of the time, as in *The Faerie Queene,* we are struck by the mingling of sensuousness and piety—but the latter is no gloomy forbidding of the joy of living, nor even a threatening of its end by death, but a trust in the Creator as frank and honest as is the delight in the world which He has made.

REVIEW OUTLINE.—The political situation in England between 1400 and 1485 should be noted as a reason for the literary decline; and the changes which followed the accession of Henry VII. and the beginning of the new monarchy, as making the conditions for the English Renaissance. What was the essential element in the Renaissance? What was the situation of the individual man under the feudal system? Under the mediæval church? What change did the Renaissance bring about in the attitude of men toward the world? Suggest several reasons for the rapid development of the Renaissance in Italy. What did other nations contribute to the Renaissance? What conditions of the fifteenth century tended to forward the Renaissance in England? What caused the revival of learning in Italy? How was it brought to England? What was its influence on literature?

In considering the progress of the Renaissance in England it may be interesting to point out some differences between the English movement and the Italian. In the first place the influence of patriotism centering about the person of the English sovereign should be noted, as limiting the exercise of personal ambition, which in Italy made for division. And in the second place, the fact that in England the Reformation took place before the Renaissance had got its full headway, should be recalled; and the influence of the new religious interest, checking the temptations of the time toward a life of pleasure, should be noted in writers from Wyatt to Spenser. It will be well also to examine rather carefully the history of the time, and observe how the religious and the national spirit, stimulated by various events, reached their height under Elizabeth in the years which saw also the appearance of the greater Elizabethan literature.

What were some of the characteristics of the court of Henry VIII? Comment on the character of the king. What influences moulded the character of Sir Thomas More? What was his purpose in " Utopia "? What are some of the features of the Utopian society? In what way is the book typical of the Renaissance? What influence did the court of Henry VIII. have on poetry? Name the chief poets of his court. What is the chief characteristic of Wyatt's verse? What were the services of Wyatt and Surrey to English poetry?

The Renaissance was in England very largely a matter of imitation. The Reformation was a more spontaneous national movement. What earlier attempts at religious reform had prepared the way for the English Reformation? What political situation in the reign of Henry

VIII. furthered it? What were the features of the Reformation under Edward VI. and Mary? What was the religious policy of Elizabeth? What was the influence of Tyndale and Coverdale's translation of the Bible on literature? What was the "Book of Martyrs"?

The years between the death of Henry VIII. and the accession of Elizabeth may be regarded as a period of reaction, between the earlier and the later Renaissance. With the accession of Elizabeth came a quickening of all the forces of the age, the individual spirit of ambition and adventure, thirst for pleasure, and love of glory, which may be illustrated from the life of Raleigh, and the plays of Marlowe, to be discussed in the next chapter; the spirit of religious patriotism, which finds its personal representation in Sidney, and its literary expression in "The Faerie Queene." Who was John Lyly? What is the character of "Euphues"? What does it illustrate? What characteristic marked its style? Outline the career of Sir Philip Sidney. What was "Astrophel nd Stella"? Why did Sidney write the "Arcadia"? Give some characteristics of the story. What was the "Defence of Poesy"? Contrast Raleigh with Sidney in character and in career. In what respects is Raleigh an illustration of the interests of his time? What are his chief works?

Outline the life of Spenser. What was the influence on him of Cambridge? of London? of Ireland? What was the "Shepherd's Calendar"? Under what circumstances did Spenser write "The Faerie Queene"? What was the purpose of the poem? What its plan? How does Spenser illustrate the dependence of English literature upon Italian? What is the Spenserian stanza?

What led to the growth of the reading public at the time of the Renaissance? What effects did this growth have upon literature? Illustrate from the career of Robert Greene. How do Greene and his friends differ from Spenser and Sidney in their attitude toward literature? In their lives? Explain the prominence of lyric verse in this period.

READING GUIDE.—All students should read at least Canto I, Book I, of the "Faerie Queene"; this portion of the poem is given in Maynard's English Classic series. If further reading is required in Spenser, it should include the "Prothalamion," and the first portion of "Colin Clout" or "The Shepherd's Calendar." Convenient texts are "Minor Poems of Spenser," in the Temple Classics, and " Selected

Poems," in the Canterbury Poets series. Lowell's essay on Spenser, in "Among My Books," should, if possible, be read.

The "Utopia" and "Roper's Life of More" are printed together in the Camelot Series and in the Temple Classics. Volunteers may be called upon to read and report to the class upon each of these.

For Wyatt, Surrey, and Sidney, the poems given in "The Golden Treasury" or in "Ward's English Poets," Vol. I, should, if possible, be read, either privately by each student or before the class.

Sidney's "Defence of Poesy" is edited by A. S. Cooke (Ginn), and in the Pitt Press Series.

Green's "Short History of the English People," chapter vii, is excellent for supplementing the student's knowledge of the times.

Kingsley's "Westward Ho" gives a vigorous picture of England's struggle with Spain by sea and in America. Tennyson's "Ballad of the Revenge" is excellent to illustrate the patriotic temper of Elizabeth's reign.

CHAPTER VI

THE RENAISSANCE: THE DRAMA BEFORE SHAKE-SPEARE

I. THE ORIGIN OF THE DRAMA: NATIVE SOURCES

Norman Shows and Pageants.—To trace the English drama from the beginning, we must go back as far as the Norman conquest. The Norman people had a great fondness for shows and spectacles. When the Norman kings were once firmly seated on the English throne, they gave full rein to their taste for splendid pageantry. If a royal wedding was to be celebrated, or a victorious monarch welcomed back from war, London was turned into a place of festival. At the entrance gate of the city, or at fixed places on the route to church or palace, elaborate structures were built, representing some mythical or allegorical scene—the gods grouped upon Olympus, an armed St. George giving combat to a golden dragon, or nymphs and satyrs sporting in enchanted gardens. Sometimes music was added, and the personators, by dialogue and action, gave welcome to the royal party. These pageants developed at the Renaissance into a special form of dramatic entertainment, the Masque. Meanwhile, by stimulating in the people a love of dramatic spectacle, they helped to pave the way for regular drama.

The Miracle Play: Its Origin and Growth.—A much more important source of the drama, however, was the mass-service of the Catholic church, especially at Christmas-tide and Easter. The ordinary services at these times were enriched with special ceremonies, such as burying the crucifix in a tomb of the church on Good Friday and disinterring it on Easter morning, with monks or choir-boys to take the parts of the three Marys, the angel at the tomb, and the chorus of rejoicing angels in heaven. These little dramatic ceremonies gradually became detached from the service, and were moved from the church into the church-yard. Later, when the crowds desecrated the graves in their eagerness to see and hear, the plays were transferred to the public green or town square. By Chaucer's time these "miracle plays" or "mysteries" had passed to a large extent out of the hands of the priests, and had come under the control of the trade-guilds, who made use of them to celebrate their annual festival of Corpus Christi. Rivalry among the guilds, and the desire of each to possess a separate play, led to the setting forth of the whole Scripture story from Genesis to Revelations, in a series or cycle forming a great drama, of which the separate plays were, in a sense, only single acts. It was the aim of these great miracle-cycles to give a connected view of God's dealings with man, from the beginning of the world until its destruction.

How Miracle Plays Were Presented.—In order to gain some idea of the impression made by the miracle plays upon the people who witnessed them, let us imagine ourselves for a moment in a provincial English town at the beginning of the fifteenth century, on the morning of Corpus Christi day. Shortly after dawn, heralds have made the round of the city to announce the coming spectacle. The places where the cars or "pageants," which form both stage and dressing-room, are to stop, are crowded with the motley population of a mediæval city. The spectators of importance occupy seats upon scaffolds erected for the purpose, or look on from the windows of neighboring houses, while the humbler folk jostle each other in the street.

Soon the first pageant appears, a great box mounted on four wheels and drawn by apprentices of the masons' guild, which guild is charged with presenting the Creation of Eve and the Fall of Man. The curtains at the front and the sides of the great box are drawn, revealing an upper compartment, within which the main action is to take place. On a raised platform sits enthroned a majestic figure in a red robe, with gilt hair and beard, impersonating the Creator. Before him lies Adam, dressed in a close-fitting leather garment painted white or flesh-color. The

Creator, after announcing his intention of making for Adam a helpmeet, descends and touches the sleeper's side. Thereupon Eve rises through a trap-door, and Adam wakes rejoicing. Again the Creator ascends to his throne, and Adam withdraws to a corner of the pageant, leaving Eve to be tempted by a great serpent, cunningly contrived of green and gold cloth in which an actor is concealed. This monster, crawling upon the stage from below, harangues Eve with lengthy eloquence. Then follows the eating of the apple, and the coming of God's angels, with gilt hair, scarlet robes, and swords waved and ridged like fire, to drive the pair from the garden into the wilderness, that is, into the lower compartment of the pageant, which is now uncovered to view.

A trumpeter advances before the car, and sounds a long note in token of the conclusion of the play. The 'prentices harness themselves to the car; and it moves off to the next station, to be replaced by others. These represent in turn, Noah's Flood, given by the guild of water-merchants; the Sacrifice of Isaac, given by the butchers' guild; the Nativity, the Crucifixion, and so on in long procession, until the crowning spectacle of the Day of Judgment. The chief feature of spectacular interest in this last is Hell-mouth, a great dragon's jaw belching flame and smoke, into which lost souls, dressed in black and yellow particolor, are tossed by the Devil—a most alarming personage with a bright red beard, a hairy body, a hideous mask, horns, and a long forked tail.

Germs of Regular Drama in the Miracle Plays.—The authors of these Miracle plays were free to embellish the biblical story with episodes drawn from the common life of their own day. Even when these added episodes took a broadly comic turn, nobody was shocked, any more than by the imps and monsters which grinned at them from the solemn shadows of their cathedrals. In the play of Noah's Flood, the patriarch causes first the animals to enter the Ark, then his sons and daughters-in-law; but when he comes to his wife, she objects. She does not relish being cooped up without her "gossips," leaving these amiable women to

drown. Remonstrances at last proving fruitless, Noah re-
sorts to the argument of blows, and drives his scolding helpmeet into the Ark, to the great delight of the crowd. In the
play of Abraham and Isaac, the yearning love of the old man
for his little son, and the sweet, trustful nature of the boy,
are brought home to us in such a way as to intensify the
pathos of the moment when Abraham makes ready, at the
Lord's command, to sacrifice the life which is dearest to him
on earth. The pleading of the boy, the gradual overmastering
of his fear of death by his pity for his father's anguish and
his solicitude for his mother's grief, are rendered with touching truth.

> "Therfor do our Lordes bydding,
>   And wan I am ded, then prey for me;
> But, good fader, tell ye my moder no-thyng,
>   Say that I am in another cunthre dwellyng."

In these episodes, and in many others which might be given,
lie the germs of regular drama. Such humorous scenes as
the quarrel of Noah and his wife, constitute in reality crude
little comedies out of which regular comedy could readily
grow. In such tragic scenes as the Sacrifice of Isaac, the
Slaughter of the Innocents, and the Crucifixion, the elements
of noble tragedy were already present.

The Morality Plays.—The miracle plays attempted to set
forth only a part of the teaching necessary to man's salvation,
namely that part contained in the history of Adam's fall, the
redemption through Christ, and the final Judgment. This
dealt with matters of belief. To complete this teaching there
was needed some treatment of the side of religion which
deals with matters of conduct; and it was this which the
"Morality plays" tried to supply. By means of such personifications or abstractions as the World, the Flesh, Mankind, Mercy, Justice, Peace, the Seven Deadly Sins, Good
and Bad Angels, Gluttony, Covetousness, Old Age, and
Death, the morality plays represented the conflict between
sin and righteousness for the possession of the human soul.
The character of Vice played a great part. He was usually
dressed in the costume of a court fool, and carried a sword

of lath. His function was to attend upon the Devil, and to worry, trick, and belabor his master for the amusement of the crowd. The Vice survived in the fool of Shakespeare's plays, though it is hard to recognize him in the philosophical Touchstone of *As You Like It*, or the musical fool who sings such charming lyrics in *Twelfth Night*.

Interludes.—Out of the moralities arose a species of play known as the Interlude. The name took its origin from the practice observed in the houses of the great, of having these little dramas performed in the intervals of a banquet. In the old play of *Sir Thomas More*, a band of strolling players is announced while Sir Thomas is dining, and they perform an interlude before him and his guests. Usually these pieces had little action, and required almost no stage-setting. For example, "The Four P's," of John Heywood, "a newe and a very mery enterlude of a Palmer, a Pardoner, a Potycary, and a Pedlar," is nothing more than an amusing series of speeches by the four impersonators, in which they vaunt their several callings, make themselves out very arrant rascals indeed, and by so doing satirize the society which they represent. The Interludes treat all kinds of undramatic subjects, such as geography, the weather, the nature of the elements, in fact all the crude natural science of the time. The stage, both at this time and later, largely took the place of the modern school and newspaper.

Robin Hood Plays and Christmas Plays.—"Robin Hood plays," setting forth the merry adventures of Robin Hood, Friar Tuck, and Maid Marian, in Sherwood Forest, were also popular; and, all over England, seasons of merry-making were enlivened by the performance of rude Christmas plays, or "mummings," in which figured certain stock characters, such as Old Father Christmas, St. George and the Dragon, Old King Cole, and the Merry Andrew. The student will find in Thomas Hardy's *Return of the Native* an account of the Christmas mummings as they still exist, or did exist until recent years, in remote corners of England.

II. CLASSICAL INFLUENCE UPON THE EARLY DRAMA

Early Plays on Classic Models.—Owing to the great revival of interest in Latin literature, which marked the beginning of the Renaissance, it became the fashion in the fifteenth century to present the Latin comedies of Plautus and Terence on the stages of grammar schools, with the students as actors. Later, these same plays began to be translated, and given in the English tongue; and from this it was but a step to the composition of simple English comedies on the Latin model. The earliest of these were *Ralph Roister Doister*, written before 1541, and *Gammer Gurton's Needle*, written about 1566. The main characters in *Gammer Gurton's Needle* are studied from real sixteenth century peasants, and the background of English village life is given with much humor and vividness.

In tragedy, Seneca was taken as a model. In 1561, two young gentlemen of the Inner Temple, Thomas Norton and Thomas Sackville, presented before Queen Elizabeth a play called *Gorboduc, or Ferrex and Porrex*, to show what could be done in handling a subject from British legend, on the lines laid down by the Latin tragedian. It is a stately production, and deserves veneration as the first regular tragedy written in English. It had a great influence upon the native drama, just beginning to take permanent form.

Latin Tragedy and Native English Tragedy Contrasted.—Latin tragedy has very little stage action; important events, instead of being directly represented, are merely reported on the stage, by messengers or others. The tendency of English tragedy, on the other hand, was from the first to present everything bodily on the stage, even the storming of cities, or battles between great armies, where the means at the disposal of the actors were often laughably inadequate. Latin drama, again, is usually careful to preserve unity of time and place, that is, to make all the action pass in a given locality, and to cover no more than the events of a single day. English playwrights, on the contrary, had no hesitation in shifting the scene to half a dozen different countries in the course of a single play; and they thought nothing of introducing in the first act a child who grew to manhood in the second act, and in the third died and handed on the story, to be acted out by his sons and grandsons in the remainder. Classic drama also drew a very sharp line between comedy and tragedy, admitting no comic element into a serious play. The English drama, on the contrary, from the miracle plays down, set comedy side by side with tragedy; it mingled the farcical with the august, the laughable with the pathetic, as they actually are mingled in life.

Good Effect of Classic Influence on the Drama.—In the end, the free native form of drama prevailed, in spite of the efforts of the University "wits" (as young men of learning and cleverness were then called) to force the Latin form upon the stage. Nevertheless, the apprenticeship of English playwrights to a foreign master, brief and incomplete though it was, was invaluable. It taught them to impose some restraint upon the riot of their fancy; it showed them the beauty and artistic necessity of good structure; in a word, it brought form out of chaos.

III. BEGINNING OF THE GREAT DRAMATIC PERIOD

The Theatre Becomes the Chief Expression of Elizabethan Life.—We now stand on the threshold of that wonderful sixty years (1580–1640) during which the Elizabethan drama ran its magnificent course. As has been shown in the last chapter, England found herself, at the beginning of this period, quickened by three of the most potent influences which can affect the life of a nation: widespread intellectual curiosity; the beginnings of an intense religious ferment; and the pride of suddenly discovered national strength. The young wits who came up from the Universities to London, tingling with the imaginative excitement of the age, seized upon the popular theatre, as the most vital form of art then existing, and the best instrument for the expression of their own swarming fancies.

Elizabethan Playhouses and Actors.—During the youth of the drama, the performance of plays had been chiefly in the hands of strolling companies, who, attaching themselves nominally to the household of some great lord, and using his name to protect them, wandered about the country, wherever, on village green, at market fair, or in the hall of some noble house, they could find an audience. But shortly before the period we are now studying, regular companies had begun to establish themselves in the suburbs of London, and to erect permanent theatres. The first of these playhouses, known simply as "The Theatre," was built in Finsbury Fields, to the north of the city, by James Burbage, in 1576. It was at this play-house that Shakespeare first found employment. Burbage's company, on the destruction of The Theatre, built the Globe, on the south bank of the Thames; and here, on the Bankside, other places of theatrical entertainment rapidly sprang up. After a time the actors became bold enough to push into the city itself. Burbage built the Black-friars, as a winter theatre. A rival company built the Fortune, also in the city limits. By the end of the century, eleven theatres existed in the city and in the free lands or "liberties" adjoining.

Performances usually took place at three in the afternoon, and were announced by the hanging out of a flag and the blowing of trumpets. The theatres were round, square, or octagonal structures, unroofed except for a shed or canopy over the stage. The winter theatres, such as the Blackfriars, were entirely roofed in. The stage extended out into the body of the house, was open on three sides, and was sufficiently elevated so that the main bulk of the audience, standing on the bare ground which formed the floor or pit of the theatre, could have a fair view. Persons who could afford to pay a higher price than the "groundlings," took advantage of the boxes built round the pit. Young gallants, for an extra fee, could have seats upon the stage itself, where they smoked their pipes, peeled oranges, cracked nuts, and often interfered with the performance by chaffing a poor actor, or by flirting ostentatiously with the fair occupant of a neighboring box. In accordance with the luxurious taste of the age in dress,

the costumes of the actors were often very rich.   All women's
parts were played by boys; actresses were not seen in England
until after the Restoration.   The stage-setting was of the
simplest, a change of scene being indicated often merely by
a placard, or at most by a roughly painted piece of paste-
board and a few stage properties.   A tree and a bench did
duty for a garden; a wooden cannon and a paste-board tower
indicated a siege.   This meagreness of stage-setting, so far
from being a misfortune, was in no small measure responsible
for the literary greatness of the Elizabethan drama; for it
threw the dramatist back upon vivid poetic expression, as the
only means of stimulating the imagination of his audience.

The Pre-Shakespearean Playwrights.—The group of young
dramatists which sprang up to supply the demand made by
the early stage included Robert Greene, George Peele, John
Lyly, Thomas Kyd, Thomas Dekker, Thomas Nash, and
Christopher Marlowe.   Of these Marlowe stands as undis-
puted leader.   He is the true founder of the popular English
drama, though himself an outgrowth of the long period of
preparation which we have been studying.

IV. CHRISTOPHER MARLOWE: 1564–1593

Marlowe's Life.—Marlowe, the son of a shoemaker in
the old cathedral town of Canterbury, was born in 1564, two
months before Shakespeare.   He was sent to Cambridge
by a patron, who had noticed his quick parts.   He graduated
at nineteen; and four years later (1587) he astonished London with his first play, *Tamburlaine*, which he brought out
with the Lord Admiral's Men, the rival company to the
Lord Chamberlain's Men, whom Shakespeare had joined a
short time before.   During the six years which intervened
between the production of *Tamburlaine* and his death, Marlowe brought out three more plays, *Doctor Faustus*, *The
Jew of Malta*, and *Edward II*.   He was killed in 1593, in a
tavern-brawl, at Deptford, whither he had gone to take
refuge from the plague then devastating London.

Marlowe's " Programme."—In the brief and haughty
prologue prefixed to *Tamburlaine*, Marlowe not only an-

nounced clearly the character of that play, but hinted at the programme which he proposed to carry out in the future:

> "From jigging veins of rhyming mother wits
> And such conceits as clownage keeps in pay,
> We'll lead you to the stately tents of war
> Where you shall hear the Scythian Tamburlaine
> Threatening the world with high astounding terms
> And scourging kingdoms with his conquering sword."

The "jigging veins of rhyming mother wits," is a sneer at the use of rhyme and awkward tumbling lines of fourteen syllables, which was customary with the popular playwrights of the time. For this "jigging vein" he proposes to substitute blank verse, which, though it had been employed previously by Sackville and Norton, in *Gorboduc,* had not established itself. It is a sign of Marlowe's artistic insight that he should have recognized at once the value of blank verse for dramatic poetry; and we can see, beneath the surface of his words, a proud consciousness of his own power over this almost untried form of verse. Out of it he built that "mighty line," which astounded and fascinated his contemporaries; and his success with it fixed it firmly henceforth as the vehicle of serious drama. By his sneer at the "conceits" that "clownage keeps in pay," Marlowe showed his determination not to pander to the pit by means of vulgar comedy and horse-play, but to treat an elevated theme with seriousness. By the "stately tents of war," to which he promises to lead his hearer, he typified the dignity and largeness of scope which he proposed to give to all his work. By the last three lines of the prologue, he foreshadowed his plan of giving unity to his dramas, by making them revolve around some single great personality, engaged in some titanic struggle for power; and likewise of treating this struggle with the rhetorical splendor, the "high astounding terms," without which Elizabethan tragedy is now inconceivable. This programme he carried out in the main with consistency.

Marlowe's Plays: "Tamburlaine."—*Tamburlaine* is a pure "hero-play." The hero is a Scythian shepherd, who conquers, one after another, the kingdoms of the East, forcing kings to harness themselves to his chariot, and carrying with him a great cage in which a captive emperor is kept like a wild beast. The huge barbaric figure of Tamburlaine is always before our eyes, and the action of the play is only a series of his triumphs. His character, half-bestial, half-godlike, dominates the imagination like an elemental force of nature, and lends itself admirably to those "high astounding terms," which fill whole pages of the play with thunderous monologue.

"**Doctor Faustus.**"—*Doctor Faustus*, Marlowe's second work, is also a hero-play, and is cast on even larger lines. It is a dramatized story of the life and death of a mediæval scholar, who sells his soul to the devil, in return for a life of unlimited power and pleasure. For a space of years, he has at his command all the resources of infernal magic. He can transport himself in a twinkling from one region of the earth to another; himself unseen, he can play pranks in the palaces of popes and emperors; he can summon up the ancient dead to minister to his delight. But at last the fearful price is demanded, and he must render up his soul to everlasting torment. The play, as it has come down to us, is disfigured by comic passages of a coarse and tasteless sort, those very "conceits of clownage" which Marlowe had formerly declared war against. But even where the workmanship is poor there is always something imposing in the design; and certain passages have hardly been surpassed for power and beauty. When Mephistopheles raises from the dead the spirit of Helen of Troy, Faustus utters one rapturous exclamation,

> "Was this the face that launched a thousand ships
> And burnt the topless towers of Ilion?"

And on his death-bed he starts up with the cry,

> "Lo, where Christ's blood streams in the firmament!"

—three lines which would alone serve to stamp Marlowe as of the company of imperial poets.

"The Jew of Malta" and "Edward II."

"The Jew of Malta" and "Edward II."—Marlowe's third play, "The Jew of Malta," is again a study of the lust of power—this time the power bestowed by great riches. Barabbas, the old Jewish merchant of Malta, is the first vigorous sketch of which Shakespeare was to make in Shylock a finished masterpiece. The first two acts are conceived on a large scale, and carefully worked out; but after these Marlowe seems again to have fallen from his own ideal, and the play degenerates into melodrama of the goriest kind. Nevertheless it shows a remarkable advance over *Tamburlaine* and *Doctor Faustus*, in the knitting together of cause and effect. Marlowe's growth in dramatic skill is even more apparent in his last play, *Edward II*. This is his masterpiece, so far as play-making goes, though for the very reason that it discards rhetorical monologue for rapid dramatic dialogue, it contains fewer passages of pure poetry than any of the others.

Marlowe a Type of the English Renaissance.—Marlowe is one of the most striking figures of the English Renaissance. He represents the Renaissance passion for life, grasping after the infinite in power, in knowledge, and in pleasure. There is something in the meteor-like suddenness of his appearance in the skies of poetry, and in the swift flaming of his genius through its course, which seems to make inevitable his violent end. When he died, at twenty-nine, he was probably only upon the threshold of his achievement; but he had already laid broad and deep the foundation of English drama, and Shakespeare was already at work rearing upon this foundation an incomparable edifice.

REVIEW OUTLINE.—The drama was the greatest and the most popular literary form of the Elizabethan age. But before it came to full flower in the work of Shakespeare and his fellow-dramatists it had to go through a long process of growth. In this chapter we go back to the earliest beginnings of the drama in England, and trace its origin from forms of entertainment and religious ceremonies only rudely dramatic in character. We then follow its development through the Miracle play, the Morality play, and the Interlude, to the time when the English drama put itself to school, during the middle of the sixteenth century, to Latin comedy and tragedy. By following classic models for a time, it became better organized, but it remained "romantic" in form and spirit, as it had been from the first. The pre-Shakespearean drama culminates in Marlowe, who marks the close of the period of preparation, and the beginning of the great dramatic period, at the end of Elizabeth's reign.

How did the ceremonial life of the Norman and Plantagenet kings contribute to the development of the early drama? Keep in mind the connection between these ceremonial shows and the spectacular and lyric form of drama known as the Masque, which we shall study in the next chapter in the work of Shakespeare's friend and rival, Ben Jonson. Trace the development of the Miracle play, from its earliest and simplest form as a part of the Catholic church service, to its culmination in the great Miracle-cycles. How did these plays come to be given in cycles? Summarize the chief facts concerning the manner in which the Miracle-cycles were presented, under a number of heads, such as Actors, Costumes, The Pageants, Stage Arrangements, The Audience, etc. Do you notice a humorous fitness in the assignment of the separate plays to particular guilds? The Miracle plays contained the germs of regular comedy and tragedy; note, however, that the comic element was introduced by the authors, to lighten the tone, but that the tragic element existed in the Bible stories themselves. Illustrate this from the instances given. How did the Morality plays supplement the Miracle plays? What stock-character of Shakespeare's plays is a survival from the Moralities? Why were the Interludes so called? What subjects did they treat?

Describe the influence of the schools, and the enthusiasm for classic studies, upon the English drama during its formative period. Name the two earliest English comedies and the earliest tragedy written under the classical influence. What were the chief differences between the Latin and the native English form of tragedy? Most of these differences arose from one circumstance, that the classic dramatists were content to treat a single episode, whereas the English dramatists who were "romantic" in feeling were eager to present a whole story made up of many incidents. Would it have been possible for Shakespeare to present the history of Julius Cæsar or of King Lear in "classic" form? What did Shakespeare think of the inclusion of humorous and tragic matters in the same play? What beneficial influences came from the struggle to impose classic forms on English playwrights?

Between what dates did the Elizabethan drama flourish? (The term

"Elizabethan drama" is used somewhat loosely. It did not begin in earnest until Elizabeth, who was crowned in 1558, had been on the throne for almost a quarter of a century; and it continued under James and Charles for about thirty-five years after her death. The later drama is sometimes called Jacobean, from Jacobus, [James], but the term Elizabethan is generally used to cover the whole.) Review what is told in Chapter V concerning the political and social conditions of Elizabeth's reign, in order to understand the high excitement of the English nation at this time, and the brilliant life which found expression in the drama. Summarize the chief facts concerning the early theatres and theatrical companies; concerning the manner in which Elizabethan plays were presented. In what poet did the long process of dramatic development reach a point of comparative completion?

Give a brief sketch of Marlowe's life. Note carefully the reforms which Marlowe proposed to carry out in play-writing—in verse-form, in rhetoric, in the kind of themes treated, and in the unifying of these themes by a single personality. Who had introduced "blank verse" into England? Where had it been already used in drama? What was the effect of Marlowe's example in the use of blank verse? Show how Marlowe's first three plays illustrate, each in its own way, the interest of the Renaissance in individual man and his thirst for conquest.

READING GUIDE.—Little reading of texts can be expected of the student in the pre-Shakespearean drama. If time serve, Marlowe's "Edward II." or "The Jew of Malta" should be read. "The Jew of Malta," arranged for school use, is included in Maynard's English Classics. "Edward II." is edited by A. W. Verity (Dent). The interest of the class work, if students are sufficiently advanced, may be much heightened by volunteer reports upon such subjects as "The Mounting and Acting of Miracle Plays," "The Early Elizabethan Theatres." Materials for the first may be found in the introduction to A. W. Pollard's "English Miracle Plays," and in K. L. Bates's "English Religious Drama"; for the second, in "Shakespeare's Predecessors," by J. A. Symonds. The study of Marlowe may be supplemented by Lowell's essay upon him, in "The Old English Dramatists."

TABULAR VIEW. THE RENAISSANCE

FROM THE ACCESSION OF HENRY VII TO THE DEATH OF ELIZABETH: 1485-1603

HISTORICAL EVENTS	NON-DRAMATIC LITERATURE	DRAMA
		MIRACLE PLAYS, MORALITY PLAYS, INTERLUDES
CAXTON prints the first book in England....................1477		Earliest preserved miracle plays in English, Abraham and Isaac (East Midland play), Fall of Lucifer, Noah's Flood, etc. (Chester Whitsun plays), about 1320-1350.
EDWARD V...................1483		
RICHARD III..........1483-1485		Miracle plays flourish until middle of sixteenth century: York, Towneley, and Coventry cycles.
HENRY VII....1485-1509 Henry marries Elizabeth of York thus uniting the Houses of Lancaster and York........1486		Earliest preserved morality plays date from reign of Henry VI. (1422-1471): The Castle of Constancy, etc.
The Cabots discover American Continent................1497		Interludes flourish, sixteenth century: JOHN HEYWOOD's Four P's, about 1520.
Beginning of the "New Learning" (Colet, Erasmus, More), about....................1499		
	MORE's Utopia...............1515	
HENRY VIII......1509-1547 Colet founds St. Paul's School..1512	Bible translated by TYNDALE and COVERDALE...........1530-1553	EARLY COMEDY AND TRAGEDY: CLASSIC INFLUENCE
Act of Supremacy makes Henry head of English Church....1535		NICHOLAS UDALL's Ralph Roister Doister, about 1541.
Bible set up in the churches....1536	ASCHAM's Toxophilus........1545 First English Prayer-book......1549	Translations of SENECA, 1560-1581.
EDWARD VI.........1547-1553	TOTTEL's Miscellany, containing poems of Wyatt, Surrey, and other courtly makers........1557	NORTON and SACKVILLE's Gorboduc, 1561.
MARY.........1553-1558 Persecution of the Protestants; Cranmer, Latimer, and Ridley burned...........1555-1556	SACKVILLE's Induction, and Complaint of Buckingham, in the Mirror for Magistrates.......1563	Gammer Gurton's Needle, 1566.
	HOLINSHED's Chronicles........1577	
	LYLY's Euphues.............1579	

TABULAR VIEW. THE RENAISSANCE (Continued)

HISTORICAL EVENTS	NON-DRAMATIC LITERATURE	DRAMA
ELIZABETH............1558–1603 "The Theatre" built.......1576 Drake sails round the globe...1577 Execution of Mary, Queen of Scots..................1587 Defeat of the Armada........1588 Globe theatre built..........1599	SPENSER's Shepherd's Calendar..1579 SIDNEY's Defence of Poesy.......1581 HAKLUYT's Voyages............1589 SIDNEY's Arcadia..............1590 SPENSER's Faerie Queene...1590–1596 SIDNEY's Astrophel and Stella....1591 SHAKESPEARE's Venus and Adonis, 1593 SHAKESPEARE's Rape of Lucrece.1594 SPENSER's Colin Clout, Epitha- lamium and Amoretti.......1595 SPENSER's Four Hymns.........1596 England's Helicon.............1600	SHAKESPEARE'S FORERUNNERS JOHN LYLY, 1554–1606. Endymion; Alexander and Campaspe; The Woman in the Moon, etc. ROBERT GREENE, 1560–1592. Friar Bacon and Friar Bungay; James IV., etc. GEORGE PEELE, 1558–1597. David and Bethsaba; Old Wives' Tale, etc. CHRISTOPHER MARLOWE, 1564–1593. Tamburlaine; Dr. Faustus; The Jew of Malta; Edward II. SHAKESPEARE, 1564–1616 Chief plays falling in this period (dates largely conjectural): Love's Labour's Lost, 1590; Comedy of Errors, 1591; Two Gentlemen of Verona, 1592–93; Midsummer Night's Dream, 1593; Romeo and Juliet; Merchant of Ven- ice, 1596; series of English history plays, 1590–1599; Taming of the Shrew, 1597; Merry Wives, Much Ado, 1598; As You Like It, 1599; Twelfth Night, 1600–1601; Julius Cæsar, 1601; Hamlet, 1602; Measure for Measure, 1603.

gratest of Plays.

CHAPTER VII

SHAKESPEARE AND HIS FELLOW-DRAMATISTS

I. WILLIAM SHAKESPEARE: 1564–1616

Shakespeare's Early Life.—William Shakespeare was born on or about the 23rd of April, 1564, in the village of Stratford. He was the third child of John Shakespeare and Mary Arden. His mother was of gentle blood, and was possessed of some wealth by inheritance. His father, though a man of consideration in the village, was of lower station, a tanner and glover by trade. Until the age of fourteen the boy attended the Stratford grammar school, where he picked up the "small Latin and less Greek," to which his learned friend Ben Jonson rather scornfully refers. The better part of his education, a wonderfully deep and sure insight into Nature, and a wide acquaintance with the folk-lore of his native district, he doubtless began to acquire in boyhood, by rambles through the meadows and along the streams of Warwickshire, and by converse with the simple folk of the country side. Only a few miles away was the picturesque town of Warwick, with its magnificent castle, to set him dreaming of the past. Within an easy day's walk lay Kenilworth Castle, the seat of Elizabeth's favorite, Leicester; and the historic town of Coventry, where one might still see miracle plays performed on certain festival days. Travelling companies of actors visited Stratford two or three times a year, and had to apply to Shakespeare's father, who was at that time a village official, for leave to play. At their performances young Shakespeare was doubtless sometimes present, drinking in his first impressions of the fascinating world of the stage.

About 1578 the fortunes of his father began to decline, and Shakespeare was withdrawn from school. In spite of the rapidly failing prosperity of the family, he was married

WILLIAM SHAKESPEARE

From the Chandos portrait

at eighteen to Ann Hathaway, a young woman eight years
his senior, the daughter of a peasant family of Shottery,
near Stratford. Some time between 1585 and 1587, he left
Stratford to seek his fortune in the capital, and until the close
of his life he returned to his native town only at intervals.
The immediate cause of his leaving is said by doubtful tradition to have been the anger of Sir Thomas Lucy, a local
magnate, over a deer-stealing prank in which Shakespeare
and other wild young blades of the village had engaged.

Shakespeare in London.—Outside the walls of London to
the north, not far from where the road from Shakespeare's
country entered the suburbs of the capital, stood The Theatre,
one of two or three play houses which London then boasted.
It had at the head of its company the famous actor James
Burbage. Tradition says that the youthful Shakespeare,
on first coming to London, picked up a living by holding
horses at the doors of The Theatre. Whether this is true or
not, he soon found himself connected with Burbage's company, as actor and as retoucher of old plays. He continued
with Burbage's company, as actor, playwright, and stock-
holder, when the Theatre was pulled down, and rebuilt as
the Globe on the south bank of the Thames.

Of the external facts of Shakespeare's life in London we
know few. Early in his career he was attacked by Robert
Greene, who, in a deathbed exhortation to Marlowe, Peele,
and others, called him "an upstart crow beautified with our
feathers, that supposes he is as well able to bombast out a
blank verse as the rest of us." The publishers of Greene's
pamphlet afterward printed a formal apology, testifying to
young Shakespeare's worth and amiability. We know of
his friendship with William Herbert, Earl of Pembroke, and
with the Earl of Southampton; of his friendly rivalry, in
art and talk, with "rare Ben Jonson," the second dramatist
of the age; of his careful conduct of his business affairs,
and of his popularity as a playwright. Except for these few
gleams of light, his external life is wrapped in mystery; and
the very breadth and dramatic greatness of his plays prevent
us from drawing from them any but the broadest inferences
concerning his personal history.

Shakespeare's Return to Stratford : His Death.—The foundation of Shakespeare's modest fortune is thought to have been laid by a gift from his friend and patron, the young Earl of Southampton, to whom he dedicated his youthful poems, "Venus and Adonis" and "Lucrece"; but it was mainly by his earnings at the Globe and Blackfriars' theatres that he was able to reinstate his parents in their old position of comfort, as well as to gain for himself a patent of gentility, and the possession of the best homestead in his native village, with broad acres of land to add to its dignity. Hither, at the age of fifty, he retired, to spend the remainder of his life in country quietude, with his wife and his unmarried daughter Judith. He died in 1616, at the age of fifty-two; and was buried in the old church by the Avon, where thousands of pilgrims now go each year to read the words on his tomb beseeching men to let his dust lie quiet in its grave.

The Period of Experiment.—Shakespeare began his dramatic work by retouching old plays, and by a number of experiments which show how eagerly interested he was in the literary fashions of the time. One of these early ventures, *Love's Labour's Lost*, sprang from his interest in the fanciful, artificial language then in vogue at Elizabeth's court and among the young fashionables of London. In another, *The Comedy of Errors*, he joins the classical enthusiasts, taking his plot from a Latin comedy of Plautus. A third, the *Two Gentlemen of Verona*, is a dramatized romance, adapted freely from one of the popular love-romances of his day.

The Earliest Masterpieces.—Shakespeare's time of experiment and probation was now over. The two plays which he next produced—*A Midsummer Night's Dream* and *Romeo and Juliet*—were, it is true, experimental, in the sense that they enter realms before unknown to drama; but both in conception and execution they are finished masterpieces. The first of these plays is thought to have been written in 1593; the second, though it did not receive its final form until 1596 or 1597, was probably produced before the poet's thirtieth year.

"A Midsummer Night's Dream."—*A Midsummer Night's Dream* is thought to have been written for some nobleman's

marriage-festival, to take the place of the masque or allegorical pageant usual upon such occasions. Theseus, duke
of Athens, and his bride Hippolita, in whose lofty figures the
noble bridal pair are perhaps shadowed forth, represent the
sentiment of love in its serene and dignified mood. About
this central pair revolve three other groups, representing
love in its fanciful and burlesque aspects. The first group
is made up of the Athenian youths and maidens astray
in the moonlight woods, loving at cross purposes, and played
upon by Puck with a magic liquor, which adds confusion
to confusion in their hearts. The second group consists of
the fairy-queen Titania and her lord Oberon; and here the
treatment of the love theme becomes deliciously satiric, as
it depicts the passion of the dainty queen for the peasant
Bottom transformed into an ass. In the third group, that
of the journeymen actors who present the "tedious brief
scene of young Pyramus and his love Thisbe: very tragical
mirth," the love-theme is modulated into the most absurd
burlesque. Then, poured over all, holding these diverse
elements in unity, is the atmosphere of midsummer moonlight, and the aerial poetry of the fairy world.

   "**Romeo and Juliet.**"—*A Midsummer Night's Dream*, like
the plays which preceded it, treats of love in a light and fanciful way, never more than half in earnest. In *Romeo and
Juliet* love ceases to be a mere sentiment, to be played with
and jested over; it becomes a passion, tragical with the issues
of life and death. Here for the first time Shakespeare was
really in earnest. The two young lives are caught in a fiery
whirlwind, which sweeps them through the rapturous hours
of their new love, to their death together in the tomb of
Juliet's ancestors. The action, instead of being spread over
months, as in the poem from which Shakespeare took the plot,
is crowded into five days; and from the first meeting of the
lovers until the end, a sense of hurry, now ecstatic, now desperate, keeps the passion mounting in a swift crescendo. Not
only is the play great as a "tragedy of fate" in the Greek
sense, but in the drawing of character the poet now for the
first time works with unerring deftness and power. The
vulgar, kind-hearted nurse, the witty, hair-brained Mercutio,

the vacillating yet stubborn Capulet, the lovers themselves, so different in the manner of their love, all these and a dozen minor figures have the very hue and gesture of life.

The Historical Plays.—Shakespeare now, at thirty years of age, proceeded to throw into dramatic form the rough masses of English history which he found in the chronicles of Holinshed. One of his youthful efforts, the blood-thirsty melodrama, *Titus Andronicus,* had been written in imitation of Marlowe; now, in *Richard III.,* again working under Marlowe's influence, he produced a portrait of elemental energy and evil pride, which the creator of Tamburlaine and Faustus might have mistaken for his own handiwork. This he followed up with *King John,* famous for the tenderly drawn and touching figure of the little Prince, Arthur; it has been thought that in writing the moving passages where Arthur begs for his life, Shakespeare perhaps had in mind his own son Hamnet, who had just died at the age of eleven. In the three connected plays, *Richard II., Henry IV.* (in two parts), and *Henry V.,* Shakespeare gave a broad picture of English history during one of its most critical periods, when feudalism was passing away, and the idea of nationality was taking its place.

"Henry IV." and "Henry V."—In planning *Henry IV.* Shakespeare hit upon the admirable notion of interspersing the historic matter with scenes from the London tavern life of his own day—a life full of racy humor fitted to afford the desired comic relief. As the presiding genius of the tavern world, he created Falstaff, the fat old knight who helps Prince Hal (afterward King Henry V.) to sow his wild oats. The immortal figure of Falstaff holds the prime place among the creations of Shakespeare's humor, as royally as Hamlet holds his "intellectual throne." In *Henry V.* we see Shakespeare in a new and very charming light; it is, indeed, hardly a figure of speech to say that we *see* the poet—for in this play, as nowhere else in his dramas, does he speak with the voice of personal enthusiasm. The manly, open character of the king, and his splendid victories over the French, made him a kind of symbol of England's greatness, both in character and in achievement. The poet transfers to the battle of

Agincourt the national pride which had been kindled by the defeat of the Armada, and makes his play a great pæan of praise for the island kingdom. In the "choruses" introducing the several acts, and even in the speeches of the characters themselves, he utters in lyric strophes an overwhelming patriotic emotion.

"The Merchant of Venice" and the "Joyous Comedies."— At this time Shakespeare seems, if we are justified in guessing his personal mood from the mood of his work, to have passed through a period of unbroken serenity and high spirits. At any rate, the fruit of these years was a succession of joyous comedies, touched with the golden light of love and romance. Even while writing the histories, he had found time to write *The Merchant of Venice*. Here, in the person of Portia, he drew his second great portrait of a woman. Portia is an elder sister of Juliet, less vehement, with a larger experience of life, a stronger and more practised intellect. The grave and noble character of Antonio shows the growing seriousness of the poet's mind. The retribution which overtakes the cruel usurer, Shylock, and the moral beauty of Portia's famous speech concerning "the quality of mercy" indicate also the ripening of Shakespeare's moral sense. Even the music of the verse shows a greater breadth, a more quiet strength, than are to be found in the poet's earlier work.

In the three comedies which now followed, Shakespeare drew three other wonderful female portraits, Beatrice of *Much Ado About Nothing*, Rosalind of *As You Like It*, and Viola of *Twelfth Night*. And, grouped around them, what a holiday company of delightful figures!—Benedick, "the married man," trying in vain to parry the thrusts of Beatrice's nimble wit; the philosophical Touchstone, shaking his head over the country wench Audrey, because the gods have not made her poetical; the meditative Jacques (a first faint sketch, it has been said, of Hamlet), with his melancholy "compounded of many simples"; Sir Toby Belch, champion of the ancient doctrine of cakes and ale, and ginger hot in the mouth; the solemn prig and egotist Malvolio, smirking and pointing at his cross-garters; Maria, "youngest wren of nine"; and the clown Feste, with his marvellous, haunting songs. All these and dozens more move here in a kaleido-scope of intense life, flooded with an indescribable poetic radiance.

The "Period of Gloom": the Sonnets.—These three com-edies were written between 1598 and 1601, that is between the poet's thirty-fourth and his thirty-seventh year. The last of them, *Twelfth Night*, has been called his "farewell to mirth." What happened to him at this time, or whether anything tangible happened, we shall never know. Certain it is, however, that in several tragedies of titanic size, and in two so-called comedies, almost more bitter and gloomy than the tragedies, he sounded one after another the depths of human baseness, sin, and suffering. The only hint that we have of the nature of that valley and shadow through which Shakespeare seems to have passed, is found in his "Sonnets." They are addressed to "a man right fair" and "a woman colored ill." What the exact relations were between the three can only be guessed at. It has been conjectured that the "Dark Lady" of the Sonnets was the evil genius of Shakespeare's life, and that to her was chiefly due the change in his spirit and in his art. Of course no such personal explanation of this change is needed. The poet's sympathy was so all-embracing, and his outlook on life so broad, that the darker aspects of human character and destiny had sooner or later, in the natural course of things, to absorb his attention. Whatever may be their personal bearing, however, the Sonnets are of inexhaustible interest, for the subtlety and depth of their thought, and for the curious mixture of oddity and artificiality, with transcendent beauty and power, in their expression. If Shakespeare had written nothing but these, he would still be a commanding figure in the literature of the English race.

The Roman and Greek Plays.—The work of this sombre middle period of Shakespeare's life includes several plays on Roman and Greek subjects. In *Julius Cæsar*, the hero's greatness is presented in a strange inverted way. While Cæsar is alive, we see only his human weaknesses and fail-ings; but after he is dead, we are made to feel the majesty of his spirit by the world-wide ruin which follows his removal. In another sense, the hero is not Cæsar, but Brutus, in whom the poet saw a political idealist and generous dreamer, used as a tool by selfish men, who bring overwhelming disaster upon the state by their murder of the only man strong enough to save it. In *Antony and Cleopatra*, Shakespeare showed the character of a great Roman general, crumbling before the breath of Eastern luxury and sensuality, personified in Cleopatra, the "worm of old Nile." In *Troilus and Cressida* he drew a picture of faithlessness in love, a picture so cynical, so fierce in its bitterness, that it is almost impossible to think of it as the work of the hand which drew Juliet, Portia and Rosalind; and at the same time he deformed the heroic figures of Homeric legend with savage burlesque.

The Great Tragedies: " Hamlet."—In *Hamlet*, the first of the four great tragedies which form the "captain jewels in the carcanet" of the master's work, we have the spectacle of a sensitive and highly intellectual youth, endowed with all the gifts which make for greatness of living, suddenly confronted with the knowledge that his father has been murdered, and that his mother has married the murderer. Even before the revelation comes, Hamlet feels himself to be living in an alien moral world, and is haunted by dark misgivings. When his father's ghost appears to him, with its imperative injunction to revenge, Hamlet takes his resolution instantly. His feigned madness, an element of the drama retained by Shakespeare from the old story whence he drew the plot, is the first device which Hamlet hits upon to aid him in his dangerous duty. He gives up his love for Ophelia because he cannot take her with him into the dark pass which he is compelled to enter; and the scathing satire which he pours out upon her when he fancies her in league with Polonius and the king to play the spy upon him, gathers its force from the greatness of the renunciation he has made. His scheme for proving the king's guilt beyond a peradventure, by means of the strolling players, is carried through with ingenious skill. His dealings with Rosencrantz and Guildenstern are those of a gifted man of action. Yet it is not wholly without reason that Hamlet has come to stand in most minds for a type of irresolution.

The exaltation of excitement in him causes his mind to play with feverish brilliancy over the questions of man's life and death. His throbbing, white-hot imagination becomes a meeting-place for grotesque and extravagant fancies. Again and again he loses hold of his enterprise in the intellectual excitement which possesses him, showing itself in bursts of fitful eloquence, in swift flashes of wit, in contemptuous irony and biting satire. From the first we feel that Hamlet is doomed irrevocably to ruin in the moral chaos where the "cursed spite" of his destiny has thrown him.

"**Othello.**"—*Othello* has a certain likeness to *Hamlet* in that here also the hero's soul is thrown into violent perturbation by the discovery of evil poisoning the very sources of his life. In Othello's case the pathos and the tragedy are heightened by the fact that the evil exists only in the hero's imagination, into which we see the demon-like Iago pouring, drop by drop, the poison of suspicion. Othello is not by nature jealous. Desdemona, in answer to Emilia's question, "Is he not jealous?" says,

> "Who, he? I think the sun, where he was born
> Drew all such humors from him,"

and he everywhere shows himself "of an open and free nature," incapable of petty suspicion. When Iago, working cautiously, with diabolic skill, has at last convinced him that Desdemona is false, the fatal rage which seizes him derives its force from the very greatness of his love. The real centre of the play is Iago, with his "honest" manners, his blunt speech, his plausible zeal in his master's service; underneath all which his nature lies coiled like a snake, waiting for a chance to sting.

"**Macbeth.**"—In *Macbeth*, Shakespeare depicted the passion of ambition working in a nature morally weak, but endowed with an intense poetic imagination. Macbeth is a dreamer and a sentimentalist, capable of conceiving vividly the goal of his evil desires, but incapable either of resolute action in attaining them, or of a ruthless enjoyment of them when attained. By the murder of the king, Macbeth is

plunged into a series of crimes, in which he persists with a
kind of faltering desperation, until he falls before the accumulated vengeance, material and ghostly, raised up to punish
him.   As, in *Antony and Cleopatra*, we are shown the slow
degeneration of the hero's character under the slavery of
sense, so here we behold the break-up of a soul under the
torture of its own sick imagination.   The ghost of Banquo,
shaking its gory locks at Macbeth from its seat at the banquet
table, is a symbol of the spiritual sickness which results
from the working of a strong fancy upon a nature morally
weak.   The witch-hags who meet Macbeth on the heath are
embodiments of the powers of evil, summoned from the four
corners of the air by affinity with the evil heart of the schemer.
Shakespeare did not, of course, consciously strive after symbolism in these things.   It is not impossible that he believed
in ghosts and witches, as did the great mass of men in his day,
from King James down.   It is certain that he was interested
in his story, here and elsewhere, as a piece of life rather than
as a moral symbol; his work is full of types and symbols
simply because life itself is full of them.

Beside Macbeth Shakespeare has placed a woman who
possesses all the masculine qualities which the hero lacks,
but who is nevertheless intensely feminine in her devotion to
her lord's interest, and in her inability to endure the strain of
a criminal life after his support has been withdrawn from her.
Her will, though majestic when in the prosperous service of
her husband's ambition, collapses in sudden ruin when he
fails to rise to the responsibilities of their grim situation.
Macbeth's feebler moral substance crumbles piecemeal; but
the firm structure of his wife's spirit, as soon as its natural
foundation is destroyed, falls by instant overthrow.

" King Lear."—*King Lear* is often put at the apex of
Shakespeare's achievement, and by many judges at the head
of the dramatic literature of the world.   The story was as old
as Geoffrey of Monmouth (see Chap. III), and, like so many
of the themes which Shakespeare handled, had already been
made the subject of a play, a crude effort by some nameless
playwright during the experimental stage of Elizabethan
drama.   As was his constant custom, Shakespeare followed

the main lines of the story given him, and incorporated into his grand edifice every bit of usable material from the building of his predecessor. Lear is an imperious nature, wayward by temperament, and made more incapable of self-government by long indulgence of its passionate whims. At the opening of the play, we see him striving to find a refuge from himself by surrendering all his wealth and power in exchange for absolute love. He demands love not only in the spirit but in the letter, and thrusts his youngest daughter Cordelia from him with cruel brusqueness, when she refuses to use extravagant terms to describe her affection. Shakespeare has made the same brusque and hasty spirit of the king precipitate upon his old head the enmity of his remaining daughters, Goneril and Regan. Before he has recovered from the shock of Cordelia's loss, this awful pair of daughters lay bare, little by little, their monstrous souls to their father's gaze. As in *Othello*, the result of the revelation is to unhinge for the sufferer the very order of nature. As if in sympathy with the chaos in Lear's soul, the elements break loose; and in the pauses of the blast we hear the noise of violent crimes, curses, heart-broken jesting, the chatter of idiocy, and the wandering tongue of madness. The sentimentalist's phrase, "poetic justice," has no meaning for Shakespeare. The ruin wrought in the old king's heart and brain is irreparable, and the tornado which whirls him to his doom carries with it the just and the unjust. The little golden pause of peace, when Lear and Cordelia are united, is followed by the intolerably piercing scene in which he bears her dead body out of the prison, muttering that they have hanged his "poor fool."

The " Period of Reconciliation " : Last Plays.—The plays which mark the closing period of Shakespeare's life are pure romances, conceived in a spirit of deep and lovely serenity, and characterized by a silvery delicacy, a tender musing touch, which is new in the poet's work. The new mood finds beautiful expression in the pastoral under-play of *A Winter's Tale*, where Prince Florizel woos Perdita, the wild-flower maid. It shines out full-orbed in *The Tempest*, where Prospero sways with his magic the elements and the wills of men to his bidding, in the service of his daughter's happiness.

In this play all the powers of the master meet together; the grace that had created the fairy world of *A Midsummer Night's Dream*, the lyric passion that had breathed through Juliet's lips on her bridal morning, the drollery and wit that had set the laughter of centuries billowing about Falstaff, the titanic might that had sent a world crashing on the head of Lear—all meet together here, but curbed, softened, silvered down into exquisite harmony.

The Tempest is believed to have been written for the wedding ceremonies of Princess Elizabeth, daughter of James I., and Prince Frederick, the Elector Palatine, in 1613. If this is true, *The Tempest* was Shakespeare's farewell to his art. When scarcely fifty years of age, with his genius at its ripest, and every faculty of his mind in full play, he laid down his pen forever, as Prospero, at the end, abjures his magic, breaks his wand, and drowns his book "deeper than did ever plummet sound." One is tempted to indulge the fanciful parallel still further, and to think of Ariel, the delicate and potent sprite whom Prospero sets free, as the spirit of Imagination, now released from its long labors in the master's service.

Appreciation of Shakespeare in His Day.—The common opinion that Shakespeare was unappreciated by his own generation, is only partly true. If other evidence were lacking to prove the esteem in which he was held, his material prosperity would be sufficient to show at least his high popularity with the theatre-going public. But there is other witness that his genius was here and there recognized. His great rival, Ben Jonson, whose burly good sense was not prone to exaggeration, and who perhaps never quite conquered a feeling of jealousy toward Shakespeare, wrote for the first collective edition of the plays a eulogy full of deep, in places even passionate, admiration; and afterward said of him in a passage of moving sincerity, "I did love and honor him, on this side idolatry, as much as any." The most significant hint we have of his personal charm is in the adjective which is constantly applied to him by his friends, "gentle," a word also often used to describe his art, in allusion evidently to its humanity and poetic grace.

Shakespeare's Carelessness of Fame.—The awe inspired by the almost unearthly power and richness of Shakespeare's mind is apt to be deepened by the knowledge that the noble plays to which English-speaking races point as their greatest single achievement, were thrown into the world carelessly, and would have perished altogether if the author of them had had his way. During his lifetime they were printed only in pirated editions, taken down by shorthand from the lips of the players, or patched up from prompters' manuscripts dishonestly acquired. He does not mention his plays in his will. Not until 1623, seven years after his death, did a collective edition appear (known as the First Folio), and then only because of the piety of two of his actor-friends. The printing of a play while it was still actable, was of course disadvantageous to the company whose property it was; and Shakespeare had probably made over his plays to his company as they were produced. Yet even when this is taken into consideration, we are filled with astonishment. We see in the working of the master's spirit not only the vast liberality but also the startling carelessness of Nature, who seems with infinite loving pains to create her marvels, and then to turn listlessly away while they are given over to destruction.

II. BEN JONSON AND THE LATER DRAMATISTS

Ben Jonson; His Life.—The most commanding figure in the group of Shakespeare's dramatic contemporaries is Ben Jonson (1573–1637). Although of humble birth, the son of a bricklayer, he was sent to Westminster School and possibly to Cambridge; and he ultimately became one of the most learned men of his time. As a young man he served a campaign with the English army in Flanders, where (as he afterward boasted) he fought a duel with a champion of the enemy in the sight of both armies, and took from him his arms. The incident is characteristic of Jonson's rugged and domineering character. As he served the foreign soldier, he afterward served the luckless poets and poetasters who challenged him to a war of words.

After returning to England, he began to work for the

theatres. His first play was *Every Man in His Humour* (1597), in which Shakespeare is known to have acted. A series of literary quarrels followed, in the course of which he wrote several elaborate plays to revenge himself upon his rather puny enemies. His three masterpieces appeared between 1605 and 1610. They are *The Silent Woman, Volpone,* and *The Alchemist*—all called comedies by him, though the second is a gloomy and biting satire. He also wrote two massive tragedies taken from Roman history, *Sejanus* and *Cataline.* For many years after his appointment by James I., in 1603, as poet-laureate, he supplied the king with court-masques. In his later years Jonson lost the laureateship, and his plays, never very popular, failed dismally. Before his death, in 1637, he was stricken with paralysis, and felt the sharp pinch of poverty. He was buried in Westminster Abbey. A pretty anecdote relates that when the workmen were putting in place the stone slab which marks his resting-place, a stranger passing by gave them money to carve upon it the words which may still be deciphered there, "O Rare Ben Jonson."

Jonson was a critic of great sanity and force, writing a perfectly simple and unadorned prose, very different from the elaborate and figurative prose-style common in his day. His volume of short reflections upon life and art, entitled *Timber,* is particularly interesting for the criticisms of Shakespeare which it contains.

It was chiefly Jonson's aggressive decision and rugged honesty which enabled him to hold for a quarter of a century his position of literary dictator, and lord of the "tavern-wits." The tavern was for the seventeenth century what the coffee-house was for the eighteenth, a rallying place for literary men; and Jonson is almost as typical a tavern figure as Falstaff. His "mountain belly and his rocky face," his genial, domineering personality, ruled by royal right the bohemian circle which gathered at "The Mermaid" or "The Devil." Here took place those famous wit-combats between Jonson and Shakespeare, described by Fuller under the simile of a sea-fight; Jonson, slow of movement and "high built in learning," being likened to a great Spanish galleon, Shakespeare to an English man-of-war, swift to strike and dart away, confounding the enemy with agility and adroitness.

Jonson's Method: His "Humors."—The chief peculiarity of Jonson's dramas is hinted at by the title of his first play, *Every Man in His Humour.* The word "humor" was a cant term in his day,* equivalent to "whim" or "hobby." He hit upon the device of endowing each one of his characters with some particular oddity or affectation, some ludicrous exaggeration of manner, speech, or dress; and of so thrusting forward this single odd trait that all others might be lost sight of. Every man, in other words, should be "in his humor." This working principle Jonson extended afterward in his two great comedies, *Volpone* and *The Alchemist.* In *Volpone* he studied, not a foible or whim, but a master-passion, the passion of greed, as it affects a whole social group; in *The Alchemist* he made an elaborate study of human gullibility. Shakespeare also has devoted whole plays to the study of a master-passion—in *Othello* that of jealousy, in *Macbeth* that of ambition. But he does this in a very different way from Jonson, with more freedom and naturalness. Jonson seems always to have a set programme: he lets us, in other words, "see the machinery," and by so doing loses in spontaneousness and charm. His ideal was strictly classical; and he tried, with all his might, to stem the tide of the romantic drama. His failure in this was one of the circumstances which embittered his old age.

Jonson's Realism.—In at least one respect the comedies of Ben Jonson are the most interesting plays in the whole Elizabethan repertory—namely, in the vivid pictures they give of contemporary London life. From Jonson's comedies alone it would be possible to reconstruct whole areas of Elizabethan society; a study of them is indispensable if one would know the brilliant and amusing surface of the most sociable era of English history. At least one of Jonson's comedies, too, gives this close and realistic study of manners with a gayety and grace fairly rivalling Shakespeare; *The Silent Woman* is one of the most sparkling comedies ever

---

* Note Bardolph's use of the word in *Henry IV.* and *Henry V.*

written, full of splendid fun, and with a bright, quick movement which never flags.

Jonson's Masques.—One of Jonson's best claims to remembrance is that he brought to perfection the court masque. Masques were an outgrowth of the ceremonial spectacles of the middle ages (see page 90), modified by the classical taste of the Italian Renaissance. They were little spectacle plays, interspersed with songs and elaborate dances, and provided with an accompaniment of instrumental music. The subjects were usually allegorical. The persons represented were either gods and goddesses from classical mythology, or abstract figures, such as Beauty, Wit, Passion, Despair. Jonson wrote nearly forty of these masques, all of them delicate in fancy and rich in lyric adornment. The titles themselves suggest their character: *Neptune's Triumph, The Masque of Blackness, The Masque of Queens, The Fortunate Islands.* They were given in the theatre of the royal palace at Whitehall, by gorgeously costumed lords and ladies. Magnificent stage-settings and transformation scenes were contrived for them by King James's architect, Inigo Jones; the music was written by the king's musician, Ferrabosco, and the dances were in charge of court dancing masters, who were men of importance at that time, when dancing was cultivated as a noble art. The masque was the forerunner of the opera, which after Jonson's death began to develop in its stead. Shortly before Jonson's death, the masque form was used by Milton in his *Comus*, and made the vehicle of one of the noblest of English poems.

Jonson displayed his lyric gift also in many short poems, which for their delicacy and sweetness are conspicuous even in the Elizabethan age, when almost every writer was capable of turning off a charming song. The best known of his lyrics are "Drink to me only with thine eyes," and "See the chariot at hand here of love"; of both these the old-time music has fortunately reached us. His verses upon Shakespeare, prefixed to the First Folio edition of his great rival's plays (1623), have furnished many phrases of common quotation, such as "Swan of Avon," and "He was not of an age but for all time."

Beaumont and Fletcher.—Francis Beaumont (1584–1616) and John Fletcher (1575–1625) are, in Lowell's phrase, among "the double stars of the heavens of poetry." Fletcher, the elder of the two, was the son of a Bishop of London. Through his father the young dramatist gained an insight into court life, and learned to paint, better than any of his contemporaries, the hollow inside, and the exquisite outer finish, of courtly manners. Another fact contributing to form his genius, was that the official residence of his father, the episcopal palace at Fulham, lay amid beautiful river and forest scenery. To the country memories gathered here in boyhood he gave expression later in the pastoral play of *The Faithful Shepherdess*, as well as in the songs with which his dramas are richly interspersed.

At the Mermaid tavern, among those "sealed of the tribe of Ben," he met the man whose name is inseparably linked with his own. Francis Beaumont was nine years younger than Fletcher, being about twenty-one at the time of their meeting. After their partnership began, tradition says that they lived together on the Bankside, sharing everything, even their clothing, in common. This at least represents a more essential truth, that they entered into a wonderfully close intellectual partnership; one mind supplying what the other lacked, to produce a rounded result. The fifty-two plays which go under their common name illustrate nearly every type of dramatic composition known to the Elizabethan stage, and constitute Beaumont and Fletcher "absolute lords of a goodly realm of romance." Nevertheless, in Beaumont and Fletcher, and still more in their fellow-workmen, Thomas Middleton (1570?–1627) and John Webster (dates unknown), we mark symptoms which tell us that the high point of the drama has been passed, and that decay and degeneration is about to set in.

The Decay of the Drama.—One symptom of decadence in the later dramatists is an obvious straining after intensity. As the ordinary "strong situations" began to be worked out, dramatists made excursions into the strained and the unnatural, in order to find new matter. A second and more fatal flaw in the later dramatists is the laxity of the moral atmosphere pervading much of their work. The moral values are not preserved with the absolute health of soul which is Shakespeare's greatest glory, but are blurred or distorted in the search after excitement. After the death of Shakespeare (1616) the decay of the drama was rapid. In John Ford (1586–1640?) the morbidness of tone becomes intolerable, and from the plays of James Shirley (1596–1666), the last of the long line, the vital fire has almost wholly departed.

The Actors and the Puritans: Closing of the Theatres.— As the drama grew weaker and more corrupt, its enemies grew stronger and more determined to root it out from the land as an abomination. Early in the history of the drama a war had begun to be waged between the actors and the Puritans. In 1576 we hear of strolling companies being kept out of London by Puritan law-makers; and when the first theatres were erected they were placed in the suburbs to the north, and in the "liberties," or exempt lands, across the Thames in Southwark. Under Queen Elizabeth's protection the actors grew strong enough to enter the city; and as long as her strong hand was at the helm, the Puritans did not assert themselves very vigorously. But when James I. came to the throne, with his lack of personal dignity, his bigoted dictum of the divine right of kings, his immoral court full of greedy nobles from Scotland and Spain, the Puritan party gained rapidly in aggressiveness. After the meeting of the Long Parliament, the Puritans quickly came to a reckoning with the theatre. In 1641 appeared a pamphlet called "The Stage-Players' Complaint," which says pathetically, "The High Commission Court is down, the Star-Chamber is down, and some think Bishops will down; but why should not we then that are far inferior to any of these, justly fear that we should be down too?" In September of 1642 an ordinance of both Houses of Parliament closed the theatres throughout the kingdom. They were not reopened until eighteen years later, when the reins of power had fallen from the dead hand of Cromwell, and Charles II. ascended the throne from which his father had been led to the scaffold.

REVIEW OUTLINE.—Give a sketch of Shakespeare's life, up to the time of his establishment in London, noting as many circumstances as possible which you think could have been useful in preparing him for his career as dramatist and poet. At the time of Shakespeare's coming to London only a few rude theatres existed, and those, owing to the enmity of the Puritans (who held control of the London municipal government) were all outside the walls of the city, to the north, in the open fields used as public playgrounds. Review what was said in the last chapter concerning the character of the early playhouses, and the manner in which plays were given. Try to imagine Shakespeare as a young man in these surroundings. For what playhouse and what manager did he do his first work? What later theatre is connected with his name? Note that the later theatres were built chiefly on the south bank of the Thames, in open spaces devoted to all kinds of public amusements. Call to mind Chaucer's connection with this part of London. Gather together from this chapter the known facts and the hints which have come down to us concerning Shakespeare's life in London: his friendships, his enemies, his business prosperity and the use to which he put it; the "Dark Lady" of the sonnets; the impression which he made upon those who knew him. Tell what you can of the close of Shakespeare's life; note in this connection what is said of "The Tempest" as his "farewell to his art."

The chronology of Shakespeare's plays is, except in a few instances, uncertain. The order in which they are given here, and their grouping, is not to be taken, therefore, as absolutely true, but only as representing, in a general way, what is probable. The same thing must be said concerning the account here given of the growth of Shakespeare's mind, based upon the chronological order of his plays. With this precaution, and recollecting that we are dealing largely with conjecture, describe the main periods and groups into which the plays fall; name two or more plays under each head. What appropriateness do you find in the title "A Midsummer Night's Dream"? In what various ways is the love-theme presented in this play? Do you remember any work of Chaucer in which "Theseus, Duke of Athens," figures? "Romeo and Juliet" is called a "tragedy of fate," that is, a play in which the tragic outcome depends upon circumstances lying outside the will of the actors; after reading the play, try to decide how far the tragedy of the lovers is due to their own characters and actions, how far to accidents, or to circumstances beyond their control.

In what two plays does Shakespeare show the influence of Marlowe? What episode of Shakespeare's personal history has been thought to be reflected in "King John"? Shakespeare was the first to write historical plays in a connected series: "Richard II." takes up English history at a time when Chaucer was a man of middle life; "Henry IV." and "Henry V." follow, bringing the story down into the first quarter of the fifteenth century; Shakespeare's youthful work (or an old work revised by him), "Henry VI.," carries on the account into the wars of the Roses; then later passages of the same unfolding national drama are treated in "Richard III." and "Henry VIII.," father of Queen Elizabeth. We see, therefore, that Shakespeare virtually covers in his historical plays the story of his country from Chaucer's time until his own. In which of these plays does Falstaff figure? What was Shakespeare's aim in introducing such a person into an historical drama? In what sense may "Henry V." be called the most personal and self-revealing of Shakespeare's plays?

How many of the characters mentioned in the text as occurring in the "joyous comedies" can you place, from your own reading? Add to the list, as many others as you can, and characterize them to your own satisfaction. Why may "Julius Cæsar" be said to have a double hero? What earlier English poet had treated the subject of "Troilus and Cressida"? Explain how "Hamlet," "Othello," and "Lear" may all be classed together as "tragedies of disillusion." The source of the Lear story is the same as that of Layamon's "Brut," of Malory's "Morte d'Arthur" of the early classical play "Gorboduc" and, in part, of Tennyson's "Idylls of the King." What is this source? What change in Shakespeare's mood is revealed by his last plays? What evidence is there that Shakespeare's genius was in some measure appreciated by his contemporaries? Tell what you can of the manner in which his plays have been preserved.

What is Ben Jonson's rank among Elizabethan dramatists? Tell what you can of him, (a) as a man, (b) as scholar, (c) as lyric poet. (d) as critic and literary dictator, (e) as dramatist. Draw together all the circumstances of his relation to Shakespeare. Name his three best plays and characterize two of them. In what way does the title of Jonson's earliest comedy give the key to his dramatic method? Taking into account the fact that Jonson's ideal was the classic one, should you expect to find in his historical plays such comic episodes as the Falstaff scenes in "Henry IV"? Why? In what respect are Jonson's comedies of supreme interest among the plays of the time? Describe the nature of the court-masque and the manner of its presentation. What modern form of entertainment has grown out of it? Who raised the masque-form to a higher beauty than even Jonson had given it?

Milton's "Comus" was suggested in part by "The Faithful Shepherdess": tell what you can of the author of this play, and of his relations with his collaborator. Note the signs of decay in the dramas of Beaumont and Fletcher and their successors. Reflect upon the phrase "health of soul" as applied to Shakespeare, and see if you can illustrate its meaning from one or more of his plays. Why were the Puritans antagonistic to the theatre? Why did their antagonism become stronger as time went on? When were the theatres closed and for how long?

READING GUIDE.—The plays of Shakespeare best adapted for school study are perhaps "Julius Cæsar," "Macbeth," "The Merchant of Venice," and "As You Like It." All these plays are included in the inexpensive Riverside Literature series (Houghton, Mifflin). Among the numberless biographies and critical studies of Shakespeare, the best for school use is the little volume by E. Dowden, in the Literature Primers series (Appleton). The many interesting illustrations in H. W. Mabie's "William Shakespeare, Poet, Dramatist, and Man," if they can be put before a class, will do much toward making the surroundings of the dramatist's life realizable. Emerson's essay on Shakespeare, in his "Representative Men," Carlyle's essay in "Heroes and Hero-Worship," and Lowell's in "Among My Books," will be found valuable in giving the student a larger understanding of Shakespeare's significance.

If time serve, and the students are sufficiently advanced, a volunteer report to the class upon one of Ben Jonson's masques should be asked for. This will be of especial interest if given in connection with the class-study of Milton's "Comus." Several of Jonson's masques, and an essay on the masque as a dramatic form, may be found in H. A. Evans's "English Masques." For advanced students a rapid reading of one of Jonson's realistic comedies, as "The Silent Woman," and one of Shakespeare's romantic comedies, such as "Twelfth Night," and a comparison of the two, will be of great interest.

Those who wish to gain a first-hand acquaintance with the work of Shakespeare's great contemporaries in the drama, will find excellent material in "The Best Elizabethan Plays," edited by W. H. Thayer (Ginn). The plays included are Marlowe's "Jew of Malta," Jonson's

"Alchemist," Beaumont and Fletcher's "Philaster" and "The Two Noble Kinsmen" (attributed in part to Shakespeare), and Webster's "Duchess of Malfi." Three of Jonson's comedies, "The Alchemist," "Volpone," and "The Silent Woman," together with his beautiful pastoral play, "The Sad Shepherd" (left unfinished at his death), and his poems, are to be had in a single volume in Morley's Universal Library.

William Black's novel, "Judith Shakespeare," gives a fresh and charming picture of rural England in Shakespeare's day.

CHAPTER VIII

THE SEVENTEENTH CENTURY: FROM THE DEATH OF ELIZABETH TO THE RESTORATION

I. INTRODUCTION

The Growth of Puritanism.—The period between the death of Elizabeth and the Restoration (1603–1660) was one of great excitement and disturbance in the national life. Puritanism, under various names, had been growing in strength since the days of Wyclif and Langland. In Henry VIII.'s reign the Bible, newly translated by Tyndale and Coverdale, had been set up in the churches. This mighty book, in which every form of literature, idyll, song, drama, and epic, was eloquently represented, became the chief food of the popular mind. Crowds gathered about the pillars in the churches to which the Book was chained, and listened eagerly while some lettered person "with an audible voice" read from its pages. Theology became the passion of the people, or at least of that portion of the people, the Puritan element, which had most deeply felt the impulse of the Reformation. Men were brought face to face with the source of divine authority; they began to feel an awful personal responsibility concerning the welfare of their souls. Out of these conditions arose the Puritans, whose black steeple-crowned hats and sombre cloaks typified the sombreness and severity of their view of life. Their distrust of forms and ceremonies in religion, and of the gayeties of social life, led them to hate the painted windows, gilded organ pipes, and carved chancel rails of old cathedrals, and to long to sweep away all traces of the "merry England" of Elizabeth's time, typified by such innocent and time-honored customs as the dance about the Maypole, and

the hanging of yew and holly at Christmas. The same
sombre zeal made of them, under Cromwell, formidable
soldiers, who advanced with hymns and with snatches of old
Hebrew war songs on their lips, to overthrow the proud cavalier armies. . It made of them wanderers and exiles, seeking
in Holland, and in the far-off wilds of America, a place where
they could worship God after their own hearts. As early as
1620, when Milton was a boy of twelve, a band of these "pilgrims" landed at Plymouth, on the coast of Massachusetts,
and began there the founding of a great Puritan commonwealth of which we are the inheritors.

Struggle Between King and Parliament.—With the demand for religious freedom, there soon became involved a
demand for greater political liberty. The struggle between
the king and parliament grew in bitterness through the reign
of James I. (1603–1625). James handed on to his son,
Charles I., his doctrine that kings govern, not by the will of
the people but by divine right, and that the church is as
much under the royal jurisdiction as are the temporal affairs of the nation. As Charles became more arrogant in
his policy, the mood of parliament became more hostile.
In 1629 Charles dissolved parliament, and for eleven years
there was no meeting of either house. With the aid of
judges of his own appointment, and of counsellors and favorites pledged to his absolute view, Charles governed without
heed to the growing wrath of the nation. He gave the direction of the church into the hands of Archbishop Laud,
who not only compelled uniformity in worship, but insisted
upon ceremonies, such as kneeling at the communion table
and making the sign of the cross, which seemed to threaten
the return of Catholicism. Milton's "Lycidas," written in
1637, expresses the indignation and fear which Laud's policy
aroused in the hearts of all Puritans.

The Civil War and the Protectorate : The Restoration.—By
1639 Charles had become involved in a war with the Scotch
Presbyterians, upon whom he had tried to force a new prayer-
book. He was compelled to summon parliament, but dismissed it angrily. The Scotch invaded England. A new
parliament, the famous Long Parliament, which met in 1640,

took affairs into its own hands and made common cause with the Scotch. The civil war followed. Oliver Cromwell, with his "Ironsides," as the flower of the stern Puritan army were called, crushed the king's forces, after three years of fighting, at Naseby, in 1645. Four years later Charles was beheaded on a scaffold outside the windows of the palace of Whitehall. In 1653, Cromwell took the reins of power into his single hands, and under the title of Lord Protector, reigned as a military despot, the excuse for his despotism being that the only alternative to it was anarchy. During all this troubled period John Milton, whose character gives us the highest and best expression of Puritanism, stood forth as champion of the cause, though often at odds both with the parliament and with Cromwell, and maintaining many independent convictions. On Cromwell's death, in 1658, the dictatorship existed for a while under his feeble son. By this time the temper of the nation had changed. Puritanism had ceased to be dominant; the people were eager for the restoration of the Stuart family. In 1660 Charles's son was recalled from exile, and mounted the throne as King Charles II.

Rise of Scientific Thought.—Along with these religious and political causes of disturbance, there went also an intellectual one. The seventeenth century saw the rise of modern scientific thought. It was a time when the foundations of knowledge were being questioned. A spirit of bold speculation was in the air. Creed clashed with creed, and theory with theory, much as they have done in our age, which has been, like the seventeenth century, an age of discovery and excited question. This new scientific spirit found its chief expression in the writings of Sir Francis Bacon.

II. FRANCIS BACON (1561–1625)

Bacon's Life and Character.—Francis Bacon was born in 1561, three years before Shakespeare. His father was Lord Keeper of the Great Seal to Elizabeth, and his uncle was Lord Burleigh, Elizabeth's prime-minister. He was thus marked out by birth for a public career. Owing to the opposition of his jealous uncle, he got little preferment under

SIR FRANCIS BACON
From an engraving by I. Houbraken

the queen; but under James I. he rose rapidly through various offices to be Lord Chancellor, with the title of Viscount St. Albans. In this position he supported his dignities by a magnificence of living altogether out of proportion to his legitimate income. In 1621 he was impeached before the House of Lords for bribe-taking and corruption in office, found guilty, and subjected to fine and imprisonment. He retired, a broken and ruined man, to his seat of Gorhambury, and spent the remaining five years of his life in scientific and philosophic pursuits; still, however, keeping up a show of his former magnificence, with an unconquerable pride which caused Prince Charles to exclaim, "This man scorns to go out in a snuff!"

For Bacon's personal character it is impossible to feel much admiration. But it is equally impossible not to admire his spacious and luminous mind, and the devotion to pure thought which constituted his deeper life. In a letter written at the outset of his career, he says proudly, "I confess that I have as vast contemplative ends as I have moderate civil ends; for I have taken all knowledge to be my province."

The "Novum Organum" and the "Advancement of Learning."—His programme was indeed a majestic one, very similar in kind to that of Herbert Spencer in our own time. As Spencer has attempted to organize the vast stores of modern science into a "synthetic philosophy," so Bacon desired to systematize the knowledge of his day, and to lay down a method for carrying that knowledge indefinitely farther. But before he could do so he had to reform the very methods of thought by which knowledge is gathered. In the philosophy of the middle ages there had been almost no attempt to examine the facts of nature, and draw conclusion from actual observation. Philosophers had begun by stating their large theories at the outset, without the long and patient process of observation, by which a modern theory, like that of evolution, for example, is built up. Bacon saw clearly that the modern method, which we call the "inductive method" of thought (as opposed to the other, or "deductive" method), was the only true one in science. He laid down the new scientific programme in the *Novum Organum,* and the *Advancement of Learning.* The change in method had to come with the rise of the scientific spirit; it is Bacon's glory that he saw and expressed the need of change before others were quite conscious of it.

The " Essays."—Bacon holds his place in literature, however, not by reason of the *Novum Organum* (which is in Latin) and the *Advancement of Learning,* but by reason of his *Essays.* The *Essays* were at first mere jottings down of stray ideas, brief note-book memoranda. As such they were first published (then ten in number) in 1597, in the author's thirty-sixth year. Fifteen years later they were issued again, with additions; and in 1625 they were put forth in final form, the essays now numbering fifty-eight, the old ones revised and expanded. It is clear that their charm grew upon Bacon, and urged him, half against his will, to put more and more serious effort into the handling of a language for which, in comparison with Latin, he had no great respect, yet of which he is one of the greatest masters.

The *Essays* deal with many subjects, of public and private conduct, of statecraft, of human passions and human relations; and with these graver themes are intermingled others of a lighter sort, on building, on the planting of gardens, on the proper mounting and acting of masques. To a modern understanding those which deal with the deeper questions of human nature are apt to seem somewhat shallow and worldly wise. We get from them few large insights or generous points of view; everywhere we find wit, keen observation, grave or clever worldly wisdom. Now and again, to be sure, Bacon startles us with an altogether unworldly sentence, such as this: "Little do men perceive what solitude is, and how far it extendeth; for a crowd is not company, and faces are but a gallery of pictures, and talk but a tinkling cymbal, where there is no love." Some of the essays, such as the one entitled "Of Great Place," show an unworldly wisdom which, if applied to Bacon's own life, would have made it a very different thing. Not seldom, too, he lifts the curtain upon that inner passion of his existence, the thirst for intellectual truth, which made him noble in spite of the shortcomings of his character: "Truth," he says, "which only doth judge itself, is the sovereign good of human nature."

Bacon's Style.—For the student of expression, Bacon's essays are of endless interest and profit; the more one reads them, the more remarkable seem their compactness and their vitality. When the bulk of English prose was being written in loose sentences of enormous length, Bacon struck out a thoroughly modern sentence, short, crisp, and clear. His style has a curious sharp emphasis, a tone of startling authority and command. The essays shock a sluggish attention into wakefulness as if by an electric contact; and though they may sometimes fail to nourish, they can never fail to stimulate.

Bacon represents the scientific curiosity of the later Renaissance. The mystical and religious thought of the age is equally well represented by a writer whose style is as ornate as Bacon's is simple—Sir Thomas Browne.

Here—

III. SIR THOMAS BROWNE (1605–1682)

Browne as a Mystic: The " Religio Medici."—Sir Thomas Browne, after studying medicine at the famous schools of Montpellier in France and Padua in Italy, settled as a physician at Norwich, in Norfolk, and there passed his life. In 1642 appeared his first work, *Religio Medici*, a confession of his own personal religious creed. It is in essence a mystical acceptance of Christianity. "Methinks," he says, "there be not impossibilities enough in religion for an active faith . . . I love to lose myself in a mystery; to pursue my reason to an *O Altitudo!*" This sense of solemn exaltation, this losing of himself in a mystery, is Browne's characteristic mood. We see in him how far the temper of men had departed from the Elizabethan zest of life, from the Renaissance delight in the stir and bustle of human activity. "Methinks," he says, "I begin to be weary of the sun. The world to me is but a dream and mock-show, and we all therein but pantaloons and antics, to my severer contemplations."

Browne as a Writer : The " Urn Burial."—It was not until long after the Civil War had ceased to shake the earth with its "drums and tramplings" that Sir Thomas Browne published his most famous piece, the *Urn Burial* (1658). It was suggested by the finding of some ancient Roman funeral urns buried in the earth in the neighborhood of Norwich. It pretends to be an inquiry into the various historic methods of disposing of the dead, but is in fact a sermon upon the vanity of earthly ambition, especially in its attempt to hand on mortal memory to future ages.

Like almost all the writers of his time, Browne is extremely uneven; his great passages come unexpectedly, but these have a pomp and majesty which even Milton has not surpassed. His English is full of large-sounding words coined from the Latin, and the music of his periods is deep, stately, and long-drawn, like that of an heroic funeral march or the full-stop of a cathedral organ. The opening of the last section of the *Urn Burial* will serve perhaps to make these comparisons clear: "Now, since these dead bones have already outlasted the living ones of Methuselah, and in a yar. under ground, and thin walls of clay, outworn all the strong and specious buildings above it; and quietly rested under the drums and tramplings of three conquests: what prince can promise such diuturnity unto his reliques?" The way in which his imagination plays through his thought and flashes a sudden illumination of beauty over his pages, may be suggested by these words, written one night when he had sat late at his desk: "To keep our eyes open longer were but to act our Antipodes. The huntsmen are up in America!"

IV. THE CAVALIER POETS, HERRICK, AND WALTON

By-Paths in Seventeenth Century Literature.—It is natural in an intensely serious age like the seventeenth century, that literature should escape here and there with delight into a world of care-free pleasure. Such a wandering in flowery by-paths we may see in the amatory verse of the Cavalier poets, Carew, Lovelace, and Suckling; in the lyrics of love and country life of Herrick; and in Walton's famous little book upon the art of angling, the humblest but one of the best-beloved of English classics.

The Cavalier Poets.—Of the three poets whose connection with the court of Charles I. have given them the title of "Cavalier Poets," the eldest was Thomas Carew (1598–1638?). His best known lyric is "Give me more love or more disdain," in which his felicity and courtly charm display themselves at their height. Carew died in 1638, just before the bursting of the storm which was to scatter the gay society of Whitehall, and bring to poverty, exile, and death the men and women for whom he had sung.

Richard Lovelace (1618–1658) and John Suckling (1609–1641) were young courtiers of wealth and great social brilliance, who practised poetry much as they practised swordsmanship, facility in turning a sonnet or a song being still, as in the Elizabethan age, considered a part of a courtier's education. Each of them wrote, it would seem almost by happy accident, two or three little songs which are the perfection of melody, grace, and aristocratic ease. Suckling's tone is cynical and mocking; the best songs of Lovelace, on the other hand, "To Lucasta, on Going to the Wars," and "To Althea from Prison," breathe a spirit of old-fashioned chivalry, of faithfulness to the ideals of love and knightly honor. Both Suckling and Lovelace met with tragic reversal of fortune; and the contrast between their careless, brilliant youth, and their wretched death, has thrown about their names a romantic glamour which has had perhaps as much to do with preserving their fame as the tiny sheaf of lyrics they left behind.

Robert Herrick.—Robert Herrick (1591–1674) was born in London, and apprenticed in boyhood to his uncle, a goldsmith in Cheapside. After some time spent at Cambridge, he returned to London in his thirtieth year, and lived on his wits in the literary bohemia of the Inns of Court. In 1629, having taken orders, he was presented by King Charles to the vicarage of Dean Prior, in Devonshire. Here, with no duties to perform save the reading of a weekly sermon to a handful of sleepy parishioners, he had ample opportunity, during the next nineteen years, to develop his lyrical gifts.

His genius was of the kind which carves cherry-stones, not of the kind which hews great figures from the living rock. Left perfectly to himself, amid the flowers of his vicarage garden, with the pretty traditional ceremonies and merry-makings of country life to look at, he spent his days carving cherry-stones indeed, but giving to them the delicate finish of cameos or of goldsmith's work. In poem after poem he enters into the homely joys and pageants of rural life—a bridal procession, a cudgel-play between two clowns on the green, a puppet-show at the fair, the hanging of holly and box at Candlemas Eve. Perhaps the most exquisite of all is "Corinna going a-Maying." This little masterpiece is drenched with the pungent dews of a spring morning. As the poet calls his "sweet slug-a-bed" out of doors, and leads her through the village streets, already decked with white-thorn, toward the fields and woods where the May-day festivities are to be enacted, we feel that the poetry of old English life speaks through one who has experienced to the full its simple charm. Even the note of sadness at the end, the looking forward to that dark time when Corinna herself and all her village mates shall "lie drowned in endless night," has a peasant-like sincerity of feeling.

Herrick's Religious Poetry.—When the parliamentary forces had gained the battle which they had been waging with the king's men, and Herrick as a loyalist was ejected from his living, he went back to London. The year of his return (1648) he published his poems, under the title of *Hesperides and Noble Numbers*, the latter half of the title referring to the religious poems of the collection. There could be no more striking sign of the immense religious ferment of the time than these poems, coming as they do from a pleasure-loving, pagan nature, whose philosophy of life is summed up in his most famous song, "Gather ye rosebuds while ye may." In the wonderful poem called "The Litany," the masterpiece among Herrick's religious poems, we see how upon even his gay and sensuous nature there descended at times that dark shadow of religious terror which later found its final and appalling expression in the *Grace Abounding* of John Bunyan.

Isaak Walton.—Isaak Walton (1593–1683) is one of the best remembered of the many seventeenth century writers who took refuge from the troubled spirit of their age, in the celebration of simple country pleasures. He was a London linen-draper, who spent his working days in measuring cloth and serving his customers over the shop counter; but who passed his holidays in quite another fashion, roaming with fishing-rod and basket along the banks of streams, and gazing with unspoiled eyes at the unspoiled peace and gayety of nature. His "Complete Angler" was printed in 1653, amid the fierce political and religious agitations of the Commonwealth; but a sweeter or more untroubled book has never been written. It is one of the most endeared of English classics, and will be read with delight when a thousand more imposing works have been forgotten.

V. JOHN MILTON (1608–1674)

Introduction.—In the great struggle between the king and parliament, between the old order and the new in government, religion, and social life, the poets ranged themselves almost to a man on the side of the king. But the greatest of all, and next to Shakespeare the mightiest spirit in the history of the English imagination, was a Puritan. In John Milton the passion for liberty and the spiritual earnestness which were at the heart of Puritanism, found themselves for once united with the poet's passion for beauty and the great artist's power of expression. The result of this fusion was a character and an achievement which, whether we regard Milton as poet or as patriot, must compel the wondering veneration of men.

Milton's Youth.—John Milton was born December 9, 1608, in Bread Street, London. His father was a scrivener (notary public), who had embraced the Puritan faith. During Milton's boyhood, England was still Elizabethan; geniality and charm of life had not yet given place to that gloomy harshness which Puritanism afterward took on. Milton was taught music, and was allowed to range at will through the English poets; among these Spenser, the poet of pure beauty, exercised

JOHN MILTON
From an engraving by Humphreys after the Faithorne portrait

over him a spell which was to leave its traces upon all the
work of his early manhood. He entered Christ's College,
Cambridge, in his sixteenth year. He had already determined to be a poet, and that too in no ordinary sense. His
mind was fixed on lofty themes, and he believed that such
themes could be fitly treated only by one who had led a lofty
and austere life. The magnificent ode, "On the Morning of
Christ's Nativity," which deals with the signs and portents
filling the world at the Saviour's birth, was written at twenty-
one. It showed clearly that another mighty poet had been
given to England.

Milton's Residence at Horton.—Two years later Milton
left Cambridge and went to Horton, a little village west of
London, whither his father had retired to spend his declining
days. Here, in a beautiful country of woods, meadows and
brimming streams, the young poet spent five quiet years.
To the outward view he was all but idle, merely "turning
over the Greek and Latin classics" in a long holiday. Really
he was hard at work, preparing himself by meditation, by
communion with nature and with the lofty spirits of the
past, for some achievement in poetry which (to use his own
words) England "would not willingly let die." The chief
immediate result was the descriptive poem in two parts,
"L'Allegro" and "Il Penseroso," the masque *Comus* and
the elegy "Lycidas."

Milton's Public Career and Prose Writings.—The twenty
years of Milton's public life were preceded by a period of
travel abroad (1638–1639), chiefly in Italy. Here he met
Galileo, was entertained by the Italian literary academies,
and pondered much upon a projected epic poem on the subject of King Arthur's wars, a subject suggested to him by
the epics of Tasso and Ariosto. His return was hastened
by news of King Charles's expedition against the Scots,
a step whose seriousness Milton well knew. Once back in
London, he was drawn into a pamphlet war on the question of church government. Then followed his marriage
to Mary Powell, the daughter of a cavalier squire. The
marriage was ill-starred. After his wife's temporary desertion of him Milton published several pamphlets on divorce.

These were received with astonishment and execration by his countrymen, who did not see that Milton was only bringing to bear, upon one issue of domestic life, that free spirit of question everywhere spreading change through the social fabric of England. Milton's revolutionary spirit next led him to attack the censorship of the press. The time-honored institution of the censorship he saw to be an intolerable hinderance to freedom of thought; and in a pamphlet entitled *Areopagitica*, the greatest of his prose writings, he launched against it all the thunders and lightnings of his magnificent rhetoric. On the execution of the king (1649) Milton was the first to lift up his voice, amid the hush and awe of consternation, in defence of the deed. His pamphlet "On the Tenure of Kings and Magistrates" was of such timely service to the Commonwealth party that he was offered the position of Latin secretary to Cromwell's government, his duties being to indite correspondence with foreign powers, and to reply to attacks by foreign pamphleteers. In the midst of a controversy of this sort his eyes failed, and in a short time he was totally blind. He continued his duties, with the help of an amanuensis, until he was dismissed in 1658 by General Monk, who was already plotting to restore Charles's son to the throne, as King Charles II. On the king's return in 1660, Milton was forced to go into hiding, and he barely escaped paying with his life for his fearless support of the Commonwealth party.

Milton's Return to his Poetic Mission.—During the long period of his public career, from 1642 to 1658, Milton wrote no poetry except a few sonnets. These are sixteen in number. Some of them, such as the famous sonnet on the massacre of the Piedmontese Protestants by the Catholic soldiery, deal with public affairs. Others are personal. Among these last the finest are two upon his own blindness, and one upon the memory of his second wife, Katherine Woodcock, who had died in the first year of their marriage.

Except for these brief returns to his poetic mission, Milton had hidden "that one talent which is death to hide." But he had more than once turned aside, in his pamphlets, to throw out a proud hint concerning the work laid upon him by the great Task-master, of adding something majestic and memorable to the treasury of English verse. Ever since his college days he had looked forward to this work, considering many subjects in turn. By 1642 he had virtually decided upon the subject of the Fall of Adam. During the sixteen years between 1642 and his dismissal from the Latin secretaryship, amid all the "noises and hoarse disputes" of the time, this subject lay in his mind, gradually gathering to itself the riches of long study and reflection. When at last his duty as a patriot was done, he turned at once to his deferred task. Forced to seek shelter from the storm of the royalist reaction, he carried with him into his hiding place the opening book of *Paradise Lost,* begun two years earlier. The poem was finished by 1665, and was published by an obscure printer in 1667.

In 1671, four years after the publication of *Paradise Lost,* appeared Milton's third volume of verse. (The college and Horton poems had been published in 1645.) It consisted of *Paradise Regained,* a supplement to *Paradise Lost;* and of *Samson Agonistes,* a drama in the Greek manner, on an Old Testament subject which Milton had thought of treating nearly thirty years before.

Milton's Last Years.—Milton lived for three years after the publication of his last poems. Much of his patrimony had disappeared in the readjustments of the Restoration, and in the great London fire of 1666; but he was still able to live in modest comfort. The painter Richardson gives us a glimpse of the poet during his last years, as he was led about the streets clad "in a gray camblet coat," or as he sat at the door of his house, near Bunhill Fields, to receive visitors. "Lately," continues Richardson, "I had the good fortune to have another picture of him from an aged clergyman in Dorsetshire. In a small house, up one pair of stairs which was hung with rusty green, he found John Milton, sitting in an elbow chair; black clothes, and neat enough; pale but not cadaverous, his hands and fingers gouty and with chalkstones." The picture makes us realize how far Milton had traveled from the world of his youth. In making himself over from Elizabethan to Cromwellian he had suffered much and renounced much; he had lost many of those genial human qualities which have won for less worthy natures a warmth of love denied to his austerity. But though some may deny him love, none can help feeling an admiration mixed with awe, for the loftiness and singleness of aim, the purity and depth of moral passion, which make him conspicuous even among the men of those moving times.

" L'Allegro " and " Il Penseroso."—The first product of the five happy and fruitful years which Milton spent at Horton, was the poem in two parts, "L'Allegro" (the joyous man) and "Il Penseroso" (the meditative man). The poem is, in a sense, autobiographical. The two parts paint the two sides of Milton's own temperament: the one urging outward, toward the brightness and vivid activity of life; the other drawing inward, toward lonely contemplation, or musings upon the dreamier, quieter aspects of nature and of human existence. To represent these two moods he imagines two typical youths, living each through a day of typical thoughts and pursuits. The first poem opens at morning, with the song of the lark, the rising sun "beginning his state," the ploughman's whistle and the hunter's horn sounding in the clear air. The day is followed through its course in a series of happy pictures, ending with merry-making and fairy tales by the evening fire. The music in which "the joyous man" delights is the rebeck (a rustic violin), and he finds his reading in the pages of gay-colored romances, in dramas and poems, through which play the sunlight of life. "Il Penseroso," on the other hand, opens at midnight, when the moon is stooping through the cloud-drift, and the song of the nightingale, "most musical, most melancholy," is flooding the air. When day appears, the "meditative man" shuns the sunlit activity of the waking world and goes to dream in shadowy groves and in the "dim religious light" of cathedral aisles. His music is that of the solemn organ, and his books are stately tragedies and epics. The poem closes with the poet's wish that he may live thus, in solitude and meditation,

> " till old experience do attain
> To something like prophetic strain."

Taken together the two little poems represent, under a slight veil, the life which Milton led during the five happy years at Horton.

" **Comus.** "—The next two poems of this period were in masque form; one a fragment, "Arcades," the other a complete masque, taking its title from the chief character, Comus, god of revelry. *Comus* was written at the request of Milton's friend Henry Lawes, a musician, who supplied the music, and played the part of the Attendant Spirit when the masque was presented (1634) at Ludlow Castle, on the Welsh border, to celebrate the installation of the Earl of Bridgewater as Lord President of Wales. It is not known whether the poet was present on the occasion; but in any case it is strange to see Milton, who was soon to become a stern fighter in the Puritan ranks, making his first great poetic effort in the drama, which the Puritan party hated, and in that form of the drama, the masque, which was most closely associated with the court. Even here, however, the seriousness of the young Puritan's view of life and art are apparent.

The plot of *Comus* is simple and very effective. Two brothers and a sister, astray by night in the forest, become separated; the girl is taken captive by Comus, the son of Bacchus the wine-god and Circe the enchantress. He leads her to the place where he dwells surrounded by strange half-bestial creatures whom he has transformed. He attempts to work upon her the same transformation. She resists him, refusing to yield to the allurements of sense, and is at length rescued by her brothers and an "attendant spirit," who takes the guise of their father's shepherd. Though in the masque form, *Comus* has none of the frivolity which usually marked the masque. It contains, in fact, a whole philosophy of conduct, and preaches the doctrine of purity of life.

" **Lycidas.** "—"Lycidas" is an elegy upon the death of Edward King, a college mate of Milton's, drowned in the Irish Sea. King had been, in his way, a poet; and it was usual among the poets of the pastoral school, to represent themselves and their art under the guise of the shepherd life. Milton, therefore, represents himself and his dead friend as shepherds driving their flocks, and piping for fauns and satyrs to dance; he calls the sea-nymphs and the gods of the wind to task for the disaster of his fellow-shepherd's death. To this "pastoral" symbolism, however, Milton adds another kind, not pagan, but Christian. King, besides being a poet, had been a preacher, or at least had been in preparation for the ministry. He was therefore not only a shepherd under Apollo, but a shepherd under Christ; a keeper of the souls of men, which are the flocks of the Good Shepherd. This second symbolism Milton boldly identifies with the first, for to him the poet and the preacher were one in spiritual aim. Still more boldly, in the strange procession of classic and pseudo-classic divinities whom he summons to mourn over Lycidas, he includes Saint Peter, the bearer of the keys of the Church; and he puts in his mouth words of solemn wrath and warning against the ecclesiastical corruption of the age. "Lycidas" is the last work of Milton's young manhood, binding together his happy and sheltered youth with his maturity of strife and renunciation.

"Paradise Lost."—The theme which Milton first seriously considered in his search for an epic subject, was the story of King Arthur, as it had been handed down by Geoffrey of Monmouth and Sir Thomas Malory. If his life as a poet had not been interrupted, he would perhaps have treated this subject, making out of it an epic of ideal England, that ideal England which swam before Milton's inward vision, as it had done before Spenser's. But with the years of his delay, Milton's ambition grew. The subject which he finally decided upon was wider than his own nation, even in its ideal aspect. It dealt with the origin and spiritual destiny of all mankind. Its action stretched beyond the created universe, into Heaven and Hell, and reached backward beyond the beginning of time.

The Story of "Paradise Lost."—The action of *Paradise Lost* begins in Heaven, before man is created, or the earth and its spheres hung out in space. Lucifer, the fairest and mightiest of the angels, jealous of the Son who shares God's throne, rebels, and draws with him a third part of the hosts of Heaven. Lucifer and the apostate angels flee to their stronghold "in the north." Tremendous battle ensues between the hosts of the rebellious and the faithful. For three days the struggle endures, and the issue is still doubtful. But now the Son goes forth to battle, riding upon a living chariot, and clad in supernal powers and glories. Lucifer and his followers are cast headlong from Heaven. For nine days and nights they fall through empty chaos, into the Hell which has been hollowed out of space to receive them. Then Christ, in the name of the Father, goes forth into chaos, and marks out the vast sphere of the universe, with Earth at the centre. The six-day process of creation follows. Man, as the first of created things, is set in the Garden of Eden, to take the place of the rebel angels in God's affection. A helpmeet is given to Adam, a woman formed from his rib while he slept. The wedded pair, perfect in beauty and innocence, dwell together in the happy garden, the favorites of nature and of God. Archangels visit them, and eat of the fruits of their pleasant toil. Heavenly warriors keep watch over their safety. But meanwhile Lucifer, now known as Satan, the Adversary, brooding upon revenge, conspires with the leaders of his host in Hell to destroy the newly-created pair or seduce them into disobedience to God.* At a great meeting at the infernal capital, Pandemonium, Satan proposes to make his way across the darkness of chaos, and to attempt some deed of enmity against Earth and its fair inhabitants. He succeeds in accomplishing his tremendous journey, in eluding the seraphic sentinels, and in entering the Garden. He perches "like a cormorant" on the Tree of Life; then, transforming himself into various shapes of serpent, beast, and bird, he spies upon Adam and Eve. Once he is found by the archangel Ithuriel, in shape "like a toad, squat at the ear of Eve," whispering evil dreams to her as she sleeps. He escapes, and circles for three days and nights through space, keeping in the earth's shadow. Again he steals into Paradise, this time

---

* It is at this point that the first book of Paradise Lost takes up the story. The earlier events are related in subsequent books by the archangel Lucifer and by Adam. Milton follows the example of Virgil in thus beginning his epic in the middle of the action.

through an underground stream. In the form of a glittering serpent he tempts Eve to eat of the forbidden Tree. She does so, and Adam shares with her the fatal fruit. A shudder runs through all creation; the face of nature is darkened; restlessness and evil passion take the place of contentment and purity in the hearts of the doomed pair. In a vision Adam is shown the future history of the world, and the coming of Christ to redeem man from his fallen state. Then flaming swords drive Adam and Eve from the garden into the gloomy wilderness, to earn their bread by the sweat of their brow, to suffer all mortal pain and sorrow and infirmity.

The Central Motive of " Paradise Lost."—The actual story of the temptation and fall, it will be seen, occupies a relatively small space in the poem; yet it is this which "motives" and organizes the whole; it is this from which it all radiates and toward which it all converges. In however vast a circle the great action may sweep outward, the human pair in the garden is the centre of the curve. Every episode of the poem, throughout its majestic course, depends for its significance upon the fate of the human pair, in whom are the issues of all human life. Only a poet of the most wonderful grasp, the most supreme sense of form, could have thus given organic shape to such vast and varied materials.

The Character of Satan.—Critics have often declared that the real hero of *Paradise Lost* is Satan. They have pointed out that, in spite of himself, Milton sympathized with Satan as an arch-rebel against authority; for was not Milton himself a rebel, not against the unchangeable will of the Almighty, but against a king who sought to wield by "divine right" an irresponsible authority? The criticism is so far true that in the earlier books the character of Satan and his outward aspects are invested with a wonderful dignity. He appears indeed not "less than archangel ruined." But as the poem progresses, Satan's figure is shorn beam by beam of all its baleful splendor. His character loses its dignity. He ceases to be the fallen "Son of the Morning." As the lust of evil gnaws deeper and deeper into his heart, he degenerates into "the father of lies," the snaky and subtle foe who cares not how he attain his hateful ends.

This degeneration of Satan under his own evil passions is one of the largest conceptions of the poem. It disposes of the often-urged objection that Satan is the hero of *Paradise Lost*, and that therefore the poem is at war with itself.

Milton's " Sublimity."—The word "sublimity," so often abused, has, in the case of *Paradise Lost*, real fitness. It was a quality to which Milton attained only after much stern experience. Without those silent years when his imagination was held back by his will, gaining momentum like the dammed-up waters of a stream, he would possibly never have attained that peculiar mightiness of imagery and phrase which causes *Paradise Lost* to deserve, as does perhaps no other work of literature, the epithet sublime. The art of "L'Allegro" and "Comus," graceful as the tracery of dancing figures about a Greek vase, gave place, in *Paradise Lost*, to an art as massive and severe as the frescoes of Michelangelo, depicting the solemn scenes of the creation and destruction of the world.

The Verse of " Paradise Lost."—For his epic Milton deliberately chose blank verse, as the most severe of English measures; but he made out of it a type of verse before unknown. The chief peculiarity of this later Miltonic verse is that the sense is held suspended through many lines, while clause after clause comes in to enrich the meaning or to magnify the descriptive effect; then the period closes, and this suspended weight of meaning falls upon the mind like the combing mass of a breaker on the shore. A second important characteristic is the extreme variety of pause; the sense comes to an end, and the suspended thought falls, at constantly varying places in the line, a device by which blank verse, monotonous when otherwise treated, becomes the most diversified of rhythms. In these and other ways Milton made for himself a sublime verse-instrument to match his sublime imagery and theme. The music of the Horton poems, compared with that of *Paradise Lost*, is like the melody of the singing voice beside the manifold harmonies of an orchestra, or the rolling chant of a cathedral organ.

" Paradise Regained " and " Samson Agonistes."—*Paradise Regained* was intended, as its title shows, as a sequel to *Paradise Lost.* In his first epic Milton had shown how mankind, in the person of Adam, falls before the wiles of the Tempter, and becomes an outcast from divine grace; in his second he shows how mankind, in the person of Jesus, wins readmission to divine grace by withstanding the temptation of Satan in the wilderness. By general consent *Paradise Regained* is given a lower place than *Paradise Lost. Samson Agonistes,* however, a venture in a new field of poetry, shows Milton's genius at its height once more. His desire was to bring over into English the gravity and calm dignity of the Greek tragedies; and, avoiding the lifeless effect of previous experiments of the sort, to give to his grave and calm treatment the passion, the conviction, the kindling breath without which poetry cannot exist. Two circumstances made this not only easy, but almost inevitable for him. In the first place his character, lofty and ardent to begin with, had now under misfortune and sacrifice taken on just that serene and melancholy gravity peculiar to the great tragic poets of antiquity. In the second place, the story of Samson was, in a sense, his own story. Like Samson he had fought against the Philistines with the strength of thirty men; he had taken a wife from among his enemies and suffered bitter loss at her hands; he sat now, blind and dishonored, amid the triumph of the Cavaliers, as Samson among the holiday-making Philistines. As he wrote, his own personal bitterness found veiled expression; and the grand choruses, with their dark and smothered music, pulsate with personal feeling.

The grandeur of Milton's character, and the grandeur of his art, become more striking when we view them against the background of the age into which he survived, and in which he did his later work. This was the age of the Restoration, an age absorbed in worldly pleasures, in love with "common-sense" and intolerant of ideals. We come now to another great Puritan writer who did his work in this same alien period, John Bunyan.

VI. John Bunyan (1628–1688)

The King James Bible.—Bunyan, the rude tinker of Elstow, who produced, without learning or literary example, one of the greatest masterpieces of imaginative English prose, can only be understood by reference to another and greater literary phenomenon of the seventeenth century, the Authorized Version of the Bible. This version was made by order of James I.; the work was divided among numerous churchmen of his appointment, and was finished in 1611. The translators used not only the original Hebrew and Greek texts, and the Latin Vulgate, but also the various English translations from Wyclif down. They succeeded in blending together the peculiar excellences of all these, with the result that we possess in the King James Bible a monument of English prose characteristic of no particular age, but gathering up into itself the strength and sweetness of all ages. The grandeur, simplicity, and force of biblical prose, acting upon Bunyan's passionately earnest imagination, made him, all unknown to himself, a great writer.

Bunyan's Early Life; " Grace Abounding."—John Bunyan was born in the village of Elstow, Bedfordshire. His father was a tinker, a trade then considered little above vagabondage. After a slight schooling, and a short experience of soldiering in the Civil War (on which side is unknown), he married a wife as poor as himself, and took up his father's trade of pot and kettle mender. Before this, however, there had begun in him a spiritual struggle so terrible and so vivid, as we see it in the pages of his *Grace Abounding to the Chief of Sinners* (published 1666), that by contrast the events of his outer life are pallid and unreal. As he wrestled and played at "tip-cat" with his village mates on the green, or stood in the tower of the church to watch the bell-ringing, he was haunted by thoughts of sudden death, of the Judgment Day, and of his soul's damnation. He saw an awful Face looking down from the clouds, and heard a Voice asking whether he would leave his sins and go to Heaven, or have his sins and go to Hell.   The tiles upon the house-roofs, the puddles in the road, spoke to him with voices of temptation and mockery.   From this religious insanity he was rescued by a Mr. Gifford, a local preacher, who gave him comfort and courage.   Soon Bunyan himself began to preach: and a revulsion of feeling now lifted him to heights of ecstatic joy in the mercifulness of God and the beauty of holiness. He saw Christ himself looking down at him through the tiles of the house-roof, saying "My grace is sufficient for thee"; and the sense of salvation came like a "sudden noise of wind rushing in at the window, but very pleasant." In all this we see in its most intense form the religious excitement of the seventeenth century, and also the qualities of imagination and feeling which make Bunyan so powerful a writer.

Bunyan's Later Life : " Pilgrim's Progress."—At the Restoration, persecution of the nonconformist sects began. Bunyan was arrested for holding illegal religious meetings; and he spent the next twelve years in confinement, earning bread for his family by putting tags to shoe laces, and keeping his mind awake by writing what he was no longer at liberty to speak.   In the midst of a sober controversial work, he happened to employ the trite metaphor of a journey, to typify the Christian life.   At once the figure began to grow and blossom; a throng of pictures and dramatic incidents started up before his mind.   Almost before he knew it the metaphor had grown into a book, and *The Pilgrim's Progress*, one of the three great allegories of the world's literature,* was written.   It was published in 1678.

It furnished the simple Bedfordshire cottagers, for whom it was written, with a reflection of their own inmost struggles and aspirations, in a form which combined the fascinations of the novel, the fairy-tale, and the romance of adventure. The novel, the great literary discovery of the next century, appears here in its germ.   Not only is the physical world through which Christian journeys from the "Wicket-gate" to the Land of Beulah, pictured with the most familiar

---

* The others alluded to are Spenser's *Faerie Queene* and Dante's *Divine Comedy*.

realism, but the wayfarers whom he meets are such as might have been seen in Bunyan's day on any English market road —portly Mr. Worldly-Wiseman, full of prudential saws; blundering, self-confident young Ignorance; "gentlemanlike" Demas; and sweet talkative Piety. The landscape, the houses, the people, are all given with quaint sturdy strokes which stamp them upon the memory forever; so that it is almost impossible for a reader of *Pilgrim's Progress* to think of the journey otherwise than as a real personal experience. And added to the charm which the book has as realism, is its charm as romance. If, in one sense, it may be said to have ushered in the eighteenth century novel, in another it may be said to have revived the mediæval romance, in which the hero was made to contend against dangers natural and supernatural, on the way to the goal of his desires. Giant Despair in his grim castle, the obscene devils creeping and muttering in the Valley of the Shadow, the dreadful enemy Apollyon, the angels and archangels who lead the way, with harpings and hosannas, from the dread River of Death to the shining gates of the Celestial City, give to the story a fascinating element of marvel and adventure. If we add to this the charm of its style, so quaintly graphic, so humorously direct, so tender and rich and lyrical when the author is moved by the beauty of his vision, it seems no matter for surprise that *Pilgrim's Progress,* before Bunyan's death, was read with delight not only throughout England, but in France, in Holland, and in the far-off colonies of America.

End of the Romantic Literature of the Century.—*Paradise Lost* and *The Pilgrim's Progress* are the two great final products of that intellectual and artistic revival which we call the Renaissance, and of that religious revival which we call the Reformation. They mark the end of the stream of literature which flows down into the second half of the seventeenth century from its source in the later reign of Henry VIII. and in the early Elizabethan age. We must in the next chapter consider a school of literature of a very different kind, which began in a revolt against the reigning "romantic" style, and which at the Restoration assumed an authority which it maintained uninterruptedly for nearly a hundred years.

REVIEW OUTLINE.—Review what is said of Wyclif and Lollardry, and of the Puritan spirit in Langland, in Chapter IV. Review also what is said of the Reformation, in Chapter V. It will be clear that the Puritan movement of Milton's age was the result of a long growth. How did the increased knowledge of the Bible during Elizabeth's reign affect the popular mind? How did the strict Puritan view of life express itself in costume, manners, etc.? Give a brief summary of the struggle between the Parliament and the King; of the Civil War, and the events leading up to the recall of Charles II. to the throne. What great intellectual revolution accompanied the political and religious disturbances of the age? Who is the chief representative of this new intellectual movement?

Give a brief outline of Bacon's life. What was the scope of the work Bacon proposed to himself? Explain the scientific principle of investigation advocated by Bacon, and contrast it with the mediæval method of reasoning, which he wished to supplant. Instance one or more modern scientific theories which have been established by the "inductive" process of investigation. By what work does Bacon hold his place in English literature? What was his opinion of English as a literary language? What kinds of subjects are treated in Bacon's essays; and what is the general character of the thought in them? If possible, compare one of Bacon's essays named in the reading-list below, with a passage of Milton's prose, and note the contrast in style between the short, crisp sentences of the former and the long, rolling sentences of the latter.

What side of the seventeenth century spirit is shown by Sir Thomas Browne? What is the theme of the "Religio Medici"; of the " Urn Burial"?

Why were the Cavalier poets so-called? They are the successors of Wyatt, Surrey, and the "courtly makers" of the age of Henry VIII. and Elizabeth; they express the lighter and brighter view of life which was held by the early Renaissance, hence the sharp contrast they present with the general tone of literature in their own time, when the Reformation had given a serious cast to the minds of most writers. If possible read, in the Golden Treasury, Lovelace's " To Lucasta," and note the evidence in it of the author's " spirit of old-fashioned

chivalry," his " faithfulness to the ideals of love and knightly honor."
Where and under what conditions was the greater part of Herrick's
poetry written ? Put in unfigurative language the judgment of Herrick's genius expressed under the metaphor of the cherry-stone. What
were the two bents of thought and feeling displayed by Herrick?
Which seems the expression of his more constant nature ? Can you
gather from what is said of Walton the reason for his occupying a permanent place in the affection of English readers ?

By a comparison of dates, select from the following writers those
who were alive during Milton's boyhood, and whom he may conceiv-
ably have met in the streets of London: Spenser, Raleigh, Shakespeare, Ben Jonson, Beaumont, Fletcher, Bacon. How old was Milton
when Shakespeare left London ? What was Milton doing in the year
of Jonson's death ? Restate the facts of Milton's early education and
surroundings which were important in determining his character. Note
that on the moral side his education was Puritan in the strict sense,
but on the literary and artistic side that it was the liberal education of
the Renaissance. May not something similar be said concerning all
Milton's poetry ? How early did Milton dedicate himself to poetry,
and what was his ideal of the poet's character ? What important
poem had he written before leaving college ? Describe his life at Horton,
and its effect upon his taste, skill, and temperament. Name the
chief poems of the Horton period. In what way do " Comus " and
" Lycidas " reflect the growing seriousness of Milton's mind ? The
date of "Comus" shows that it may have been a part of the dem-
onstration made by sympathizers with the theatre as a reproof to
Puritan persecution of the stage. Connect this with the sympathy
for the drama expressed in " L'Allegro " and " Il Penseroso." Show
how unlike the sour and narrow view of life held by the more fanat-
ical Puritans is the view taken by Milton in these two pieces. What
later work of Milton's is in dramatic form ? In connection with
"Comus" review what is said of the masque-form as developed by
Jonson, and note the particulars in which Milton's poem answers to the
general description. Where, and on what occasion was "Comus" presented ? What is the " teaching" of " Comus," and what allegorical
means are taken to bring it out ? What are the two forms of symbolism used in " Lycidas ? " Which of these was conventional ?
What moved Milton to add the second form ?

What important events intervened in Milton's life between his sojourn at Horton and his life in the diplomatic service? Did Milton write any poetry while engaged in work for the government? Name the sonnets of Milton which have the greatest autobiographic interest. How do we know that he was not forgetful of his great purpose? To what circumstance is his blindness attributed?

What subject did Milton at first intend to use for a great epic? By what poet of our own time has this subject been treated? What national events finally gave Milton leisure to write " Paradise Lost " ? When was it published? How long had he had the subject in mind before he began to write? Restate in your own words the story of " Paradise Lost." The story is not presented in the poem in the natural order of events; explain what the difference is, and upon what literary tradition it rests. Notice that the theme of " Paradise Regained " is suggested at the end of " Paradise Lost " ; by what means? By what "central motive" is the whole action held together? Why is it an untrue criticism to say that Satan is the hero of the epic? What connection is here traced between the personal experiences of Milton and the grandeur of style in his later work? Why did he choose blank verse? For what purpose had blank verse been chiefly used up to this time? Describe as clearly and simply as possible the two great characteristics of Milton's blank verse. Compare the first fifteen or twenty lines of "Paradise Lost" with a passage from one of Shakespeare's plays, such as the speech of Portia before the judges; notice how much longer the sense is suspended in Milton, and how much less simple is the grammatical structure of the sentences. Make clear in what way Milton's second epic supplements the thought of the first. In what respects may his last poem be taken as an allegory of his own life, private and public?

When was the King James or Authorized version of the Bible made? Review the history of the English Bible up to this point, beginning with the partial translations made in Anglo-Saxon times. What was the effect of the Bible upon Bunyan as a writer? Narrate the facts of Bunyan's early life which typify the religiou excitement of the period. In what work has he made a revelation of his religious state of mind? How did Bunyan's masterpiece come to be written? Explain the double connection of " Pilgrim's Progress " with the obsolete mediæval romance and the future eighteenth century novel. Review the great names which make up the line of imaginative writers beginning with Wyatt and Surrey, and ending with Bunyan. Notice that only one of these, Ben Jonson, is " classic " in his sympathies; he is the only one who insists first of all on correctness and restraint; all the others are " romantic," that is they care for beauty and energy of expression first of all. Milton holds a middle position; can you explain how ?

READING GUIDE.—Milton.—All members of the class should read, at least, " L'Allegro " and " Il Penseroso," " Comus," the first three books and the ninth book of "Paradise Lost." Good school editions are abundant. The most convenient complete editions are the Globe (Macmillan), and the Cambridge (Houghton, Mifflin). If a supplement is desired for the biographical matter given in the text, either the life of Milton by R. Garnett, in the Great Writers series, or that by M. Pattison, in the English Men of Letters series, will furnish abundant material. An excellent short biography, by D. Masson, is prefixed to the Globe edition. Lowell's essay on Milton, in " Among My Books," and Matthew Arnold's, in " Essays in Criticism," will be found of value in giving a larger view of Milton's place in English poetry. Macaulay's essay on Milton gives an admirable study of the social and political aspects of Puritanism. This may be supplemented by Chapter IX. of Green's " Short History of England," and by Macaulay's " Conversation Between Mr. Abraham Cowley and Mr. John Milton Touching the Great Civil War." In Ruskin's " Sesame and Lilies " may be found an illuminating passage in interpretation of " Lycidas." Interpretative studies of all Milton's poems, and a translation of his Latin and Italian verses, are given in the Cambridge edition.

The routine of class work will probably allow little time for the firsthand study of the other writers of this period; but ambitious students will be interested to do some reading in them independently. Among Bacon's essays the following are recommended: Truth, Adversity, Envy, Love, Great Place, Travel, Wisdom for a Man's Self, Friendship, Discourse, Gardens, Studies. Bacon's Essays are included in Cassell's National Library, and in Morley's Universal Library, and a good selection from them is given in Number 3 of Maynard's English Classics.

The pieces of Herrick and the Cavalier poets given in Palgrave's Golden Treasury or in Ward's English Poets, should by all means be read. For those who wish to learn more of Herrick, the selections from his poetry published in the Golden Treasury series is recommended. A delightful essay upon Herrick can be found in E. Gosse's "Seventeenth Century Studies." Walton's "Complete Angler" and, Bunyan's "Grace Abounding" can be had in Cassell's National Library. "The Pilgrim's Progress" is published in the Riverside Literature series. "Grace Abounding," in spite of its somewhat dry-sounding title, is a most picturesque and absorbing book. Bunyan's "Holy War" is certain to prove interesting to students, especially to boys. Volunteer reports upon these two, or portions of them, and upon "The Pilgrim's Progress," or some portion thereof, can hardly fail to furnish an interesting hour.

TABULAR VIEW

FROM THE DEATH OF ELIZABETH TO THE RESTORATION: 1603-1660

HISTORICAL EVENTS

JAMES I............1603-1625
James proclaims "divine right"....1604
The King James Bible.......1611
Pilgrims land at Plymouth......1620
Commons protest against the King's arbitrary rule......1621
CHARLES I......1625-1649
Strafford and Laud institute the policy of "Thorough"......1635
Charles tries to force a new liturgy upon Scottish Church......1637
Expedition against the Scots......1639
Long Parliament meets......1640
Civil War begins......1642
Cromwell organizes "Ironsides"......1645
Defeat of Charles at Naseby......1645
Execution of Charles......1649
The Commonwealth......1649-1653
Cromwell Protector......1653-1658
Richard Cromwell......1658-1659
Charles II. recalled......1660

NON-DRAMATIC LITERATURE

FRANCIS BACON......1561-1626
Advancement of Learning......1605
Essays......1597-1625
JOHN DONNE......1573-1631
Poems, amatory and satirical, published 1633, but circulated much earlier.
JEREMY TAYLOR......1613-1667
Holy Living and Holy Dying......1650-1651
SIR THOMAS BROWNE......1605-1682
Religio Medici......1642
Urn Burial......1658
THOMAS CAREW......1598-1638
JOHN SUCKLING......1609-1641
RICHARD LOVELACE......1618-1658
ROBERT HERRICK......1591-1674
Hesperides and Noble Numbers......1648
ANDREW MARVELL......1621-1678
GEORGE HERBERT......1593-1632
The Temple, published......1633
RICHARD CRASHAW......1613-1650
HENRY VAUGHAN......1621-1695
Silex Scintillans......1650
ABRAHAM COWLEY......1618-1667
JOHN MILTON......1608-1672
Earlier Work falling in this period:
Ode on the Morning of Christ's Nativity......1629
L'Allegro and Il Penseroso......1632
Arcades......1633
Comus......1634
Lycidas......1637
Sonnets....chiefly between 1642 and 1658
Areopagitica......1644
Paradise Lost......begun 1658
(For Milton's later work, and for Bunyan, see next table.)

DRAMA

BEN JONSON......1573-1637
Alchemist, Volpone, and Silent Woman......1605-1610
SHAKESPEARE:
Great tragedies and Roman plays (except Julius Cæsar and Hamlet) and later romantic plays......1603-1613
THOMAS HEYWOOD....died about 1650
A Woman Killed With Kindness, The Fair Maid of the West.
THOMAS MIDDLETON......1570-1627
BEAUMONT, 1584-1616, and FLETCHER, 1575-1625
Joint plays written......1605-1616
JOHN WEBSTER:
White Devil......1612
Duchess of Malfi......1616
JOHN FORD......1586-1640
The Broken Heart, Perkin Warbeck.
JAMES SHIRLEY......1596-1666
Hyde Park, The Cardinal, The Lady of Pleasure.
Theatres closed......1642

CHAPTER IX

THE RESTORATION

I. INTRODUCTION

Political History of the Restoration Era.—The year 1660 marks the return of Charles II. to the throne which his father had lost, and the beginning of an era known as the period of the Restoration. Historically the age is in sharp contrast with the grea century that began in 1558 with the accession of Elizabeth. That epoch was, as we have seen, one of intense national and individual energy, of zealous devotion to religious and political ideas which finally involved the country in civil war. In the age of the Restoration men were weary of all this excitement and turmoil, and ready to accept any system which promised order and peace. The king himself was idle and pleasure-loving, indisposed to take the trouble to push his royal prerogative to extremes, and inclined to a do-nothing foreign policy. Under his rule England sank from the great position in European affairs which she had held under Cromwell, to that of paid ally of the French king. The reign of Charles II. was marked by such public calamities as the Great Plague in 1665, and the Fire of London in 1666; but neither these nor the misfortunes of foreign war, in the course of which the Dutch fleet entered the Thames, stirred the English people from its lethargy. Only when, after the death of the king in 1685, his brother, who succeeded him as James II., attempted to undo the work of the Reformation, did the nation rise, and, by the Revolution of 1688, set aside the male line of the House of Stuart and placed upon the throne the daughter of James II., Mary, and her husband, William of Orange.

Social and Literary Tendencies.—The contrast between the age of Elizabeth and that of Charles II. is as strongly marked in social and intellectual life. The former period was a time when the unmeasured possibilities of the new world of the Renaissance gave scope to the far-reaching desires of men. The imagination, whether dealing with knowledge as in Bacon, or with human power as in Marlowe, or with the things of faith as in Milton, took wings to itself and flew. In the Restoration era, on the contrary, men were content to remain at peace within the limits of the world of things which they could see and touch. In science they gave themselves, not to visions of all knowledge, but to patient investigation of facts immediately about them; in statecraft they imagined no Utopias, but worked out principles of practical politics and party government; in social life they had learned to fear the spirit of individualism, leading to such violent contrasts as that between Cavaliers and Puritans, and therefore tried to set up ideals of life in accordance with reason and " common-sense," to which all men should conform. The literature of the time is a faithful reflection of these tendencies. It is largely concerned with the facts of the immediate world of London, with contemporary men and politics, and with social life. And it reflects the spirit of uniformity in the agreement of writers, both in prose and poetry, upon rules and principles in accordance with which they should express themselves. The acceptance of these literary conventions, drawn from the practice of writers of the past, marks the difference between the *classic* age of Dryden and Pope, and the *romantic* epoch of Spenser and Shakespeare.

French Influence.—In this difference the influence of France counted for much. There the reaction against the poetic license of the Renaissance had set in somewhat earlier. Its result is seen in the work of Corneille and Racine, who developed a drama on the lines of Latin tragedy, succeeding where the English classicists of the sixteenth century had signally failed. It must be remembered that many Englishmen of the class which cared for literature and the stage, spent years of exile in France, and naturally came to accept the principles of French taste. Through the new artistic conceptions brought back to England by the exiles, French influence upon English literature, especially upon the English drama, was strengthened. To their notions of refinement the license of the older dramatists seemed uncouth. "I have seen *Hamlet*," wrote Evelyn, "but now these old plays begin to disgust this refined century, since their majesties have been so long abroad."

The Heroic Couplet.—The most striking way in which English poetry reflected the spirit of the new era, was in its substitution of a single form for the lawless variety of the age which had gone before. This form, called the heroic couplet, consisted of two pentameter lines connected by rhyme. It had been used in earlier periods, for example by Chaucer; but in his hands the couplet had not been necessarily a unit, the thought having often been drawn out into the succeeding pair of verses, with no pause at the rhyming word. The literary ideals of the Restoration may be illustrated by the comparison of a few lines from the prologue to the *Canterbury Tales*,

> " A knight ther was, and that a worthy man,
> That fro the tyme that he first bigan
> To ryden out, he loved chivalrye,
> Trouthe and honour, fredom, and curteisy,"

with these from the chief poet of the Restoration, John Dryden:

> " A milk-white hind, immortal and unchanged,
> Fed on the lawns, and in the forest rang'd;
> Without unspotted, innocent within,
> She fear'd no danger for she knew no sin."

In the first, it is clear, the couplet exerts little control over the thought, which runs on into the second pair of verses; in the second the thought is limited and regulated by the acceptance of a precise and narrow form; and this limitation and regulation were the chief qualities of Restoration poetry.

II. JOHN DRYDEN (1631–1700)

Dryden's Early Life.—Dryden was born in 1631 at Aldwinkle, in Northamptonshire, his parents being of the upper middle class, and of Puritan sympathies. He was sent to Westminster School, and thence, in 1650, to Trinity College, Cambridge, where he remained seven years. During this time his father died, leaving him a small property. His first important verse was an elegy on the death of Cromwell, written in 1658. Two years later, however, Dryden, with the mass of Englishmen, had become an ardent royalist; and he welcomed the return of Charles, in a poem in couplets called "Astræa Redux"—("The Return of the Goddess of Justice"). In 1663 he married Lady Elizabeth Howard, a woman of higher rank than his own. It may have been the desirability of increasing his income that, just before this marriage, drove Dryden to write his first comedy, *The Wild Gallant*. It certainly was his accumulating financial necessities that kept him writing for the stage constantly down to 1681. During this period his only poem of importance was "Annus Mirabilis" (1667), ("The Wonderful Year"), a chronicle of events of the preceding year, which had been distinguished by several victories at sea over the Dutch, and by the great London fire.

Dryden's Satires.—In 1681 Dryden began the succession of political poems which have generally been accounted his best works. The times were troubled. The court and the country were divided between the partisans of the king's brother, who, though a Papist, was recognized as the heir to the throne, and those of the king's illegitimate son, the Duke of Monmouth, whom certain persons zealous for the Protestant faith were disposed to set up as a rival candidate. The leader of the latter party was the Earl of Shaftesbury. In the Bible story of the revolt of Absalom against King David, Dryden found an apt parallel to existing circumstances in England; and his satire *Absalom and Achitophel* exposed the relations of Monmouth, the prince, and Shaftesbury, the evil counsellor, with merciless humor. The poem became im-

JOHN DRYDEN

mensely popular. The next year Dryden followed it with a second blow at Shaftesbury in *The Medal*. Then he turned aside in *MacFlecknoe* to attack a rival poet, Shadwell, who had been employed by the Whigs to reply to *The Medal*. In this year, also, Dryden extended his range into the field of religious controversy, with *Religio Laici* ("The Religion of a Layman"), a very temperate statement of a layman's faith in the Church of England. Three years after this confession of faith Dryden became a Roman Catholic, and in 1687 he published a political defence of the Church of Rome called *The Hind and the Panther*.

Dryden's Later Life.—This political and religious writing brought Dryden distinction and a modest income. In 1670 he was made Historiographer Royal and Poet Laureate, with a salary of two hundred pounds a year. Later he received a pension of a hundred pounds a year, and in 1683 he was made Collector of the Port of London. All these honors and emoluments he lost in consequence of the Revolution of 1688. He was obliged to betake himself again to the stage as the most lucrative department of literature, to accept aid from private patrons in place of the royal bounty, to contract with Tonson, the book-seller, to produce and deliver ten thousand lines of verse for three hundred guineas, and to undertake various jobs of translation for the same employer. In short, in his old age Dryden was compelled to attempt almost all the methods by which a literary man could live. Nevertheless, his production in these years added much to his fame. Whatever may be thought of his poetical qualities, at least his literary energy lasted well. His work of this time includes his translation of Virgil, and his renderings into modern English verse of stories from Chaucer, among which the *Palamon and Arcite* is best known. These twice-told tales were published in 1700, in a volume of *Fables*, which contained also his best lyrical poem, "Alexander's Feast."

Dryden as a Literary Dictator.—During these last years Dryden lived constantly in London. The coffee-house of that day was the chief place of resort for literary men, much as the tavern had been in Elizabeth's time. At Will's or Button's the wits gathered for exchange of courtesies or for combat; there their admirers or patrons met them; and thence went forth the criticism that made or marred the fortunes of rising men. Dryden frequented Will's, where he was as much a monarch as Ben Jonson had been at the Mermaid, or as, a century later, Samuel Johnson was at the Literary Club. At Will's he is pictured for us by tradition, sitting in his arm-chair on the balcony in summer, and before the fire in winter, burly of figure, shrewd and kindly of feature, altogether a sound, stalwart, wholesome man. It was to Will's that young Pope was brought to gaze on greatness and be inspired; and it was there also that Dryden dismissed his youthful relative with the pitying words, "Cousin Swift, you will never be a poet." In an age when the form of poetry was all but rigidly fixed, the acknowledged master of that form could be as much of a despot as he chose.

Dryden's Character.—The life of Dryden seems at first sight to have been an unheroic, and in some ways an ignoble one. His changes of side from Cromwellian to Royalist, from Protestant to Romanist, stand out in unfavorable contrast to the devotion of men like More and Milton. His concern with the details of party strife is sharply opposed to the ideal morality of Sidney and of Spenser. His indifference in matters of belief seems tame and watery after the flame-like faith of Bunyan. But we must not let such comparisons carry us too far. Dryden illustrates the change from the virtues of Elizabethan chivalry and Cromwellian fanaticism, to the sober commonplace ethics of an era of reason. His tendency to shift his influence to the winning side was in part the patriotism of a sensible man who argued that it mattered comparatively little whether the country was ruled by Protector or King, whether it worshipped according to Anglican or Catholic rites, so long as it was at peace under institutions which were strong enough to curb individual ambition.

Dryden's Poetry.—There is also a temptation to extend the first harsh judgment of Dryden's life, to his poetry. It, too, lacks elevation, and the subject-matter of much of it, the affairs of church and state, is remote from what we regard as poetic. But in his writing also Dryden responded to the demands of his age. In the days of Charles II. men were weary of revolution. To them the kingship and the church, Anglican or Catholic, were interesting and beautiful because they represented, for the mass of the nation, an ideal of order and restraint; just as to an earlier time the boundless self-assertion of Faustus and Tamburlaine had been interesting and beautiful for the opposite reason.

Not only the substance, but the form of Dryden's verse has been a ground for detraction from his fame. Few poets of the modern world have maintained such strict uniformity. With the exception of the lyrics in his dramas, of several odes, and of two early poems in the heroic stanza, Dryden cultivated steadily the heroic couplet. This kind of verse appealed with irresistible force to an age which desired, above all, uniformity and regularity. When at the close of *Religio Laici* Dryden says,

> " And this unpolished rugged verse I chose
>   As fittest for discourse, and nearest prose,"

his second line may be taken as referring to his poems in general. In them we look for the virtues of prose rather than for those of poetry; for the useful qualities, exactness, clearness, energy, rather than for imagination and suggestion; for epigram in place of metaphor; for boldly marked rhythm instead of elusive harmony.

Dryden as Prose Writer.—Dryden was not only the foremost poet, but also the most copious dramatist, and the chief critic, of his time. The age of the Restoration was a period of criticism rather than of creation, a time when men were interested in testing the product of earlier ages, and in winnowing the good from the bad. This interest accounts for the fact that to many of his works Dryden prefixed one or more critical essays in the form of dedications or prefaces, in which he discussed the leading artistic questions of the day. Among these essays the most important are "An Essay of Dramatic Poesy" (1668), the "Essay on Satire" (1693), and the Preface to the "Fables" (1700). In these essays Dryden set a model for simple, practical prose style. By his adoption of the modern sentence in place of the unit of great and unequal length used by Raleigh and Milton, he carried out in prose a change exactly analogous to that accomplished in verse by his adoption of the couplet in place of the stanza. In short, he did for prose what he did for poetry; he reduced the unit of treatment to manageable size; he set an example of correctness; and finally, by his authority, he did much to establish such a standard of taste as should render henceforth impossible the eccentricities to which the preceding century had been indulgent.

III. SAMUEL BUTLER (1612–1680), SAMUEL PEPYS (1633–1703), AND THE DRAMATISTS

Butler's " Hudibras."—Like Elizabeth and Charles I., Charles II. held in some sort a literary court, of which lyric poetry and satire were the language. The courtly poets of the time, the successors of the Cavaliers, caught from the king an attitude of moral indifference. In their circles the most popular work was a fierce and scurrilous satire upon the Puritan, Samuel Butler's *Hudibras*. Butler was doubtless meditating his attack during the years of the Protectorate, when he was acting as private secretary to a Puritan nobleman. Three years after the accession of Charles II., he published three cantos of a poem in which the vices of the Puritan period, hypocrisy, sanctimoniousness, and intolerance, are presented with savage exaggeration in the person of Sir Hudibras. This knight, with his squire Ralpho, passes through a series of quixotic adventures, which are continued in further instalments of the poem, published in 1664 and 1678.

Pepys's Diary.—While Butler and the Cavalier poets were embodying the mood of the aristocracy, Bunyan was writing his *Pilgrim's Progress* for the serious lower class, where Puritanism still survived. Between these extremes, however, we have an order that was to make its presence felt increasingly from this time on, the upper-middle class; and as it happens, this class had, in the late seventeenth century, a figure almost as representative as Bunyan. Samuel Pepys was a busy man of affairs, a clerk of the Navy Board, and secretary of the Admiralty under James II. Between 1660 and 1669 he kept a diary in cipher, which he left with his library to Magdalen College, Cambridge. It was deciphered and published in the nineteenth century, and was recognized at once as a personal document of great interest.

Pepys's diary is scarcely to be called literature. It is a transcript of the observations, doings, thoughts, and feelings of a commonplace burgher, all set down with the greatest fidelity. If Pepys goes on a picnic he mentions the time of starting, the dishes of the luncheon, the substance of the conversation by the way, the company he met, the sheep which he saw ("the most pleasant and innocent sight that ever I saw in my life"), the shepherd whose little boy was reading the Bible to him, the flowers, the glow-worms which came out in the evening, and the slight accident by which he sprained his foot. In its detail the diary reflects the patient, industrious habits by which business and science were to thrive in the next century—for Pepys was a scientist and President of the Royal Society. In its uniformity of tone, its lack of emphasis and dramatic interest, it illustrates again the sober modernity which the citizen's life was beginning to assume. In its worldliness, its reflection of perfectly unashamed delight in mere comfort, well-being, and success, it shows the bourgeois ideal of life. And finally, the pleasure in his own life, which sustained the author in the mechanical toil of recording its happenings, is to be connected with the interest in human life in general, which was the force behind the development of realistic fiction in the following century.

The Restoration Drama.—One result of the Restoration was to re-open the theatres of London, which had been closed since 1642. Though the great generation of dramatists had come to an end, the drama had retained its hold on the masses. Dryden found the production of plays the most lucrative of literary employments, and he wrote many, both comedies and tragedies, in prose, blank verse, and rhyme. His most characteristic dramatic works are his "heroic plays" in rhyme, the use of which he defended on the ground that "it bounds and circumscribes the fancy. For imagination in a poet is a faculty so wild and lawless that it is like an high ranging spaniel, it must have clogs tied to it lest it outrun the judgment." Dryden's two dramatic masterpieces, however, *All for Love* and *Don Sebastian* are in blank verse.

In the main, the tragedy of the period interests us only as a survival. The Restoration comedy, however, is a genuine reflection of the temper, if not of the actual life, of the upper classes of the nation. As practised by Shakespeare, English comedy had been romantic in spirit. However seriously it concerned itself with the essentials of human nature, it had comparatively little to do with the circumstances of actual human life. In Ben Jonson we find more realistic treatment of the setting, the social surroundings, of the play. Following his lead, the comedians of the Restoration, of whom William Wycherley and William Congreve are the chief, devoted themselves to picturing the external details of life, the fashions of the time, its manners, its speech, its interests. For scene they turned to the most interesting places they knew, the drawing-rooms, the coffee-houses, the streets and gardens of London. Their characters were chiefly people of fashion, and their plots, for the most part, were love intrigues,—both often enough uninteresting and improbable. For these deficiencies, however, the dramatist made up in part by the brilliancy of his dialogue. In tendency these plays are, almost without exception, immoral; they represent the reaction of the play-going public against Puritanism. They are anti-social, in that they represent social institutions, particularly marriage, in an obnoxious or ridiculous light.

This anti-social influence of the plays of the time was clearly perceived, and protest was not lacking. In 1698 a clergyman, Jeremy Collier, published his "Short View of the Profaneness and Immorality of the English Stage," and Dryden, who was one of the dramatists particularly attacked, admitted the justice of the rebuke. Its immediate effect was not sufficient to do away with the coarseness of Restoration comedy, but in Steele's plays, early in the next century, the drama is in full alliance with the forces which were making for morality and decent living.

REVIEW OUTLINE.—The Restoration is held by some writers to mark the beginning of modern English history. In the period which followed, English life begins to assume its modern form, and to show the beginnings of that political, commercial, industrial, artistic, and social development, the results•of which make the England of to-day.

It was, in the main, a period of peaceful growth. How do you account for its calmness? What was the character of Charles II.? What were some of the events of his reign? What caused the Revolution of 1688? Contrast the age of Charles II. with the century which preceded it. Why was the former a period of interest in society? How did the ideal of social conduct as opposed to that of individual expression affect literature? Where did men find rules for writing? What was the influence of France? How did poetry in its form reflect the tendency of the time? What is the heroic couplet? How did the writers of this period differ from Chaucer in their use of it?

Outline the early life of Dryden, and mention his early poems. What is the general subject-matter of these poems? Sketch the political situation out of which Dryden's great series of satires arose. What was his position before and after 1688? Mention his chief later works. What was the place of the coffee-house in the literature of the time? In what sense was Dryden a literary dictator? Give your view of Dryden's personal character. Explain that character in the light of his age. State your opinion of his poetic quality. Why did Dryden choose political subjects? What is the form of his poetry? What virtues has it? What was the importance of criticism in Dryden's time? Compare his reform in prose with that in verse?

What is Hudibras? Look up several passages from it in a book of quotations. Who was Samuel Pepys? Of what class was he representative? What is the nature of his diary? How does it reflect the ideals of the time? Who were the chief writers of comedy in the Restoration? What is the difference between the Restoration comedy and the comedy of Shakespeare? What is the moral tendency of the former? Who protested against it? Was the protest effective? (See also page 201.)

READING GUIDE.—"Palamon and Arcite" is an excellent example of Dryden's poetry, and if the poem be compared with its original, Chaucer's "Knight's Tale," the result of making over a story to suit the classic taste of the time may be observed. Numerous school editions are accessible. Of Dryden's other poems, "Alexander's Feast" should be read as an example of his power of sustaining lyric effects through a variety of metres. The poem is included in The Golden Treasury. Of Dryden's prose, examples may be found in Craik's English Prose. Selections from Pepys's Diary may be chosen from the several volumes in Cassell's National Library, and no better pictures of English life of the time are to be found.

For fuller treatment of the general condition of society in the Restoration, the third chapter of Macaulay's "History of England" will be found crowded with interesting details. The life of Dryden, by Mr. Saintsbury in the English Men of Letters series (Harper), is satisfactory; and the pupil will enjoy R. L. Stevenson's vivid portrait of Pepys in "Memories and Portraits" (Scribner). Extended criticism of the Restoration writers is given in Mr. Edmund Gosse's "From Shakespeare to Pope." An appreciation of the comedy of the Restoration may be gained from Thackeray's lecture on Congreve, in "The English Humourists of the Eighteenth Century."

TABULAR VIEW

FROM THE RESTORATION TO THE DEATH OF DRYDEN: 1660-1700

HISTORICAL EVENTS	NON-DRAMATIC LITERATURE	DRAMA
CHARLES II............1660-1685. Severe laws against Dissenters, 1660-1663 War with the Dutch........1665 Great Plague (afterwards described by Defoe)........1665 Great Fire of London........1666 Persecution of Catholics..1678-1679 Rise of Whigs and Tories, about 1680 JAMES II............1685-1688 James flees, and William of Orange invited to take the throne................1688 WILLIAM AND MARY......1688-1702 James II. defeated at Battle of the Boyne..........1690 Freedom of the Press........1695	JOHN MILTON, 1608-1672. Later work falling in this period: Paradise Lost, 1667; Paradise Regained, 1672. Drama (not intended for the stage), Samson Agonistes, 1672. JOHN BUNYAN, 1628-1688. Grace Abounding, 1666; Pilgrim's Progress, 1678. JOHN DRYDEN, 1631-1700. Astrea Redux, 1666; Annus Mirabilis, 1667; Ode on St. Cecilia's Day, 1667; Absalom and Achitophel, 1681; Mac-Flecknoe, 1682; Religio Laici, 1682; The Hind and the Panther, 1687; Alexander's Feast, 1687; Fables (including Palamon and Arcite), 1699. SAMUEL BUTLER, 1612-1680. Hudibras, 1663-1678. SAMUEL PEPYS, 1633-1670. Diary, written 1660-1669.	JOHN DRYDEN. The Wild Gallant, 1663; The Indian Emperor, 1665; The Conquest of Granada, 1670; All for Love, 1678. WILLIAM WYCHERLEY, 1640-1715. The Country Wife, 1673; The Plain Dealer, 1674. THOMAS OTWAY, 1651-1685. The Orphan, 1680; Venice Preserved, 1682. WILLIAM CONGREVE, 1670-1729. Love for Love, 1695; The Way of the World, 1700.

CHAPTER X

THE EIGHTEENTH CENTURY

I. INTRODUCTION

Political History of the Eighteenth Century.—Almost at the opening of the eighteenth century the crown passed, by the death of William III., to the second daughter of James II., Anne (1702–1714). Her reign was marked by political struggles between the Whigs, who wished to secure the Protestant succession to the throne by recognizing the Elector of Hanover as next heir, and the Tories, who hoped to see the kingdom revert to the son of James II. In spite of the fact that the Tories were led by one of the cleverest men of the time both in politics and literature, Lord Bolingbroke, the Whigs triumphed, and on the death of the queen in 1714 the Elector of Hanover succeeded as George I. The supporters of the Stuart heir, or Jacobites, revolted twice, once in 1715, and again against George II. in 1745, but fruitlessly. The House of Hanover was continued by George III., in whose reign England won her imperial domain from France in America and India, only to lose the greater part of the former by the American Revolution.

The Social Importance of Literature.—The early eighteenth century shows a continuation of the literary tendencies which marked the Restoration. Literature on its serious side was largely concerned with politics. The Revolution of 1688 had made Parliament supreme in the government of the nation, and had fixed the system of party government. In the days before newspapers, the services of writers were of great importance in determining public opinion; accordingly they were employed largely by both parties and liberally rewarded. In a sense, political service took the place of patronage as the chief resource of authors. It gave them a place of independence and power in the state such as they have at no other time enjoyed. Moreover, thoughtful men saw in literature a means of improving social life and purging society of evils which threatened the peace and order of the community. The violence of party spirit engendered by the expulsion of the Stuarts, the survival of religious fanaticism among the lower orders, the licentiousness of private life among the aristocracy, which is reflected in the Restoration drama—against all these the literature of the age made protest, partly by the use of ridicule and satire, partly by an appeal to common sense. In minor respects, also, the civilization of the time was imperfect. London was so filthy that the plague was always imminent, so badly paved that traveling was dangerous, so poorly guarded that footpads and highwaymen operated freely, and wild young bucks, who called themselves Mohocks, kept peaceful citizens in terror. The crude, immature nature of the masses, as it expressed itself in vulgar amusements and cruel practical jokes, is portrayed in the realistic writings of the time, as it is with still more vivid satire in the pictures of Hogarth—always with the intention of making things better.

Eighteenth Century Style.—To serve such ends the writers of the time found their most acceptable form in the regular style which had characterized the period of Dryden. The reign of law and order, which was so much desired after the turbulence of the seventeenth century, had already been achieved in the realm of letters. Literary men had only to practise what they preached, the cultivation of perfect manners instead of the assertion of personal peculiarities, the attainment of regularity and correctness of form instead of originality of thought. If the literary fashion of the time seems to us to stifle real feeling under formality, we must remember that men needed this formality, as they did their wigs and ruffles and their stately courtliness of manner, to remind themselves that they were not barbarians, like Shakespeare and his friends, but almost as fine gentlemen as the French or the Latins. Indeed, it was the boast of Queen Anne's time that it resembled the first century of the Roman Empire, whence it called itself the Augustan Age.

The Age of Queen Anne.—Queen Anne has given her name to an age in English history only less glorious than that of Elizabeth. Her short reign is famous for the wonderful victories of the Duke of Marlborough over the French, and for the writers who are known as Queen Anne's men. These form the most compact group in the history of English letters. They all shared the same interests and wrote after the same models. They were all more or less in politics; they lived as much as possible in London; they met constantly in coffee-houses and clubs where they formed partnerships and alliances, or quarrelled and went away to attack each other with lampoons and epigrams. All this gives a peculiar sense of intimacy to literary society in the early eighteenth century, the days of Swift, Addison, Steele, Pope.

II. JONATHAN SWIFT (1667–1745)

Swift's Early Life.—Jonathan Swift was born in Ireland of English parents, in 1667. He was a posthumous son, and he grew up to share his mother's poverty. He was sent to the University of Dublin, where, as he says, he was "stopped of his degree for dulness and unsufficiency; and at last hardly admitted, in a manner little to his credit." In 1689 he left Ireland to take a position as under-secretary to a distant relative, Sir William Temple, with whom he remained intermittently for some years, reading aloud to his patron, writing at dictation, keeping accounts, and cursing his fate. At Moor Park, Temple's country-seat, he met Esther Johnson, who was also a dependent on the bounty of Temple, and there began the long friendship between them which later gave rise to the story of their secret marriage. While in the service of Sir William Temple, Swift wrote *The Battle of the Books*, a contribution to the controversy which Temple was carrying on with Bentley, the great scholar, as to the comparative merit of ancient and modern writers. About this time, also, he wrote a satire on the divisions of Christianity, called *The Tale of a Tub*. Neither work was published until 1704. Before this time, in despair of any other career, he had entered the church; and after his patron's death he returned to

Ireland as chaplain to Lord Berkeley, by whom he was given the living of Laracor.

Swift's Political Career.—Then began the great period of Swift's life, the time of his political power. During the reign of William III., party strife was bitter between the Whigs, who supported the king's foreign policy of resistance to Louis XIV. of France, and the Tories, who opposed it; and this struggle was continued in the reign of Queen Anne. Almost all the prominent literary men of the time were engaged on one side or the other. Swift, who was frequently in London promoting his candidacy for offices in the church as they fell vacant, at first wrote on the Whig side; but in 1710 he joined the Tories, who were just coming into power. The Tory ministry, of which Lord Bolingbroke was a member, was resolved to stop the war with France; and in defence of this policy Swift put out one of his strongest political writings, *The Conduct of the Allies*. His life during these years is reflected in his *Journal to Stella*, a daily account of his doings which he wrote to his friend, Esther Johnson. Here we find Swift playing the part in which he most delighted, that of a man of affairs, active, successful, and powerful. He records with gusto his hours spent with the rulers of the country; their politeness, and his own half contemptuous familiarity; his pleasure in his ability to serve his friends and to punish his enemies. In 1713, as the price of his support of the Tory government, he was named Dean of St. Patrick's in Dublin, a promotion little to his taste. The next year the Tories went out of power, discredited by Bolingbroke's intrigues with the Pretender; and Swift returned to Ireland.

Swift in Ireland.—Here his unconquerable activity found vent in defending the Irish from the careless tyranny of the home government. In this endeavor he published *The Drapier's Letters*, most of them in 1724, as a protest against turning over the right to coin money for Ireland to a private individual, for his own profit. In 1726 he took the manuscript of his most famous work, *Gulliver's Travels*, to London for publication, and the next year he returned thither to taste the pleasure of a great literary success. This, as all else in his life, seemed to turn only to disappointment. In 1728 Miss Johnson died, and her death left him desolate. As the years passed, his hatred of the world grew more intense, and his satire more bitter. A disease from which he had suffered at intervals gained rapidly upon him, resulting in deafness and giddiness; and he suffered also from attacks of epilepsy and insanity. After years of gloom and agony, death came slowly upon him. He died in 1745.

Swift's Character.—It is evident from this narrative that, to a great extent, Swift's writings were occasional, and grew out of the circumstances of his life. He was not a professional writer; with one or two exceptions, his works were published anonymously. He was a man of affairs, who became a man of letters because literature was a means by which affairs could be directed. His writings must be regarded, then, as one expression among others of energy turned to practical ends; as one evidence among others of his extraordinary activity. For Swift lived hard. "There is no such thing," he wrote to a friend, "as a fine old gentleman; if the man had a mind or body worth a farthing they would have worn him out long ago." We are not surprised to read of Swift that while he was at Moor Park with Sir William Temple he used to leave his study every two hours for a half mile run. As an old man, imprisoned in his deanery, he found relief in rushing over the house and up and down stairs with incredible speed.

This need of exercise is the explanation of much that is singular in Swift's life. It shows itself not only in his serious concern with important affairs of state, but also in his gigantic sense of play. The anecdotes related of him by his earlier biographers are legion, most of them turning upon the translation of some whim into practical form, usually as a grotesque joke. The tale of his dispersing a crowd gathered to witness an eclipse, by sending a message that, according to the Dean's orders, the eclipse would be put off for a day; of his impersonating a poor usher at a reception, to draw the contempt of a rich fool; and of his disguising himself as a fiddler at a beggar's wedding, to discover the arts by which impostors live—all these bear testimony to that restlessness which could not be satisfied by work alone. With this lighter side of Swift's nature are to be connected the works by which he is chiefly known, his satires—*The Tale of a Tub* and *Gulliver's Travels*.

"The Partridge Predictions"; Swift's Literary Method.— Once, indeed, this love of a practical joke was directly responsible for some of Swift's most characteristic writing. A certain Partridge was in the habit of issuing an almanac, with predictions of events to fall out in the next year. This impostor Swift exposed in a set of "Predictions for the year 1708," one of which was the death of Partridge himself, who, according to the prophecy, should "infallibly die upon the 29th of March, about eleven at night, of a raging fever." This pamphlet was published over the name of Isaac Bickerstaff. On the 30th of March, Swift published a letter supposed to be written by a revenue officer to a certain nobleman, giving an account of Partridge's last days and death. He also wrote "An Elegy of Mr. Partridge." Of course, Partridge hastened in triumph to assure the world that he was not dead; but Swift promptly came back with "A Vindication of Isaac Bickerstaff," in which, after rebuking Partridge for his impudence, he proved by various logical demonstrations that Partridge certainly died "within half an hour of the time foretold."

This skit is broadly characteristic of the whole spirit and method of Swift's work, in that it exposes a sham or an evil by setting up a more monstrous imposition against it, and defends the latter with ironical seriousness; the whole being permeated so thoroughly by contemptuous fooling that one hesitates to say whether it may or may not have been written with a certain amount of reforming zeal. In Swift's works generally there is this double aspect of earnestness and play. In the "Modest Proposal, for Preventing the Children of the Poor in Ireland from being Burdensome," the terrible suffering of the Irish is revealed in the mocking suggestion that the poor should devote themselves to rearing children to be killed and eaten. *The Tale of a Tub* represents the three leading sects of Christians in the story of three stupid brethren, Peter, Martin, and John, and their quarrels as to how they shall wear the coats left them by their father. *Gulliver's Travels* is, in form, a romance of marvelous adventures, yet it is full of satire against all mankind.

"**Gulliver's Travels.**"—Gulliver is shipwrecked first at Lilliput, where the inhabitants are six inches high—except their emperor, "taller by almost the breadth of my nail than any of his court, which alone is enough to strike an awe into the beholders." Here the satire consists in showing human motives at work on a small scale, and in suggesting, by the likeness of the Lilliputians to ourselves, the littleness of human affairs. The arts by which the officers of the government keep their places, such as cutting capers on a tight-rope for the entertainment of the emperor, remind us of the quality of statesmanship both in Swift's day and in our own; the dispute over the question at which end an egg should properly be broken, that plunged Lilliput into civil war, is a comment on the triviality of party divisions in the greater world. Gulliver's next voyage, to Brobdingnag, brings him to a people as large in comparison with man as the Lilliputians are small. Once more his adventures are a tale of wonder, behind which lurks Swift's contempt for humanity. Gulliver tells the giant beings by whom he is surrounded, and in comparison with whom he is a mere manikin, of the world from which he has come. Among other things, he tells of the invention of gunpowder, and the use of instruments of warfare. "The king was struck with horror at the description I had given of those terrible engines. He was amazed how so impotent and grovelling an insect as I (these were his expressions) could entertain such inhuman ideas." Finally, after a third voyage to Laputa and other curious places, Gulliver makes his fourth journey, to the land of the Houyhnhnms, where horses are the rulers and masters, and where the human animal is in a state of servitude and degradation. Here again Gulliver relates to his incredulous hosts the follies and cruelties of men. But the fiercest satire is in the picture of the Yahoo, the human beast, in which the worst of man is once for all told.

Swift as a Moralist.—It is interesting to compare the sketches of imaginary kingdoms in *Gulliver's Travels* with the picture of society in *Utopia*. While More constructs an ideal commonwealth, and commits himself heartily to its exposition and defence, Swift occupies himself entirely with railing at the follies and frailties of humanity. Even the Houyhnhnms, who are as intelligent as the Utopians, and conduct their lives as reasonably, lead an existence so devoid of charm that we wonder whether, in picturing it, Swift was not satirizing the ideals of men, as keenly as in the Yahoos he scores the realities. In other words, we miss entirely the enthusiastic confidence in the future of mankind which marked the early Renaissance. Swift's criticism is wholly destructive. He sees the evils and follies of men, but he has no hope that they will outgrow them. Indeed, in his wavering between jest and earnest, it seems as if he never felt quite sure that the world was worth his zeal, as if he were always a trifle ashamed to declare himself a reformer. Yet it would be useless to deny that in Swift's ironical playfulness there is something awakening. The fact that we are never quite sure of his aim keeps us on the watch lest he take us by surprise; his clever artifice calls for an answering alertness in his readers. And even in Swift's downright pessimism there is a certain wholesome stimulus, perhaps because it is a change from the conventional light in which we are taught to look at the world. Even his coarseness contains something of vigorous challenge that forces us to prove everything, and to call things by their true names.

III. JOSEPH ADDISON (1672–1719), AND SIR RICHARD STEELE (1672–1729)

The Early Periodicals.—The practical tendency of eighteenth century literature, its direct concern with existing affairs, is shown by the development of the various forms of the periodical, from the newspaper to the magazine. The first English newspaper was Butter's *Weekly Newes from Italy and Germanie*, which appeared in 1622. Later the periodical form was used for political purposes. Swift conducted a paper in the Tory interest known as the *Examiner*, and the Whigs replied with the *Whig Examiner*. The lighter

JOSEPH ADDISON
From a painting by G. Kneller, S. R.

side of journalism which lies between news and politics was not adequately represented, until, in 1709, there appeared a periodical of which the object was to "observe upon the pleasurable as well as the busy part of mankind." This was *The Tatler*, founded by Richard Steele, who was soon joined in the enterprise by his friend, Joseph Addison.

"**The Tatler.**"—*The Tatler* appeared three times a week. Each number consisted of several letters dated from the different coffee-houses of London; those from the Saint James being devoted to foreign and domestic affairs, those from Will's, to poetry and the drama, those from White's to "gallantry, pleasure, and entertainment." There were also papers dated "From my own apartment," which dealt with miscellaneous topics, personal or social. It was in these last that the authors carried out most fully the object which they set before themselves, "to expose the false arts of life, to pull off the disguises of cunning, vanity, and affectation, and to recommend a general simplicity in our dress, our discourse, and our behavior." Although *The Tatler* appealed to the public without distinction of party, it was colored by Steele's Whig views. Accordingly, when the authors wished to avoid politics altogether, they abandoned *The Tatler*, replacing it by *The Spectator* (1711), in which Addison took the chief part.

Addison's Life.—Joseph Addison was born in 1672, at Milston. He was educated at the Charterhouse School, London, where his friendship with Richard Steele began, and at Christ Church College, Oxford. At Oxford he first attracted notice by a Latin poem on the Treaty of Ryswick, receiving for it a pension of three hundred pounds a year, which enabled him to travel abroad. After his return, the Whigs needed a poet to celebrate the Duke of Marlborough's victory of Blenheim, and the commission fell to Addison. His poem, "The Campaign," gained for its author various honors and preferments. He was made Under Secretary of State, Member of Parliament, editor of various Whig journals, and later Secretary for Ireland. Indeed, Addison's career affords the best example of the high rewards which the service of party offered in the early eighteenth century to literary men. Even his tragedy, *Cato*, which was presented in 1713, owed its great popularity to a supposed parallel between the struggles of parties at Rome and the political situation of the time in England; and as neither party could allow the other to take to itself the platitudes about liberty with which the play is strewn, Whigs and Tories alike attended the performances, rivalling each other in the violence of their applause.

Addison was the great literary man among the Whigs and the centre of a group of minor writers belonging to that party. As a young man he was a satellite of Dryden at Will's coffee-house, but later he set up his headquarters at Button's, where, to quote the contemptuous line of Pope, he "gave his little senate laws." His worldly success, and especially his marriage to a noblewoman, the widow of the Earl of Warwick, raised him above the status of a literary man, and perhaps for that reason he drew upon himself the enmity of his rivals. He died in 1719.

No character in English letters is to-day better known or more generally admired than Addison. This power of attracting admiration is largely due to a certain classic quality which showed itself in his literary ideals, in his pure, regular style, in the just appreciation of his criticism, and in his singularly correct sense of conduct. His taste was nearly faultless, and taste did for him what it should do for anyone, it saved him from blunders and follies. In his life as in his writing, what he did was well done. Every stroke that went to the presentation of his character in bodily form seems to have been made with conscious care and conscious pride. The last touch of all, as he lay on his death-bed, and turning to his step-son bade him "See in what peace a Christian can die," expresses the mood in which his whole life was lived.

"The Spectator."—The papers which Addison contributed to *The Spectator*, are for the most part essays in the art of living. They illustrate the practical nature of his own culture, his easy mastery of life. To the world of the eighteenth century, with its crudeness, its coarseness, its grotesqueness, as revealed in the pictures of Hogarth, Addison came as a missionary, to enforce ideas of civilization, and in particular to overcome the anti-social tendencies of both Puritan and Cavalier, preserving the zeal for conduct of the former without his gloom and intolerance, and the lightness and gaiety of the latter without his license. Thus we find many of Addison's papers directed against the coarser vices of the time, against gambling, drinking, swearing, indecency of conversation, cruelty, practical joking, duelling. Others attack the triviality of life, special follies and foibles of dress, of manners, or of thought; others, the lack of order and comfort in the life of the community. Addison cared also for the literary cultivation of his readers, as is shown by such papers as the famous series of criticisms on Milton. Finally, he made a novel contribution to literature in a series of sketches of character and contemporary types—of himself as the Spectator, of Sir Andrew Freeport the merchant, of Sir Roger de Coverley the country gentleman, of Will Honeycomb the man of fashion. These figures are not only types of the public to which *The Spectator* appealed; more than this, they define themselves as persons, fitting members of the great company of characters who live in English fiction from Chaucer to George Eliot. One of them at least, Sir Roger de Coverley, to whose presentation both Addison and Steele contributed, is drawn with genuine affection, as an embodiment of healthy, kindly, natural virtue, touched with just enough humor to make the picture real and wholly winning.

Addison's Style.—In his treatment of these various subjects Addison displays the graces of style which are the expression of his character. His sense of humor always gives him deftness and lightness. Even such a serious subject as the division of men on political grounds, he treats by a playful comparison with the fashion of ladies in wearing black patches of different shapes on their faces. This easy tone comes from Addison's moderation and reasonableness, and from his genuine good-nature. Satirist though he is, he is never misanthropic.

Addison's style has always been a model of the more regular virtues,—clearness, facility, grace Benjamin Franklin was only one among the many who have learned to write by imitating it. The praise of Addison as the school-

master of English prose was pronounced by Dr. Johnson
when he wrote, "Whoever wishes to attain an English style,
familiar but not coarse, and elegant but not ostentatious,
must give his days and nights to the volumes of Addison."

Richard Steele.—Despite the close connection between
Addison and Steele, in friendship, political interests, and
literary work, the two men were very different. Addison's
father was a clergyman, and Addison himself intended (at
one time) to take orders. "He looked," as a contemporary
said with some scorn, "like a parson in a tie-wig." Steele,
on the contrary, was for some years a soldier, and never lost
the bearing of his profession. He was Captain Steele and
wore a sword to the end of his days.

Steele was born in Dublin, in the year of Addison's birth,
1672. He was sent to Charterhouse School, and then to
Oxford, which he left without a degree, to become a soldier.
He gave up the army for literature, failed as a dramatist,
and became a journalist in the interest of the Whigs. In
1709 he began *The Tatler* and his literary partnership with
Addison, which was continued in *The Spectator* and *The
Guardian*. Steele's services to the Whigs brought him
various offices. He was more than once Member of Parliament, was appointed director of Drury Lane Theatre, and
became Sir Richard Steele. But in the end his ventures,
both in business and in politics, all turned out badly. He
retired to Wales, where he died in 1729.

Altogether Steele's life was a thing of fragments. His
character, too, showed certain flaws and lapses, faults of a
generous, whole-hearted nature; and to these his writings
in a measure served to call attention. While a soldier he
wrote *The Christian Hero*, a manual of personal and domestic virtues; his plays were entirely moral; in *The Tatler*
he appeared as a preacher. The discrepancy between his
personal life and the tenor of much of his writing, laid Steele
open to gibe and sneer; but there is an honest human quality
about his inconsistencies that gives him, after all, a charm
which his greatest contemporaries lack. This charm is reflected in his papers in *The Tatler*, some of which, like the
181st, which describes his feelings on the death of his father,

have an intimate and personal quality that suggests Charles Lamb or Thackeray.

IV. ALEXANDER POPE (1688–1744)

Pope's Early Life.—Alexander Pope, the greatest poet and the most brilliant man of letters of the early part of the century, was born in London, in 1688, of Catholic parents. By reason of the sweeping laws against the entrance of Catholics into public service, he was shut out from the ordinary career of Englishmen, in Parliament, the church, or the army; and he was, moreover, from his youth feeble, almost a cripple. In consequence he is, among his contemporaries, almost the sole example of an author who was entirely a man of letters; the events of his life were altogether literary events. Like Spenser and like Milton he early consecrated himself to poetry. His *Pastorals*, written when he was seventeen, were published in 1709. The *Essay on Criticism* two years later, attracted Addison's notice; and Pope's other early poems, *Windsor Forest, Eloisa to Abelard*, and above all *The Rape of the Lock*, of which the first draft appeared in 1712, confirmed him in his position at the head of English poetry. About 1713 he undertook the greatest venture of his life, the translation of Homer, which he did not complete until 1726. From the publishers and from his sales to subscribers, Pope obtained more than five thousand pounds for the *Iliad*, and two-thirds of this sum for the *Odyssey* (on which most of the work was done by others)—much the greatest pecuniary reward which up to that time had been received by any English author. It made Pope independent of patronage and politics; and it marks the opening of a time in which literature looked to the public alone for support.

Pope at Twickenham.—The profits of his translation enabled Pope to buy a small estate at Twickenham, on the Thames near London. This he fitted up in the mock classical style which the age affected in other things besides literature. He subdued nature to taste by landscape gardening, until his few acres must have seemed a miniature Versailles. He scattered statuary and temples about in artistic contrast to the woods and lawns; and as his crowning achievement he built a famous grotto ornamented with mirrors. Against this artificial background we catch the most characteristic glimpses of Pope,—"a lively little creature," as he describes himself, "with long legs and arms; a spider is no ill emblem of him." At Twickenham Pope lived the remainder of his life, secluded from the world which he affected to despise, but very constantly occupied with his own relations to it. Here he entertained his friends, Swift, Arbuthnot, Gay, and others, with whom he formed a literary partnership known as the Scriblerus Club. It was in connection with this partnership that he published in 1728 a great onslaught on their literary foes, entitled *The Dunciad*. At Twickenham also Pope saw much of Bolingbroke, and under his influence wrote the *Essay on Man*, published in 1732 and 1734. The remainder of his work consists of the *Moral Epistle* (satires in imitation of Horace), the *Epistle to Dr. Arbuthnot*, which is Pope's chief defence of himself, and the *Epilogue to the Satires*. These were published before 1737, after which date Pope wrote little. He died in 1744.

Pope's Character as a Poet.—Pope's claim to the first place among the poets of his time cannot be gainsaid, but his true place among the poets of all time is a matter of dispute. At the outset it must be recognized that certain sources of power were denied him, partly in consequence of the nature of the period in which he lived, partly by reason of the deficiencies of his own temperament. The age was one in which sympathy for nature and for humanity was limited, and in this matter Pope shared the blindness of his age. Moreover, Pope was from birth sickly and feeble; strong passion, great emotion, richness of life, were beyond his experience. Accordingly, we miss in his poetry greatness of feeling for the natural world and for the world of man, as well as greatness of human personality. That such a man should become a poet at all is as wonderful as that a deaf man should be a composer, or a blind man a sculptor. That he should be the typical poet of his age shows how limited was the con-

ALEXANDER POPE
From a painting by A. Pond

ception which then prevailed of the nature and function of poetry.

But though certain qualities which we expect to find in poetry are necessarily absent in Pope, these were replaced, at least for his contemporaries, by others. First of all, he owed his success to his marvellous skill in managing the heroic couplet. He declared that as a child he "lisped in numbers, for the numbers came." But he was not satisfied with mere facility. One of his earliest friends and critics, William Walsh, pointed out to him that "though we had had several great poets we never had any one great poet that was correct." Correctness, accordingly, Pope made his aim from the first. Nor did he sacrifice to mere exactness of metre and rhyme the other virtues of couplet verse, compression, epigrammatic force, and brilliancy of phrase. In his *Essay on Criticism*, he sets forth the artistic principles of the time with special reference to poetry. In this discussion he bids the poet follow Nature, but Nature methodized by rules, for "to copy Nature is to copy them." The substance of the poem is made up of commonplaces, for Pope and his readers believed that there was nothing new under the sun; but these commonplaces are given the most apt, the most chiselled form, a form in which they are fitted to survive as part of the common wisdom of the race.

Pope's Homer.—Pope's comprehension of the artistic demands of his time, and his rhetorical skill, fitted him admirably for his work of translating Homer. His own knowledge of Homer was, it is true, second-hand and inaccurate; but the impossibility of making a literally faithful rendering left him the freer to turn the material of the Greek poems into the form in which it was most fitted to become a part of the culture of his own time. Not only does Homer, in Pope's hands, become an eighteenth century poet, by virtue of his submission to the literary fashions of the day—the heroic couplet, and conventional poetic diction—but even the characters, the manners, the ethical ideals of primitive Greece are run over into eighteenth century moulds. Just as to the cloudy mediæval imagination the heroes of Troy became knights, so in Pope's conception they are statesmen and party leaders, treating each other with parliamentary courtesy, and talking of virtue, patriotism, and fame, as glibly and eloquently as Bolingbroke himself.

"The Rape of the Lock."—The works of Pope thus far mentioned are chiefly remarkable for their literary qualities. But even more important is the group of poems in which, with no loss of artistic finish, he dealt directly with the life of his time. Of these *The Rape of the Lock* stands first. The poem was suggested by a trivial occurrence, the rude behavior of Lord Petre in cutting a lock from the head of Miss Fermor. Only the excessive interest of the age in social matters, combined with the sympathetic genius of a poet, could have made such gossip as this outlast the centuries. Pope wrote first a rapid account of the card-party at Hampton at which the theft took place. Later he expanded the poem by introducing the sylphs, who guard the lady's bed, make her toilet, and attend her in public—admirable suggestions of the artifice which directed each act, however trivial, of a belle of Queen Anne's day. *The Rape of the Lock* is not only a satire on society; it is a witty parody of the heroic style in poetry. Even the verse form is treated humorously, especially through its tendency toward anti-climax, as in the lines,

> " Here thou, great Anna! whom three realms obey,
> Dost sometimes counsel take—and sometimes tea."

Pope's Satires.—In *The Rape of the Lock* the satire is general, and, on the whole, good-natured. Pope's later poems, however, are intensely personal, and grew out of the circumstances of his life. As has been said already, his character was not a great one. We listen in vain in his poetry for the deeper notes of individual human experience. But his lack of absorption in his inner life made him morbidly sensitive in his external contact with the world. No man ever had more elaborate relations with people than Pope, or got more out of his friends, or changed more often from friendship to enmity, or pursued his enemies with more unwearied spite. The *Moral Epistles* and *Imitations of Horace* are crowded with satiric allusions to contemporaries. The *Epistle to Dr. Arbuth-*

not contains the savage sketch of Addison under the name Atticus. Countless personal grudges were paid off by the several editions of *The Dunciad*, an elaborate satire in which, after the fashion of Dryden in *MacFlecknoe*, the dullards, pedants, and bad poets are presented in ridiculous surroundings and attitudes. All this morbid following of "miserable aims that end with self" seems remote enough from the dignity of a great poet. Yet it must not be forgotten that the age itself was largely preoccupied with small things. Pope's satiric genius came to him as of right, at a time when the eyes of men were turned away from the wonders of nature and of the human heart, and were fixed on themselves and their worldly concerns.

"The Essay on Man."—One of Pope's last friendships, that with Bolingbroke, proved the inspiration of the best remembered of his poems, the *Essay on Man*. Bolingbroke was the representative of eighteenth-century scepticism in its effort to substitute a religion of reason for one of revelation. Pope's poem is in reality an application of common-sense to the problems of the universe and to the life of man; and where common-sense refuses to carry us, "beyond the flaming ramparts of the world," there Pope closes his inquiry.

> " Know then thyself, presume not God to scan,
>   The proper study of mankind is man."

The first epistle is concerned with man's place in nature; the second with individual ethics; the third with the origin of society and politics; the fourth with the question of man's happiness. In all four appear the satisfaction of the century with things as they are, its dislike of those speculative differences which lead to fanaticism, its trust in downright utility.

> " For forms of government let fools contest;
>   Whate'er is best administered is best:
>   For modes of faith let graceless zealots fight,
>   He can't be wrong whose life is in the right."

In short, the *Essay on Man* is a marvellous collection of happily phrased couplets, pointing neatly and exactly the beliefs of the age of which Pope was so eminently the voice.

V. DR. JOHNSON, AND HIS CIRCLE

Social Position of Writers in the Later Eighteenth Century.—The social conditions under which literature was ordinarily practised in the second period of the century, were very different from those of Queen Anne's day. By this time, owing to the decisive victory of the Whigs, literature had lost in large part its value as a political weapon in party strife, and authors were obliged to rely entirely upon the public. And the reading public was of slow growth. The writers who depended upon it were compelled to live in a squalid Bohemia—not unlike that inhabited by the popular group of authors in the age of Elizabeth—and to put forth a mass of bad poetry, criticism, and journalism merely for bread. The name of the street where many of them lived, Grub Street, became a synonym for hack writing and poverty. The aristocratic traditions of the profession were supported by men of the highest reputation, like Pope, who could approach the public directly through the subscription list; but for the ordinary writer there was no resource except servitude to the literary broker or bookseller. Under these hard conditions Samuel Johnson and his friends slowly made their way to distinction; from that Grub Street which Pope and Swift had scornfully lampooned, came their successors in power and reputation.

Johnson's Life.—Samuel Johnson was born in 1709, the son of a Lichfield bookseller. He was at Oxford for a time, but his father's failure in business obliged him to leave the University. After vainly trying to win his bread as a teacher, he tramped to London. Here he lived in a state of wretchedness which is reflected in his *Life of Savage*, a poet who was his companion in Grub Street misery. Often the friends walked the streets from dusk to dawn for want of mere shelter. One resource was, indeed, open to them. Following the success of *The Tatler* and *The Spectator*, had come the periodical magazines of miscellaneous literature, for one of which Johnson wrote reports of the debates in Parliament. His first poem, *London* (1738), gave him some reputation, which was increased by *The Vanity of Human Wishes*

DR. SAMUEL JOHNSON

From a painting by Sir Joshua Reynolds

(1749). He also wrote essays after the *Spectator* model, called *The Rambler* (1750–1752). But his pre-eminent position came to him after the publication of his *Dictionary of the English Language* in 1755. When he had announced this work seven years before, Johnson had sought the support and patronage of Lord Chesterfield, but the latter had been contemptuously cold toward the project. When the work was about to appear, however, the nobleman let it be known that he would accept and reward the dedication of the work to himself; but it was now Johnson's turn, and in his famous letter to Chesterfield he wrote for English literature its final declaration of independence from the institution of patronage.

The *Dictionary* made Johnson's fame and state secure. In 1764 he formed with Burke, Goldsmith, Reynolds, and others, the famous Literary Club, as chief member of which he held the unquestioned headship of contemporary letters in England. Still, Johnson was poor; and to the end of his life he was forced to labor to support himself and the various persons who fell dependent upon him. When his mother died, in 1759, he wrote his oriental apologue, *Rasselas*, in a week, to pay for the funeral. He edited Shakespeare, and undertook the preparation of a series of *Lives of the English Poets*, which was completed in 1781. He died in 1784.

Johnson's Style.—Johnson continued the literary traditions of the Age of Queen Anne. In his poetry he followed Pope's use of the heroic couplet. His essays are modelled upon the form set by *The Spectator*, though Johnson's papers are longer, heavier, and duller than Addison's. The *Rambler* essays show, perhaps more clearly than any other of Johnson's writings, those peculiarities which have made his style a by-word for heaviness. The diction involves a large proportion of Latin words, due, as has been humorously suggested, to the fact that Johnson was then at work on his lexicon, and used his *Rambler* as a track where he could exercise the words that had grown stiff from long disuse. But this elaborate manner is not always out of place. It occasionally gives to Johnson's writing a sombre eloquence, as in the opening passage of *Rasselas*. Moreover, he could be simple and colloquial when he chose; and his later works, possibly because they were written more hurriedly, are much more terse and rapid.

Boswell's " Life of Johnson."—Johnson had in him a force of character far greater than he succeeded in bringing to bear on any of his literary undertakings. This force of character strongly impressed his contemporaries through his powers of conversation, and has been transmitted to later times by the extraordinary zeal and ability of the greatest of all biographers, James Boswell, whose *Life of Johnson*, published in 1791, is one of the classics of the century. From his first meeting with Johnson, in 1763, Boswell followed the great man's doings and sayings with unwearied attention. In his effort to draw Johnson out and to make him expressive, he was deterred by no rebuffs, and he was not ashamed to offer himself as the butt of his master's wit. For twenty years he worked with his eye constantly upon his subject, and was then prepared to write the biography which still keeps Johnson in his place as the most striking figure of his epoch. Of no man in the past is our perception so extraordinarily keen and first-hand. His bulky, awkward appearance, his brusque, overbearing manner, his portentous voice, his uncouth gestures and attitudes, his habits of whistling or "chuckling like a hen" in the intervals of speaking, and of "blowing out his breath like a whale" when he was "exhausted by violence and vociferation"— all these have come down to us, together with the record of a great mass of his conversation. It is in this last that Johnson's power and Boswell's skill are most strikingly manifested. Johnson wrote much, but nearly always under the spur of necessity; he talked spontaneously. His reputation, indeed, rests largely upon such sayings as "Being in a ship is like being in gaol with the chance of drowning," or "A woman's preaching is like a dog's walking on his hind legs. It is not done well, but you are surprised to find it done at all." In such scraps of homely comment the practical sense of the age expressed itself as vividly and rememberably as in Pope's couplets.

To Boswell's "Life," then, Johnson owes his reputation

as an original character, and as a sayer of good things. But there is another Johnson whom Boswell knew without comprehending — the stricken, hopeless, much-enduring, brave, pious soul, who exemplifies so much of what is wholly admirable in human nature. Johnson suffered grievously in life. What with poverty, ill-health, and the necessity of toil, which to his indolent spirit meant torture, it is no wonder that he came to believe with Rasselas that the world is almost barren of joy. Yet he faced life always with energy and courage. In his strenuousness, his morality, his refusal to yield ground anywhere to the evils without or the foes within, in his resolve to draw inspiration from his own shortcomings, in all this Johnson is a great man, and for this he deserves his fame.

Goldsmith; His Life.—Johnson's dictatorship of English letters was partly the result of his conversational supremacy in the Literary Club, which included nearly all the famous writers of the time. Next to Johnson himself its most notable figure was Oliver Goldsmith. Goldsmith was born in 1728 in Ireland, where his father was a clergyman. He was a dull boy at school, and had an undistinguished career at the University of Dublin. After a succession of attempts to get a start in life he went to Edinburgh to study medicine, and afterward to Leyden. Thence he worked or begged his way over a large part of Europe, returning to London in 1756. He wavered for a time between the practice of medicine and school teaching, but finally took to literature as it was practised in Grub Street, and became a hack writer for various magazines. His papers called *The Citizen of the World* (1760–1761), consisted of observations upon English life written from the point of view of a Chinaman. He lived in extreme poverty. Johnson found him one day in lodgings, the prisoner of an unpaid landlady, with the manuscript of *The Vicar of Wakefield* by him. Johnson sold the book, which appeared some fifteen months later, after Goldsmith had published his first successful poem, *The Traveller* (1764). His second venture into poetry, *The Deserted Village*, appeared in 1770. Meanwhile Goldsmith yielded to his necessities, and at the bidding of his tyrants, the booksellers,

OLIVER GOLDSMITH

After a painting by a pupil of Sir Joshua Reynolds

produced a number of histories and other works of information. He was well paid for these comparatively worthless
labors; and two of his plays were fairly successful, *The Good-
Natured Man* (1768), and *She Stoops to Conquer* (1773).
No success, however, could keep pace with his improvidence.
He died in 1774 of a fever which was aggravated by anxiety
over his debts.

Goldsmith and Johnson. — Goldsmith is almost as well
known to us as Johnson, and largely through the same
agency, the industry of Boswell. The two figures are in
the strongest possible contrast — Johnson, large, strong of
feature, with a certain dignity of bearing in spite of his
oddities; Goldsmith, under-sized, ill-formed, frightfully disfigured by smallpox, and with a more than childlike simplicity.
Again, Johnson's ponderous thought, sturdy virtue, and strong
common-sense were at the farthest remove from Goldsmith's
mental vivacity, moral laxness, and practical folly. When
they joined in combat of words at the club, where Goldsmith
was the only member who dared persistently to provoke the
wrath of the dictator, Johnson sometimes bore down his
opponent by sheer weight; but often Goldsmith sent his stone
to its mark and made good his retreat, as when he doubted
Johnson's ability to write a fable because he would inevitably
make the little fishes talk like whales.

Goldsmith's Humanity. — Goldsmith's lack of practical ability brought him both scorn and pity in his own day, but in
our eyes his incapacity is in rather refreshing contrast to the
hard common-sense of that age. His difficulties came partly
from generosity, partly from his blind trust in the world. For
Goldsmith threw himself upon life with the naïve impru-
dence of a child. Whether traversing Europe as a penniless
student, or selling his masterpieces, Goldsmith took no
thought for the morrow. And with this confidence in his
fellows went a great love for them, a love apparent in all the
writings into which he put his real self. His papers in *The
Citizen of the World*, though, like Addison's, often directed
against the faults and absurdities of men, have a tenderness
which goes beyond Addison's mildness, a note of kinship
with humanity that is very different from the Spectator's

aloofness. Goldsmith's poems are written in the heroic couplet, but in spirit they are far removed from Pope's. *The Traveller* is a survey of the countries of Western Europe, those which Goldsmith had visited in his journeyings; but instead of the complacent optimism of the *Essay on Man*, we find pictured both the evil and the good in man's situation. *The Deserted Village* is also a "prospect of society," more powerful because more detailed. The village of Auburn is described with its happy, humble life, centering around the two characters of the village parson and the schoolmaster, both drawn with tenderness and no little humor. But the village is depopulated by order of its landlord, and Goldsmith follows the exiles, compelled to wander over seas to remote America, "where wild Altama murmurs to their woe." In this protest on behalf of the individual against the institution which crushes him Goldsmith was a prophet of the approaching revolution.

Goldsmith's Plays.—Goldsmith's sympathy, however, did not lead him into extravagant appeals to emotion. His plays were an effort to substitute for the prevailing "comedy of tears" a healthy comedy of laughter. Goldsmith, indeed, took his own misfortunes with so much spirit and humor that he could not be much concerned about imaginary griefs, and his trust in the goodness of the world was so perfect that with him sorrow was always turned into joy. This optimism gives its color alike to his novel and to his plays. *She Stoops to Conquer*, the best known of the latter, is a charming idyl, in which the rough edges of the world are ground smooth, in which faults turn out to be virtues, and mistakes prove blessings. At times the stage-land copies the actual world with fidelity, as in the riotous scene at the "Three Pigeons," with which the play opens. But the magic of comedy is over all, a magic much subdued, indeed, from the brilliant romance of Shakespeare's day, but still potent.*

Sheridan.—Goldsmith's plays are a reflection of the idealism which was beginning to manifest itself in the realistic

---

* Goldsmith's *Vicar of Wakefield* will be discussed in the next chapter, together with other eighteenth-century fiction.

age. Opposed to him is Richard Brinsley Sheridan (1751–1816), whose dramas are written in a mood of satirical observation of the surface of life. Sheridan was born at Dublin, of English-Irish stock. After a romantic runaway marriage he settled in London; and when only twenty-three he produced *The Rivals* (1775). In 1777, after his assumption of the directorship of Drury Lane Theatre, he put on his best play, *The School for Scandal,* and in 1779 *The Critic.*

The School for Scandal sets forth the eighteenth-century world of fashion, which, in its frivolous artificiality, lent itself readily to the purposes of the comedian. In this corrupt society Lady Teazle has, for form's sake, provided herself with an admirer, Joseph Surface. Meanwhile Joseph, a cold hearted hypocrite, has plans of his own, one of which is to marry Sir Peter Teazle's niece Maria, and another to supplant his own brother Charles, a good-natured spendthrift, in their uncle's affection. The uncle, Sir Oliver, returns from India, introduces himself, as a money-lender, to Charles, whom he finds ready to sell even his family portraits, except that of Sir Oliver himself. This modest bit of loyalty serves to reinstate the prodigal in his uncle's good opinion; while Joseph, discovered on all sides, fades out of the play in disgrace. At first sight, *The School for Scandal,* with its opening scenes in which gossip runs wild, seems to revive the world of the Restoration drama, but there is a difference. Light, trifling, frivolous as is Sheridan's society, it is not fundamentally immoral. His people play with fire, but they are not burned. So much had the moral and social force of the century accomplished, in the years since Jeremy Collier's attack on the stage.

VI. EDMUND BURKE (1729–1797)

Burke's Early Life.—Burke was born in Ireland, in 1729. He was educated at Trinity College, Dublin, and thence, after taking his degree in 1748, went up to London to study law, but soon turned aside into literature. His first important work was an *Enquiry into the Origin of our Ideas of the Sublime and the Beautiful* (1756). In 1765 he became secretary to the Whig prime-minister, the Marquis of Rockingham, and Member of Parliament. Although he never held high office, he was for years the brain of the Whig Party in its effort to deal with the new problems arising from the growth of England as a colonial power both in America and in India. The view of his contemporaries, that he was a man wasting the greatest powers on passing affairs of the day, is expressed in Goldsmith's epigram:

> "Who, born for the universe, narrowed his mind,
> And to party gave up what was meant for mankind."

Yet so profound was Burke's thought, and so noble its presentation, that his writings are of value to-day, irrespective of the occasions which called them forth.

Burke's Views on America and India.—It is Burke's peculiar distinction that he saw the dangers gathering over England from all quarters, and strove to avert them. He pointed out the one way of escape in the American situation. His first speech in Parliament was in favor of the repeal of the stamp tax. His speech on American taxation was delivered in 1774; his great speech on Conciliation with America in 1775. When England emerged from the war against the coalition of European powers, with the loss indeed of America, but with victory in other quarters, Burke instantly began to press his inquiry into the circumstances of that triumph. The chief success of England had been in India, and the man who had won it was Warren Hastings. Against him Burke levelled his attack. Instead of thanking God that things had turned out so well, he asked why they had turned out well, on what principles the Indian Empire had been conquered and administered, and whether those principles were founded upon justice and humanity. In 1785 he delivered his arraignment of English methods in India, in his speech on *The Nabob of Arcot's Debts;* and the following year he moved the impeachment of Warren Hastings for his cruel and mercenary treatment of his Indian subjects. Two years later he opened the case before the House of Lords, and he continued to manage it until the acquittal of Hastings in 1795.

Burke's Views on France.—In the last year of his life Burke led the opposition to the French Revolution. This attitude involved a separation from his party, but Burke took the step without flinching. His *Reflections on the Revolution in France*, published in 1790, and the reviews of French affairs which followed, did much to check the rising sympathy with the movement, in England and on the continent. In this opposition Burke took a larger point of view than that of mere prejudice. He believed that England had a world mission in stemming the tide of the revolution and in marshalling the forces of order in Europe. Right or wrong, the struggle of England against France between 1794 and 1815 is a splendid act in the drama of nations. It is scarcely too much to say that the leading rôle which England played in those years was cast for her by Burke. He wrote the lines which the cannon declaimed at Trafalgar and Waterloo.

Burke has been criticised for his attack on the French Revolution, as being behind his age. Nevertheless his attitude was the result of his principles, and rested on the same philosophy that guided his action in other matters. For Burke was in character essentially practical. His speeches on the American crisis testify to his power of seeing a situation as it really was, and tossing aside all abstract considerations. "I think it may be necessary," he told Parliament, "to consider distinctly the true nature of the peculiar circumstances of the object which we have before us. Because after all our struggle, whether we will or not, we must govern America according to that nature, and to those circumstances; and not according to our own imaginations; nor according to abstract ideas of right; by no means according to mere general theories of government." This is the best expression of what may be called Burke's genius for facts, a quality which he shared with other great men of his century, notably with Swift. It was this sense of fact which impelled his opposition to the abstract political theories of the French Revolution.

Burke's Connection with Romanticism.—The great difference between Swift and Burke is to be found in the imaginative power of Burke's sympathy—a sympathy which penetrated to the uttermost parts of the earth, and made the wrongs of the American colonist, the sufferings of the Hindu peasant, and the sorrows of the queen of France as vividly real to his hearers as the sights of London. In short, Burke, like Scott and Wordsworth, was a romanticist in feeling, though a conservative in political thought.

It is the feeling behind his thought that gives to Burke's style its far-reaching eloquence. The subjects with which he dealt are not those which we think of as lending themselves to imaginative treatment. Burke got up his facts carefully, and built the arguments of his speeches and papers out of solid material with the most careful regard to logical structure. But playing over this seemingly refractory substance of fact, constantly bringing it to white heat, is the flame of his passion, now a burning love of justice, now a consuming fire of hatred of all the hypocrisies, oppressions, cruelties, treacheries under the sun. Swift had as fierce an indignation against the ungodly; but while Swift's world was the petty world of the eighteenth century, Burke's world, geographically and intellectually, was the great one of modern thought. And while Swift masked his feeling behind a style of severe plainness and restraint, Burke gave his fervent spirit utterance in a rhetoric which included in its range visions as gorgeous as the East, the sound of words as of many waters, effects of pathos and invective that moved the hearts of his hearers to pity, terror, and wrath.

REVIEW OUTLINE.—The writers of Queen Anne's day, Swift, Pope, Addison, Steele, represent the classical impulse; they illustrate the literary treatment of social topics with a view to artistic perfection according to definite standards and in approved forms,—standards and forms which they believed to have behind them the authority of the classical writers.

Explain the connection between literature and politics in this period. Was it a benefit to literature? What elements in the life of the time stirred the reforming zeal of writers? What was their method of dealing with abuses? What example of law and order did literary men themselves set? How does the literary style compare with fashions of the time in dress and etiquette ? Why is the age of Queen Anne called the Augustan age ? Why is the age memorable in English history ? Explain the close association of writers of this period.

How was Swift's early life unhappy ? Can you trace any connection between his experience in these years and his later attitude toward the world ? Name his early satires. Outline Swift's connection with the political parties of the day. What was his reward ? Name his chief works after his retirement to Ireland. Who was " Stella " ? To what personal peculiarity was Swift's writing due ? With what personal trait is his satire to be connected ? Tell the story of Swift and Partridge. How do the Partridge tracts illustrate Swift's method ? Outline " Gulliver's Travels.". Point out the opportunities which it affords for satire. Compare Swift's Utopia with Sir Thomas More's. Was Swift a genuine reformer ? What purpose do his writings serve ?

Explain the growth of periodical literature in the eighteenth century. What was the peculiar field of " The Tatler " ? Why was it replaced by " the Spectator " ? Outline the life of Addison, noting his connection with political affairs. What is the source of his attractiveness ? Can you suggest in what ways his character appears in his writing ? What was Addison's main object in " the Spectator " ? With what subjects did he deal ? What characters did he create ? Contrast his satire with Swift's. Why is Addison's style a good one to imitate ? (Note the passage in Franklin's Autobiography in which he describes his use of " the Spectator.") Contrast Addison and Steele in character.

Why is there no sharp division between prose and poetry of the eighteenth century ? Discuss the life of Pope. What is the importance of Pope's Homer in the social history of authorship ? Describe Pope's life at Twickenham. Mention Pope's later works. Was Pope a great man ? Was he a great poet ? What are his limitations as a poet and what his virtues ? What is the poetic creed of the " Essay on Criticism " ? What was his aim in the translation of Homer ? In what poems did Pope deal with the life of his own day ? What is " The Rape of the Lock." ? Wherein does its satire consist ? What part did personal relations play in Pope's life ? What was the " Dunciad " ? Outline the " Essay on Man." To whose influence on Pope is the latter ascribed ? What is the value of the poem to-day ?

In the second half of the eighteenth century, literary men of London gathered about Johnson as a centre; but it must be remembered that there was a growing spirit of revolt from the classical ideals which he represented. Against the diminished realm of authorship which Johnson ruled must be set the romanticists, Collins, Gray, Blake, Cowper, and Burns, to be discussed in Chapter XII.

How is Johnson's life typical of the social status of authors in the middle of the century? What resource was left to them after the decline of their political influence? What were Johnson's relations with Chesterfield? Mention Johnson's chief works. In what ways does Johnson continue the work of the classical school? To what qualities does Boswell's " Life of Johnson" owe its greatness as biography? What personal impression does it give us of Johnson?

Sketch the life of Goldsmith. What were his personal relations to Johnson? How does his character differ from Johnson's? Contrast the philosophy of the two men. Summarize " The Deserted Village." How do its personal sketches differ from those in Pope's satires? In what ways does the poem suggest the rise of romanticism? Why is Goldsmith called an " idealist "? In what does Sheridan's realism consist? How does Sheridan differ from the Restoration dramatists?

What part did Burke play in the history of the time? What did he contribute to literature? Discuss the three periods of his political activity. In which was Burke successful according to the point of view of the time? To which do his most valuable writings belong? Can you trace any unity in Burke's intellectual attitude during all three periods? Note the points of contact between Burke's thought and the romantic movement. To what is the greatness of Burke's style due? Contrast his outlook at the close of the century with that of Swift at the beginning.

READING GUIDE.—The works of the eighteenth century generally read in school are Addison's " Sir Roger de Coverley Papers," and Burke's " Speech on Conciliation with America." In addition, pupils should read " Gulliver's Travels, " or some abridgment of it, and Goldsmith's " Deserted Village." If possible Pope's " Rape of the Lock " should be added. Addison's papers furnish a great amount of detail from which pictures of eighteenth-century life both in town and country may be constructed. Additional papers from " The Spectator " may be chosen from Morley's one-volume edition (Routledge). " Gulliver's Travels," should be read, of course, primarily for its interest as a tale.

In addition, however, the real meaning of the book as the most vigorous criticism of life which the century has left us should be perceived. Many of the references to contemporary things (especially in the third book) are to be understood only by careful study, but the scope of the general attack upon human nature is obvious. It may be compared not only with More's "Utopia," but with "Sartor Resartus," the theme of which was indeed partly suggested to Carlyle by Swift's "Tale of a Tub." "Gulliver's Travels" is published in Henry Morley's Carisbrook Library (Routledge & Co.). An excellent volume of selections from Swift is edited by F. C. Prescott (Holt's English Readings). In contrast with Swift's works, Goldsmith's "Deserted Village" affords evidence of the wider view of humanity and deeper sympathy which were characteristic of the new poetry. It may be compared interestingly with Pope's "Rape of the Lock." Burke's speech also bears witness to the breadth of thought which supplanted the narrow interests of the first half of the century.

No group of authors is capable of being presented to a class more attractively than those of Queen Anne's day. They are far enough away in point of time to have something of the fascination of antiquity, and yet not so remote as to be altogether removed from our interest or comprehension. The biographies in the English Men of Letters series are generally good, and in the case of Steele Mr. Dobson's volume in English Worthies (Scott) is excellent. The appreciations in Thackeray's "English Humourists of the Eighteenth Century" are always suggestive and picturesque. For fuller accounts of the history of the time Green's "Short History of the English People" may be recommended to the pupil. The teacher will find Lecky's "History of England in the Eighteenth Century" valuable. Of histories of literature in the eighteenth century T. S. Perry's (Harper) is useful as containing much out-of-the-way information. Edmund Gosse's "From Shakespeare to Pope" is also valuable. Of importance to scholars is A. Beljame's "Le Public et les Hommes de Lettres en Angleterre." There are many books which deal with the social life of the age of Queen Anne, among which Sydney's "England and the English in the Eighteenth Century" and Ashton's "Social Life in the Reign of Queen Anne" are likely to prove of special use to a class reading Addison's essays. The most important source of social information and personal gossip for the latter part of this century is Boswell's "Life of Johnson." It does for us in its period what Pepys's "Diary" and Addison's essays do in the two epochs preceding, that is, puts us directly into contact with the life of the time through the records of a close observer. If pupils cannot be expected to read Boswell for themselves, some selections, at least, should be read aloud in class. Birkbeck Hill's edition (Clarendon Press) is best furnished with notes.

CHAPTER XI

THE EIGHTEENTH-CENTURY NOVEL

I. INTRODUCTION

The Novel and the Drama.—As the drama was the characteristic and natural form of literature in the Elizabethan age, so the novel has been the prevailing type in the last two centuries. For this change many reasons may be assigned. In the first place, the novel allows the author greater freedom in handling his story. Instead of relying solely on the words and acts of his characters, as in the drama, the novelist can deal with their thoughts also; and instead of leaving these characters to explain themselves, he can give his own comment upon their lives. Thus the novel in some ways lends itself more easily than the drama to the presentation of the complicated problems and characters of modern life. Moreover, in the diffusion of English-speaking people over the world, the public which is interested in literature has become too widely scattered to be dependent in large measure upon the theatre. The magazine and the circulating library have come to occupy the place which for the Elizabethan was filled by the stage. This latter fact in itself is sufficient, though other reasons may be given, to explain the predominance of the novel in modern literature.

Early Fiction.—For the beginning of the modern novel we must go back to the stories of the Middle Ages. These were in general of two kinds, adapted to two audiences, the nobles and the people. Of the first class were the romances clustering about such heroes as Charlemagne and King Arthur, and dealing with knightly adventure, mystical religious experience, and courtly love. These were told first in verse, later in prose. Being written for an aristocratic class, the romances of chivalry presented a highly idealized view of life, in which strength and virtue were exaggerated. The fiction of the common people was decidedly more in the spirit of actual life, or, as we should say, *realistic*. For them, the stories of the knightly epics were in part retold, often in a spirit of burlesque. Sometimes the vices and follies of men were represented in short tales; the hypocrisy of the clergy, for example, being a favorite subject. Many tales were brought into Europe from the Orient, and others grew up about popular characters. Such stories as these abounded in Italy, where they were called *novelle*, from which word comes the term novel.

Although the novel drew its name from Italy, it first attained something like its modern form in Spain. There the spirit of burlesque aroused by the contrast between the ideals of chivalry and the affairs of actual life, led to the production of stories known as picaresque romances. In these the hero is a rascal (*picaro* = rogue) who wanders from place to place, finding all manner of adventures, amusing and scandalous; he is not, like the knight-errant, bent upon finding the Holy Grail, nor upon rescuing injured princesses, but is intent merely upon satisfying his personal wants. The typical Italian *novella* and the Spanish rogue story resembled each other in their realism, in the faithfulness with which they reproduced the motives of actual men and the manners of actual life. They are the source of the realistic novel of to-day, while what we call the romance looks back to the epic of chivalry for its origin. Both Italian and Spanish stories were translated into English in large numbers during the Renaissance.

In the seventeenth century Bunyan's *Pilgrim's Progress* is the best example of fiction written for the Puritan middle class. In the eighteenth century the demand of that class for reading matter which should deal with actual life, in a way productive both of amusement and profit, resulted in the stories of Daniel Defoe.

II. DANIEL DEFOE (1659–1731)

Defoe's Life.—Daniel Defoe was born in London in 1659. His father was a butcher, and by religion a Dissenter. He intended his son for the ministry, but Daniel preferred to go into trade, which he followed for some years with fortunes varying from prosperity to bankruptcy. He became interested in politics, and held various minor offices under William III. One of his early political writings showed his native talent for fiction. The Tory party believed in punishing persons who did not attend the services of the English Church. Defoe, pretending to write as a Tory, put forth a pamphlet called *The Shortest Way with Dissenters,* in which he advised treatment so severe that people generally were disgusted with the policy of persecution. Although Defoe concealed his real personality, the trick was discovered; he was arrested and sentenced to exposure in the pillory and a long imprisonment. While in prison he edited the *Review,* one of the earliest English newspapers. He was released to become a servant of the government which had imprisoned him, and was employed almost until the close of his life by both parties as a secret agent, perhaps as a spy.

Defoe continued to write for newspapers, and as an enterprising journalist he published the lives of various people of interest to the public: of Peter the Great for one; of Jonathan Wild, a notorious criminal and thief-taker, for another; of Captain Avery, a famous pirate, for a third. His life brought him into contact with all sorts of adventurers; being gifted with curiosity and a retentive memory, he listened to their stories and afterward wrote them out. When his material failed he drew upon his imagination; but he realized that he was writing for people who demanded fact, who perhaps thought it wrong to read fiction, and accordingly he tried to give every appearance of reality to his narratives.

"Robinson Crusoe."—While working on the border line between biography and fiction, Defoe was attracted by the story of a sailor, Alexander Selkirk, who had been wrecked on an island in the Pacific, and had remained there for many years. This story suggested *The Surprising Adventures of Robinson Crusoe*, which was published in 1719. The book proved immensely popular. Defoe added a sequel, *The Further Adventures of Robinson Crusoe*, and many imitations appeared in England and throughout Europe.

In *Robinson Cru oe* Defoe shows what a contemporary described as "the little art he is so truly master of, of forging a story and imposing it on the world for truth." The secret of his success lies in his skill in taking the point of view of his hero. Defoe throws himself completely into the situation of Crusoe, wrecked on the island. He foresees the dangers incident to such a situation, takes measures of precaution against them, indulges the natural hope of escape, and makes the wonderfully human mistake of building a boat too heavy for him to launch. He is absorbed in the trivial events of a solitary existence; he is filled with satisfaction at his miniature conquest of nature, and with horror at the frightful discovery of the human footprint in the sand. In fact, so utterly did Defoe merge himself in Crusoe that, when his work was finished, he came to see in the struggles of the York mariner an allegory of his own toilsome and dangerous experience of life.

Robinson Crusoe is one of the great stories of the world, and one of those most typical of the English race. As Bunyan's Pilgrim represents the spiritual, so does Crusoe the practical element in the English character. Crusoe is indeed a man of piety, but his religious experience lacks warmth. His real significance is as a model of the virtues which make civilization possible,—courage, patience, ingenuity, prudence. Bunyan and Defoe were both Puritans, and the difference between them serves to show how far the spiritual tide had ebbed in a generation. Bunyan is concerned with the winning of heaven; Defoe, with the problem of staying in the present world and living successfully in it.

"The Journal of the Plague Year."—The success of *Robinson Crusoe* led Defoe to put out a number of minor novels, founded upon the lives of various adventurers. The only one of Defoe's fictions, however, which ranks with Robinson Crusoe is *The Journal of the Plague Year*, published in

1722. The Great Plague visited London in 1665, and Defoe as a boy must have heard many of the experiences of survivors. A historian would have endeavored to base his account directly upon these various authorities, but Defoe, as a story-teller, presents all the facts which he has gathered as the experiences of a single imaginary character,—a citizen of London who, when the tide of pestilence rose high, shut himself and his family in his house, having provisioned it as if to stand a siege, and from this point of safety viewed the events of that dreadful time. As in *Crusoe*, Defoe throws himself entirely into the situation of his character, making us hear with his ears the rumble of the carts, the call "Bring out your dead," the blasphemous railing of the men in the tavern, and the cry of "Death, Death, Death!" from the window in Token House Yard; making us believe on his authority every gruesome anecdote, in which the misery, terror, or madness of the time expressed itself. Indeed, the personality of this character, the plain, careful, God-fearing citizen, comes to be to the reader the ultimate reality in the book. We believe in the actual horrors of the plague because we believe in the truth of this imaginary spectator of them.

One very important element of the modern novel is lacking in Defoe's stories—that is, *plot*. The first great example of a work of fiction guided throughout its course by a single motive, a story in which all the incidents serve to bring about a certain result, was *Pamela*, by Samuel Richardson.

Here

III. SAMUEL RICHARDSON (1689–1761)

"Pamela."—Richardson was a London printer, already over fifty years old when an accident discovered to him his power as a writer of fiction. A publishing firm asked him to write a series of letters which should serve as models for people in the lower walks of life. In order to add interest to this "complete letter-writer," Richardson hit upon the plan of making it the correspondence of a young serving-girl who writes to her parents, telling the story of her temptation by her master, and of her resistance. In the end the evil-hearted master reforms and marries Pamela, thus justifying the sub-title, "Virtue Rewarded." The book appeared in 1740. Its popularity encouraged Richardson to publish a sequel two years later, and two other long novels, *Clarissa* (1748), and *Sir Charles Grandison* (1753).

"**Clarissa.**"—The former is the story of a young lady, Clarissa Harlowe, who, as the result of the attempt of her family to force her into an unwelcome marriage, flees from her home.   In her flight she accepts the assistance of a certain Lovelace, who has long been in love with her, and this gentlemanly reprobate virtually kidnaps her.   After many attempts to escape, and much suffering, she dies, leaving her relatives to repent of their cruelty, and Lovelace to suffer the punishment of his guilty conscience.

Like *Pamela*, *Clarissa* is told by means of letters in which the different characters speak for themselves.   Indeed, it is clear that Richardson thought of the novel as an elaborated drama.   He calls *Clarissa* "a dramatic narrative"; and he does so very properly, for, as in a play, there is in *Clarissa* a definite catastrophe, every step toward which is carefully prepared for by something in the environment or the characters of the actors.   Richardson could not, however, forego entirely the novelist's right to personal communication with his audience.   He introduced footnotes in which he enforced his own view of the story when he thought his readers likely to go astray.   Especially in the long negotiation between Clarissa and Lovelace in regard to the latter's offer of marriage, the heroine needed the personal defence of the author from the charge of squeamishness. Though Richardson is not entirely successful in securing his heroine's acquittal, he has won a greater triumph in making her so real that we are willing to discuss with him the wisdom of her conduct, and pity her mistakes.   Impatient as we may be of her uncertainties, scruples, and hesitations, we accept them as part of the character of a living woman—one who, in her humiliation and suffering, makes an appeal to which our human sympathy responds.

Richardson's Character.—*Sir Charles Grandison* is the story of the hero's love affair with Miss Harriet Byron, its various obstacles, and happy conclusion.   In this novel

Richardson undertook to study the heart of a man with the same minute analysis that he had practised earlier in the case of his heroines, but his success is not the same. Grandison, for all the ingenuity expended upon him, remains like Lovelace, a machine. Richardson knew women better than men. As a youth he used to write love-letters for the girls of his village. As a novelist he worked in close connection with the feminine part of his audience. His circle of admirers began with his wife and a young lady visitor, who stimulated him to his task by inquiring daily, "Haven't you a little more 'Pamela,' Mr. Richardson?" It widened with his fame until it included even great ladies of fashion, who, in person or by letter, communicated with the old printer upon the progress of his tales. They petted him and flattered him until the good Richardson lost himself in the seclusion which they provided, and forgot the world of action outside. So retired did he become that at last he would communicate with the foreman of his printing-house only by letter. We think of him naturally as an indoor man, always in dressing-gown and slippers. Because of this seclusion Richardson's novels lack breadth and freshness. They deal with a small world of trifles and scruples, of feminine niceties of sentiment and deportment.

Richardson's Purpose.—Like Defoe, Richardson was of the English middle class, and wrote primarily to minister to its interest in morality and in behavior. He began his work with the humble design of teaching his readers to write, but his plan broadened until it covered the essentials of the art of living. Pamela serves as a model for servants; Clarissa is perfection in a higher sphere. Richardson's characters are all involved in intricate questions of conscience. Clarissa's course is determined after elaborate discussion of the right and wrong of each step. In *Sir Charles Grandison*, it is only after the hero has dealt with a succession of difficult circumstances arising from the claims upon him of his friend, his friend's children, his sister, and his ward, that he yields to his passion for Miss Byron. Richardson surely did not exaggerate when he declared the inculcation of virtue to be his first object.

IV. HENRY FIELDING (1707–1754)

Fielding's Life.—Something like disgust for Richardson's moral pretensions led Henry Fielding, the greatest of eighteenth-century novelists, to enter the field of fiction. Fielding was of higher birth than Richardson, his father being a soldier of some renown, and his grandfather the son of a peer; he had, too, a far wider and more varied experience of life. He was born in 1707, was educated at Eton, and afterward went to Leyden to study law. In 1727 he returned to London, where he supported himself for awhile by writing plays. He married a lady of fortune, and lived for a time as a country gentleman; but he at length exhausted his wife's money, and returned to London in poverty. Deprived of his profession of playwright by the restrictions of the licensing act of 1737, he betook himself again to the study of law, meanwhile supporting his family by miscellaneous writing. His wife died in 1743, leaving him with two children. He struggled on until life was made somewhat easier for him by his appointment as police magistrate in London, in which office he was highly efficient. In 1754, broken in health, he left England for Portugal; a journey of which he has left a pathetic account in his *Voyage to Lisbon*. He died the same year.

"Joseph Andrews."—While Fielding was earning his bread by various literary ventures, he was moved to write a burlesque upon Richardson's *Pamela*. The hero, who is described as Pamela's brother, Joseph Andrews, is, like his sister, a model of virtue, but unlike her he is turned out of doors for his pains, and left to make his way from London to his home in the country. The course of this journey brings Joseph and his companion, Parson Adams, into manifold adventures, and introduces them to men and women who, as Fielding sketches them for us, are as vivid as the figures in Hogarth's prints. Mrs. Towwouse, the innkeeper's wife, Trulliber, the hog-raising parson, and Mrs. Slipslop are drawn with a broad humor which becomes caricature, but they are essentially true to the crude life of the English country-side. In his wide vision of the world, in the fertility with which his imagination peoples it, and in his power to individualize types of human life, often with a touch of comedy, Fielding is a realist of the company of Chaucer.

" Jonathan Wild."—*Joseph Andrews* appeared in 1742. Possibly before this Fielding had written the story called *Jonathan Wild the Great*, suggested by the life of a famous rascal whom Defoe had also celebrated. Here, also, Fielding began his work as a burlesque on other writers, in this case the biographers, who find every trait in their heroes a sign of greatness. Both these earlier stories are written loosely, with little care for construction, but in his last two novels, *Tom Jones* (1749), and *Amelia* (1751), Fielding developed genuine plots.

" Tom Jones."—*Tom Jones* opens with the discovery of the hero as a babe in the house of a virtuous gentleman named Mr. Allworthy. He grows up with Allworthy's nephew Blifil, who out of jealousy ruins Tom's reputation with his benefactor, and gets him turned out into the world. Meanwhile, Tom has fallen in love with the daughter of a neighbor, Sophia Western. He travels to London, meeting adventures in plenty by the way; he passes through temptations, not unscathed; and finally, by the discovery of the secret of his birth and the revelation of Blifil's villainy, he is advanced to his happy fortune, the favor of Allworthy, and marriage with Sophia.

Tom Jones may be taken as an account of Fielding's own experience, the vigorous, careless, adventurous life of a good-hearted, thoughtless youth, turned loose upon the rough life of English villages, inns, post-roads, and country houses. If we think of Richardson as always in his arm-chair, shod with slippers, we must fancy Fielding on horse-back, in jack-boots and spurs. Richardson's scenes are usually laid within doors, and the characters are engaged in working out some complication of private life. Fielding keeps his story out of doors, and his characters in contact with the larger world. His novels thus gain in movement and freshness, in breadth and picturesqueness. Again, Richardson's characters appeal to us chiefly by virtue of their mental struggles and sufferings; Fielding's, by their external appearance and bearing. The most fascinating element in *Tom Jones* is the brilliant figure of the hero as he rides across England in the days when travel was little less exciting than war.

"**Amelia.**"—In Fielding's last book, *Amelia*, we behold this brightness somewhat dimmed. Captain Booth, the hero, is Tom Jones grown older, but no wiser. Like Fielding himself, he has spent his wife's fortune, and is compelled to resort to all manner of shifts to live. His adventures lack the picturesqueness of those in *Tom Jones*. They are the reflection of the sordid life of poverty in London, which Fielding knew only too well. The heroine, Amelia, is the counterpart of Fielding's wife, a developed portrait for which Sophia Western was a first sketch. Her constancy and devotion save Booth from the ruin to which his light character tempts him.

Fielding's Satire.—Fielding has been taken to task for the frankness with which he portrayed man's life, both in the case of Booth and that of Tom Jones. For the honesty of his picture he is not to be blamed; but the indifference which he shows toward moral considerations, and his lack of concern for a life higher than that of worldly enjoyment, are to be regarded as serious shortcomings. But if Fielding is deficient in the spiritual virtues, he has in abundance those that belong to mere human nature. With his broad view of the world of men went an immense sympathy with them that always saves his satire from cynicism. He laughs, but his laughter is never inhuman like Swift's; and it is always ready to give place to tenderness and pity. For him the tragedy of life lay in the appearance of virtue and innocence in a world of evil, cruelty, and deception. In his presentation of this tragedy Fielding is always direct, sincere, and simple. The scene in which Amelia prepares supper for Booth, and when he does not come puts aside the wine untasted to save a sixpence, while her husband is losing guineas at the gaming-table, is more moving than are the complicated woes of Clarissa. It is this humanity, the most essential quality of the novelist, that makes Fielding's work permanently winning and powerful.

V. LATER NOVELISTS

Smollett.—Fielding's successor, Tobias Smollett (1721–1771) was a Scotchman, a physician who failed in his profession on account of his irascible temper, and who accordingly took up the practice of literature. His first novel was *Roderick Random* (1748), a tale of adventure, in which he made use of much of his own experience. He had been surgeon's mate on a man-of-war; accordingly, after describing Roderick's youth in Scotland, he sends his hero to sea, taking the opportunity to insert some vivid descriptions of naval life. Of much the same type as this first novel is *Peregrine Pickle* (1751). Smollett's last novel, *Humphrey Clinker*, published in 1771, is his best. The story consists of the adventures attending the journeys of a Welsh family through England and Scotland. The adventures are mild enough, but the plan of the story gives Smollett an opportunity to describe men and things; and as a contemporary record, and comment on life and manners, the book is of decided interest. Moreover, in *Humphrey Clinker* appear some of Smollett's best characters, humorous figures who stand each for a single quality or mannerism,—Matthew Bramble, the irascible Welsh misanthropist, his sister Tabitha, and Win Jenkins the maid, who exhausts the possibilities of fun in English misspelling. To these should be added the admirable sailor characters of the earlier stories: Admiral Trunnion in *Peregrine Pickle*, and Bowling and Pipes in *Roderick Random*.

Sterne.—Laurence Sterne (1713–1768), was the son of a petty officer in the army, and he himself, born in barracks, spent his sickly youth in moving from one military station to another. He was sent to Cambridge, and thence drifted into the church, obtaining a small living in Yorkshire, where, he says, "books, fiddling, painting, and shooting were my chief amusements." He began *Tristram Shandy*, as he says, "with no clear idea of what it was to turn out, only a design of shocking people and amusing myself." The first two volumes, published in 1760, made him famous. He was courted and flattered in London, promoted in the church, and well received at Paris, for his book was an international success. Meanwhile he continued to issue volumes of his masterpiece, putting into them material of any sort which he happened to have on hand. His health failing, he spent a year in southern France. Part of the experience of his journey he turned into the seventh volume of *Tristram Shandy*, part he saved for a book of travels called *The Sentimental Journey*, of which two volumes appeared in 1768, just before his death.

"Tristram Shandy." *Tristram Shandy* is not a novel in the proper sense of the word. The book is without plan; without beginning, progress, or end. In the fourth volume the hero laments that though he is a year older than when he began to write, his story has not got beyond the life of his first day. The author shifts arbitrarily from one character to another, begins conversations in the middle, interrupts them with little essays full of odd learning, prepares for stories which are never told and scenes between his characters which are never acted. He introduces a new character, the Widow Wadman, with whom Tristram's Uncle Toby falls in love, by a blank page, on which the reader may write his own description. The style is given over to mannerism; it abounds in trick and innuendo, and has none of the formal regularity that had marked written prose since the time of Dryden. Like Sterne's life, the book is an exaltation of whim. In his life and in his art Sterne was without a sense of propriety, without respect for the conventions that the eighteenth century was so much interested in establishing.

Sterne's Sentimentality.—Writing thus, at the instance of his moods, Sterne is curiously sentimental. Tears and laughter follow each other in his pages, and sometimes are incongruously mingled. He sits down to weep beside the poor insane Maria, who stares alternately at him and at her goat. "What resemblance do you find?" he asks. His pathos is not the sympathy of the strong man who weeps because he must; on the contrary, he goes about seeking occasion for feeling. He is thus the chief of sentimentalists, of those who write not to picture the world as it is, but to draw from it suggestions for certain moods and feelings. This attitude, which became for a time a leading fashion in literature, found its model largely in *Tristram Shandy*.

"The Vicar of Wakefield." Goldsmith's *Vicar of Wakefield* (1766) represents a reaction against the extreme sentimentality of Sterne. The book has feeling in abundance, but it is the natural, wholesome sentiment of English domestic life. The Vicar and his family have griefs enough. They fall from their happy state into poverty. Worse misfortune comes in the flight of the eldest daughter, Olivia, lured away by an unworthy lover; in the burning of their poor home; in the arrest of the Vicar for debt. But the Vicar's confidence in life is steadfast. Like Goldsmith himself, he believes that to laugh is better than to weep. Many of the ills of life are but the humors of comedy, as when Moses sells the horse for a gross of green spectacles. Others are blessings in disguise. For Goldsmith's world is an ideal one. Troubles and disasters accumulate like threatening clouds, but only to resolve themselves into beneficent showers. Suffering is not a problem; it is little more than an artistic device to make the world seem more beautiful. Evil loses its essential quality; Olivia is married to a rake who does not love her, but even this we accept confidently as a part of the happy outcome, so contagious is Goldsmith's optimism, so triumphant the Vicar's faith in the best of all possible worlds. One element of great importance in the modern novel makes its appearance in *The Vicar of Wakefield*—that of *scene*. Richardson had shown skill in arranging his interiors; Fielding had given a few set pieces of description, showing the preference of eighteenth-century taste for artificial over natural beauty; but Goldsmith pictured nature with real feeling for it, and it is, throughout the book, a symbol of the eternal goodness of the world, another reason for putting trust in life.

The Romantic Novel.—Eighteenth-century fiction from Richardson onward shows the demand of the reading public for a more sympathetic treatment of life than the hard, matter-of-fact temperament of men like Swift and Pope could give. As we have seen, both Richardson and Fielding appealed to the emotions of their readers, and in

Sterne and his followers we have a school of writers who are properly called sentimentalists, who write merely to play upon the feelings.   Toward the close of the century the novel reflects that re-awakening of the imagination known as the romantic movement (see next chapter), and the deeper feeling for man as an individual which was one of the forces beneath the upheaval of the French Revolution.   The mediæval or "gothic" romance, which sought to excite emotions of wonder and terror by the use of material drawn from the superstitions of the past, finds its chief representative in *The Castle of Otranto* (1765) by Horace Walpole.   The humanitarian novel, which seriously undertook to right the wrongs of the individual, and cure the evils of society, was developed by a group of writers more or less in sympathy with the Revolution, of whom William Godwin, the author of *Caleb Williams* (1794), was the chief.   In these two schools we find the beginnings of two great classes of the fiction of to-day, the historical novel and the novel of purpose.

REVIEW OUTLINE.—What are the causes of the predominance of the novel in modern English literature ?   What forms did fiction assume in the Middle Ages for different classes ?   What name was given to the Italian tales ?   What was the picaresque romance ?   In what sense was it the forerunner of the modern novel ?   To what class did the novel especially appeal ?   Why was Defoe especially fitted to write for that class ?   What qualification for writing fiction did he show in his early political articles ?   How did his later life provide him with the material for his stories ?   On what was the story of " Robinson Crusoe " founded ?   In what does the art of the book consist ?   What is " The Journal of the Plague Year " ?   What element of imagination is involved in the narrative ?

What narrative method does Defoe employ ?   What element of structure do his works of fiction lack ?   Under what circumstances did Richardson write " Pamela " ?   What purpose appears in the sub-title ?   What is the plot of " Clarissa " ?   How does Richardson's method suggest that of the drama ?   Wherein does the strength of Richardson's character-drawing appear ?   Why did he succeed better with women than with men ?   What limitation did his character put upon his work ?   What place does moral purpose take in his novels ?

Outline the life of Fielding. What led him to undertake fiction? For what is "Joseph Andrews" notable? What is the element of satire in "Jonathan Wild"? Sketch the plot of "Tom Jones." How does the book differ in atmosphere from Richardson's works? What relation have "Tom Jones" and "Amelia" to Fielding's own career? In what does Fielding's pathos consist?

Mention three of Smollett's novels. What can be said of his portrayal of character? Give an idea of the method of "Tristram Shandy." Of its style. What is meant by Sterne's sentimentalism? How is "The Vicar of Wakefield" a reaction against it? How does the story illustrate Goldsmith's view of life? What use does Goldsmith make of scene? In what ways does the novel mark an advance upon the treatment of life by Swift and Pope? In what ways does it reflect the romantic movement?

READING GUIDE.—Every one should read "Robinson Crusoe," "The Journal of the Plague Year," and "The Vicar of Wakefield." Beyond this the reading in eighteenth-century fiction must be left largely to the initiative of the pupil. It is the aim of the text to present the substance and quality of a few of the greater books like "Clarissa," "Tom Jones," and "Tristram Shandy" in such a way that reading the works themselves may be dispensed with until pupils are of college age.

Lives of the novelists (except Smollett) appear in the English Men of Letters series, and in addition should be mentioned Austin Dobson's "Life of Goldsmith" in the Great Writers series (Scott). Sir Leslie Stephen in "Hours in a Library" has essays on Defoe, Richardson, Fielding, and Sterne. Thackeray's "English Humorists" contains lectures on Fielding, Sterne, and Goldsmith.

Of general works on the history of fiction the teacher or advanced student will use Jusserand's "English Novel in the Time of Shakespeare" (Unwin), W. L. Cross's "Development of the English Novel" (Macmillan), F. H. Stoddard's "The Evolution of the English Novel" (Macmillan), and W. E. Simond's "Introduction to the Study of English Fiction" (Heath).

CHAPTER XII

THE REVIVAL OF ROMANTICISM

I. INTRODUCTION

Literature at the Death of Pope.—When Pope died (1744), the classical ideal had been dominant for three-quarters of a century. As we have seen, the civilizing effect of this era upon literature had been great. But in its zeal for law and order the Augustan Age had sacrificed too much. It had marked as forbidden too many things which, sooner or later, men were bound to find excellent and desirable. It had set up standards of taste which, in their narrowness and inflexibility, were bound in time to bring about a revolt.

Signs of Reaction Against the Classical Ideal.—As soon as Pope's commanding presence was removed, and the fascination of his brilliant example began to be a little dimmed, signs of such a revolt were not long in making themselves apparent. Even before Pope's death, the reaction against the order of things for which he stood, had set in. Here and there a poet, tired of the sharp click and hard polish of the classic couplet, had begun to turn back to Milton and Spenser, and to imitate that fuller and freer music. Shakespeare, the "splendid barbarian," began once more to cast his spell upon adventurous readers, and to fill them with a new wonder and admiration. Things as they were, in the world of London coffee-houses and drawing-rooms, began for some minds to lose their charm, and things as they had been in the mysterious past, or as they might still be in remote regions of the earth, began to attract men's curiosity. Chosen spirits, gifted somehow with a new vision, looked out upon the world of nature, and found that it was good. They looked into their own hearts, and found there a thousand wayward impulses which conventions had long stifled, but which clamored now for expression. With the new feeling for nature there went a new feeling for man, a greater tenderness for the unfortunate, a greater sympathy with the humble and obscure, a livelier curiosity concerning man's life in distant regions and far-off times.

The Romantic Movement Broadly Viewed.—This great awakening we call, for lack of a better word, the "Romantic Movement." It was a slow awakening, for it covered the whole period from about 1725 to the end of the eighteenth century. It was as broad as it was slow, for it covered nearly the whole of Western Europe, and brought in its train no less a world-shaking event than the French Revolution. It was in essence, as the Renaissance had been, a reassertion of the freedom of the individual, but this assertion was made now in a more spiritual sense, and with a profounder conception of what freedom means to the spirit and the imagination.

The Romantic Movement in Literature.—In literature the Romantic revival expressed itself in three main directions. In the first place, it brought with it a new interest in the past, especially in the Middle Ages, because the life of the Middle Ages, with its turbulence, its strong passions, its rich barbaric color, was in strongest contrast to the well-ordered life of the "classic era," and it therefore ministered to that hunger for the "picturesque," which the formality of the Augustan Age, by a natural reaction, had engendered. In the second place, the Romantic revival brought with it a new interest in nature, especially in the wilder and more desolate aspects of nature— again, by reaction from the Augustan indifference to everything which had not been pruned and ornamented by the hand of man. In the third place, the Romantic movement brought with it a new human sympathy, especially toward such human lives as by reason of their humbleness or their rudeness had been treated with contempt by an aristocratic age.

II. THE ROMANTIC PIONEERS (FROM THOMSON TO BURNS)

Thomson's " Seasons " and " Castle of Indolence."—The earliest poet in whom the workings of the new romantic spirit can be seen, was James Thomson (1700–1748). Thomson was a Scotchman, who came up to London in 1725. The following year he published the first section, "Winter," of a poem which he afterward continued under the titles "Summer," "Spring," and "Autumn," and which was published in 1730 as *The Seasons*. To the readers of his own day the novelty of this poem was great. For two generations the first-hand study of nature had been neglected. Literature had found its interests in city life; or, if it ventured into the country at all, it was into a country conventionalized and unreal, a country clipped and trimmed like a formal garden in the Italian style. Accordingly, Thomson's poem had an aspect of daring innovation. His views of English landscape, his description of the first spring showers, of the summer thunderstorms, and of the terrors of the wintry night, showed an honest understanding and love of that to which the eye had long been blind. In *The Castle of Indolence*, published in 1748, Thomson went back to Spenser for his inspiration. The poem is in the Spenserian stanza, and recaptures something of the master's rich, long-drawn music. The same golden atmosphere which enwraps Spenser's "land of faery" steeps the embowered castle of the enchanter Indolence, with its "listless climate," where the plaint of stock-doves mingles with the sighing of hillside pines.

Gray : His Letters and Diaries.—Among the early bearers of the banner of Romanticism, the most important name is that of Thomas Gray (1716–1771). Gray lived the life of a scholar and recluse at Cambridge, where in his later years he held a professorship of history, but delivered no lectures. He was sensitive to all the finer influences of the time. He was a delightful letter-writer and diarist, and his letters and journals give a very complete view of the intellectual movements of the period. Particularly interesting are those passages which show in him the new sensibility to picturesque scenery and to Gothic architecture, two of the great enthusiasms of the romantic innovators. In a letter written in early life from Switzerland, during a tour which he made with his friend Horace Walpole, he writes of the scenery about the Grande Chartreuse: "Not a precipice, not a torrent, not a cliff, but is pregnant with religion and poetry. One need not have a very fantastic imagination to see spirits there at noonday." Years after, in the Scotch highlands, he writes of the mountains as "those monstrous creatures of God," and declares that they "ought to be visited in pilgrimage once a year." A generation before Gray wrote from the Grande Chartreuse, Addison had crossed the Alps, and dismissed the experience thus: "A very troublesome journey. You can't imagine how I am pleased with the sight of a plain." Gray's enthusiasm over the marvels of mediæval architecture at Rheims and Sienna, contrasts also with Addison's comparison of the nobility of the classic Pantheon with the "meanness of manner" in the Gothic cathedrals. Toward the end of his life Gray made one of his "Liliputian journeys" to the English lake country afterward made famous by Words-worth's poetry. The journal which he kept on this occasion is remarkable for the intimate sympathy which it shows with the changes of mood in the landscape, under variations of weather and time of day. Gray sees nature with a modern eye, as a living thing full of sentiment and meaning.

Gray's Poetry.—Gray's most important poems are the "Elegy in a Country Churchyard" and "The Bard." The "Elegy" is perhaps the most widely known and loved of English poems. A large part of its charm comes from the poet's personal, sensitive approach to his subject. He lingers in the churchyard, noting the signs of approaching nightfall, until the atmosphere of twilight musing is established, after which his reflections upon life and death have a tone of sad and intimate sincerity. In its recognition of the dignity of simple lives lived close to the soil, and in its sympathy with their fate, the "Elegy" shows the breaking-up of the hard forms into which social feeling had stiffened, and looks forward to the enthusiasm for humanity which marked the later phases of romantic poetry. "The Bard" is more distinctly romantic, both in subject and treatment. An ancient minstrel, the last of the Welsh singers, escaped from Edward's massacre, stops the king in a wild mountain pass, and prophesies the terrors which are to gather over his descendants. This poem, with its imaginative rekindling of the passion of an ancient and perished people, shows that re-awakened interest in the Middle Ages which soon became the leading feature of romantic art.

Percy's Reliques.—In 1765 Bishop Percy, an antiquarian scholar with literary tastes, published a ballad collection entitled *Reliques of Ancient Poetry*. These old ballads, which spoke in tones of primitive freshness and passion out of the distant past, had a great effect in quickening the romantic impulse. Long afterward, Wordsworth said of these ballads that they had led English poetry back to the truth from which it had wandered.

"Ossian": Chatterton's Imitations.—About the same time appeared an epic poem in irregular chanting prose, entitled *Fingal*, purporting to have been originally written in the ancient Gaelic tongue of the Scotch highlands, by Ossian, the son of Fingal, in a dim heroic past. It seems to have been in large part a clever literary forgery, the work of a young Scotchman named Macpherson, but its influence was enormous in furthering the new taste for the mysterious past.

Of a similar nature were the series of literary forgeries put forth by Thomas Chatterton (1752–1770). These consisted of poems and prose pieces in the mediæval style and diction, which he palmed off upon the good burghers of Bristol as originals which he had unearthed in the ancient coffers of their church. Chatterton ended his morbid and amazingly precocious life by suicide in a London garret, at the age of nineteen. When the battle of the new poetry had been fought and won, Keats dedicated *Endymion* to his memory, and Shelley placed him in "Adonais" among the "inheritors of unfulfilled renown."

Cowper: "The Task."—William Cowper (1731–1800), though he was not conscious of being an innovator, marks the advent of a new realism in the poetic treatment of nature and human life. His early life was spent at Westminster School, and as a law-student in London. Fits of gayety, and states of mystical exaltation, were succeeded in him by periods of terrible depression. At the age of fifty-two, he was living in the obscure village of Olney, where, under the care of a widow, Mrs. Unwin, several years his senior, he was spending a peaceful interval between two attacks of religious melancholia. At the suggestion of one Lady Austin, he began a long poem in blank verse, in which he described the landscapes, the changes of seasons, the human types and employments of the rural world about him, as well as his own simple pleasures and occupations. The poem was published in 1785, as *The Task*. A large portion of *The Task* is conventional enough, but here and there one comes upon little vignettes,—the figure of a teamster driving homeward in a snowstorm, a postman hurrying through the village with his eagerly awaited bag of news from the great world, ploughmen at work in the flat fields by the river Ouse,—which are instinct with vivid natural life. The amusing ballad of " John Gilpin" also belongs to this bright period of Cowper's life. He afterward relapsed into melancholia, broken at intervals by a ray of poetic inspiration such as produced his touching lines, "On the Receipt of my Mother's Picture out of Norfolk," deservedly the best known of his poems. His last poem, entitled "The Castaway," is a cry of despair from the depths of visionary anguish into which he was now hopelessly plunged.

Blake.—William Blake (1757–1827), was by profession an engraver, and the most important part of his work is his drawings, many of which are in illustration of his own poems and the strange mystic writings which he called "prophecies." When a very young child, he one day screamed with fear, because, he said, he had seen God put his face to the window. In boyhood he saw several angels, very bright, standing in a tree by the roadside. In his manhood, the earth and the air were for him full of spiritual presences, all concerned with his fate or with that of his friends. He saw everywhere about him "armies of angels that soar, legions of demons that lurk." His fame as a poet rests chiefly on his *Poetical Sketches*, and on his *Songs of Innocence and Experience*. Amid much that is unfinished, and no little that is obscure, these little volumes contain some of the simplest and sweetest, as well as some of the most powerful, short poems in the language. At his best, as in "The Tiger," and "Hear the Voice of the Bard," Blake has a simplicity as great as Wordsworth's, and a magic which reminds us of Coleridge, together with a startling depth and intensity. Like a true mystic, he moves us less by what he says than by what he hints, and these hints are often so shadowy that they elude us at the very moment when we seem about to grasp them.

III. ROBERT BURNS (1759–1796)

Burns's Early Life and Poetry.—Robert Burns was born in a two-roomed clay cottage in Ayrshire, West Scotland, in 1759. His parents were God-fearing peasants of the best Scotch type, who worked heroically to keep the wolf from the door, and to give their children an elementary education. There have been preserved to us many glimpses of the family life which Burns shared, and all of them show us how earnest and wholesome was its atmosphere. The father, as he walked to the morning's labor with his sons Robert and Gilbert, would talk to them as man to man, drawing their thoughts to serious themes of conduct and belief; and he would often visit his daughter, where she tended the flock afield, to teach her the names of the plants and herbs which grew about. The local schoolmaster brought books to the family and read to them regularly. Once, when he was reading from Shakespeare's *Titus Andronicus*, and had reached a particularly harrowing passage, with one voice they cried out for him to desist, as they could not endure the cruelty of the pictures which the drama evoked. In all this we see that Burns's early life, though full of privation and harsh toil, was passed among gentle influences.

The privation, however, was severe, and the toil bitter. At fifteen Robert did a grown man's work in ploughing and reaping. The various farms which the elder Burns leased in succession, proved too poor to repay the labor put upon them. In spite of all frugality and industry, ruin was seldom far away. Looking back upon his youth in after years, Burns described it as the "cheerless gloom of a hermit, with the unceasing toil of a galley-slave." But this is clearly an exaggeration, for we have his youthful poems to prove him wrong.

He had had a few books of poetry to read, and had heard, as every Scotch peasant hears, the floating ballad verse of

small service is true service while it last.

ROBERT BURNS
From a painting by Nasmyth

the country-side. Then he had begun to rhyme, almost as spontaneously as a bird begins to sing, or, as he says himself, "for fun," as he followed his plough "in glory and in joy, along the mountain-side." The youth who wrote the lines "To a Mountain Daisy" and "To a Mouse," with their searching sympathy, the "Epistle to Davie," with its manly philosophy and genial temper, the "Address to the De'il," with its rich humor and fun, "The Cotter's Saturday Night," bathed in its tender light of fireside happiness,—was neither a hermit nor a galley-slave, but simply a healthy, impetuous farm-lad, with a warm heart, a rich nature, and a God-given genius for song.

Between his twenty-third and his twenty-sixth year, at Mossgiel, Burns wrote the larger number of those poems which have made his name loved wherever the lowland dialect is understood. In these he revealed with wonderful completeness the rural Scotland of his day. He illuminated with a blended light of humor and tenderness the common experiences of his peasant world. He celebrates "Scotch Drink," holds up to laughter the praying hypocrite "Holy Willie," and paints the riotous games of Hallowe'en; but he turns also to mourn over the "wee, modest, crimson-tippèd flower" uprooted in the furrow on the mountain-side, and finds in a field-mouse whose snug home has been broken up by the ploughshare, a thing to touch the springs of human pity.

Burns's temporary residence at Irvine, whither he went in 1782, with the plan of learning the flax-dressing industry, marks a great change in his life, and the beginning of those dissipations into which his eager and abounding temperament only too easily led him. Here and at his home-village of Mauchline his reputation as poet and wit threw him into the company of "buckish young squires, roaring lawyers and half-heretical divines," who welcomed him as a brilliant addition to their circle, and spurred him on to wild extravagances of word and deed. His was a nature which loves to shine, to which the exercise of its charm and power is a necessity. Even in his sober earlier years he had "worn his plaid in a particular manner, and of a particular color," and had had "the only tied hair in the parish." Now he threw himself headlong into pleasure; it was not long before he had earned his title of "Ranting Rob."

Publication of the "Poems": Burns in Edinburgh.—By the time he reached his twenty-sixth year, his wild ways had got him into desperate trouble. His father was dead, and the hand-to-hand fight which he and his brother Gilbert were waging with poverty, bade fair to end in absolute failure. Distracted and despairing, Burns determined to go to the West Indies. In order to raise the passage money, someone suggested that he should publish the poems which lay in his desk in the cottage at Mossgiel. Neither the author nor anyone else hoped for more than a local popularity. The little book was published at Kilmarnock in 1786, with the title, *Poems, Chiefly in the Scottish Dialect*. The few pounds brought in by the small edition were in his pocket, his trunk was sent forward, and he had written the solemn and moving song, "The Gloomy Night is Gathering Fast," as his farewell word, when a letter from Edinburgh arrived which changed the whole face of his fortunes. It was from an eminent scholar and critic, who praised the book highly and called for another and larger edition. Burns posted to Edinburgh, heralded and fêted on the way like a hero of romance. A winter in the Scotch capital followed, during which he was petted and lionized by the brilliant society gathered there. Learned doctors, famous critics and men of letters, not to speak of "Duchess Gordon and all the gay world," were eager to flatter and amuse the "ploughman poet." In this sudden revolution of his fortunes, his powerful sense and his native dignity never deserted him. His head was not turned; he refused to be anything but himself. Walter Scott, then a young boy, on one occasion saw Burns at close range in an Edinburgh drawing-room, and has left a charming description of him as he looked at this time—the burly figure in boots and buckskins, blue coat and buff-striped waistcoat, "like a farmer in his Sunday best," the large head with its air of thoughtful melancholy, the great dark eyes which "literally glowed" as he spoke. "I never saw such another eye in a human head," Scott adds, "though I have seen the most distinguished men of my time."

Burns's Later Life : His Songs.—Burns left Edinburgh after a second winter, somewhat richer in money and prospects, but with his energy relaxed. The flattery of the great had not turned his head, but the dissipations of the capital and the long period of idleness had weakened his purpose. Nevertheless he made a strong effort to recover the lost ground. He returned to Ayrshire with an appointment as "gauger" (inspector of the liquor customs) in his pocket, married Jean Armour, and took a farm at Ellisland, with the design of combining farming and revenue service. His duties covered ten parishes and compelled him to ride two hundred miles a week. What was worse, they threw him constantly into riotous company, where his wit and eloquence were always in uproarious demand. His farm naturally went to ruin, and he found time for little poetry except short snatches of song. With the exception of the "Jolly Beggars" and "Tam O'Shanter," Burns did no more sustained work. But he poured out in recompense hundreds of songs—love-songs, drinking songs, songs of patriotism, many of which are among the eternal possessions of the race. They have given Burns rank as the first of English song-writers. Their range is as wonderful as their quality. "From the loud flowing revel in 'Willie Brewed a Peck o' Maut,' to the still rapt enthusiasm of sadness for 'Mary in Heaven'; from the glad kind greeting of 'Auld Lang Syne,' or the comic archness of 'Duncan Gray,' to the fire-eyed fury of 'Scots Wha Hae Wi' Wallace Bled,' he has found a tone and words for every mood of man's heart." * Although pressed for money, he refused to accept any pay for these songs. In the fast-gathering ruin of his life, he wished to dedicate this its noblest part to Scotland, and would take no wage for that which was indeed above all price.

Sincerity and Vividness of Burns's Work.—The quality of Burns's poetry which first arrests a reader's interest, and which makes perhaps the most lasting impression, is its sincerity. In his English verse, to be sure, he often expresses himself in the stilted manner which was then fashionable. Even "The Cotter's Saturday Night" is hurt by passages where Burns deserts the Scotch dialect for conventional

* Carlyle : Essay on Burns.

English speech. But it is not in his English verse that we find the real Burns. Everything that he wrote in his native dialect has the ring of absolute honesty. He expresses the truth of life as it appears to him, with penetrating frankness. His words have an indescribable intonation of heartiness, of careless conviction. His lyric strain has a curious arresting power, like that of certain human voices in whose tones there seems to vibrate an inner assurance of truth, though the words themselves are lightly, perhaps mockingly, spoken.

Allied to this sincerity, but more external and easier to lay hold of, is the vividness of Burns's speech. In "The Twa Dogs" he not only gives us with a few airy touches a lively likeness of the Scotch collie Luath and the squire's St. Bernard, but fixes, as it were, the universal traits of doghood. In "The Holy Fair" there are scores of groups and single figures, touched in with marvellous lightness and rapidity, but as vivid as if bitten with aqua-fortis upon an etcher's plate. The infernal dance which Tam o'Shanter views in the ruined kirk, and his flight from the witches, show the same graphic power employed in portraying scenes of wild action. In "The Brigs of Ayr" and a score of other poems, it is manifested in the description of natural scenes. And where not an image but a feeling is to be evoked, Burns has the same energy of utterance. His words "go home" with an inevitable force and directness.

Burns's Sympathy and Humor.—But it is neither his energy nor his sincerity which has made Burns the most widely beloved of English poets. It is rather his sympathy, the bright, warm geniality of nature which prompted him not only to accept everything human in the world of men about him, but to draw the life of beast and bird and flower into the circle of his humor and tenderness. For humor pervades his poetry, keeping it fresh and tonic and free from sentimentality. In "The Holy Fair" Burns tells us how he once met Fun come "skelpin' up the way," gay in her Sunday best. She came toward him

> "lap, skip, and loup,
> As light as onie lambie,
> And wi' a curchie low did stoop,"

offering to go with him to the fair, and promising him some "famous laughin'." She went with him, indeed, through life, even to the dark end; but the laughter which she brought him was never harsh or bitter; it was always generous and gay and kindly.

Burns and the Romantic Revival.—In Burns, the eighteenth century had at last produced a man able to deliver literature from the bonds of convention. His vindication of the natural life, the natural instincts, humors, and affections, made untenable the narrow fortress of eighteenth-century taste. His glowing democracy of heart, which reached out to include in fellowship not only the least well-seen among men, but even the beasts of the field and birds of the air, robbed the aristocratic eighteenth-century ideal of its attraction. After Burns, the triumph of "romantic liberty," through the length and breadth of English letters, could not be long delayed.

REVIEW OUTLINE.—It is important to note that the literary movement traced in this chapter was, as the title of the chapter indicates, a "revival." Romanticism, in the broad sense, was no new thing in English literature. "Beowulf" is "romantic"; so is the work of Chaucer, of Spenser, of Marlowe, and of Shakespeare; so is "Pilgrim's Progress"; so, in almost all respects, are "Comus," and "Paradise Lost," and even where Milton adopted "classical" standards he did so in a far freer way than did Dryden or Pope. The Romantic revival, therefore, is to be thought of as a return to the freedom which the great writers of earlier times had enjoyed. But the tyranny of the classical school was so excessive that the return to freer ways of thought, feeling, and speech took on the aspect of a conscious revolt. It became, toward the end of the eighteenth century, a kind of crusade, and poets fought for it as for a holy cause. It went hand in hand with a great religious revival under John Wesley, and with a great struggle for social and political freedom in France; and this gave to the literary movement extraordinary depth and intensity.

To what earlier poets did the pioneers of the Romantic revival especially turn back? To what was due the renewed interest in the Middle Ages? In natural scenery? In strange lands and distant peoples? In the life of humble men? What parallelism is noted here between this period and that of the Renaissance? In what respects does the spirit that underlay this reaction indicate that the period between the sixteenth and the eighteenth centuries had been one of progress?

Note the statement that for two generations the first-hand study of nature had been neglected. In what poem did it first reappear? To what earlier poet did Thomson recur in his "Castle of Indolence"? Who is the most important poet of the new school among the writers of this period? Consider carefully what is said about his " seeing nature with a modern eye, as a living thing full of sentiment and meaning." Find something to illustrate this from the quotations given from Gray's prose. For which of these aspects of the spirit of the Romantic revival is Gray's "Elegy" best known? For which "The Bard"? What is "Percy's Reliques"? At what period were the most important of the early English ballads produced? (See Chap. IV.) In what esteem did Wordsworth hold these ballads? What was the current literary interest that inspired McPherson and Chatterton to make their famous literary imitations? What evidence is there from the opinions of other poets that Chatterton's gifts as a poet would have entitled him to high rank if he had lived? What is Cowper's most famous poem? Which of the interests of the Romantic revival does he show in "The Task"? What is the special character of the genius of William Blake?

Among what conditions did Burns pass his early life? What influence did his father exert on him? What did Burns say of the character of this portion of his life? What evidence of its influence on him is to be gathered from his poems? At what time of his life did he do his best writing? What effect did his residence at Irvine have on his mind and character? For what purpose was Burns's first book of poems published? What was the immediate consequence of the publication of this volume? How did the life at Edinburgh affect Burns? What effects did this experience have on his after life? What portion of his literary work was done after his final retreat from Edinburgh? Find from your own reading illustrations of the qualities of Burns's poetry spoken of in the text.

READING GUIDE.—The reading prescribed for the class upon this period will naturally be devoted chiefly to Gray and Burns. Gray's "Elegy" and "Bard" should be read by all. The following poems of Burns are recommended: "The Cotter's Saturday Night," "Tam o'Shanter," "Address to the Unco Guid," "The Twa Dogs," "To a

Mountain Daisy," "To a Mouse," "Is There for Honest Poverty"? "John Anderson," "To Mary in Heaven," "Of a' the Airts," "A Red, Red Rose," "Bonnie Doon," and "Scots Wha Hae Wi' Wallace Bled." A convenient edition of Gray is that edited by W. L. Phelps, in the Athenæum Press series (Ginn). Selections from Cowper and Gray are given in the Riverside Literature series ; Cowper's "Task" and other poems are included in Cassell's National Library. Lowell's essay upon Gray in " Latest Literary Essays," and Matthew Arnold's essay in " Essays in Criticism," are valuable. The life of Gray, by Edmund Gosse, in the English Men of Letters series, is entertaining. The Riverside Literature series (Houghton, Mifflin), includes a volume of selections from Burns with glossary of Scotch words. Carlyle's essay on Burns is not only invaluable as a commentary, but is itself a classic in the literature of the essay. R. L. Stevenson's " Familiar Studies of Men and Books " contains an excellent study of Burns's character, which may be supplemented by the widely different view taken by W. E. Henley, in the biography prefixed to the Cambridge edition of Burns (Houghton, Mifflin).

TABULAR VIEW

EIGHTEENTH CENTURY

HISTORICAL EVENTS	CLASSICAL SCHOOL	ROMANTIC SCHOOL	NOVELISTS
QUEEN ANNE....1702–1714 First daily newspaper.1703 Battle of Blenheim ...1704 GEORGE I. .....1714–1727 Jacobite rising in Scotland, in favor of the Old Pretender....1715 Modern cabinet system begins.......1721 GEORGE II. .....1727–1760 Rise of Methodists under Wesley.......1738 Jacobite rising in Scotland, for the Young Pretender. .....1745 Foundation of England's Indian Empire. . ...1757 England gains Canada, at the Battle of Quebec.......1759 GEORGE III. ....1760–1820 Spinning machinery invented....1764–1768 Watt invents steam engine........1765	JONATHAN SWIFT, 1667–1745. Tale of a Tub, 1704; Journal to Stella, written 1710–1713; Gulliver's Travels, 1726. JOSEPH ADDISON, 1672–1719. The Campaign, 1704; Cato, 1713; Essays in Tatler, Spectator, and Guardian, 1709–1714. RICHARD STEELE, 1672–1729; Essays in Tatler, Spectator, and Guardian, 1709–1714. ALEXANDER POPE, 1688–1744; Essay on Criticism, 1709; Rape of the Lock, 1713; translation of Homer, 1713–1726; Dunciad, 1728; Essay on Man, 1732; Epistle to Arbuthnot, 1737. SAMUEL JOHNSON, 1709–1784; London, 1738; Vanity of Human Wishes, 1749; Dictionary, published 1755; Rasselas, 1759; Introduction to Shakespeare, 1765;	JAMES THOMSON, 1700–1748. Seasons, 1730; Castle of Indolence, 1748. EDWARD YOUNG, Night Thoughts, 1742–1744. WM. COLLINS, 1721–1759. Odes, 1747; Ode on Superstitions of the Highlands, 1749. THOMAS GRAY, 1716–1771. Elegy in a Country Churchyard, 1750; The Bard,1757.	DANIEL DEFOE, 1659–1731. Robinson Crusoe, 1719; Captain Singleton, 1720; Moll Flanders, 1722; Journal of the Plague, 1722. SAMUEL RICHARDSON, 1689–1761. Pamela, 1740; Clarissa 1748; Sir Charles Grandison, 1753. HENRY FIELDING, 1707–1754. Joseph Andrews, 1742; Jonathan Wilde, 1743; Tom Jones, 1749; Amelia, 1751; Voyage to Lisbon, posthumous. TOBIAS SMOLLETT, 1721–1771

TABULAR VIEW

EIGHTEENTH CENTURY *(Continued)*

HISTORICAL EVENTS	CLASSICAL SCHOOL	ROMANTIC SCHOOL.	NOVELISTS
Declaration of American Independence..1776 Independence of United States acknowledged...........1783 French Revolution begins. . . . . .1789 Reign of Terror in France. . . . . .1793 England declares war on France.......1793 Battle of the Nile....1798	Lives of the Poets, 1779–1781. JAMES BOSWELL, 1740–1795. Tour to the Hebrides, 1786; Life of Johnson, 1791. OLIVER GOLDSMITH, 1728–1774. Traveller, 1764; Vicar of Wakefield, 1766; Deserted Village, 1770; She Stoops to Conquer, 1773. RICHARD BRINSLEY SHERIDAN, 1751–1816; Rivals, 1775; School for Scandal, 1777; Critic, 1779. EDWARD GIBBON, 1737–1794. Decline and Fall of Roman Empire, 1776–1788. EDMUND BURKE, 1729–1797. On the Sublime and Beautiful, 1756; Conciliation with America, 1775; Nabob of Arcot's Debts, 1785; Reflections on Revolution in France, 1790; Letters on a Regicide Peace, 1796–1797.	MACPHERSON's Ossian, 1760–1763. PERCY's Reliques, 1765. THOMAS CHATTERTON, 1752–1770. Rowley poems, begun 1764. GEORGE CRABBE, 1754–1832. The Village, 1783 (The Borough, 1810). WM. COWPER, 1731–1800. The Task, 1785; later short poems, John Gilpin, Boadicea, On his Mother's Portrait, The Castaway. WM. BLAKE, 1757–1827. Poetical Sketches, 1783; Songs of Innocence, 1789; Songs of Experience, 1794. ROBERT BURNS, 1759–1796. Poems, 1786; other editions with added poems, 1787, 1793; Later songs published in the Musical Museum and Scottish Airs, which began to appear in 1787.	Roderick Random, 1748; Peregrine Pickle, 1751; Humphrey Clinker, 1771. LAURENCE STERNE, 1713–1768. Tristram Shandy, 1768. Sentimental Journey, 1768. FANNY BURNEY, 1752–1840. Evelina, 1778; Cecilia,1782. ROMANTIC NOVELISTS HORACE WALPOLE, 1717–1797. Castle of Otranto. 1765. WM. BECKFORD, History of the Caliph Vathek, 1784. MATTHEW GREGORY LEWIS (Monk Lewis), The Monk, 1795; (The Bravo of Venice, 1804). ANNE RADCLIFFE, 1774–1823. Mysteries of Udolpho, 1794; The Italian, 1797. WILLIAM GODWIN, 1756–1836. Caleb Williams, 1794.

CHAPTER XIII

THE NINETEENTH CENTURY: THE ROMANTIC TRIUMPH

I. INTRODUCTION

The Revolutionary Era: the First Group of Poets.—
Toward the end of the eighteenth century there occurred two
events of world-wide consequence, long prepared for by circumstances but only vaguely foreseen; America threw off her
political bondage to England, and the French people, in the
name of freedom and universal brotherhood, rose up to
destroy the old fabric of the state, founded upon privilege
and caste. In 1776 the Declaration of Independence was
signed at Philadelphia; in 1789 the Bastille, the famous French
prison which stood as a symbol of tyranny and oppression, was
levelled by the revolutionists. The American revolution,
though destined to have an incalculable effect upon the world's
progress, was of far less immediate moment than the French
revolution. This terrible upheaval affected the whole of Europe. It brought in its train a series of bloody wars, in the
course of which the map of the continent was remade, and
both government and the social spirit were everywhere profoundly changed. In England alone, by reason of her detached
position, the fabric of government stood firm. England's task,
politically, was a repressive one. She took it upon herself to
hold in check the powers which were making for violent
change, especially when the bright dreams of the early revolution gave place, during the Reign of Terror, to an unbridled
frenzy of destruction, and later to the gigantic military ambitions of Napoleon. It was English diplomacy, English
gold, and English arms which held back the tide of Napoleonic
conquest, and finally sealed Napoleon's fate at Waterloo
(1815). But while the British government, under the guid-

ance of Pitt and the inspiration of Burke, was hostile to the revolution, the French cry of "Liberty, Equality, Fraternity" found an echo in thousands of English hearts. Burns lived long enough to greet the dawn of the revolutionary struggle, and to become actively involved in sympathy with the cause to such a degree as to draw official reproof upon his head. Of the three great literary figures of the next generation, Wordsworth, Coleridge and Scott, the first two were, during their young manhood, ardent champions of the doctrines of the revolution. Wordsworth especially watched with enthusiastic hope the early stages of the great drama which was being played in France, and he came near to throwing himself personally into the struggle, in the year preceding the Reign of Terror. "Bliss was it in that dawn to be alive," he writes, "and to be young was very heaven." When the fair dawn had given place to a noon blood-red with violence and crime, and later, when the sun of liberty seemed to have set forever in the barren military rule of Napoleon, Wordsworth passed through a period of gloom and despondency, from which he emerged as a conservative of the school of Burke.

The Second Group of Poets.—This reaction toward conservatism was shared by almost all the men of the generation of Wordsworth, Coleridge, and Scott. But the next generation contained a group of poets who were destined to take up the torch of revolutionary doctrine, after the actual Revolution as a political fact had failed. Byron, born 1788, was only a year old when the Bastille fell, Shelley was born in 1792, the year before the Reign of Terror, and Keats two years after it (1795). Of these three, Keats stands apart from the political agitation of the time, but Byron and Shelley were passionate revolutionists, who spent their lives in storming the citadels of ancient prejudice, and attempting to plant upon stronghold after stronghold of tyranny, bigotry, and blind custom, the flag of the new thought. Though dead as a political experiment, the revolution lived on in them, as an inspiration and a beckoning light; nor has it ever ceased so to live, from then until now, though taking on new forms and expressing itself in new ways.

II. SAMUEL TAYLOR COLERIDGE (1772–1834)

Coleridge's Early Life.—Samuel Taylor Coleridge was born in 1772, at Ottery St. Mary, a Devonshire village. His father was an eccentric and unworldly country parson. Of Coleridge's childhood we have some vivid glimpses, one in particular which shows him "slashing with a stick at rows of nettles representing the Seven Champions of Christendom." He tells us that he "never thought or spoke as a child," and his precocity made him solitary in the midst of his boisterous brothers. At nine he became a "blue-coat boy" at Christ's Hospital, an ancient charity school in the heart of London. One of his fellow-pupils was Charles Lamb, who has left us a picture of the school and of Coleridge, in his essay "Christ's Hospital Five and Thirty Years Ago." Lamb tells us that casual visitors in the halls of the school would stop spell-bound to listen while Coleridge talked or recited Greek hexameters, and "the walls of old Greyfriars re-echoed the accents of the inspired charity boy." At nineteen he entered Cambridge. With his friend Robert Southey, then a student at Oxford, he took an excited share in the enthusiasm for social progress which the French Revolution had kindled. Before long, anxiety over some college debts drove him to London, where he enlisted as a cavalry soldier, and spent two wretched months in barracks. Fortunately, he was a favorite with his mess-mates, who groomed and saddled his horse in return for the charming letters which he wrote home for them. A Latin lament scribbled under his saddle-peg by "Private Cumberback" (as he signed himself in humorous allusion to his poor horsemanship) gained him his release. The incident shows his impulsiveness and human charm, as well as the weakness of will which was to be so fatal to him.

After leaving college, Coleridge and Southey evolved a radiant scheme for establishing a Utopian community across the ocean, on the banks of the Susquehanna. There, in a virgin Paradise, they and their fellow colonists were to spend the few hours of daily toil necessary to make the wilderness bloom as a rose, and to devote the rest of their time to higher things. Southey, whose nature was at bottom very practical, soon abandoned this grand scheme of "Pantisocracy," and his desertion alienated for a time Coleridge's friendship.

In 1795 Coleridge married Miss Sarah Fricker, sister of the girl who soon after became Southey's wife. To support his new household Coleridge wrote a volume of *Juvenile Poems* and attempted to eke out the few guineas thus earned, by preaching and lecturing. To get subscribers for a projected periodical, called "The Watchman," he made a tour of the Midland counties, preaching on Sundays "as a tireless volunteer in a blue coat and white waistcoat," holding his hearers spell-bound with that marvellous eloquence for which he was already famous. A part of his early married life was spent in the village of Clevedon, in a little rose-covered cottage by the sea; the time was a happy one for Coleridge, but an ominous sentence or two in his letters show that he had already, in order to escape the pain of neuralgia, begun the fatal habit of opium-taking.

Friendship of Coleridge and Wordsworth; "The Ancient Mariner."—Early in 1797, Coleridge removed, with his wife and baby, to a tiny cottage in the village of Nether Stowey, in the green Quantock Hills; and a month later they were joined by Wordsworth and his sister Dorothy, who took a house near by at Alfoxden. Coleridge was then twenty-five, his brother poet twenty-seven. For both of them the companionship was in the highest degree stimulating. In little more than a year Coleridge wrote all the poems which place him among the immortals. This was the year of "Genevieve," "The Dark Ladie," "Kubla Khan," "The Ancient Mariner," and the first part of "Christabel"—truly, as it has been called, an *annus mirabilis*, a year of wonders.

"The Ancient Mariner" was undertaken, singular to say, as a mere "pot-boiler." Coleridge and the Wordsworths had in mind a little autumn walking tour from Alfoxden over the Quantock Hills to Watchet. To defray the expenses of the trip, some five pounds, they determined to compose together a poem to be sent to the *New Monthly Magazine*. Coleridge suggested, as a starting point, a dream which had

SAMUEL TAYLOR COLERIDGE
From a painting by Washington Allston

been related to him by his friend Mr. Cruikshank, a dream "of a skeleton ship, with figures in it." To this Wordsworth added something he had just read in Shelvocke's *Voyages*, an account of the great albatrosses, with wings stretching twelve or thirteen feet from tip to tip, which Shelvocke had seen while doubling Cape Horn. Taking a hint from the same account, he suggested that a sailor should kill one of these birds, and that the guardian spirits of the region should take vengeance on the murderer. Wordsworth also suggested the navigation of the ship by the dead men.

Coleridge seized eagerly upon all these hints, and began to weave them into unity. The composition of the poem began at once, the two poets co-operating line by line. But they had not progressed far before their styles and manners of thought were seen to be so divergent that the idea of joint composition had to be abandoned. As "The Ancient Mariner" bade fair to take on dimensions too large to allow it to be put to the modest use originally intended, it was proposed to make a little volume by adding to it other poems which the friends had in manuscript, or were contemplating. In the course of the following year, the volume appeared, under the title *Lyrical Ballads*.

The "Lyrical Ballads."—The ideal which underlay this famous little volume was that of fidelity to nature, and the use of the least artificial means possible in reproducing nature. But nature, rightly conceived, is two-sided. There is first the world of external fact, the visible world of men and things; and there is further the inner world of thought and imagination. It was a part of the philosophy which lay back of the Romantic movement, that this inner world was just as "real," just as truly existent, and therefore just as worthy of being talked about, as the outer one,— perhaps more so. This double aspect of the Romantic school is illustrated by the contents of the *Lyrical Ballads*. Wordsworth writes in simple language of simple incidents and simple people, though he does not fail to find a suggestion of strangeness and mystery in them as they are seen by the spiritual eye of the poet; in other words, he makes the usual appear strange simply by fastening our gaze intently upon it. Coleridge writes of fantastic, supernatural things, but also so simply, with so many concrete and exact details, that the world of imagination into which he leads us seems for the time the only real one. The *Lyrical Ballads*, contained four poems by Coleridge, only a small portion of the whole; "The Rime of the Ancient Mariner," however, has the place of honor at the beginning.

Coleridge's Later Life.—The rest of Coleridge's life, though he wrote a good deal of verse, has little importance in the history of poetry. He made a trip, in the Wordsworths' company, to Germany, and there became absorbed in the philosophy of Kant. So far as his later life had any definite purpose, it was spent in interpreting this philosophy to his countrymen. He settled at first in the Lake Country, where he shared a house with his brother-in-law, Southey. The dampness of the lake climate brought on his old neuralgic troubles, and as an escape from pain he resorted again to opium. His bondage to the opium habit, made his life a heartrending succession of half-attempts and whole failures. He planned many books, and partly executed a few; but his chief influence was exerted in talk with his friends, and with those young men who, as his reputation for transcendental wisdom increased, resorted to him as to an oracle of hope and faith, in the years which followed the failure of the French Revolution. In 1814 he voluntarily put himself under the care of a London physician, Dr. Gillman. He lived in the doctor's house, at Highgate Hill near London, from this time forth, and gradually shook himself free from his bondage to the drug which had wrecked him, "the most golden genius born in that age."

Contemporary Glimpses of Coleridge.—William Hazlitt, the critic and essayist, who in his youth saw and talked with Coleridge, says, "His genius had angelic wings, and fed on manna. He talked on forever, and you wished him to talk on forever. His thoughts did not seem to come with labor and effort, but as if the wings of imagination lifted him off his feet. His voice rolled on the ear like a pealing organ, and its sound alone was the music of thought." Of his appearance the same observer says, "His forehead was broad and high, as if built of ivory, with large, projecting eyebrows; and his eyes rolled beneath them like a sea with darkened lustre." Carlyle, who saw him in his later years at Dr. Gillman's, writes: "Coleridge sat on the brow of Highgate Hill, in those years, looking down on London and its smoke-tumult, like a sage escaped from the inanities of life's battles. A sublime man, who, alone in those dark days, had saved his crown of spiritual manhood. The practical intellects of the world did not much heed him, or carelessly reckoned him a metaphysical dreamer. But to the rising spirits of the young generation, he had this dusky, sublime character; and sat there as a kind of Magus, girt in mystery and enigma."

Characteristics of Coleridge's Poetry.—Coleridge's poetry transports us into a world of strange scenery and of supernatural happenings, illuminated by "a light that never was on sea or land." "Kubla Khan" paints an oriental dream-picture, as splendid and as impalpable as the palaces and plunging rivers and "caverns measureless to man," which we sometimes see lifted for a moment out of a stormy sunset. "Christabel," which seems in its fragmentary form to have been planned as the story of a young girl fallen under the spell of an unearthly demon in woman's shape, moves in a mediæval atmosphere blended of beauty and horror; a horror poignantly vague, freezing the heart with its suggestion of all that is malign and cruel in the spirit world. "The Ancient Mariner," Coleridge's one finished masterpiece, stands alone in literature for the completeness with which it creates an illusion of reality while dealing with images and events manifestly unreal. Its great pictures of night and morning, of arctic and tropic seas; its melodies of whispering keel and rustling sails, and of dead throats singing spectral carols; its strange music, richer and more various even than that of "Kubla Khan," though not so grand and spacious—these characteristics, to say nothing of the fruitful lesson lying at its heart, make "The Ancient Mariner" a poem without an equal in its kind. It is manifestly a dream, but a dream caught in a magic mirror, which holds it spellbound in immortal freshness.

Here

III. WILLIAM WORDSWORTH (1770–1850)

Wordsworth's Early Years and Education.—William Wordsworth was born in 1770, at Cockermouth, in Cumberland, on the borders of the Lake region in which he was to spend the greater part of his long life, and the scenery of which he was to weave into all his poetry. His family was of ancient Saxon stock, settled at Peniston in Yorkshire probably from before the Norman Conquest. His mother died when the poet was eight years old, and his father five years later, after William had finished his early school-days at Hawkshead, at the other extremity of the Lake country from his birthplace. After he had grown to manhood, Wordsworth wrote, in a long poem called *The Prelude*, the history of his growth and education. From this "epic of a soul's growth," we learn the influences which moulded his nature, from the time of his earliest conscious experiences to the time when his character was formed and his course decided. Chief among these influences were the mountains, lakes, and streams in the midst of which he was born and reared. His first recollections were of the grassy holms and rocky falls of the Derwent, with Mount Skiddaw, "bronzed with deepest radiance," towering in the eastern sky. At Hawkshead, the place of his schooling, on the banks of Esthwaite Water, he led a life of open-air adventure; but already there was in nature more for him than for his companions. Setting springs for woodcock on the grassy moors, scudding from snare to snare in the night, he felt himself "a trouble to the peace" of the moon and stars; and when he was tempted to take a bird from another's trap he heard low breathings and ghostly footsteps coming after him through the solitary hills. As he clung to the windy face of a cliff, to rob a raven's nest, he felt himself swing loose from the world, suspended in a sky which was "not a sky of earth." As he rowed upon the starlit bosom of Esthwaite Water, the huge peak of Wetherlam seemed to follow him, and visions of "unknown modes of being" frightened his spirit. As he "hissed along the polished ice" in winter games, he would stop suddenly, and feel dizzily the motion of the rolling world. In all this we see the impassioned love of nature, mingled with the sense of some moral and spiritual life behind the face of things, which it was his lifelong task to interpret in poetry. These early days at Hawkshead also made him acquainted with the sturdy dalesmen, whose simple life, with its deep primitive joys and sorrows, he was to make his own.

In 1787 he entered St. John's College, Cambridge. His college life meant little to him, for his lore was not of a kind that can be learned from books. One of his summer vacations he spent in a walking trip through Switzerland; another in revisiting the scenes of his boyhood, taking part in country merry-makings. Once, he tells us, he had danced till morning, and walked home in a glorious dawn. As he walked there came upon him for the first time the full sense of his mission as a poet.

> "My heart was full; I made no vows, but vows
> Were then made for me; bond unknown to me
> Was given, that I should be, else sinning greatly,
> A dedicated spirit."

Wordsworth and the French Revolution.—After graduation he spent some time in London. Late in 1791 he went to France, intending to pass the winter at Orleans, learning French. France was then "standing on the top of golden hours"; the Revolution was in its first stage; the Bastille had fallen, symbol of all the tyranny and injustice of the past, and men stood as in the dawn of a new day, flushed with visions of a world from which "man's inhumanity to man" should be forever banished. Wordsworth passed through Paris, and spent the greater part of the year at Orleans and Blois, returning to Paris late in 1792, when the excesses of the Reign of Terror were already beginning. During his year of residence in France Wordsworth had become a fervid revolutionist. He dimly foresaw the awful anarchy toward which France was drifting, but his confidence was as yet unimpaired. He had wild dreams of throwing in his lot with the revolutionists, and striving for a place of control. His friends in England, seeing no other way to compel him to

WILLIAM WORDSWORTH
From a painting by W. Boxall

return, took the prosaic but effectual course of stopping his remittances of money. He returned to England at the close of 1792. The later course of the revolution induced in him a profound despondency and pessimism. During this critical period, he says, his sister Dorothy's influence kept alive the poet in him, by directing his mind toward the sources of permanent strength and joy, which lie in nature and in human sympathy:

> "She gave me eyes, she gave me ears;
> And humble cares, and delicate fears;
> A heart, the fountain of sweet tears,
> And love, and thought, and joy."

Real Beginning of Wordsworth's Poetical Career.—The residence of Wordsworth and his sister at Alfoxden, with Coleridge, 1797–1798, marks the true beginning of Wordsworth's poetic career; for up to this time, though he had written much, he had not found his genuine voice. In "We are Seven," "Expostulation and Reply," "Lines in Early Spring," "Tintern Abbey," and other pieces written at this time, the true Wordsworth is apparent. During the winter in Germany which followed, he added to these pieces some of his most characteristic poems, such as "She Dwelt Among the Untrodden Ways," "Three Years She Grew in Sun and Shower," and "The Two April Mornings."

Wordsworth at Grasmere and at Rydal Mount.—On his return, he settled with his sister in a cottage at Grasmere. In 1802 he married his cousin, Mary Hutchinson, to whom the poem beginning, "She Was a Phantom of Delight" is addressed. At Grasmere, and afterward at Rydal Mount at the other end of the lake, he lived for fifty years among the Cumberland dalesmen, leading an existence as pastoral and as frugal as theirs, reading little and meditating much, looking with deep, unwearied delight upon the mountains and skies and waters which had fascinated him in boyhood. A legacy of nine hundred pounds from a friend, Raisley Calvert, and later an appointment as distributor of stamps for Westmoreland, made him independent, and left virtually his whole time free for the pursuit of poetry.

Though living apart from the world, he was surrounded

by his friends. Southey had made a home a few miles over the hills, at Keswick. De Quincey, the essayist, took the Wordsworth cottage at Grasmere, after the poet's removal to Rydal Mount. Coleridge "came to and fro in those fruitless, unhappy wanderings which consumed a life that once promised to be so rich in blessings and in glory." As Wordsworth's reputation grew, many pilgrims found their way to his quiet retreat. Sir Walter Scott and his young wife visited him, and in later years (1833) Emerson came from New England, to talk with one of the five great men whom he had crossed the Atlantic to see.

The heights of his poetic achievement are marked successively by such pieces as "Michael" (1800); "The Leech-Gatherer," the sonnets to Milton, to Toussaint L'Ouverture, "It is a Beauteous Evening," and "Westminster Bridge" (1802); "The Solitary Reaper" and "Yarrow Unvisited" (1803); the "Ode to Duty," "To a Skylark," and *The Prelude* (1805); "The World Is Too Much With Us," and "The Ode on the Intimations of Immortality" (1806); "Song at the Feast of Brougham Castle" (1807), and *The Excursion* (1814). For many years his poetry met with neglect and ridicule, but he gradually drew to himself the attention and veneration of the best minds. The crowd turned aside to follow first Scott, then Byron, and then Tennyson; but those whose suffrages were of most value rallied in increasing numbers about the "good old steel-gray figure" of the Cumberland poet; and before his death in 1850, he enjoyed a late but sure renown.

Wordsworth as Portrayed by Emerson and Carlyle.— Emerson has left us a delightful account of his meeting with Wordsworth at Rydal Mount. The white-haired, grey-clad poet led his visitor out into the garden, and showed him the gravel walk where thousands of his lines had been composed. Then, without solicitation, he offered to recite three sonnets which he had just written. "He recollected himself for a few moments," continues Emerson, "and then stood forth and repeated, one after another, the three entire sonnets with great animation. This recitation was so unlooked for and surprising—he, the old Wordsworth, standing apart and reciting to me in a garden walk like a school-boy declaiming—that I was at first near to laugh; but recollecting myself, that I had come thus far to see a poet, and here he was chanting poems to me, I saw that he was right and I was wrong, and gladly gave myself up to him." Beside this we may well place Carlyle's portrait of him, as he appeared ten years before his death. "A fine, wholesome rusticity, fresh as his mountain breezes, sat well on the stalwart veteran. His face bore marks of much, not always peaceful, meditation; the look of it not bland or benevolent, so much as close, impregnable, and hard. He was large-boned, lean, but still firm-knit, tall, and strong-looking when he stood; a right good old steel-grey figure, with a fine rustic simplicity and dignity about him and a veracious *strength* looking through him."

The Nature-Poetry of Wordsworth.—Wordsworth was gifted with an eye and an ear marvellously sensitive to those elusive impressions which most persons pass by without noticing at all. This sensibility was increased by a long life spent in the country, in a region full of charm and even of grandeur. His poetry is full of exquisitely noted sights and sounds—the shadow of the daisy on the stone, the mist which follows the hare as she runs across a rain-drenched moor, the echo of the cuckoo's voice, the varying noise of waters, and the many voices of the wind. "To read one of his longer pastoral poems for the first time," it has been said, "is like a day spent in a new country." And all these sights and sounds are given with absolute truthfulness to the fact. Wordsworth writes "with his eye on the object," content to portray what he sees. He learned from Burns that "verse can build a princely throne on humble truth"; and everywhere he gives an impression of unquestioning faithfulness to the fact which his senses have perceived. It follows that the greater part of his nature-studies are in a low key. Especially noteworthy is the predominance in Wordsworth of broad elementary impressions—mere darkness and light, the silence of the sky, the moon "looking round her when the heavens are bare," the twilight with its one star, the breathlessness of the evening sea, the lonesomeness of upland fields, the "sleep that is among the lonely hills." It is the keenness of Wordsworth's sensibility to nature, and his quiet, religious acceptance of her as she is, and his unwearied delight in her broadest and simplest phases, which together make him the first of her poets.

Wordsworth's Treatment of Human Nature.—This same sobriety and truth of tone, this same reverent regard for the great commonplaces of life, characterize also Wordsworth's treatment of human nature. He deals with the broad elementary passions, the everyday affections, occupations, and duties, in a state of society where man is simplest and nearest to the soil. In many of his best poems, indeed, the human beings whom he pictures seem almost a part of the landscape, an emanation from nature herself, like the trees or the rocks. The figure of the Leech-gatherer on the moor seems as much a part of the natural landscape as the pool by which he stands. The woman who speaks to the poet in "Stepping Westward" seems a part of the sunset, so blended is she with the scene. In "The Highland Reaper" the singing of the girl comes out of the heart of the day, like the spirit of ancestral Scotland telling over its "old unhappy far-off things, and battles long ago"; she is hardly more of a human personality than the cuckoo or the nightingale to which the poet compares her voice. Even when he looks closer at his human characters, and shows us their passions and the accidents of their life, they still partake of the simplicity and breadth of external nature. The story of Margaret, in the first book of *The Prelude*, illustrates this, as does in a still better way "Michael," the greatest example of Wordsworth's power to give to the simple tragedies of the peasant world a kind of biblical majesty. He is the poet of that joy and sorrow which is "in widest commonalty spread." He looks to find the true significance of life on its lower levels. The best praise he can give his own wife is that she is a "being breathing thoughtful breath," in whose countenance meet sweet household records and promises. For Milton his best praise is that, although his "soul was like a star and dwelt apart," yet it laid upon itself "the lowliest duties" along "life's common way."

Wordsworth's Mysticism : " Tintern Abbey."—Yet nature is for Wordsworth, even when he portrays her external aspect with the most naked truth, never merely a physical fact; nor has man, even when most blended in with her external features, merely a physical relation to her. On the contrary, nature is everywhere full of spiritual meaning, and speaks mysteriously to the spirit in man, working upon him by the power of kinship and mutual understanding. Perhaps the most complete expression of this aspect of his thought is "Tintern Abbey," which appeared in the *Lyrical Ballads*. "Tintern Abbey" was written during a walking tour which Wordsworth took in 1798, in company with his sister, through a country familiar to him in earlier years. The well-remembered scenery of the river Wye calls up before his musing thought the picture of his boyhood. He shows how the influences of nature, acting upon the plastic soul of youth, bear fruit in later life, in "sensations sweet felt in the blood and felt along the heart," and "little nameless unremembered acts of kindness and of love"; and how they lift the spirit which remembers them, to

> " that blessed mood
> In which the burden of the mystery,
> In which the heavy and the weary weight
> Of all this unintelligible world
> Is lightened . . .
> While with an eye made quiet by the power
> Of harmony, and the deep power of joy,
> We see into the life of things."

And he suggests an explanation for this strange power which nature has to soothe and ennoble the human soul, namely, that throughout nature there is diffused the active spirit of God:—

> " Whose dwelling is the light of setting suns,
> And the round ocean, and the living air,
> And the blue sky, and in the mind of man;
> A motion and a spirit, that impels
> All thinking things, all objects of all thoughts,
> And rolls through all things."

In many noble poems Wordsworth developed the three themes here given out: the eternal beauty of nature, which waits everywhere about us "to haunt, to startle, and waylay"; the power of that beauty to heal, gladden, and fortify whoever gives it welcome; and the mystic source of this power, the spirit of God, hidden yet apparent in all the visible creation. Perhaps the most exquisite expression he has given to the idea of nature's formative power upon the soul, and through the soul upon the body of man, is the poem beginning "Three Years She Grew in Sun and Shower."

"Ode on the Intimations of Immortality."—In Wordsworth's school-days at Hawkshead, the world would sometimes, he tells us, seem suddenly to dissolve, and he would fall into an abyss of idealism from which he had to bring himself back to reality by grasping at the wall by the roadside, or by stooping to pick up a stone. This ideal habit of mind, sobered and strengthened by reflection, gives to his poetry a peculiarly stimulating character. In reading him, we never know when the actual landscape and the simple human story will widen out suddenly into some vaster theme, looking beyond space and time; so that he awakens in us a kind of apprehension or expectancy which forces us to look below the surface of his simplest poem, and to be on the alert for a meaning deeper than its primary one. His greatest poem, the "Ode on the Intimations of Immortality," is also the one in which speculation is the boldest. In this wonderful ode, which Emerson called the "high-water mark of poetry in the nineteenth century," the poet looks back with passionate regret to the lost radiance of his childhood, and tries to connect childhood reassuringly not only with manhood and old age, but also with a previous existence, whence it brings its light of innocence and joy. The poem is a product of that majestic kind of imagination which transcends space and time, and makes

> "Our noisy years seem moments in the being
> Of the eternal silence."

IV. OTHER ROMANTIC POETS OF THE FIRST GROUP: SOUTHEY AND SCOTT

Southey.—It has long been the custom to associate with Wordsworth and Coleridge, to form the triad of "Lake poets," the name of Robert Southey, Coleridge's colleague in the youthful scheme of pantisocracy. Southey was a man of amiable and nobly upright character, and of unwearied industry; he had a pure-hearted passion for literature, and an unfaltering belief in his own mission. He wrote several very long and ambitious romantic poems, of which *The Curse of Kehama* is perhaps the best; and many prose works, among which his *Life of Nelson* holds a worthy place in literature as a model of succinct and vivid biography. Some of his short poems have an assured place with posterity, especially his verses "To My Books," in which his devotion to the literary life finds classic expression. But his long poems have lost most of their interest, and he holds his place in the Lake triad less by poetic gift than by personal association.

Scott's Career as a Poet.—The interest in the Middle Ages and the storied past, which we have traced through Gray, Chatterton, and Ossian, culminated in the works of Sir Walter Scott. Scott was born in Edinburgh in 1771; his father was a lawyer, but was descended from a vigorous and war-like border clan. Scott developed early a passion for the ballad minstrelsy of his land; and he spent many days of his youth roaming over the country, gathering ballads and scraps of ballads from the lips of Lowland peasants. His collection was published under the title *Border Minstrelsy*. Scott wrote very little original poetry until his thirty-fourth year. In 1805 appeared *The Lay of the Last Minstrel*, in which a thread of "gothic" superstition is woven into a tale of Scotch border life in the Middle Ages. This was followed in 1808 by *Marmion*. *Marmion* exhibited in much greater measure the brilliant descriptive color, the swift and powerful narrative movement, and the ringing, energetic music, which had made the "Lay" instantly popular; and it showed a great advance over the earlier poem in life-likeness and breadth. Scarcely more than a year later appeared *The Lady of the Lake*, a story softer and more idyllic than *Marmion*, yet not lacking in wild and stirring episodes; in it Scott came far nearer than he had done in his earlier poems, to the broad imaginative handling of mediæval Scotch life which he afterward gave in his prose romances.

Qualities of Scott's Poetry.—These three poems, presenting many of the new romantic motives in popular and attractive form, were greeted with delight. The diction employed in them was fresh, but not, like the language of Coleridge and Wordsworth, so startlingly novel as a literary medium that it repelled the unaccustomed ear. The metre was strong and buoyant, appealing powerfully to a public weary of the monotonous couplets of the preceding age, but unable to appreciate the delicate melodies of the "Songs of Innocence and Experience" and the "Lyrical Ballads." The wild scenery, brightly and firmly painted, the character delineation, picturesque and broad; and the vigorous sweep of the story—all contributed to give these stirring verse-tales a popularity which they have never lost. Scott himself described the peculiar excellence of his poetry truly enough, though with characteristic modesty, as consisting in a "hurried frankness of composition which pleases soldiers, sailors, and young people of bold and active disposition."

Scott's metrical tales did much to win the battle for romantic poetry. He was, however, not much in earnest as a poet; and when the public turned to the more highly colored verse-tales of Byron, Scott cheerfully resigned his place to the younger man, and began his far greater work in prose.*

First and Second Poetic Groups Contrasted.—The group of poets who came to manhood when the French Revolution was at its height, reacted during the Napoleonic wars into settled conservatism. The two poets whom we now approach, Byron and Shelley, took up the torch of revolution which had been kindled in France during their childhood, and carried it flaming into new regions of thought and feeling.

* (For the discussion of Scott's prose work, and a fuller account of his life, see Chapter XIV.)

Here

V. GEORGE GORDON, LORD BYRON (1788–1824)

Byron's Life.—George Gordon, Lord Byron, was born in 1788, of a family of noblemen notorious for their pride and their passionate temper. Their family seat was at Newstead Abbey. They had come to England with the Conqueror, and their names had figured in a score of battle-rolls. The poet's great-uncle had been forced to flee from society, after being convicted of manslaughter. The poet's father, Captain John Byron, was a rake and spendthrift, who deserted his wife after the birth of their son; and the mother to whose care Byron was left was a woman of weak and violent disposition. With these antecedents and under these influences, it is not strange that the boy grew up proud, sullen, and reckless. He was of extraordinary physical beauty, and a lameness of one foot added to this a touch of pathos. Personal fascination was his from the first. He mastered his little world of school-fellows at Harrow with the same enthralling power of personality which later took captive the imagination of Europe. His first volume of poems, *Hours of Idleness* (1807), was faithful to the school of Pope, a poet for whom Byron throughout his life professed an unswerving admiration. The immature little book was mercilessly ridiculed in the *Edinburgh Review*. Byron nursed his revenge, and in 1809, after he had taken his hereditary seat in the House of Lords, he published a vigorous onslaught upon his critics, entitled *English Bards and Scotch Reviewers*. It is significant that his first note-worthy performance should have been in a satiric vein, and occasioned by a blow to his personal pride.

Two years later the young poet set off upon his travels. Not content with the conventional "grand tour," he pushed on into Turkey, Greece, and the islands of the Ægean; sharing the hospitality of robber chieftains, rescuing distressed beauties from the harem, and doing many other romantic things. The public, at any rate, was eager to ascribe all these adventures to him, incited thereto by the lurid verse-romances, *The Giaour* (1813), *The Corsair* (1814), and others, which he poured out with prodigal swiftness after his return

LORD BYRON

From a painting by J. Phillips, R. A.

to England in 1812. These verse-tales were preceded, however, by the first two cantos of *Childe Harold*, the publication of which brought instant applause. " I awoke one morning," says Byron, " and found myself famous."

Byron's marriage to Miss Milbanke, in 1815, was followed a year later by a separation from his wife and by his final departure from his native country. The next years he spent in Switzerland and Italy, part of the time in company with Shelley. To this period belong his most important works, the later cantos of *Childe Harold* (1816–1818), the dramas *Manfred* (1817) and *Cain* (1821), and his satiric masterpiece, *Don Juan* (1819–1824). The romance of his life was crowned by a romantic and generous death. In 1824 he went to Greece, to join the revolutionary forces gathered to liberate that country from the tyranny of the Sultan. He was given command of an expedition against the Turkish stronghold of Lepanto, but was seized with fever in the swamps of Missolonghi, and died before he had had time to prove his ability in the field. On his death-bed he imagined himself, in his delirium, at the head of his Suliote troops, leading an attack upon Lepanto, and cried, " Forward, forward, follow me ! "

Byron's Eastern Tales and Dramas.—In his Eastern tales and his dramas, Byron presents under many names one hero—himself, or rather an exaggerated shadow of himself. The Conrads and Laras of the tales are all imperious and lonely souls in revolt; mysteriously wicked, infernally proud, quixotically generous, and above all melancholy. In *Manfred* and *Cain* these crude outlines became imposing silhouettes, thrown out sharply against a back-ground half real and half supernatural. The scene of *Manfred* is laid in the high Alps, where the hero lives in his castle in gloomy and bitter isolation, communing with unearthly powers, and scornfully working out his dark fate. In the drama of *Cain*, we follow the earthly rebel and first shedder of human blood, under the guidance of Lucifer, the rebel angel, into Hell and Chaos, where he finds grounds for his hatred of God and man. It was by these plays that Byron earned his title as founder and chief exemplar of the "Satanic school" of poetry. They are perhaps the most terrible expression of egoism to be found in our literature.

Byron as a Descriptive Poet: " Childe Harold."—*Childe Harold* presents the Byronic hero in a softer mood, as a pensive wanderer through Europe and the East. In the third and fourth cantos, the scene of which is laid among the lakes and mountain solitudes of Switzerland, the decaying glories of Venice, and the imperial ruins of Rome, the poet's imagination is genuinely kindled, and the passages which celebrate these scenes are among the triumphs of descriptive poetry in our language. Doubtless Shelley's inspiring companionship had much to do with the elevation of mood and style which these later cantos show. Byron paints his pictures in free, bold strokes, and with a pomp of rhetoric well suited to his grandiose subjects. His music, too, is loud and sonorous; without the heartfelt, searching beauty of greater melodists, but with an orchestral sweep and volume which stir the blood.

Byron as a Satirist: " Don Juan."—In *Don Juan*, however, Byron first found his genuine voice, and it proved to be neither dramatic nor lyric, but satiric. *Don Juan* is a comprehensive satire upon modern society. The hero is a Castilian youth, a light-hearted, irresponsible, pagan creature, who wanders through Turkey, Russia, and England, meeting all sorts of adventures, particularly such as exhibit the social corruption which the world attempts to hide under a conventional veneer. The poem was, in effect, a long peal of scornful laughter flung at British cant, at that famous British cant which Byron declared was in his day the main-spring of his countrymen's life, both national and private.

Byron's Relation to his Age.—We cannot hope to understand Byron without taking into account the state of England, and of continental Europe, in his day. England, in her struggle against the social chaos which the French revolution threatened, had entrenched herself in conservatism. Her one desire was to preserve her ancient institutions, however false they had become. Her ruling classes, taking advantage of this mood of the people, used it to their own selfish ends.

Hypocrisy, bigotry, misgovernment, and oppression were the order of the day. Against this state of things Byron revolted with all his strength.

After the defeat of Napoleon at Waterloo, the governments of Europe, under the leadership of Metternich, the Austrian prime-minister, entered into a "Holy Alliance" to crush the spirit of democracy, and to hold the continental peoples in much such a bondage as England had voluntarily assumed. The spirit of revolution, however, was still alive, no longer joyous and hopeful, but gloomy and bitter. So long as it had been possible for men to dream of freedom and justice for all mankind, the revolutionary spirit had been social, but when these large dreams were shattered, society became the enemy of the freedom-loving soul. This mood of personal rebellion, in which the individual stands apart in lawless isolation, waging dark and hopeless war against a hateful world, is the mood of Byron. His rebellion had in it an element of the theatrical and the spectacular, but at bottom it was terribly sincere. All Europe felt its sincerity, and worshipped him as the embodiment of its own unhappy ideal. His fascinating personality, his brilliant, defiant life, the romantic mystery which surrounded him wherever he went, the audacity and energy of his verse, all united to make him the idol of his age. Even his loose-flowing neckerchief, his trick of deranging his hair and leaving his shirt collar unbuttoned, became as signs and portents to his generation. But this Byron-worship, for all its extravagance, was founded upon a real greatness in the man, a greatness which all men felt, from the janitor who kept his rooms at college to Shelley and Goethe. Goethe declared that Byron's personality was the greatest which the world had seen, and he enshrined him in the second part of *Faust* as Euphorion, the genius of modern poetry.

Byron in Our Day.—Byron's reputation as a poet has now considerably declined. In the first place, we miss in his poetry the pleasure which comes from perfected art; for Byron was a careless and hasty worker. *Lara* he wrote "while undressing after coming home from balls and masquerades, in the year of revelry, 1814. The *Bride* was written in four, the *Corsair* in ten days." He would not or could not revise.

"If I miss my first spring," he said, "I go growling back to my jungle." All his poetry is, so to speak, an improvisation. But while it has the defects, it has also the charm of whatever is impromptu and spontaneous; it has force and fire; at its best, it rushes on in a splendid stream, as if rejoicing in its own unbridled might.

Another, and a more serious flaw in Byron's work to the reader of to-day, is that we miss in it some of the sincerity which his own age felt. A suspicion of "pose," of empty rhetoric, of false exaggeration, troubles us. His scorn of his fellow men seems morbid; his constant quarrelling with life, his bitter mockery of society, seem one-sided, even a little childish. To do him justice, we must think ourselves back into the age for which he wrote, and see him struggling against what was really hateful in his world. His life, thus viewed, takes on real heroism; we recognize that he battled, after all, for society and not against it. We see him, as has been said, engaged in "the struggle which keeps alive, even if it does not save, the soul."

Here

VI. PERCY BYSSHE SHELLEY (1792–1822)

Shelley's Early Life.—Percy Bysshe Shelley was born just when the eyes of all Europe were fixed in hope and fear upon France, and the "stars fought in their courses" for the triumph of a new order. His home contained no elements to control his peculiar temperament. His father was a Whig squire of narrow views; his mother bequeathed to him nothing except her extraordinary beauty. At Eton, among the tyrannies of a great public school, where the "fagging" system was still in force, his sensitive nature was thrown into a fever of rebellion. "I have seen him," wrote a schoolfellow, "surrounded, hooted, baited like a maddened bull"; and when thus set upon, the gentle, high-spirited, excitable boy would be seized with a frenzy and paroxysm of rage which frightened even his persecutors. His shyness and strangeness of manner won him the nickname of "Mad Shelley." In the "Hymn to Intellectual Beauty" he gives a glimpse of his boyhood, when in the awakening spring he pursued through the starlit woods "hopes of high talk with the departed dead," and felt, in the midst of the bright season, the shadow of an "awful loveliness" fall upon him. It is no wonder that his schoolmates thought him strange, or that in the judgment of the world he remained "Mad Shelley " to the end of his life.

He went to Oxford in 1810. Here his closest friend was Thomas Hogg, son of a North-country Tory farmer, and as keen-sighted and shrewd as Shelley was dreamy and idealistic. Hogg has left us a vivid picture of Shelley at Oxford; of his chambers, wildly littered with books, manuscripts, and apparatus for scientific experiments; of his favorite sports of skimming stones and sailing paper boats; of his outbursts of enthusiasm over ideas of justice, and of indignation at any sight of cruelty or oppression; of his rapt search into the mysteries of matter, and his high impassioned discourse concerning the deeper mysteries of mind. Together with his friend, Shelley read the French philosophers of the revolutionary period, and the two young enthusiasts published their views of religion in a pamphlet entitled "The Necessity of Atheism." For this they were expelled, and for a time lived together in London. In August of the same year, 1811, Shelley, then nineteen, eloped to Scotland with Harriet Westbrook, a girl of sixteen, and was married in Edinburgh. Then followed a quixotic attempt to arouse Ireland to seek redress for her national wrongs. The young couple carried on their mission by throwing from the windows of their lodging in Dublin copies of Shelley's "Address to the Irish People," "to every passer-by who seemed likely." They continued the campaign later in Wales, by setting tracts adrift in the sea in sealed bottles, or sending them down the wind in little fire-balloons. The curious mixture in Shelley of the real and the unreal is sharply brought out by the fact that the writings thus fantastically put in circulation are often of grave and simple eloquence, wise in counsel and temperate in tone, and that some of the reforms which they advocate have since been enacted into law.

An acquaintance with William Godwin, a revolutionary philosopher and novelist, led Shelley to write *Queen Mab*,

PERCY BYSSHE SHELLEY
From a painting by Geo. Clint, R. A.

a crude poem attacking dogmatic religion and the social state. The scandal which it created was soon increased by incidents of another kind. Shelley's marriage with Harriet Westbrook had not only been hasty and rash; it had been founded upon no sympathy of nature or genuine love, but had come from Shelley's impetuous offer to release her from what he deemed the "oppression" of her parents. They separated, and Shelley formed a union with a daughter of William Godwin. This was followed by Harriet Westbrook's suicide, and the departure of Shelley and Mary Godwin from England into lasting exile. The shock of the tragedy dealt a blow to Shelley's already delicate health, and pursued him with dark thoughts in the bright land of Italy, where he spent the short remainder of his life.

Shelley in Italy.—In Italy his powers developed rapidly. At Este, near Venice, where the Shelleys had gone to be near Byron, the beautiful "Lines Written Among the Euganean Hills," were composed, as well as "Julian and Maddalo," a poem in which Byron figures. At Rome, amid the tangle of flowers and vines which at that time covered the mountainous ruins of the Baths of Caracalla, Shelley wrote his lyrical drama, *Prometheus Unbound*. "The blue sky of Rome," he writes, "and the effect of the vigorous awakening of spring in that divinest climate, and the new life with which it drenches the spirit even to intoxication, were the inspiration of this drama."

In the same wonderfully fruitful year he produced *The Cenci*, a drama intended for the stage, and written in much more simple and every-day language than his other works. This was composed in a villa near Leghorn, in a glazed terrace at the top of the house, overlooking the Mediterranean and flooded with the sun of the Italian summer, in the almost overpowering intensity of which Shelley's tropic nature took a singular, not to say an uncanny, delight. At Florence, where he went in the fall of the same year, the great "Ode to the West Wind" was composed, in a wood beside the Arno, on a day of magnificent storm, when the wind was collecting the vapors which pour down the autumnal rains.

The next two years, 1820–1821, were spent chiefly at Pisa. Several congenial friends gathered about Shelley. Among them were Lord Byron, Edward Williams, who was to share Shelley's tragic death, and Captain Trelawney, a picturesque and adventurous character, who has left us in his "Reminiscences," a record of Shelley's last days as vivid as Hogg's memorial of the poet's life at Oxford. To this happy period belong some of Shelley's most memorable poems; "The Sensitive Plant," suggested, we are told, by the flowers which crowded Mrs. Shelley's sitting-room, exhaling their fragrance to the rich Italian sunlight; "The Witch of Atlas," written after a trip to the pilgrimage-shrine of Mount San Pellegrino; the "Ode to a Skylark," the most popular of all Shelley's lyrics; and "Epipsychidion," a rhapsody addressed to a beautiful young Italian girl, Emilia Viviani, whom the Shelleys found immured against her will in a convent. This last poem is remarkable as embodying the poet's conception of love, on its ethereal and mystic side. Speaking of "Epipsychidion" to a friend, he said, "It is a mystery; as to real flesh and blood, you know I do not deal in these articles;" and he complained that even the elect among his readers, in their interpretation of the poem, reduced him to the level of a servant-girl and her sweetheart.

"Adonais": Shelley's Death.—Shelley's last days were spent in a bare, high-ceiled, white-washed villa at Lerici, on the Gulf of Spezia. With his friend Williams he had built a sail-boat, christened by Byron the "Don Juan." Shelley was passionately fond of sailing, and much of the poetry of his last months was written while gliding over the flashing blue waters of the gulf. In April of 1821 the news of Keats's death at Rome reached Shelley; and the unfounded belief that it had been accelerated by a sneering review of *Endymion* in the *Quarterly* led him to write the wonderful threnody "Adonais," in the dead poet's memory. At the close of "Adonais," Shelley sees himself swept out by a tempest upon some vast ocean of the spirit:

> "My spirit's bark is driven
> Far from the shore, far from the trembling throng
> Whose sails were never to the tempest given.

The massy earth and spherèd skies are riven!
I am borne darkly, fearfully afar:
Whilst burning through the inmost veil of Heaven,
The soul of Adonais, like a star,
Beacons from the abode where the Eternal are."

In July of 1822, a few months after these prophetic lines were written, Shelley's boat, returning from Leghorn to Lerici, with himself, his friend Williams, and a sailor-boy, was overwhelmed by one of those swift storms which sweep the Mediterranean during the summer heats. Some days later Shelley's body was washed ashore at Viareggio. It was burned by Trelawney and Byron on the beach; the ashes were placed in the Protestant cemetery at Rome, near the grave where, a few months before, Keats had been laid.

Shelley as Seen by his Contemporaries.—Shelley's figure was slight and fragile. His wavy brown hair became gray very early in life, but his face remained to the end strikingly smooth, fresh-colored and youthful. "His features," says Hogg, "were not symmetrical, but the effect of the whole was extremely powerful. They breathed an animation, a fire, an enthusiasm, a vivid and preternatural intelligence, that I never met with in any other countenance." His passion for study was so intense that to open a great book for the first time threw him into a violent excitement—"his cheeks glowed, his eyes became bright, his whole frame trembled, and his entire attention was immediately swallowed up in the depths of contemplation." Trelawney's account of his first meeting with Shelley brings him vividly before our eyes. "Swiftly gliding in, blushing like a girl, a tall, thin stripling held out both his hands; and although I could hardly believe, as I looked at his flushed, feminine, and artless face, that it could be the poet, I returned his warm pressure. After the ordinary greetings and courtesies he sat down, and listened. I was silent from astonishment. Was it possible this mild-looking, beardless boy could be the veritable monster, at war with all the world? excommunicated by the fathers of the church, deprived of his civil rights by the fiat of a grim Lord Chancellor, discarded by every member of his family, and denounced by the rival

sages of our literature as the founder of a 'Satanic school'"?
Among the circle of his Pisan friends, the poet was known
by two nicknames, "Ariel" and "The Snake." Both are
highly descriptive. The first suggests his unearthliness and
spirituality; the second was given him because of his sinuous
figure, noiseless, gliding movement, bright eyes, and perhaps,
too, because of a slight touch of the uncanny in him. Yet it
would leave us with a false impression not to remember that
all his friends testify to his manliness, his genuineness, his
virile mind. The fibre of his nature was as strong as it was
delicate and strange.

The " Prometheus Unbound."—Shelley's most characteristic work, both in thought and style, is *Prometheus Unbound*. The subject was suggested by a lost drama of
Æschylus, in which Prometheus, the heroic friend and lover
of mankind, was unchained from a bleak precipice where
the tyrant Zeus had hung him. In Shelley's treatment Prometheus represents, not a superhuman helper of mankind,
but Mankind itself, heroic, just, gentle, sacredly thirsting
after liberty and spiritual gladness, but chained and tortured
by the ruler of Heaven. In the fulness of time Demogorgon
(Necessity) hurls the tyrant from his throne; and Prometheus,
amid the songs of Earth and the Moon, is united to Asia,
the spirit of love in nature. Here as elsewhere, Shelley
shows himself a child of the French Revolution, in believing
that it is only some external tyranny—the might of priests
and kings, the weight of "custom," the dark dreams of superstition—which keeps mankind from rising to his ideal stature.
But if the philosophy of *Prometheus Unbound* is immature,
and tinged with the misconceptions of the time, the nobility
of its mood, the heroic enthusiasm which it voices, make it
eternally inspiring. And for its spirit of sacred passion the
verse of the poem is a glorious vesture. The unearthly beauty
of its imagery, the keen ethereal music of its songs and
choruses, make this not only Shelley's highest achievement,
but a fixed star in the firmament of poetry.

Shelley as a Lyric Poet.—It is in its lyrics that *Prometheus*
reaches its greatest altitudes, for Shelley's genius was essentially lyrical. In all his best songs and odes, the words

seem to be moved into their places in response to some hidden tune, wayward and strange in its movement, but always rounding into a perfect whole. Such a poem as that beginning "Swiftly Walk Over the Western Wave" obeys a higher law than that of regularity, and with all its waywardness it is as perfect in shape as a flower. The rhythmical structure of the "West Wind" should be studied as an example of Shelley's power to make the movement of verse embody its mood. In this ode, the impetuous sweep and tireless overflow of the *terza rima*,* ending after each twelfth line in a couplet, suggest with wonderful truth the streaming and volleying of the wind, interrupted now and then by a sudden lull. Likewise in the "Skylark," the fluttering lift of the bird's movement, the airy ecstasy and rippling gush of its song, are subtly mirrored in the rhythm.

Shelley's Myth-making Power; His "Unreality."—Another main peculiarity of Shelley as a poet is what may be called his "myth-making" power. His poetry is full of "personifications" which, although in origin not different from those which fill eighteenth-century poetry with dead abstractions like "smiling Hope" and "ruddy Cheer," are imagined with such power that they become real spiritual presences, inspiring wonder and awe. Such are the "Spirits of the Hours" in *Prometheus Unbound,* such is the spirit of the west wind in the ode just mentioned, the latter a sublime piece of myth-making. It is in "Adonais," however, that this quality is best exhibited. To mourn over the dead body of Keats there gather Splendors and Glooms, grief-clad Morning and wailing Spring, desolate Hours, winged Persuasions and veiled Destinies, and the lovely dreams which were the exhalation of the poet's spirit in life.

Shelley deals less with actualities than does any other English poet. His imagery is that of a dream world, peopled by ethereal forms and bathed in prismatic light. He is at the other pole from Wordsworth's homeliness and large acceptance of nature as she is. Hence an air of unreality rests over Shelley's work, an unreality made more conspicuous by his unpractical theories of conduct and of society. Matthew

* Ten-syllable lines rhyming a b a, c b c, d c d, etc.

Arnold called him "a beautiful and ineffectual angel, beating in the void his luminous wings in vain." But beauty such as Shelley's verse embodies cannot be ineffectual; and his burning plea for freedom, for justice, and for loving-kindness, has never ceased to be potent in the deepening earnestness of this century's search after social betterment.

VII. JOHN KEATS (1795–1821)

Keats's Early Life and Poetry.—John Keats was born in Finsbury, London, in 1795. His parentage was humble: his father had been head hostler in a livery stable, had married the daughter of his employer and succeeded to the business. At first the family lived over the stable, but as their affairs prospered they removed to a house in the neighborhood. Keats and his two younger brothers were sent to a good school, kept by the father of Charles Cowden Clark, the poet's intimate friend throughout life. As a schoolboy Keats was a spirited, pugnacious lad, a favorite with all for his "terrier courage," as well as for his "high-mindedness, his utter unconsciousness of a mean motive, his placability, his generosity." A little later his impulsiveness and animal spirits turned into a headlong interest in books, which he devoured in season and out of season. He took up "for fun" the task of translating the entire *Æneid* into prose. His father had died when the boy was ten years old; on the death of his mother he was removed from school, at fifteen, and apprenticed to a surgeon at Edmonton, for a term of five years. He was released a year before this term was concluded, and went up to London to study in the hospitals, and to pass his examination for a surgeon's license. But his growing passion for poetry distracted him from his profession. His last operation was the opening of a man's temporal artery. "I did it," he told a friend, "with the utmost nicety; but reflecting on what passed through my mind at the time, my dexterity seemed a miracle, and I never took up the lancet again." An acquaintanceship with Leigh Hunt opened up to him a circle of friends where his dawning talents found recognition. The circle included Haydon, the painter, who gave the poet his first introduction to Greek art. Hunt turned his attention to the Elizabethans, to Milton, and to the great Italian poets. In these newly discovered glories of literature Keats revelled to intoxication. We are told that, in company with Charles Cowden Clark, he sat up one whole night reading Chapman's Homer; the next morning Keats sent his friend the magnificent sonnet, "On First Looking into Chapman's Homer," by far the finest thing which had yet come from his pen. In 1817, a year after he gave up surgery, he published a little volume containing, besides this sonnet, a number of other early poems. The most interesting of these juvenile pieces is the one beginning, "I Stood Tiptoe Upon a Little Hill," which shows that his feeling for nature was already exquisite, and his observation keen; and "Sleep and Poetry," where his young devotion to his art is beautifully apparent.

"**Endymion.**"—After the publication of his first volume of poems, Keats went to the Isle of Wight, and later to Margate on the seashore. He writes from there that he "thinks so much about poetry, and so long together, that he cannot get to sleep at night," and is "in continual burning of thought." By this time he was deep in his first long poem, *Endymion*, which tells the story of the Latmian shepherd beloved by the moon-goddess. *Endymion* was published in 1818. The opening passage of the poem, the Hymn to Pan, and many other lines and short passages, are worthy of the Keats that was to be; but as a whole *Endymion* is chaotic, and too full of ornament. Nobody knew this better than Keats himself, as is testified to both by his letters and by the proudly humble preface in which he describes the poem as a "feverish attempt rather than a deed accomplished," and hopes that "while it is dwindling I may be plotting, and fitting myself for verses fit to live." This preface should have disarmed the most unfriendly of critics, but it did not. The *Quarterly* printed a sneering review, and *Blackwood's* rudely ordered him "back to the shop, Mr. John, back to plasters, pills, and ointment-boxes!"

Keats's Last Volume; His Death.—To what purpose Keats "plotted," the wonderful volume published two years

JOHN KEATS

From a painting by Joseph Severn

later, in 1820, shows. It was entitled *Lamia, Isabella, The Eve of St. Agnes, and other Poems;* besides the pieces named, it contained the great odes, "On Melancholy," "On a Grecian Urn," "To Psyche," and "To a Nightingale," and the heroic fragment, "Hyperion." Two years had done wonders in deepening and strengthening his gift. During these two years he had had experience of death, in the loss of his beloved brother Tom, by consumption; he had met Fanny Brawne, and conceived for her a consuming and hopeless love. The funds which he had inherited were all but exhausted, and he was confronted with poverty. His health began to fail; the disease which had carried off his brother progressed with dreadful rapidity in his highly-strung physique. To Shelley, who had invited him to stay at Pisa, he wrote in the summer of 1820, "There is no doubt that an English winter would put an end to me, and do so in a lingering and hateful manner." In September, under the care of his generous friend, the artist Joseph Severn, he took passage for Naples. While detained by contrary winds off the English coast he wrote his last sonnet, the beautiful one beginning "Bright Star, Would I Were Steadfast As Thou Art," with its touching veiled tribute to Fanny Brawne, whom he was not to see again. The poet's eyes were already darkening when he reached Rome. In February of 1821, in a house overlooking the Piazza di Spagna, he died, and was buried in the Protestant cemetery by the Aurelian Wall, where Shelley's ashes were soon to be laid. On his tomb are carved, according to his own request, the words, "Here lies one whose name was writ in water." In a hopefuller time and in a mood of noble simplicity, he had said, "I think I shall be among the English poets after my death."

Keats as a Man.—Keats's appearance is thus summed-up by one of his later biographers, from the many descriptions left us by his friends: "A small, handsome, ardent looking youth—the stature little over five feet; the figure compact and well-turned, with the neck thrust eagerly forward, carrying a strong and shapely head set off by thickly clustering gold-brown hair; the features powerful, finished, and mobile; the mouth rich and wide, with an expression at once combative and sensitive in the extreme; the forehead not high, but broad and strong; the eyebrows nobly arched, and eyes hazel-brown, liquid-flashing, visibly inspired—'an eye that had an inward look, perfectly divine, like a Delphian priestess who saw visions.'" Of his impulsive generosity of nature all his friends have left warm testimony. "He was the sincerest friend," says one, "the most lovable associate, the deepest listener to the griefs and distresses of all around him, that ever lived."

Although the body of Keats's work lies remote from everyday human interest, it is a serious mistake to think of him as indifferent to human affairs, or in any sense effeminate. His wonderful letters, with their rollicking fun, their quick human sympathy, their eager ponderings upon life and clear insight into many of its dark places, show a warm and most vital nature. Through many of his later poems, especially the great odes, there breathes a poignant human undertone, which suggests that if he had lived he might have turned more and more to themes of common human experience. Dying as he did at twenty-five, after only three or four years of opportunity, he yet left behind him a body of poetry which has had a greater influence than any other upon subsequent verse. From the youthful work of Tennyson and Browning down to the present day, the poetry of the Victorian age has been deeply affected by Keats's example.

Qualities of Keats's Poetry.—The essential quality of Keats as a poet is his sensitiveness to beauty, and the singleness of aim with which he seeks for "the principle of beauty in all things." He worships beauty for beauty's sake, with the unreasoning rapture of a lover or a devotee. In his first volume he tells of the "dizzy pain" which the sight of the Elgin marbles gave him, of the "indescribable feud" which they "brought round his heart." He opens his second volume with the memorable line, "A thing of beauty is a joy forever"; and in his last volume, at the close of the ode "On a Grecian Urn," he declares that beauty is one with truth.

It is this passion for beauty, working through a very delicate and powerful temperament, which gives to Keats's poetry its richness, and which makes it play magically upon all the senses of the reader. The pure glow of his color reminds us of the great Italian painters; and the music of his best verse has a wonderful mellowness and depth, as if blown softly through golden trumpets. From the first, his poetry has extraordinary freshness, energy, gusto. His use of words is, even in his earliest volume, wonderfully fresh. He revived old words, coined new ones, and put current ones to a new service, with a confidence and success unequalled by any other English poets except Chaucer, Shakespeare, and Spenser.

The sense of form, which is so conspicuous in Keats's later work, was a matter of growth with him. *Endymion* is formless, a labyrinth of flowery paths which lead nowhere. But the great odes, especially the "Nightingale" and the "Grecian Urn," and the later narrative poems, the "Eve of St. Agnes" and "Lamia," have a wonderful perfection of form, a subordination of part to part in the building up of a beautiful whole, which is the sign of the master-workman. This is particularly true of "St. Agnes' Eve," that latest and perhaps most perfect flower of the old Spenserian tree. The story of Madeline's dream on the haunted eve, of its magical fulfilment through young Porphyro's coming, and of their flight from the castle, is set in a framework of storm and cold, of dreary penance and spectral old age, of barbarous revelry and rude primeval passion, which by a series of subtle and thrilling contrasts marvellously heightens the warm and tender radiance of the central picture; then, when the illusion of reality is at the height, the whole thing is thrown back into the dim and doubtful past by the words

> "And they are gone; aye, ages long ago
> These lovers fled away into the storm."

Keats's strength, which we see in "The Eve of St. Agnes," "Lamia," and the Odes, working in the service of perfect grace, impelled him in *Hyperion* to attempt a theme of the largest epic kind, the overthrow of the old Titan sun-deity Hyperion by the new sun-god Apollo. The subject proved too large for his undeveloped powers, and he threw it aside, on the ground that there were "too many Miltonic inversions in it." Probably the deeper reason was that he felt as yet unequal to the task of giving form to his mighty subject, and his artistic sense would no longer permit him to be content with formlessness. As the poem stands it is a superb fragment, an august portal to a temple which will never be built.

VIII. THE ROMANTIC ESSAYISTS

Lamb and De Quincey.—The leading exponents of the new romantic school of criticism were Charles Lamb and Thomas De Quincey. Lamb was a pioneer in the Elizabethan revival, and De Quincey was one of the earliest champions of the Lake school of poetry. Both of these writers united the criticism of literature with the criticism of life, and it is in the latter province that their most important work was done.

Life of Lamb; His Early Critical Work.—Charles Lamb was born in London in 1775, and was brought up within the precincts of the ancient law-courts, his father being a servant to an advocate of the Inner Temple. From the cloisters of the Temple he was sent to the cloisters of Christ's Hospital, where he had for a classmate Coleridge, his lifelong friend.* At seventeen he became a clerk in the India House, and here he spent the working hours of the next thirty-three years, until he was retired on a pension in 1825.† His lifelong devotion to his sister Mary, upon whom rested an hereditary taint of insanity, has done almost as much as the sweetness and gentle humor of his writings to endear his name. He died in 1834, his sister outliving him and gradually sinking into that mental darkness from which his patience and tenderness had upheld her.

Lamb's first successful literary venture was his *Tales from Shakespeare* (1807), written in collaboration with his sister,

* See Lamb's "Recollections of Christ's Hospital" and "Christ's Hospital Five and Thirty Years Ago," in the Essays of Elia.
† See Elia Essay, "The Superannuated Man."

and intended for children. A year later he published his
Specimens of English Dramatic Poets, with critical comments. His reading in the Elizabethan drama was extensive, his appreciation of its qualities subtle and penetrating, and his enthusiasm for it unbounded. The book did
much to revive the almost extinguished fame of the lesser
dramatists grouped about Shakespeare. It is one of the
earliest, as well as one of the most significant products of the
new romantic criticism.

The " Essays of Elia."—But it is not as a critic of literature, but as a commentator upon life, recording his moods,
his memories, his witty and tender observations, that Lamb
reveals his true greatness. The *Essays of Elia,** published
at intervals in the *London Magazine,* were at length gathered
together and republished in two series, the first in 1823, the
second ten years later. The essays cover a great variety
of topics, but the approach to the subject is always a personal
one; and it is this intimate quality, communicating to us
the author's odd and lovable personality, which constitutes
their chief charm. Many of them are confessions of personal prejudice, such as the essay entitled "Imperfect Sympathies," where Lamb's dislike of Scotchmen and his taste
for Quakers is made matter of delicious mirth. In "Old
China" Lamb gives a winning picture of his home life with
his sister, who appears here and elsewhere as " Cousin
Bridget." In "Dream Children," a beautiful and deeply
affecting essay, he talks with two children conjured from
nothingness to solace for an hour his lonely hearth. To
turn from an essay like this to the famous extravaganza
entitled "A Dissertation on Roast Pig," is to sound the full
gamut of Lamb's pathos and humor.

The style of these essays is in part borrowed from older
writers, especially the quaint and eloquent essayists of the
seventeenth century; but it is nevertheless wholly new and
individual, betraying its remote origin only by a certain rare-
ness and charming oddity of flavor. The "Elia" papers

---

* The pseudonym Elia was borrowed by Lamb from an Italian clerk in
the South Sea House, named Ellia. The change of spelling has led to the
broadening of the initial letter in pronunciation.

continue the traditions of essay writing fixed by Addison and Steele, but their range is wider, and their treatment of human life is marked by the more searching pathos, the more sensitive and flashing humor, which belong to Lamb as a partaker in the spiritual awakening of the nineteenth century. Like the Queen Anne's men from whom he borrowed the idea of the essay, he cared little for natural beauty, and was essentially a Londoner. London, its streets, its shops, its theatres, was the place of his affection, and he has pictured many of the phases of its life with the vividness that comes from personal delight.

De Quincey: His Life.—In Thomas De Quincey the romantic element is more pronounced, and displays itself not only in his writings, but in the circumstances of his life. He was born in Manchester in 1785, the son of a prosperous merchant in the foreign trade. At sixteen he ran away from the Manchester grammar-school, and spent a summer wandering in North Wales, often sleeping on the open hills or in the tents of gypsies. When the cold weather came on, he made his way to London, where he led a starved and vagrant existence, until he was reclaimed by his family and sent to Oxford. He was one of the earliest converts to the "Lake poetry," and after leaving college he established himself at Grasmere, in the neighborhood of Wordsworth and Southey. Here he lived for more than twenty years, reading prodigiously and eating vast quantities of opium. By reason of some peculiarity of his constitution the drug was less fatal in its workings than is commonly the case; but the splendid and tumultuous dreams which it brought were paid for by periods of awful gloom and lassitude. In his thirty-first year De Quincey married. Forced to earn money by his pen, he published in 1821–1822 the famous *Confessions of an English Opium-Eater*, and from this time forth he poured out magazine articles on almost every conceivable topic. In 1830 he removed, with his wife and children, to Edinburgh, where he resided until his death in 1859.

"Confessions of an Opium-Eater."—His best-known work is also his most characteristic, the *Opium-Eater*, and its sequel, *Suspiria de Profundis*. Only a small portion of the

Opium-Eater deals with the subject of opium-taking. It is an extended autobiography, covering the life of the author from early childhood to about the year 1819, when his bondage to opium became absolute. The most powerful portion of the narrative, aside from the description of his opium sensations, is that which tells of his life of vagrancy and starvation in London, and of his nightly wanderings with "poor Ann" through the crowded desolation of Oxford street. The *Suspiria de Profundis* (Sighs from the Depths) is made up mainly of dream-phantasies transcribed from the wanderings of his mind under the spell of opium, or suggested by them.

De Quincey's Style.—In such strange imaginings as "Levana and Our Ladies of Sorrow," in the *Suspiria*, and the "Dream-Fugue" appended to the *English Mail-Coach*, De Quincey developed a kind of prose closely resembling verse, in its rhythm and its rich imagery. In doing so, he revealed new possibilities in the English tongue. The following passage from the "Opium-Eater" will illustrate the poetical quality of his style. It describes a series of dreams suggested by the sight of a mysterious Malay, who appeared one day at De Quincey's door—"I brought together all creatures, birds, beasts, reptiles, that are found in all tropical regions. . . . I was stared at, hooted at, grinned at, chattered at, by monkeys, by paroquets, by cockatoos. I ran into pagodas, and was fixed for centuries at the summit, or in secret rooms; I was the idol; I was the priest; I was worshipped; I was sacrificed. I fled from the wrath of Brama through all the forests of Asia; Vishnu hated me; Seeva lay in wait for me. I came suddenly upon Isis and Osiris: I had done a deed, they said, which the ibis and the crocodile trembled at. Thousands of years I lived and was buried in stone coffins, with mummies and sphinxes, in narrow chambers at the heart of eternal pyramids. I was kissed, with cancerous kisses, by crocodiles, and was laid, confounded with all unutterable abortions, amongst reeds and Nilotic mud." Upon this and similar passages of richly colored, chanting prose, De Quincey's fame as a writer rests. The qualities of style exhibited in them have had a great influence upon the prose writing of the century, an influence which can be traced in such widely different writers as Bulwer and Ruskin.

Transition to the Victorian Era.—From the death of Byron in 1824 until the decisive appearance of Tennyson in 1842, there was a period of comparative exhaustion in English literature. Keats and Shelley were dead; Coleridge was lost in metaphysics, and Wordsworth had almost ceased to produce poetry of value; Scott died in 1832, and the best work of Lamb was done before that date. During this period of lull, the new forces which were to go to the making of literature during the reign of Victoria, were gathering strength. Tennyson, Browning, and Carlyle had already appeared; and, although they remained as yet comparatively obscure, they were doing some of their greatest work. Thomas Hood (1798–1845), in his "Bridge of Sighs" and "Song of the Shirt," had struck the note of sympathy with the unfortunate and oppressed, which was to swell in volume and depth through the whole course of Victorian literature. We must consider in the next chapter that body of literature, gigantic in bulk and almost infinite in variety, which places the era of Victoria beside that of Elizabeth in literary importance.

REVIEW OUTLINE.—The introduction to this chapter first sets forth briefly the political conditions in England and France during the French Revolution and the Napoleonic wars. It next defines the relation of hostility borne to the Revolution by England as a nation, and the attitude of sympathy which the first group of poets, with Wordsworth at their head, held toward the struggles of France to realize a new form of society. It then shows that after this first poetic group abandoned their revolutionary tendencies and swung back into a conservative position, a second group of writers, of whom Byron and Shelley were the chief, arose to proclaim anew the doctrines of the revolutionists. Only a small portion of the poetry of the age was directly inspired by the Revolution; the influence was for the most part indirect, or rather it was the same impulse toward freedom and truth of life which expressed itself on the one side in social revolution, and on the other in that literary revolution which we call the Romantic movement.

Give a brief account of Coleridge's early life, his friendship with Southey, and his earliest literary efforts. Tell what you can of the relations between Coleridge and Wordsworth. At what time of his life was Coleridge's best poetry written? How did " The Ancient Mariner " come to be written? What was the purpose of Wordsworth and Coleridge in projecting the volume of "Lyrical Ballads"? What aspect of the " Romantic imagination " did each present? Illustrate from " The Ancient Mariner " and " We are Seven." Why were the " Lyrical Ballads " an important landmark in the history of English poetry?

Describe the influences of Wordsworth's earlier and later life which helped to give him his peculiar insight into nature. Give an account of Wordsworth's relation to the French Revolution, in its earlier and its later phases. During what period of his life was Wordsworth's best work done? The three qualities of Wordsworth's nature-poetry noted here are its sensitiveness, its truth, and its breadth; find for yourself passages which illustrate each of these qualities. In what respect is Wordsworth's presentation of nature and his presentation of human nature similar? Consider the suggestion made here of the union of Wordsworth's love of nature, with his love of man and of God. Point out some expression of this threefold and united sentiment in the quotation given from " Tintern Abbey " and if possible, in passages found in your own reading. What is the theme of Wordsworth's greatest poem? What quality of Wordsworth's mind does it especially illustrate?

How did Southey's name come to be closely associated with the names of Wordsworth and Coleridge? In what department of literature was Southey's best work done? What general aspect of the Romantic revival of the eighteenth century found its culminating expression in the poetry of Sir Walter Scott? In what way did Scott's poetry serve as an intermediary between that of the preceding age and the delicate melodies of Wordsworth and Coleridge? What value did Scott put on his own poetry? In what field was his most important work to be done?

Give a brief biographical sketch of Byron. For what common attribute are the names of Byron and Shelley associated? What was the cause of Byron's immense popularity? Who was Byron's persistent hero? Say what you can of Byron's strength and weakness as a poet. What was the most significant quality in his earlier verse-tales? What in his " Childe Harold " ? What in his " Don Juan " ?

Give a sketch of Shelley's life. How do Shelley's manifestations of the spirit of revolution differ from Byron's? Why is Shelley's "Prometheus" said to be his most characteristic work? What is the underlying thought of this poem? Where is its greatest beauty to be found? Explain the metrical structure of Shelley's "Ode to the West Wind." Of whom is Shelley's poem "Adonais" a memorial? What other important English threnodies were written in honor of personal friends who were also poets? (See pages 145 and 306). Study the "Adonais" and explain how it exemplifies Shelley's myth-making power. In what respect is Shelley said to be at the antipodes from Wordsworth?

Give a brief sketch of Keats's life. What were his relations with the following persons: Leigh Hunt, Haydon, Charles Cowden Clark, Fanny Brawne, Shelley, Joseph Severn? What was his own estimate of his first ambitious poem, "Endymion"? What circumstances intervened between the publication of "Endymion" and his last volume to deepen his nature and strengthen his art? From what may it be inferred that Keats, if he had lived, would have turned to poetic themes of a more directly "human" sort? What is Keats's essential quality as a poet? How may we trace the growth of his feeling for artistic form?

Who were the most important prose writers of the new Romantic school? Give a brief account of the life of Lamb. What is the quality that gives to Lamb his peculiar influence? How do Lamb's little studies of life differ from those of Addison and Steele? What is meant by saying that these studies reveal Lamb's participation in the spiritual awakening of the nineteenth century? In what respect does Lamb resemble the Queen Anne essayists?

Give a brief account of De Quincey's life. What is his best-known work? How did De Quincey impart a new impetus to English prose?

READING GUIDE.—For class work upon this period the following list of reading, or as large a portion of it as can be accomplished, is recommended. Coleridge: "The Ancient Mariner," "Kubla Khan," the first part of "Christabel." Wordsworth: "Michael," "The Leech-Gatherer," "Ode on Intimations of Immortality," "Tintern Abbey," "We are Seven," "Lines Written in Early Spring," "To a Sky-lark," "The Solitary Reaper," "Strange Fits of Passion I Have Known," "Three

Years She Grew," "She Dwelt Among the Untrodden Ways," "A Slumber Did My Spirit Seal," "I Travelled Among Unknown Men"; and the sonnets, "Milton, Thou Shouldst Be Living At This Hour," "Scorn Not the Sonnet," "It Is a Beauteous Evening," sonnet on Westminster Bridge, and to Toussaint L'Ouverture. Southey: "Life of Nelson." Scott: "The Lady of the Lake" or "Marmion." Byron: "Childe Harold," third canto, "Mazeppa," "The Prisoner of Chillon." Shelley: "Ode to the West Wind," "To a Sky-lark," "Adonais," "Swiftly Walk Over the Western Wave." Keats: "Ode to a Nightingale," "Ode to a Grecian Urn," "Eve of St. Agnes," "La Belle Dame Sans Merci," sonnet on Chapman's Homer. Lamb: "A Dissertation on Roast Pig," "Mackery End," "Christ's Hospital," "The Superannuated Man," "Old China," "Dream Children." De Quincey: "Revolt of a Tartar Tribe" (or "The English Mail-Coach"), a portion of the "Confessions," the "Dream Fugue."

EDITIONS: "The Ancient Mariner" can be had in the Riverside Literature series, and many other good school editions. The best selection of Wordsworth's poetry is that edited by Matthew Arnold, in the Golden Treasury series (Macmillan). A cheaper volume, also good, is included in Cassell's National Library. Selections from Shelley, from Byron, and from Keats exist in Cassell's Library, and in the Golden Treasury series. Southey's "Life of Nelson" exists in Morley's Universal Library, and many school editions. "Old China" and eight other Elia essays and Lamb's "Tales from Shakespeare," are to be had in the Riverside Literature series; selected essays also in the Camelot series. For the study of De Quincey, the comprehensive volume of selections by M. H. Turk, in the Athenæum Press series (Ginn) is recommended. Volume LXIX of Cassell's National Library contains "The English Mail-Coach" and "Murder as a Fine Art." "The Revolt of a Tartar Tribe," edited by C. W. French, is published by Scott, Foresman; other school editions are numerous.

BIOGRAPHY AND CRITICISM: For advanced biographical study, the English Men of Letters series will furnish abundant material. Essays upon Coleridge, Wordsworth, and Keats may be found in Lowell's works. Matthew Arnold's "Essays in Criticism" contain valuable studies of Wordsworth, Byron, Shelley, and Keats. Many of Lamb's essays have an autobiographic interest: "The Old Benchers of the Inner Temple," "Christ's Hospital Five and Thirty Years Ago" (with its picture of Coleridge's boyhood), "The South Sea House," "Blakesmore," and "Mackery End" all deal with places associated with Lamb's history; "Old China," " Dream Children," and "The Superannuated Man" are more directly personal. For De Quincey's biography, his " Autobiographic Sketches," and the "Confessions of an Opium-Eater" are of fundamental interest.

CHAPTER XIV

THE NINETEENTH CENTURY: THE VICTORIAN ERA

I. INTRODUCTION

Social Changes and Their Effect Upon Literature.—Never before, not even in the troubled seventeenth century, have there been such rapid and sweeping changes in the society of the English-speaking races as have taken place since the beginning of the long reign of Victoria (1837–1901). Among the many circumstances making for change the chief one has been the growth of democracy. The Reform bill of 1832 placed the political power of England in the hands of the middle class, and since that date the ballot has been gradually extended to the working classes. With the growth of democracy has gone the spread of popular education, and a great increase in the number of readers of books. Literature has become in consequence more democratic. It has attempted more and more to reach out to all manner of men, to move, instruct, and inspire them. The great change from hand-labor to machine-labor, which began in the latter half of the eighteenth century, and has continued throughout the nineteenth, has kept the economic basis of society unsettled. Labor troubles have been frequent. Social unrest, and the demand for social justice, have appeared in the work of nearly all the great writers of the time. The growth of manufacture and commerce has brought a great increase of wealth, and added greatly to the comfort and luxury of living; but it has also exposed men to the danger of losing themselves in these external things, at the expense of the inner life. Against this danger the prophets and preachers of the time have striven with all the earnestness that is in them.

During the nineteenth century the means of communication between distant places have been vastly increased. In 1819 the first steamship crossed the Atlantic; in 1830 the first railroad was opened, between Liverpool and Manchester; in 1838 the electric telegraph was introduced into England, and twenty years later the first Atlantic cable was laid. By subsequent inventions and improvements, town has been knit to town, county to county, nation to nation. The telegraph and the modern printing press have laid the news of the world day by day before even the humblest reader. Literature, in consequence, has become broader in its interests. A community of ideas has been established throughout the civilized world; sympathy with life in all its forms has been widened. Historical science has brought, as never before, the buried past before our eyes, and writers have presented the past with a truthfulness not possible in former times. The mental sciences have led to a deeper study of character, a closer analysis of human motives, a broader interest in all kinds and types of human life. Novelists and poets have vied with each other in throwing light upon the secret places of man's soul.

The Growth of Science.—Another great cause of change and unrest has been the growth of science, which has made more gigantic strides in this age than in all the past history of the race. Especially the world-shaking doctrine of evolution, dating from the publication of Darwin's *Origin of Species* in 1859, has given men a new idea of their own origin, of the prehistoric past of the human race. In so doing it has unsettled many old beliefs. It has brought "obstinate questionings" concerning life and death, and has led many men, against their wills, into religious doubt. But here again there have been voices lifted up to declare anew the truths of religion, and to interpret the teachings of science in a spiritual sense.

The " Time-Spirit" in the Great Victorian Writers.—Each of the writers whom we are about to study illustrates some phase of the "time-spirit" which we have tried briefly to describe. Macaulay made it his life-work to put his vast stores of knowledge into a form easy for common men to understand.

Carlyle's rugged figure stands as a protest against the self-satisfied, external view of life to which an age of commerce and of mechanical science is prone. He preaches the dignity of the individual as opposed to the crowd; he utters fierce warnings against the levelling process of democracy. Tennyson took the facts of natural science, and showed the poetry hidden in them; he helped to fight the battle of faith against doubt, and to break down the opposition between science and religion. Browning, and the great novelists, Dickens, Thackeray, and George Eliot, studied the souls of men as they reveal themselves in the actual life about us; or summoned up men and women from the past to reveal their inmost natures. Arnold, in the poetry of his youth, voiced the unrest, despondency, and doubt which afflicted so many sensitive souls in this age of change; his later life he spent in preaching to Englishmen the necessity of being alert to new ideas. Ruskin waged unending war against the vulgarity and ugliness which he believed to be an outgrowth of the commercial basis of modern life, and sought earnestly for some better foundation upon which might be built the society of the future.

here

II. THOMAS BABINGTON MACAULAY (1800–1859)

Life of Macaulay.—Thomas Babington Macaulay was born in 1800 at Rothley Temple in Leicestershire. His father, Zachary Taylor, was an anti-slavery reformer, of a family of Scotch Presbyterians, many of whom had been preachers. His mother was of Quaker descent, and a woman of vigorous intelligence. Many anecdotes are related of the boy Macaulay's startling precocity. He made at seven a "compendium of universal history"; at eight he knew Scott's *Lay of the Last Minstrel* by heart, and himself composed several long epic poems in imitation of it. Histories, odes, and hymns flowed with astonishing facility from his boyish pen. Throughout life he was a prodigious reader, and his memory, surprising to start with, became by cultivation one of the most marvellous on record. He declared that if every copy of *Paradise Lost* or the *Pilgrim's Progress* were destroyed, he would be able to replace them from memory.

At Cambridge, whither he went at nineteen, he took a prominent part in the excited discussion which was then going on all over England concerning the reform of the suffrage laws. He was then, as afterward, a Whig; that is to say, he believed in the gradual extension of liberty, but distrusted violent and revolutionary methods. Before leaving college, he began writing for the reviews. In 1825 his essay on Milton appeared in the *Edinburgh Review*. This essay made him instantly famous. Even the potentates of the critical world, such as Jeffrey, the much-feared editor of the periodical in which the "Milton" appeared, wondered where the brilliant newcomer had "picked up that style."

From this time on Macaulay's career was one of uninterrupted success, both in literature and politics. In 1830 he entered Parliament, in time to take a prominent part in the passage of the Reform bill. Four years later he went to India, as legal adviser to the Supreme Council. He found time from his legal duties to write the essay on Bacon; the essays on Machiavelli, Dryden, Byron, and Dr. Johnson had already appeared. He returned in 1838, with a comfortable fortune saved from his salary, to play once more a leading rôle in the Whig party. He was made Secretary of War and a member of the Privy Council. During these years of active political life he wrote several of his most famous essays, notably those on Addison and on Sir William Temple, and the splendid ones on the Indian pro-consuls, Clive and Warren Hastings, the materials for which he had gathered during his stay in the east.

In 1847 he published his *Lays of Ancient Rome*, dignified and vigorous celebrations, in ballad verse, of the antique civic virtues, as shown in Horatius, Virginius, and other Roman worthies. The next year, after long delay, he began to realize the dream of his life, in the publication of the first part of his *History of England*. This was instantly and immensely popular; and the remainder of the work which he lived to complete increased his success. The History was translated into most of the languages of Europe, and at home took a permanent place as a classic among historical writings. In 1857 he was made a peer of the realm, with the title of Baron Macaulay of Rothley. He died of heart disease, at Holly Lodge, Kensington, in 1859, and was buried in the Poet's Corner in Westminster Abbey.

Character of Macaulay.—Macaulay's nature was practical and unromantic. Carlyle, who was in nearly all respects his opposite, once observed Macaulay's face in repose, as he was turning the pages of a book. "I noticed," he says, "the homely Norse features that you find everywhere in the Western Isles, and I thought to myself, 'Well, any one can see that you are an honest, good sort of fellow, made out of oatmeal!'" The biography of Macaulay written by his nephew Trevelyan, shows him to have been, in his private life, even more "honest and good" than Carlyle knew. When his father's affairs, owing to the old reformer's unworldliness, fell into ruin, Macaulay, then a very young man, quietly shouldered the burden of debt, and set about retrieving the family fortunes. Many of his own hopes were thus frustrated, but he took up the load of responsibility with the sunniest radiance, with the most contagious gladness and high spirits. He made those about him doubt "whether it ever crossed his mind that to live wholly for others was a sacrifice at all." His loyalty to his father led him to break with his party on an anti-slavery bill which was too moderate to suit the old enthusiast's views. In his public career he more than once gave evidence of high and unselfish virtue. He voted for a reform of the bankruptcy laws, though the reform included the suppression of his own Commissionership, and reduced him to such straits that he was forced to sell the gold medals he had won at college. Plainly, he had in him a strain of heroism like that of the Roman worthies of his "Lays"; though his prosperous life kept it for the most part hidden.

Macaulay as Orator and Essayist.—Gladstone has told us that an announcement of Macaulay's intention to speak in Parliament was "like a trumpet call to fill the benches" His powers as an orator were superb, and they furnish a key to his fascination as a writer. In a speech the meaning must be so clearly stated, so skilfully emphasized, that misunderstanding shall be impossible, and the attention of the audience must be continually kept awake by strong contrasts and striking figures of speech. In all these respects Macaulay's essays resemble good oratory. Probably no writer has ever been more skilful than Macaulay in making his whole meaning clear; none more successful in keeping the reader's attention alert, and his dramatic sense excited. He is always vivacious, loud, and positive, never in doubt, and never at a loss. These qualities served him well in his work of popularizing knowledge. From the stores of his capacious memory, he presented in lucid and entertaining form a great mass of fact and opinion, the educative power of which was and still continues to be very great.

The best of the essays are those in which the author paints us the picture of an era, of a social group, or of a single person, addressing his story more to the eye than to the mind. In dealing with the great facts of the inner life Macaulay is often weak. The essay on Bacon, for instance, is an attack upon all higher speculations; Bacon as a master of pure thought is belittled, and the real passion of Bacon's life, philosophy, is held up to ridicule. The essay on Dr. Johnson gives us a very wonderful picture of the old doctor's appearance, manners, and surroundings, but we get from it no insight into his deeper nature. Macaulay is also weak in literary criticism, as he himself, always frank and modest, was the first to declare. "I am not successful," he said, "in analyzing the works of genius. I never have written a page of criticism on poetry or the fine arts which I would not burn if I had the power." In the essay on Milton, which made him famous, he is soon drawn aside from his real subject into a long and heated defence of the Puritan party, with one eye always upon the political conditions of his own time. He is at his best in historical portraiture, and in this field his essays are incomparable. He was most at home in the seventeenth and eighteenth centuries. In his series of brilliant studies on this period he did for it, in the prose essay, almost as much as Shakespeare did for the fifteenth century in his historical plays.

Macaulay as Historian.—In his History he carried these talents into a larger field, and won even a more striking success. His aim was to write a history of England from the accession of James II to the end of George IV's reign, in a manner so concrete, picturesque, and dramatic, that his narrative of actual events should have the fascination of romance, or, as he himself put the case, that it should have the power "to supersede the last fashionable novel upon the dressing-table of young ladies." The portion of the story which he lived to complete is, in fact, presented with a wealth of detail concerning particular persons, places, and events, such as a writer of fiction uses to embody the creations of his fancy. But all this detail is wonderfully merged together, and the whole effect is that of a canvas covered with luminous pictures, which change before our eyes into new groupings, and give place to other spectacles, as in a magic diorama. In the art of story-telling, of chaining the reader's interest with the exciting sweep of events, Macaulay stands first among English historians. He cares little for underlying causes. Not *why*, but *how* things happened, is his concern. But he gives us the story itself with the skill of a great novelist, and in as great fulness. The five volumes which he completed cover only fifteen years. To have covered the whole period which he at first intended, would have filled fifty volumes and—even at the rapid rate at which he worked—would have taken a century and a half in the writing.

Macaulay's Material View of Life.—Macaulay's view of life is extremely practical. He wrote at a time when men were inclined to exchange the longings and aspirations of the Romantic era for a satisfied acceptance of the benefits which commerce, liberal government, and the mechanical sciences were bringing to English life. "A half-acre in Middlesex," he says, "is better than a peerage in Utopia." Of the Crystal Palace exhibition, one of those great industrial fairs upon which this century has lavished so much effort, he can hardly find words to express his admiration. The spread of comfort and of material prosperity, constantly arouses him to eloquence. He flattered his age by his satisfaction with its practical achievements. But meanwhile another voice was raised in fierce protest and warning. Thomas Carlyle, son of one of "the fighting masons of Ecclefechan," arose to scourge and lament over the age like a prophet of old Israel, bidding men ponder what their boasted progress was progress toward, and whether, in their zeal for material improvements, they were not perchance bowing down to heathen idols, forgetting the God of the spirit.

Here   Here

III. THOMAS CARLYLE (1795–1881)

Carlyle's Early Life.—Thomas Carlyle was born in 1795, at Ecclefechan, a village of the Scotch Lowlands. His father was a man of strong character, and of a picturesque and rugged speech to which Carlyle traced his own literary gift. His peasant mother learned to write in order to communicate with her son in absence, and followed his career with more than a mother's devotion. Though the family was very poor, Carlyle received an excellent schooling. At fourteen he walked the eighty miles from his native village to Edinburgh, and entered the university, to prepare himself for the ministry. After graduation, however, he renounced the church career, to his father's deep disappointment, and determined to be "a writer of books." He lived for a number of years in or near Edinburgh, earning a living as school teacher, private tutor, and afterwards as a writer for the magazines.

In these early days of privation and loneliness, with dyspepsia ' gnawing like a rat at the pit of his stomach,' he fought the battle which he afterward described in *Sartor Resartus*. The "Everlasting No," the voice of unfaith denying God and the worth of life, he put from him; the "Everlasting Yea," the assurance that life could be made divine through labor and courage, he accepted once for all. The climax of this struggle, he has told us, came one day in Leith Walk, as he was going down to bathe in the sea, after three weeks of total sleeplessness. The "Everlasting Yea" sounding suddenly in the depths of his despairing soul, made him "strong, of unknown strength, a spirit, almost a god."

At twenty-five he began the study of German, and writes

a friend about "the new heaven and new earth" which German literature has revealed to him. His *Life of Schiller* and his translation of Goethe's *Wilhelm Meister* got him a hearing with the publishers; but his earnings remained extremely small. In 1826 he married Jane Baillie Welsh, a woman of genius hardly inferior to his own, a descendant on her father's side from the religious reformer, John Knox, on her mother's from the patriot, William Wallace. After marriage, the young pair went to live at Craigenputtoch, a farm-house amid miles of high dreary moor, in a "solitude almost druidical." Here Carlyle passed six years (1828–1834). During this time he produced *Sartor resartus*," and wrote several masterly essays, notably those on Burns and on Dr. Johnson. But the public would have none of him. The wonderful essay on Burns, which has been called "the very voice of Scotland, expressive of all her passionate love and tragic sorrow for her darling son," was saved from editorial mutilation only by the author's angry protest; and the still more wonderful *Sartor Resartus* fell, as it seemed, dead from the press.

Carlyle and Emerson.—One August day in 1833, as Carlyle sat despondent, a carriage drove up to the door of the lonely house, and a young American alighted. It was Emerson, come over-seas in search of a wise man—the first human being, said Mrs. Carlyle, who had visited those moors on such an errand since Noah's flood. The Carlyles found Emerson "one of the most lovable creatures we have ever looked upon." He brought with him the welcome news that Carlyle's writings had already reached America, and had found there the warm recognition which the British public refused to give them. During the years which followed, Emerson helped in many practical ways to further Carlyle's interests in America, and, in spite of their differences of character, their friendship continued throughout life.

Carlyle in London; Later Life.—In 1834, Carlyle decided to seek his fortune in London. He had already had a glimpse of the great metropolis, and had written, "It is like the heart of all the universe, and the flood of human effort rolls out of it and into it with a violence that almost appalls

THOMAS CARLYLE
From a painting by Whistler

one's very senses." He settled with his wife in the suburb of Chelsea, taking the house in Cheyne Row where he was to spend the long remainder of his life. Of the new home he wrote to his mother: "We lie safe at a bend of the river, away from all the great roads, have air and quiet hardly inferior to Craigenputtock, an outlook from the back windows into mere leafy regions with here and there a red high-peaked old roof looking through; and see nothing of London, except by day the summits of St. Paul's Cathedral, and Westminster Abbey, and by night the gleam of the great Babylon affronting the peaceful skies." Here Carlyle gathered about him all that was best in the new intellectual life now stirring in the nation—John Stuart Mill, the political economist; the youthful Tennyson, who had published two slender volumes, but was as yet unknown to fame; Leigh Hunt, the essayist and friend of Keats; Browning, whose star had not yet risen, though he had already done some of his most wonderful work; Dickens, in the full tide of his fame; and Ruskin, who was to be Carlyle's greatest disciple.

In 1837 Carlyle published his *French Revolution.* With this book he at last gained the ear of the public, and from this time on his reputation grew apace. For more than thirty years after this, he stood as teacher and preacher to the people of England and America, thundering above them wrath, warning, and exhortation. The chief works of this long period were *Chartism* (1839), an anti-democratic deliverance on the labor troubles then agitating England; *Heroes and Hero-Worship* (1841), a great sermon on veneration, calling upon the world to love, honor, and submit in childlike obedience to its great men, whether they appear as warrior, poet, or priest; *Cromwell* (1850), *Latter-Day Pamphlets*, the *Life of John Sterling* (1851), a masterpiece of intimate biography, in which he enshrined the memory of a friend in a work as noble in its kind as that which Milton had dedicated to Henry King, or Shelley to Keats. His last work of importance was the *History of Friedrich II* (1858–1865), a vast picture of the life and times of the founder of the Prussian empire.

From 1865 until his death in 1881, the veneration in which

Carlyle's name was held steadily increased. In 1866 he was installed as Lord Rector of his own University of Edinburgh, having been elected by the students to succeed Gladstone. The day of his installation was the proudest of his life. Youths and gray-haired scholars hung upon the calm and noble words of the old seer "like children held by a tale of fairyland"; and when his address was concluded, the students crowded about him, some shedding tears. In the same month his wife died. Carlyle never recovered from the shock and grief of her death. On the bright shores of the Mediterranean, and later in his desolate house at Chelsea, he wrote his "Reminiscences," intended chiefly as a memoir of his lost wife. As he lay upon his death-bed he was heard to murmur "Honesty, honesty"; the word which gives the keynote of his teaching and of his life.

Carlyle's Personality.—Carlyle had a most caustic tongue, and hardly any even of his best friends escaped from the biting humor of it. As he grew older, his petulance grew upon him, and the lightning strokes of his wit and anger spared neither friend nor foe. Yet underneath this bitter surface was a nature of the deepest tenderness. The first volume of his *French Revolution,* which he had lent to John Stuart Mill to read, was accidentally destroyed. The labor of rewriting it was so enormous as at first entirely to crush his courage. Yet when Mill had left the room, after telling him and his wife of the loss, all that Carlyle said was, "Poor Mill! We shall have to conceal from him how very serious this is to us." The last letters written to him by his friend Sterling he speaks of as "brief, stern, loving, altogether noble, never to be forgotten in this world," and some verses sent him from the same hand, he refers to as "verses written for myself alone, as in star-fire and immortal tears." Perhaps nowhere does the deep tenderness of his rugged, volcanic nature appear so exquisitely as in the sentences written about his mother after he had been called to her death-bed in 1853. "It was my mother and not my mother. The last pale rim or sickle of the moon which had once been full, sinking in the dark seas." His rugged, deeply-chiselled features bore always the marks of spiritual pain. In moments of excitement and eloquence his eye, we are told, would "beat like a pulse," under his abrupt, cliff-like forehead and bushy brows. But there was in him, along with all that is fiercely earnest, with much that is sardonic and grim, a spring of genuine and ever-flowing fun. In general temper he reminds us, as has been often said, of some old Hebrew prophet, Isaiah or Jeremiah; but he could also be genial, graceful, full of sly, delicious humor. It was this mingling of rude strength with tenderness and humor that Emerson probably had in mind when he described Carlyle quaintly as "a trip-hammer with an Æolian attachment."

Underlying Spirit of Carlyle's Work.—The actual doctrines which Carlyle preached with such intensity—his "Gospel of Work," his political dogma of "Government by the Best" (instead of "government by the worst," as he held democracy to be), and all the other war-cries of his unending battle with his age—are of less moment than the spirit which underlies his writing. This spirit may be defined as an intense moral indignation against whatever is weak, or false, or mechanical; an intense moral enthusiasm for whatever is sincere and heroically forceful. From this point of view his two typical books are *Sartor Resartus* and *Heroes and Hero-Worship*. The first is an attack upon all those social shams and mechanisms which defeat the sincerity of life; the second is a pæan of praise for those chosen heroic spirits who join earnestness with power. *Sartor Resartus* is pre-eminent in philosophic interest among all his books. It is also extremely ingenious in plan, and is written with a wonderful mingling of wild sardonic humor, keen pathos, and an eloquence and elevation almost biblical.

" Sartor Resartus."—"Sartor Resartus" means "the tailor re-tailored," and its theme is clothes. It purports to be the fragment of a great "Clothes-philosophy," the life-work of an eccentric German scholar and recluse, Herr Diogenes Teufelsdröckh, professor of Knowledge-in-general at the university of None-knows-where. This philosophy has been left in wild confusion, scribbled on scattered leaves, and stuffed helter-skelter into twelve bags signed with the twelve signs of the Zodiac. Carlyle represents himself merely as editor and commentator of this weltering mass of words, endeavoring desperately to extract order out of chaos, and to lighten a little, with much head-shaking and consternation, the dark abysses of the German professor's thought. This whimsical fancy of Carlyle's enables him to be both author and commentator; to state astounding paradoxes and then to shrug his shoulders in sign of his own irresponsibility; to take the side of his opponents against what he, as a well-regulated editor, pretends to find extravagant and crazy doctrine, but what is really his own heart's belief.

The book has a two-fold meaning. In the first place, it is a veiled attack upon the shams and pretences of society, upon hollow rank, hollow officialism, hollow custom, out of which life and usefulness have departed. These are, Carlyle hints, the fantastic, outworn garments which stifle the breath and health of the social body. Under the shield of this novel idea, he attacks the mechanical view of life, mechanical education, mechanical government, mechanical religion; and he preaches, now with drollery and paradox, now with fiery earnestness, a return to sincerity in all things. In the second place, Carlyle applies the Clothes-philosophy to the universe at large; showing that as clothes hide the real man, and as custom and convention hide real society, so Time and Space and all created things hide the real spiritual nature of the universe.

Carlyle's Style.—The pretence that he was translating from the German gave Carlyle an excuse for developing in *Sartor Resartus* a style of expression full of un-English idiom, of violent inversions, startling pauses and sharp turns —a style which he employed to rouse the attention of his reader as by a series of electric shocks. He himself refers humorously to this odd new use of language, as a "rumfus-tianish roly-poly growlery of style," and says that his mood in evolving it, was that of "a half-reckless casting of the brush, with its many frustrated colors, upon the canvas." However recklessly or humorously evolved, the style continued to be his for the remainder of his life. It has been said that "henceforth he wrote English no more, but 'Carlylese.'"

The " French Revolution."—*Sartor Resartus* proved Carlyle to be a great literary artist.   This title was broadened and confirmed by his historical masterpiece, *The French Revolution*.   Here we see to best advantage what Emerson calls the "stereoscopic imagination" of Carlyle, which detaches the figures from the background, brings them, as it were, close to our eye, and gives them startling vividness. The stupid, patient king, the "lion Mirabeau," the "sea-green incorruptible Robespierre," Marat, the "large-headed dwarfish individual of smoke-bleared aspect,"—not only these chief figures, but the minor ones, a multitude of them, stand out in the reader's memory unforgettably.   The larger pictures are equally admirable; the Storming of the Bastille, the Feast of Pikes, the long-drawn agony of the Night of Spurs.   Above all, the unity and sweep of the story, reminding us of a play of Shakespeare or of Æschylus, only acted by millions of figures on a gigantic stage, place this with Macaulay's History as the two greatest examples in English of the dramatic portraiture of an era.   The smoothness and lucidity of Macaulay's narrative, in comparison with the ruggedness, the deep glooms and sudden splendors of his own, is brought out by Carlyle's humorous exclamation upon reading Macaulay for the first time—"Flow on, thou shining river!"

Carlyle's Service to His Age.—Carlyle poured into the life of his time a stream of intense moral ardor and indignation which broke up the congealed waters and permanently raised the standard of feeling.   He united in remarkable degree the artistic and the moral impulses; and he is in this respect typical of the Victorian era, during which, more than ever before, art has been infused with moral purpose.

Here

IV. ALFRED TENNYSON (1809–1892)

Tennyson's Early Life and Poetry.—Tennyson was born in 1809, at Somersby Rectory, Lincolnshire.   His father was a vicar of the Established Church, holding his living by gift from a large landed proprietor; so that Tennyson was from birth in close connection with the main conservative interests of England, the church and the land.

The country about Somersby is a typical English country, softly rolling, richly wooded, full of green lanes and quiet streams. Here, and on the sea-coast of Lincolnshire, where the family spent a part of each summer, Tennyson gathered his first impressions of nature, and began to cultivate those powers of observation which, ripening with his years, made him so wonderful an interpreter of nature's moods. Pictures of Lincolnshire landscape, inland and sea-coast, can be traced in the poetry even of his latest years.

At Cambridge, where he matriculated in 1828, he was a member of a remarkable group of undergraduates, called "The Apostles," all of whom attained eminence in later life. Among these his closest friend was Arthur Henry Hallam, himself a poet and a youth of splendid promise. Tennyson had already determined to devote his life to poetry, and had published, in conjunction with his brother, a small volume entitled *Poems by Two Brothers*. While at Cambridge, in 1830, he published his first independent volume, a group of little verse-studies in melody and picture, including "Claribel," "Mariana," and the "Recollections of the Arabian Nights," which revealed a new music, rich, dreamy, and delicious. In 1831 Tennyson and Hallam made a quixotic journey to the Pyrenees, with the aim of carrying money to the Spanish revolutionists. The project miscarried, but Tennyson found in the scenery of the Pyrenees the inspiration of his "Œnone." In 1832 he published a second volume, which showed, in "The Lady of Shalott," "The Lotus-Eaters," "The Dream of Fair Women," and "Œnone," a rapidly developing and already exquisite art. In this volume, too, he began, with "The Miller's Daughter" and "The May Queen," his long series of idylls of English life, with which he was destined to gain his widest popularity.

These early poems won for Tennyson the enthusiastic admiration of a small group of young men, with Hallam as leader of the chorus of praise. The critics, however, were differently minded, and greeted the new poet with an outburst of ridicule. Tennyson, now and always intensely sensitive to criticism, determined to be silent until he could overwhelm his opponents by a splendid and decisive triumph. For ten years he published nothing. These were years of privation, for the family property was swept away by an unfortunate investment; and they were also years of sorrow. In 1833, Arthur Hallam, for whom Tennyson had a love "passing the love of women," died suddenly at Vienna. This tragic loss threw Tennyson back upon the deeper problems of human life and destiny. In the struggle to relay the shaken foundation of his existence, his nature grew strong; his work took on a lofty seriousness of tone and a new depth of meaning. He worked away, at his bachelor lodgings in London and with his family in the country, until 1842, when his long probation was over, and he was ready to lay the fruit of his toil before the world.

Tennyson's Triumph; The Poems of 1842.—The two volumes which appeared in 1842 contained the best of his previously published work, jealously revised, and many new poems of maturer power. These volumes took the critics and the world by storm. The range and variety of work in them was extraordinary. Almost every province of poetry was touched upon, from the lyric simplicity of "Break, Break, Break," to the largely moulded epic strength of "Morte d'Arthur." The series of idylls and eclogues picturing English home and country life, and pervaded by the atmosphere of familiar affections, was increased by such poems as "The Gardener's Daughter," "Dora," "Lady Clare," and "The Lord of Burleigh." "Ulysses," in which Tennyson gave a magnificent new wording to an old legend, deals with the closing episode of the wandering hero's life. The picture of the aged Ulysses, determined to employ the remnant of his days in pushing out into the unknown waters of the West, rather than "rust unused" in barren Ithaca, was an outgrowth, Tennyson has told us, of his own need of taking heart and pushing forward, after Hallam's death. The new seriousness of the poet's mind, induced by the calamity of his loss, is shown also in such poems as "The Two Voices" and "The Vision of Sin." In the first we are shown the struggle of a despairing mind, as it beholds the misery of

ALFRED, LORD TENNYSON

After a painting by G. F. Watts

life, and questions whether or not it shall take refuge in self-destruction. The second touches upon a more awful subject, "the end, here and hereafter, of the merely sensual man." In "Locksley Hall" Tennyson infused into a story of broken love, a story in its main features as old as poetry itself, ideas drawn from recent discoveries of science, visions of the "increasing purpose" which runs through the ages, by which "the thoughts of men are widened." In the poems "Of Old Sat Freedom on the Heights," and "Love Thou Thy Land," Tennyson made a declaration of his political faith, in which a stern and ardent love of freedom was mingled with a veneration for old institutions, a distrust of violence and revolution. Finally, the 1842 volumes displayed Tennyson's gift of pure song, wonderfully refined and deepened during this ten years' silence, in such poems as "Move Eastward, Happy Earth," and "Break, Break, Break." The latter, "made in a Lincolnshire lane at five o'clock in the morning between blossoming hedges," is as moving and lovely a lyric as had been written in England since the age of Elizabeth.

Tennyson's Later Life and Poetry.—In 1847 appeared *The Princess*. This was followed in 1850 by *In Memoriam*, begun seventeen years before, soon after the death of Arthur Hallam, whose memory it celebrates. *In Memoriam* made Tennyson's fame and material prosperity secure. In the year of its publication, Wordsworth, who had been poet laureate, died, and Tennyson took the laurel. A government pension enabled him to marry Emily Sellwood, to whom he had been engaged for many years. They settled at Farringford, in the Isle of Wight. Here, and at Aldworth, in Surrey, Tennyson lived for the rest of his life, retired from the world, but constantly binding himself by his work closer with the thoughts and affections of all English-speaking people. The most important landmarks of the long literary life still before him were: *Maud* (1855); *Enoch Arden* (1864); *The Idylls of the King* (begun with "Morte d'Arthur" before 1842 and completed in 1872); a series of dramas including *Queen Mary, Harold, Becket,* and *The Foresters;* a splendid volume of *Ballads* (1880), including "The Revenge," "The Defense of Lucknow," and "Rizpah"; and such striking single poems as "Locksley Hall Sixty Years After," "Merlin and the Gleam" and "Crossing the Bar." "Merlin and the Gleam" he intended as an allegory of his own poetical career; "Crossing the Bar" he wished to be printed last in all editions of his poetry, and to stand as his farewell word, spoken with solemn gladness as he put off into the mysterious sea of death.

During the forty-two years in which he held the laureateship, Tennyson stood as the spokesman of his people in times of national sorrow and rejoicing. In such poems as "The Charge of the Light Brigade," "The Revenge," "The Relief of Lucknow," and the "Ode on the Duke of Wellington," he ministered to national pride, fired the national courage, and brought poetry nearer to the national life than it had been since the age of Elizabeth. In 1883 he was raised by Queen Victoria to the peerage, an honor which he accepted in a large spirit, as a tribute less to himself than to literature. He died in 1892, and was buried beside Chaucer in Westminster Abbey, with a pomp and solemnity unparalleled in the case of any other English man of letters.

Tennyson's Appearance and Personality.—Many of Tennyson's friends have recorded personal impressions concerning him which enable us to see him vividly as he lived. Carlyle, about 1842, described him to Emerson thus: "Alfred is one of the few British and foreign figures who are and remain beautiful to me, a true human soul, to whom your own soul can say, 'Brother!' One of the finest looking men in the world. A great shock of rough dusky dark hair; bright, laughing, hazel eyes; massive aquiline face, most massive yet most delicate; of sallow brown complexion, almost Indian looking; clothes cynically loose, free-and-easy; smokes infinite tobacco. His voice is musical, metallic, fit for loud laughter and piercing wail, and all that may lie between; speech and speculation free and plenteous; I do not meet in these late decades such company over a pipe!" A friend once protested to Tennyson that it was unfair he should be "Hercules as well as Apollo"; and Fitzgerald (the translator of Omar Khayyam) notes: "Alfred could hurl the crow-bar farther than any of the neighboring clowns, whose humors, as well as those of their betters, knight, squire, landlord, and lieutenant, he took quiet note of, like Chaucer himself." Of his simplicity and candor, Mr. T. Watts-Dunton says: "The charm of Tennyson lay in a great veracity of soul, in a simple single-mindedness, so child-like that you could not have supposed but that all subtleties—even those of poetic art—must be foreign to a nature so simple." And again, "Behind his uncompromising directness was apparent a noble and splendid courtesy of the grand old type. As he stood in the porch at Aldworth, meeting a guest or bidding him good-bye—as he stood there, tall far beyond the height of average men, his skin showing dark and tanned by the sun and wind—no one could mistake him for anything but a great forth-right English gentleman." To the end of his life he was excessively sensitive to criticism; but his distaste for adulation was equally marked, and this, together with a certain unconquerable shyness, often made his manner gruff and abrupt, especially toward strangers. All who knew him in his daily walks about his country homes testify to his marvellous knowledge of the world of nature; every flower, bird, and insect was known to him; his knowledge of geology was profound, and a lifelong study of the stars and their seasons gave him a grasp of astronomy unequalled by any other poet except Dante. Humor is seldom apparent in his writings, it is in fact rather conspicuously absent; but many good sayings and amusing anecdotes bear out the testimony of his friends that his daily life was illuminated by abundant humor, very quaint and dry.

"**The Princess.**"—Tennyson's first long poem, *The Princess*, deals with the question, then beginning to be much discussed, of the higher education of women. It has for its sub-title "A Medley," and no description could be more just. The story is set in a graceful framework of modern English life; it is supposed to be "improvised" by a group of young people gathered on the lawn of an English country-house during the afternoon of a popular holiday. A modern and realistic atmosphere is thus established, in which the modern "teaching" of the story may emerge without a sense of discord. The story itself deals with the quixotic attempt of a

noble-spirited maiden and her women associates to establish
a female college and to realize an ideal of intellectual life in
which love and marriage shall have no part. The college is
invaded by the maiden's suitor in disguise, and love finally
triumphs over learning. The story is fantastically mixed,
of elements brought from many ages and countries; and the
style, always musical, dreamy, and richly colored, often wanders from the "mock heroic" key in which the poem is
supposed to be pitched. Tennyson gives a fair hearing to
both sides of the vexed question of the emancipation of
women. His solution, however, given in the noble concluding
passage of the poem, is practically the old solution, broadened
and clarified, that "woman's cause is man's," that "either
sex alone is half itself" but united they form a "two-celled
heart, beating with one full stroke, life." The songs which
divide the various parts of the little mock-epic are among the
most beautiful and best-loved of all Tennyson wrote. "Blow,
Bugle, Blow," "Sweet and Low," and "Tears, Idle Tears"
are miracles of pure and lucent melody.

"**In Memoriam.**"—*In Memoriam*, the greatest work of
Tennyson's younger manhood, may be called an epic of
the inner life, on its religious side. Epic in its boldness
and sweep, it is, however, purely lyrical in form. It consists of a hundred and thirty-one lyrics, "short swallow-
flights of song," composed in the intervals of other work.
In the beginning of the poem, the early phases of grief are
touched upon, moods of stunned and bewildered sorrow.
Gradually the personal pain merges into anxious speculation
concerning the mystery of death and the hope of immortality. Through states of doubt, despair, and anguished question, the poem slowly mounts into a region of firm though
saddened faith; and it ends in full hymnal music breathing
hope and fortitude of heart. In it we see exemplified, in the
struggle and hardly-won triumph of a single soul, the world-
wide struggle of our age to preserve its faith in the spiritual
significance of life and death, in the face of the revelations
of modern science, at first view so appalling. When *In
Memoriam* was written, Darwin's theory of the evolution of
human life from lower forms had not yet been given to the

world; * but the idea was already in the air, and in numberless ways Science had begun to sap the old foundations of
religious faith. Tennyson courageously faced the facts of
science, as revealed in geology and biology; and he succeeded
in wringing religious consolation from the very things which
were dreaded as a fatal menace to religion. A majestic
movement is given to *In Memoriam* by the fact that the
poem follows the year twice through its revolutions, so that
the succession of day and night, the moon's changing phases,
the lapsing of the stars in their courses, the slow pageant of
the seasons, seem at last to enfold with their large harmony
and peace the forlorn heart of the mourner. Although, in
helping to break down the false opposition between science
on the one hand, and poetry and spiritual faith on the other,
In Memoriam did a great service to the age, its definite
religious teaching is of minor import beside its general nobility of mood, the solemn beauty of its portrayal of the
inner life, its wonderful pictures of English landscape and the
English home, and the full deep tide of music upon which all
is borne along. With Milton's "Lycidas" and Shelley's
"Adonais" it forms the height and crown of English elegiac
verse.

"**Idylls of the King.**"—The greatest work of Tennyson's
later life is the *Idylls of the King*, in which he painted anew
the character of the first English national hero, King Arthur,
and gave new meaning to the cycle of legends which had grown
up in the middle ages about the Knights of the Round Table.
These legends had been gathered together by Geoffrey of
Monmouth, added to by Layamon in his *Brut*, woven into
romances by the Anglo-Norman *trouvères*, and combined
into a splendid prose romance by Sir Thomas Malory. A
great tangled mass of legend, the King Arthur stories had lain
for centuries awaiting the hand of some poet able to give them
a monumental treatment. Milton had looked at the subject
longingly in his youth, and had abandoned it only to take
up the greater theme of *Paradise Lost*. Tennyson began
early in his career to dip into its treasure-house of fancy, and

* *The Origin of Species* appeared in 1859, the *Descent of Man* in 1871.

to make short lyric studies, such as "The Lady of Shalott" and "Sir Galahad and Queen Guinevere," upon its themes. As early as 1842 he had written the wonderful narrative of Arthur's death, which in the completed series of "Idylls," was changed in title from "Morte d'Arthur" to "The Passing of Arthur," and was put last of the twelve poems making up the epic. The others were written at long intervals apart, and in a very different order from that in which they now appear. They are bound together by the persistence through them all of Arthur's personality, the attempt which he made to build up an ideal kingdom, and the defeat of this attempt by the forces of sin and violence. Taken together, the "Idylls" form a body of blank verse which, for splendor and charm, had not been equalled since Milton. The quality of poetry in them is like that of the *Faerie Queene*, a beauty of dream, of cloudland, of " Celtic magic." Their whole effect may be best described by Keats's phrase, "huge cloudy symbols of a high romance."

Tennyson as Representative of His Age.—Tennyson is the supremely representative figure of the Victorian era, first because he held for fifty years of Victoria's reign the poetic supremacy almost unchallenged, and second because he was for that long period the recognized spokesman of the English people in matters both public and personal. His position was always at the midway of extremes in thought, and he was able to include and reconcile a greater number of the age's diverse interests than any other single writer. He spiritualized and poetized its science. He voiced its religious struggle. He shared its interest in the storied past, and its vivid curiosity concerning the future. He gave inspiration to its search after broader and more humane politics. He deepened his country's patriotism and the sense of her national mission. He poured a hallowing light over her familiar affections. And he did all this in a medium of verse always fine, with an artistic devotion equalled in English literature only by Keats and Milton.

V. ROBERT BROWNING (1812–1889)
ELIZABETH BARRETT BROWNING (1806–1861)

Browning's Early Life and Poetry.—Robert Browning, who disputes with Tennyson the first place among Victorian poets, was born in London in 1812. English, Scotch and German blood was mingled in his veins with a more distant strain of Creole. This mixed ancestry has been often pointed out as an explanation of his wide sympathy with different races and types of men. His father, a clerk in the Bank of England, was a man of literary sensibility, and full of odd learning. From him Browning gained, almost without knowing it, a knowledge of out-of-the-way corners of history, and of little-known by-ways of literature. To the end of his life the influence of this early training was evident both in his choice of themes and in the immense stores of curious information which he lavished upon them. Browning's boyhood and youth were passed in the suburb of Camberwell, where Ruskin also was brought up. Camberwell was then a green, and almost a rural neighborhood, and the youthful poet's life seems to have been as freshly romantic as any that was ever lived. He was fond of following gypsy caravans as they passed through the country-side; the refrain of a gypsy song which he once heard, "Follow the Queen of the Gypsies, O!" formed the kernel of a poem which he wrote years after, "The Flight of the Duchess." He would sometimes, at night, climb into the elms above Norwood, and gaze with a strange wonder and excitement at the lights of London on the horizon; by day and night the nearness of the vast city was a reminder of the complex human life he was to interpret more subtly and deeply than any other poet had done since Shakespeare. When a lad of fourteen he picked up by chance on a London book-stall a pamphlet labelled "Mr. Shelley's Atheistical Poem—'Queen Mab.'" Shelley had been dead four years, but was still so little known to the world at large that none of Browning's family, though really cultivated people, could tell him who this strangely fascinating poet was. By perseverance, however, he obtained the rest of Shelley's poetry,

Photograph, Copyright, by Frederick Hollyer, London.

ROBERT BROWNING
From a painting by G. F. Watts

and through "Adonais" came into a knowledge of Keats. The two together kindled Browning's latent genius, and made a poet of him.

His first long poem, *Pauline*, published in 1833, is a half-dramatic study of the type of spiritual life which Shelley's own career embodied; and Shelley's influence is clearly traceable both in its thought and in its style. After a trip to Russia and Italy, Browning published *Paracelsus*, in his twenty-fourth year. This, like *Pauline*, is the "history of a soul." It gives the life-story of Paracelsus, a mediæval scholar and alchemist, and shows how his absorption in the things of the intellect, to the neglect of the things of the heart, causes him to fail.

Paracelsus gained Browning the attention of the discriminating few, and led to a request from the actor Macready for a play. In response to the invitation Browning wrote the first of his dramas, *Strafford*, which had a moderate success upon the stage. In 1840 appeared his third long poem, *Sordello*, obscure and difficult by reason of its youthful, unmastered abundance of thought and feeling. Of the reception which *Sordello* met with, several amusing stories are told. Carlyle wrote that his wife had read the work with much interest, and desired to know whether Sordello was a man, a city, or a book. Tennyson declared that he could understand but two lines, the first and the last, "Who will shall hear Sordello's story told," and "Who would has heard Sordello's story told,"—and that they both were lies! In *Pippa Passes*, however (1841), Browning shook himself free from these faults of manner, and produced a poem of sustained beauty, as clear as sunlight, a work of simple, melodious, impassioned art. Between 1840 and 1845 Browning was chiefly occupied with attempts in the acting drama, of which the most interesting are perhaps *Colombe's Birthday*, *A Blot in the 'Scutcheon*, and *The Return of the Druses*. He had also begun those short poems dealing with special moments in the lives of various men and women, historical or imaginary, which constitute the most important division of his work. These were published under the titles *Dramatic Lyrics* and *Dramatic Romances*.

Browning's Marriage; Life in Italy.—In 1846 Browning married Elizabeth Barrett, whose poetic reputation was then far greater than his. She was a frail invalid, living in a darkened room, and awaiting the coming of death. Browning's love rescued her from the grave; and their married life was one of happiness so high and clear that it has already become one of the glorified facts of literary history. Owing to the opposition of Miss Barrett's gloomy and tyrannical father the marriage was secret. The pair settled in Italy, where for the remainder of Mrs. Browning's life they lived, entering intimately into the life of the country, and sharing with intense sympathy in the struggle it was then waging for freedom from Austria. They made their home at Florence, in the house called Casa Guidi, from which was taken the title of Mrs. Browning's poem on the Italian liberation, *Casa Guidi Windows*. Here Browning wrote his great series of dramatic monologues, entitled *Men and Women*.

" The Ring and the Book."—One day in Rome Browning picked up from a street-stall a faded seventeenth century pamphlet narrating the trial of Count Guido Franceschini for the murder of his wife Pompilia. He saw in the sordid police record the material for a great picture of human life. After his wife's death in 1861 he threw himself, for distraction from his grief, into the composition of the vast poem in twelve parts, *The Ring and the Book* (1868–69), in which he told the tragic story of Pompilia from many different points of view, from her own and her husband's, from that of a young priest Caponsacchi, who aids her in her distress, from that of the lawyers upon both sides, from that of the Pope who gives the final judgment, and from that of various onlookers and gossips. It is a monumental study of a chain of human circumstances as they appear to minds looking from many different angles, with various degrees of insight, and with various warping prejudices. It is the crowning effort of Browning's genius for the vastness of its scope, its intense humanity, its grasp of the complex elements of human nature. The imperfect understanding which Browning's work met with even thus late in his career is illustrated by Carlyle's exclamation upon reading *The Ring and the*

Book, "It's a wonderful poem, one of the most wonderful poems ever written. I have re-read it all through—all made out of an Old Bailey story that might have been told in ten lines, and only wants forgetting!" Carlyle missed in it its main significance, the infinite importance of that which, from the ordinary point of view, seems unimportant.

Browning's Later Life.—After the death of his wife Browning spent his time chiefly in England. He wrote much, with a steady gain in intellectual subtlety but with a corresponding loss of poetic beauty. Many of his later poems, such as *Bishop Blougram's Apology*, *Prince Hohenstiel-Schwangau*, and *Mr. Sludge the Medium* take the part, dramatically, of dubious characters, and attempt to justify them from their own standpoint. He made an exhaustive study of Greek life and literature, and produced several remarkable poems upon Greek subjects. The most enjoyable of these is a free translation of the *Alcestis* of Euripides, set in a beautiful framework of original narrative, and entitled *Balaustion's Adventure*. To the last his genius continued to throw out, in his short poems, bursts and jets of exquisite music, color, and feeling. Such, for instance, are the little pieces called "Wanting is—What?" and "Never the Time and the Place," written in his seventy-first year; and "Summum Bonum," written just before the pen dropped from his hand in 1889, at Venice, in the seventy-seventh year of his age. He had had to wait long for recognition, but during the latter years of his life his fame overshadowed even that of Tennyson, and his works were studied with an enthusiasm seldom accorded to a living poet.

Browning as a Man.—Although Browning spent a large portion of his literary effort in defending what society has generally regarded as indefensible, his conduct of his own life, before and after his secret marriage and elopement, was thoroughly plain and usual. He even prided himself upon being a man of the world. He was open and abundant in conversation; he was fond of society; he discharged all the common duties of life with thoroughness and relish. A lady who saw him at a dinner-table, without knowing him, asked, "Who is that too exuberant financier?"

and Browning was flattered by the question. Yet, notwithstanding all this, his romanticism was as vivid as Shelley's or Byron's, and perhaps deeper than theirs. Macready, the actor, said of him in his youth that he looked and spoke more like a poet than anyone he had ever known. Carlyle tells how, on one of his solitary gallops he was stopped on Wimbledon Common by a young man, singularly beautiful, with dark Italian face and black hair flowing in the wind, who poured out to him, without preface or apology, his admiration for the philosopher's writings. The anecdote, besides giving us a picturesque glimpse of Browning in his ardent youth, shows the impulsiveness and generous admiration for others which characterized him always, and which made him the friend of men whose differences of temperament estranged them from each other. There was in him, also, an almost savage virility and force of feeling, capable at rare intervals of transforming the affable man of the world into a primeval creature, violent and terrible. Much of Browning's work is intellectual; but we cannot rightly understand him unless we remember that the core of his nature was simply and glowingly human; that he was, first of all, a poet, and therefore one in whom feeling and imagination were the moving forces, and thought was only a secondary thing.

Browning's Poems as " Soul Histories "; " Pippa Passes." —Browning's earliest poem, *Pauline,* was, he tells us, intended as the first of a series of "mono-dramatic epics," each of which was to present the "history of a soul." Broadly viewed, the whole of Browning's work is what his youthful ambition dreamed of making it. In three forms, pure drama, dramatic narrative, and dramatic lyric, he gave the history of hundreds of souls; or if not their whole history, at least some exciting moment of it. In his earlier life he made many attempts to present these high moments in regular drama, but the form was not perfectly suited to his peculiar task. In *Pippa Passes,* however, he threw aside many of the conventional demands of the stage, and presented four special moments of soul-history, connected with each other by only a slight thread. The germ of the poem came to him in youth, while listening to a gypsy girl singing in the Camberwell woods. He imagined someone walking alone through life, apparently too obscure to leave any trace behind, but unconsciously exercising at every step a determining influence upon other lives. This conception he afterward connected with the personality of a little work-girl in the silk-mills of Asolo, a mountain town which he had visited on his first journey to Italy. Pippa walks through Asolo on New Year's Day, her one holiday in the year, unconsciously dropping her divine songs into the lives of various people, just at the moment when their fates are trembling between good and evil, courage and cowardice. By the touching purity and gladness of her voice, or by the significant words she utters, she saves in turn each of the four persons whose lives are at the turning point. At evening she goes back to her bare room, and sinks to sleep with a final song on her lips, still ignorant of the service she has done.

Browning's Short Poems: Peculiarities of His Method.—Browning is less a dramatist than an exhibitor of single dramatic situations, such as the four which are bound loosely together by Pippa's chance-heard songs. It follows that his most vital work is, generally speaking, in his short poems. In these he not only selects a special moment in the life of his characters, but as a rule he views his theme from some odd and striking point of view. Perhaps the best example of his skill in selecting a point of view, is to be found in the "Epistle of Karshish." The aim of the poem is to present the state of mind of Lazarus, who has beheld the mysteries of existence beyond the grave, and who has brought back into mortal life a sense of immortality so strong that every act and every judgment is determined by it. The time is about thirty years after the death of Christ; and the speaker, Karshish, is an Arab doctor who in travelling through Palestine has met Lazarus, and who sends a report of the strange case to his old master in leechcraft, Abib. Through the vain struggle of Karshish to maintain his scientific scepticism in the face of Lazarus's story and bearing, we are made to feel the reality of the miracle with overwhelming force, and are brought strangely near to the conditions of life in Palestine in the next generation after Christ. Another peculiarity of Browning's method in his short poems is that he throws the reader into the midst of the theme with startling suddenness, and proceeds with a rapidity which is apt to bewilder a reader not in the secret of the method. There are no explanations, no gradual transitions. A capital example of this peculiarity is the "Soliloquy in a Spanish Cloister," which has to be read to the end before we see it for what it is, the self-revealed picture of a narrow-minded, superstitious, sensual monk, stirred to hatred by a brother monk, whose mild, benignant ways and genuine piety we gradually discern through the speaker's jeers and curses. If we add to these peculiarities of method the fact that Browning's best work is very compressed in style, we see why many persons have found obscure in him what is in reality clear enough, but is not to be perceived clearly without alertness on the reader's part. Perhaps the poem which best illustrates all Browning's peculiarities of method, harmoniously combined, is "My Last Duchess," a marvellous example of his power to give a whole life-history, with a wealth of picturesque detail, in a few vivid, suggestive lines.

Some of Browning's Themes.—In "Caliban upon Setebos," taking a hint from Shakespeare's *Tempest*, Browning has shown the grotesque imaginings of a half-human monster, groping after an explanation of the universe. In "Childe Roland," starting with a snatch of song from the fool in *Lear*, he has shown the heart of mediæval knighthood, fronting spectral terrors in its search after the stronghold of sin, the Dark Tower, where lurks the enemy of life and joy. In "Abt Vogler," and "A Toccata of Galuppi" he has touched upon the inner meanings of music, and has painted for us permanent types of the musical enthusiast. In "The Grammarian's Funeral" he has shown the poetry and heroism hidden underneath the gray exterior of the life of a Renaissance pedant. In "Fra Lippo Lippi," "Andrea del Sarto," and "Pictor Ignotus," he has given the secret workings of the painter's nature, and has flashed illumination upon the sources of success and failure in art which lie deep in the moral being of the artist. In "Balaustion's Adventure" he has revealed the inner spirit of Greek life in the fourth century before Christ. In "A Death in the Desert" he has led us into the mystical rapture of the early Christians; and in "Christmas Eve" and "Easter Day" he has approached Christian faith from the modern standpoint. In "Saul" he has shown us, against the splendid background of patriarchal Israel, the boy David singing, in the tent of the great king, songs of human joy which rise, in a sudden opening of the heavens of prophecy, into a song of the coming of the Messiah. Nowhere out of Shakespeare can be found a mind more wide-ranging over the outer circumstances and the inner significance of man's life.

Love, as the supreme experience of the soul, testing its temper and revealing its probable fate, holds the first place in Browning's thought. In such poems as "Cristina," "Evelyn Hope," "The Last Ride Together," "My Star," "By the Fireside," and a multitude more, he has presented love in its varied phases; and has celebrated its manifold meanings not only on earth, but in the infinite range of worlds through which he believes that the soul is destined to go in search after its own perfection. By the intensity and positiveness of his doctrine he has influenced his age profoundly, and has made his name synonymous with faithfulness to the human' love which life brings, and through that to the divine love which it implies and promises.

The robustness of Browning's nature, its courage, its abounding joy and faith in life, make his works a permanent storehouse of spiritual energy. In an age distracted by doubt and divided in will, his strong unfaltering voice has been lifted above the perplexities and hesitations of men, like a bugle-call to joyous battle, in which the victory is to the brave.

Elizabeth Barrett Browning.—One of Browning's most perfect short poems, "One Word More," is addressed to his wife, Elizabeth Barrett Browning (1806–1861), and is a kind of counter-tribute to her most perfect work, the *Sonnets from the Portuguese,* which contain the record of her courtship and marriage. Her early life was shadowed by illness and affliction; and her early poetry (*The Seraphim,*

ELIZABETH BARRETT BROWNING

From a drawing by Field Talfourd, Rome, March, 1859

1838, *Poems*, 1844) shows in many places the defects of unreality and of overwrought emotion natural to work produced in a sick-chamber. The best known of these early poems are perhaps "Lady Geraldine's Courtship," where she works under the influence of Tennyson's idylls, and "The Cry of the Children," where she voices the humanitarian protest against child-labor in mines and factories. After her marriage and removal to Italy her health improved, and her art greatly strengthened. The *Sonnets from the Portuguese* (1850) are among the noblest love-poems in the language. Mrs. Browning was deeply interested in the struggle of Italy to shake off her bondage to Austria, as is shown by her *Casa Guidi Windows*, published in 1851. In 1856 appeared her most ambitious work, *Aurora Leigh*, a kind of versified novel of modern English life, with a social reformer of aristocratic lineage for hero, and a young poetess, in large part a reflection of Mrs. Browning's own personality, for heroine. *Aurora Leigh* shows the influence of a great novel-writing age, when the novel was becoming more and more imbued with social purpose. The interest in public questions also appears in Mrs. Browning's *Poems Before Congress* (1860), and in her *Last Poems* (1862).

Mrs. Browning's touch is uncertain, and her style sometimes vague or extravagant. But she had a noble sympathy with noble causes, her emotion is elevated and ardent, and her expression, at its best (as in the *Sonnets from the Portuguese*), is as lofty as her mood. Her characteristic note is that of intimate, personal feeling; even *Casa Guidi Windows* has been called "a woman's love-making with a nation."

VI. MATTHEW ARNOLD (1822–1888)

Arnold's Life.—Browning's robust optimism in the face of all the unsettling and disturbing forces of the age is thrown out in sharp relief when we contrast him with a somewhat younger poet, Matthew Arnold, in whom the prevailing tone is one of half-despairing doubt. Arnold was born in 1822, the son of Dr. Thomas Arnold, the famous head-master of Rugby. The Arnolds had a house in the lake country, near Wordsworth, and the two families were on friendly terms. In his later life as a critic Matthew Arnold was to do much toward fixing Wordsworth's high place in the minds of his countrymen. From the first the influence of Wordsworth's poetry upon Arnold was strong. Arnold went up to Oxford in 1840, and five years later won a fellowship at Oriel College. His first volume appeared in 1849, with the title, *The Strayed Reveller, and Other Poems.* This was followed by *Poems* (1853), *Merope,* a drama in Greek form and on a Greek subject (1858), and by *New Poems,* in 1867. From his thirtieth year until shortly before his death, he held the position of inspector of schools. To the demands and responsibilities of this official position were added, in 1857, those of a professorship of poetry at Oxford. These outer circumstances were largely instrumental in turning his energies away from poetry into the field of prose criticism, where, for the last twenty years of his life, he held the position of a leader, almost of a dictator. His most important work in prose is the *Essays in Criticism* (1865). Toward the end of his life he made a lecturing tour in America, the chief outcome of which was the brilliant address on Emerson, published, with other essays, in *Discourses in America.* He died in 1888.

Arnold as a Poet.—Arnold may be described as a poet of transition. He grew up in the interval between the first and the second outburst of creative energy in the century. Carlyle, Browning, Tennyson, and others, were, each in his way, already building anew the structures of spiritual faith and hope; but by Arnold, as by many others, the ebbing of the old wave was far more clearly felt than the rising of the new one. Standing, as he says,

> " between two worlds, one dead,
> The other powerless to be born,"

he fronts life wearily, or at best stoically. He seeks consolation in the intellect; and his poetry, which addresses itself to the cultivated few, is rather thoughtful than impassioned. His religious dejection is expressed very beautifully in " Dover

Beach" and "Obermann." It is this same dejection applied to the facts of human intercourse, which breathes sadly but calmly through the series of love lyrics entitled "Switzerland." The imperfections and unrealized ideals of life, in which Tennyson found cause to "faintly trust the larger hope," and in which Browning saw the "broken arcs" of heaven's "perfect round," Arnold made a reason for doubt, declaring that men should put away delusion, and expect in the future only what they see in the past. Other phases of this stoic melancholy and of the struggle which it wages with the restless craving for joy, are to be studied in the pieces called "Self-Dependence" and "A Summer Night."

For his ideal of form, Arnold went to the literature of Greece. When he works more deliberately in the Greek spirit and manner, his style is often cold and dry. In his long poems, especially, he is apt to sacrifice too much to his reverence for classical tradition. Only one of them, *Sohrab and Rustum*, which tells an oriental story of a duel between a father and his lost son, and their recognition of each other in death, combines classic purity of style with romantic ardor of feeling. The truth of its oriental color, the deep pathos of the situation, the fire and intensity of the action, the strong conception of character, and the full, solemn music of the verse, make "Sohrab and Rustum" the masterpiece among Arnold's longer poems. The same unity of classic form with romantic feeling characterizes his two shorter masterpieces, "The Scholar Gypsy" and "Thyrsis," written to commemorate his college friend, Arthur Hugh Clough.

Arnold as a Prose Writer.—Arnold's prose has little trace of the wistful melancholy of his verse. It is almost always urbane, vivacious, light-hearted. The doctrine which he spent his later life in preaching is based upon a classical ideal, the ideal of symmetry, wholeness, or, as he daringly called it, *perfection*. Carlyle had preached the value of conduct, the "Hebraic" element in life; Arnold set himself to preach the value of the "Hellenic" element—open-mindedness, delight in ideas, alertness to entertain new points of view and willingness to examine life constantly in the light of new theories. Wherever, in religion, politics, education, or literature, he saw his countrymen under the domination of narrow ideals, he came speaking the mystic word of deliverance, "Culture." Culture, acquaintance with the best which has been thought and done in the world, is his remedy for all ills. In almost all of his prose writing he attacks some form of "Philistinism," by which word he characterized the narrow-mindedness and self-satisfaction of the British middle class. His ideal was that of balanced cultivation, the ideal of the trained, sympathetic, cosmopolitan gentleman. In his own way he was a prophet and a preacher, striving whole-heartedly to release his countrymen from bondage to mean things, and pointing their gaze to that wholeness and balance of character which has seemed to many noble minds the true goal of human endeavor.

Arnold's tone is admirably fitted to the peculiar task he had to perform. He makes his plea for the gospel of ideas with urbanity and playful grace, as befitted the Hellenic spirit, bringing "sweetness and light" into the dark places of British prejudice. Arnold's most important work of literary criticism is the series of lectures "On Translating Homer," which deserve careful study for the enlightenment they offer concerning many of the fundamental questions of style. The essays on Wordsworth and on Byron, from *Essays in Criticism*, and that on Emerson, from *Discourses in America*, furnish good examples of Arnold's charm and stimulating power as a critic.

VII. JOHN RUSKIN (1819–1899)

Ruskin's Early Life; Art Criticism.—The dictatorship of taste which Arnold held in matters of literature, was held in matters of art by John Ruskin, who also broadened his criticism, as did Arnold, into the region of social and moral ideals. He was born in 1819. His father, a London wine-merchant of wealth and liberal tastes, gave him every early advantage of education and travel. Family carriage trips through England, France, and Switzerland, enabled him to gather those impressions of landscape beauty and of architectural effect which he afterward put to remarkable use in his critical writings. A boyish enthusiasm for the paintings of Turner ripened with years into an ardent championship of that wonderful artist, then obscure and neglected. In the first volume of *Modern Painters*, published in his twenty-fourth year, Ruskin enshrined Turner as the greatest of landscape painters. In doing so, however, his powers of analysis led him deep into the theory of art; and in the remainder of his work, published at intervals during the next eighteen years, he examined many types and schools of painting, separating what he held to be true from what he held to be false, with eloquence and haughty assurance. Meanwhile, in *The Seven Lamps of Architecture* and *Stones of Venice*, he made a similar examination of the principal types of European architecture, and attempted to establish similar underlying principles concerning their growth and decay, their worth and worthlessness. He believed the springs of art to lie deep in the ethical nature of the artist, and in the moral temper of the age and nation which produced him. This is the pervading idea of all Ruskin's art criticism. By insistence upon this view, by eloquent illustration and fiery defence of it, he gradually led his readers to a new understanding of the spiritual meaning of art, and awakened them to a new understanding of the beautiful.

Ruskin's Later Life; Ethical and Economic Teaching. —In 1860, at forty years of age, Ruskin finished *Modern Painters*, and practically closed that series of works which had given him repute as a writer upon art. From this time on he used art mainly as illustration and text, by means of which to enforce some ethical, economic, or religious lesson. He became more and more absorbed in the problems of socialism, being led thereto by the conviction at which he had arrived in his previous work, that all great art must be national and social, and must spring from healthy and beautiful conditions of life in the society where it arises. Modern art he held to be, with a few exceptions, debased; and he gradually came to believe that this debasement was due to our commercial organization of society. In two books, *Munera Pulveris* and *Unto This Last*, he protested against the received theories of political economy. The substance of his teaching is that economics must be looked at from the stand-point of what does and what does not constitute true "value," that is, of what does and what does not contribute to the true good of man. He includes, therefore, in his "political economy" many things not included in the previous "commercial economy," as he insists that the science of the old economists should be called. In thus broadening the basis of discussion, and giving a new significance to the term "value," Ruskin did a real service for the economic thought of the future.

His most popular book, *Sesame and Lilies*, was a side-product of his thinking on political economy. In the first division of the book, entitled "King's Treasuries," he holds up to censure England's absorption in worldly success as opposed to the real success which comes only from a life beautifully and humanely lived. To the "gospel of getting-on," which depends for its appealing power upon the idea that money constitutes the only real "value," he opposes the gospel of spiritual wealth, especially as deposited in books, those King's Treasuries which are the real centre of the realm of "value." The second part, "Queen's Gardens," is Ruskin's contribution to the "woman problem" of the century, the theme being the same as that of Tennyson's *Princess*. *Sesame and Lilies* is written in a style of wonderful strength and richness. It affords perhaps the best example of Ruskin's prose.

As he went on in years, Ruskin's sympathy went out more and more to the oppressed and unjustly treated of this world; and he spent a large part of his time and energy, as well as the bulk of his large fortune, in attempting to help the working classes by word and deed. After his removal in 1872 to Brantwood, in Wordsworth's country among the English lakes, his chief connection with the outside world was through a series of letters to working men, entitled *Fors Clavigera*, which contain some of his ripest teaching, as well as much humorous and sweet-minded familiar talk. In *Fors Clavigera* first appeared the sketches afterward brought together as an extended autobiography, with the title *Præterita*, where a delightfully naïve and candid account is given of his boyhood and youth. He died in 1899.

Ruskin as Writer and as Teacher. — Ruskin combined many gifts and qualities: a subtle intellect, an intense susceptibility to beauty and ugliness, great moral ardor, marked impatience and dogmatism, and a marvellous power of prose expression. His style is based on the prose of the English Bible, modified by the religious writers of the seventeenth century, and it is enriched by a unique gift of description, lyrical in movement and splendid in color. His best descriptive passages, for example the famous dithyramb on St. Mark's cathedral in *Stones of Venice*, that on the Falls of Schaffhausen in *Modern Painters*, or that on the Rhone at Geneva, in *Præterita*, are among the greatest examples of descriptive eloquence in the language.

In the use to which he put his powers, Ruskin shows the strong sociological drift of the Victorian era. The first half of his life was taken up with the effort to vivify and spiritualize his countrymen's perceptions of the beautiful, an effort parallel with that of Arnold to combat the sloth of their intellect, with that of Carlyle to make more sincere and valiant their personal character. The latter half of his life was taken up with a protest against modern civilization, and with a search after some better basis of society than the present commercial one.

The Nineteenth-Century Novel. — While tracing, in this chapter and the preceding, the literary history of the nineteenth century, we have omitted all but casual mention of that form of literature which has been most popular, most widely cultivated, and perhaps most influential of all, — the novel. We must in the next chapter retrace our steps, take up the novel as it was handed on from the eighteenth century, and consider its manifold development during the last hundred years.

REVIEW OUTLINE. — With the close of the Revolutionary era, political events cease to have a preponderating influence upon literature, and social changes become of greater importance. Summarize the chief circumstances making for social change during the Victorian period, and describe briefly the influence which these changes have had upon the readers and makers of books. Note the unusual conjunction in Victorian literature of romantic feeling with a serious aim.

State briefly the facts of Macaulay's life up to his departure for India. When and how did he make his first reputation as a writer? What did the Reform Bill aim to accomplish, and what was Macaulay's connection with it? What were the literary fruits of Macaulay's residence in India? Give a short account of his life from his return to England until his death. In what respects does Macaulay's success as a speaker furnish a key to his popularity and power as a writer? In what province of essay-writing is Macaulay strongest? In what province is he, by his own confession, weakest? How much ground did he propose to cover in his " History," and how much did he actually cover? It has been said that Macaulay derived his ideal of what historical writing should be from the novels of Sir Walter Scott. What light does this throw upon his aim and method as a historian? Give some account of Macaulay's personal character; of his attitude toward his own time. How is he contrasted with Carlyle in this latter respect?

Give an account of Carlyle's life up to the time of his removal to London. From what source did he gain his greatest intellectual stimulus? What is the meaning, in Carlyle's own early history, of the phrases, " Everlasting No " and " Everlasting Yea "? What famous book, and what two notable essays had he written before leaving Craigenputtoch? It has been said that the sympathy which Carlyle shows in his essay on Burns is due in part to a resemblance between them. Can you instance a leading trait of Burns's character, as man and as poet, which gives him kinship with Carlyle? Narrate the chief facts of Carlyle's life after coming to London; name and characterize briefly some of his most important writings in their proper order. Give some instances of Carlyle's wit and caustic temper; of his generosity of character; of his tenderness. Pick out from your own reading some examples of his humor. In what respects may " Sartor Resartus " and " Heroes and Hero-Worship " be looked upon as his two typical books, embodying his view of life? Describe the plan of " Sartor Resartus." Compare Carlyle's attitude of irresponsibility and sly masquerading with what is said in Chapter X of Swift's method of satire. Explain the twofold meaning of the " Clothes philosophy," as developed in " Sartor." What is meant by the

phrase " Carlylese " ?   Carlyle takes rank with Macaulay as a master
of picturesque historical narrative; in what main respect do they
differ ?   State in broad terms the service which Carlyle rendered
to his age.

Note the circumstances of Tennyson's parentage and youth which
contributed to form his character as a poet. What was his first publication ?   When did his first independent volumes appear ?   What
circumstances of Tennyson's life during his ten years' silence, from
1832 to 1842, tended to give his work greater humanity and seriousness ?   In what poems of the 1842 volumes is this particularly apparent ?
How is " Ulysses " connected with Tennyson's personal history ?
What was Tennyson's political attitude, as shown in such poems as
" Love Thou Thy Land," and " Of Old Sat Freedom on the Heights " ?
Tell what you can of the relations between Tennyson and Arthur Hal-
lam.   How long was Tennyson engaged upon " In Memoriam " ?   Nar-
rate briefly the course of Tennyson's life from the publication of " In
Memoriam " until his death.   How long was he engaged upon the
" Idylls of the King " ?   What can you say of Tennyson as a laureate ?
What is the bearing of " Merlin and the Gleam " and " Crossing the
Bar " upon the poet's personal history ?   Describe the plan of " The
Princess."   With what question does " The Princess " deal, and what
is Tennyson's view of the question?   In what form is " In Memoriam " written ?   Note the admirable fitness of this form for presenting the many different moods, the many thoughts and memories which
the poem aims to present.   What, in general terms, is the course of
thought in the poem ?   Why was its religious aspect of peculiar importance at the time when it was written ?   With what two other
poems is it commonly grouped, and why ?   Review the history of
the King Arthur legends up to the time when Tennyson took them up.
By what central theme did Tennyson seek to give unity to the " Idylls
of the King " ?   In what respect is Tennyson the representative poet
of the Victorian age ?

Give a brief outline of Browning's life.   What was the first poetical
influence under which he fell, and how is this reflected in his first
volume ?   What is the theme of " Paracelsus " ?   What is his most
perfect long poem ?   Which is the greatest in scope and human meaning ?   Give the titles of two or three of his most successful dramas.
What was Browning's conception, in his youth, of the work he wished
to do; in what way did he realize his ambition ?   In what peculiar

kind of dramatic writing is Browning most successful? Explain in what respect " Pippa Passes " is typical of his peculiar dramatic genius. State some of the peculiarities of Browning's method in his short poems, illustrating the general points, if possible, from your own reading. Find for yourself further illustration, besides that given in the text, of Browning's sympathy with widely different types of human. life. What aspect of human life held the first place in his thoughts ? As an epitome of Browning's courage and optimism read the " Epilogue to Asolando," the last lines which Browning published; they are his farewell word in the same sense that " Crossing the Bar " is Tennyson's. Read in the same connection " Prospice," in which poem also he faces the fact of death, and utters his personal feeling concerning it. In what two poems did Browning and his wife leave to the world a memorial of their love for each other ? If possible read these two works together. Give a brief outline of Mrs. Browning's life, with her chief works. Where does she show the influence of Tennyson; where the humanitarian interest of her age; where her enthusiasm for Italian liberty; where the influence of the novel-writers of her time ?

State the leading facts of Arnold's life. What, in general, is his poetic attitude toward religion and human life ? How, in matters of faith, does he stand contrasted with Browning; how with Tennyson ? Note that, though he is in feeling a romantic poet, and born in an age when romanticism was prevalent in literature, he attempts to give his work classic form. What great poet of the seventeenth century does he resemble in this respect ? If possible read " Sohrab and Rustum," the masterpiece among Arnold's longer poems, noting particularly the romantic strangeness and picturesqueness of the story, together with the classic calmness and " poise " of the style in which it is told. With what three other great English elegies may " Thyrsis " be grouped ? With what kind of writing was Arnold chiefly occupied in his later years ? Explain, as clearly as possible, what Arnold meant by the catch-words, " Perfection," " Culture," and " Philistinism."

What point of resemblance is noticeable between the literary positions of Arnold and Ruskin. Into what two main periods was Ruskin's literary life divided ? Name two or three works of each period. Note Ruskin's theory of the relation between art and the ethical nature; between art and the society where it is produced. What was Ruskin's great service to political economy ? Read " Sesame and Lilies " as a typical example of Ruskin's style and thought. In what respect does Ruskin's later life reflect the social conscience of the Victorian age?

READING GUIDE.—Class reading of the authors treated in this chapter will naturally vary greatly, according to the taste of the teacher and of the student, and the time at their disposal. A selection from the following list will meet most cases.

Macaulay: Essays on Milton, on Addison, and on Johnson. These, together with the essay on Goldsmith, are given in Numbers 102, 103, and 104, of the Riverside Literature series.

Carlyle: Essays on Burns, on Boswell's "Johnson" (contrast with Macaulay's treatment); "The Hero as Poet" and "The Hero as Man of Letters," from "Heroes and Hero-Worship." These are included in the Selections from Carlyle by H. W. Boynton (Allyn & Bacon).

Tennyson: "The Lotus-Eaters," "The Lady of Shalott," "A Dream of Fair Women," "The Palace of Art," "The Miller's Daughter," "Locksley Hall," "Ulysses," "Charge of the Light Brigade," "The Revenge," ode on the Duke of Wellington, "Rizpah," "The Daisy," "Bugle Song" and "Tears, Idle Tears" from "The Princess"; "The Coming of Arthur," "Guinevere," and "The Passing of Arthur," from "Idylls of the King"; "The Poet," "Of Old Sat Freedom on the Heights," "Flower in the Crannied Wall," "The Higher Pantheism," "Merlin and the Gleam," "Crossing the Bar." All these poems, with selections from "Maud" and from "In Memoriam," are included in a volume edited by H. van Dyke, in the Athenæum Press series (Ginn).

Browning: Short Poems—"How They Brought the Good News from Ghent to Aix," "Cavalier Tunes," "The Lost Leader," "Meeting at Night and Parting at Morning," "Evelyn Hope," "Home Thoughts from Abroad," "My Star," "Memorabilia," "The Patriot," "The Boy and the Angel," "The Englishman in Italy," "One Word More," "Abt Vogler," "Rabbi Ben Ezra," "Prospice," "Hervé Riel," "Over the Sea Our Galleys Went" (from "Paracelsus"), "Never the Time and the Place," "Epilogue to Asolando." Longer Poems—"Fra Lippo Lippi," "Andrea del Sarto," "Epistle of Karshish the Arab Physician," "Saul," "The Flight of the Duchess," "Pippa Passes," "Pompilia" and "Caponsacchi" from "The Ring and the Book." A good selection from Browning's shorter poems is edited by F. T. Baker, in Macmillan's Pocket series.

Mrs. Browning: "The Cry of the Children," "Cowper's Grave,"

"Rhyme of the Duchess May," "The Great God Pan," a few of the "Sonnets from the Portuguese." Selections from Mrs. Browning's Shorter Poems, by H. E. Hershey, in Macmillan's Pocket series, is recommended.

Arnold: Poetry—"Dover Beach," "Obermann," "A Summer Night," "Self-Dependence," "The Scholar Gypsy," "Thyrsis," "Sohrab and Rustum." Selected poems in Maynard's English Classics. Prose— "On Translating Homer," essays on Wordsworth, on Milton, and on Gray (from "Essays in Criticism"), essays on Emerson and on Numbers (from "Discourses in America"), selections from "Culture and Anarchy," given in Number 68 of Maynard's English Classics.

Ruskin: "Sesame and Lilies," "Crown of Wild Olive," "Unto This Last," selections from "Modern Painters," given in Number 48 of Maynard's English Classics. Comprehensive selections from Ruskin, with critical comment, are edited in one volume, by Mrs. L. G. Hufford (Ginn).

Texts: Besides the editions already mentioned, the following may be found useful—"Macaulay's Essays" (twenty-seven essays), and "Lays of Ancient Rome," in a single volume (Longmans); "Carlyle's Critical and Miscellaneous Essays," in one volume (Appleton); "Heroes and Hero-Worship" (Athenæum Press series, and in Cassell's National Library); "Past and Present" and "Sartor Resartus," in one volume (Harpers); "Selections from Tennyson's Shorter Poems," edited by C. R. Nutter, in Macmillan's Pocket series; "The Princess" and "Idylls of the King" in same series, also in Maynard's English Classics, Riverside Literature series, etc.; "Browning's Selected Poems" (Harpers), "Principal Shorter Poems" (Appleton), selections also in Maynard's English Classics; Arnold, "Selected Poems" in Golden Treasury series, "Selections from Prose Writings," by L. E. Gates (Holt); Ruskin, "Wild Olive" and "Munera Pulveris," in one volume (U. S. Book Co.), "Wild Olive" and "Sesame and Lilies," one volume (Burt).

Biography and Criticism.—Life of Macaulay, by J. A. C. Morison, in the English Men of Letters; the "Life of Macaulay," by G. O. Trevelyan, is one of the great biographies of English literature, but is too voluminous for school use. The life of Carlyle, by R. Garnett, in the Great Writers series, is more satisfactory than the one given in the English Men of Letters; an essay on Carlyle occurs in Lowell's "My Study Windows." The life of Tennyson, by A. Lyall, English Men of Letters, is the best for ordinary use; H. van Dyke's study,

"The Poetry of Tennyson," is the best among the many commentaries upon his work. The life of Browning, by W. Sharp, Great Writers series, and by G. K. Chesterton, English Men of Letters, supplement each other well; the best aid to an understanding of Browning for beginners, is H. Corson's "Introduction to the Study of Browning" (Heath). An excellent study of Arnold is prefixed to the volume of "Selections" by L. E. Gates, mentioned above. Of Ruskin's life, especially his early years, his autobiography entitled "Præterita" is the best account; Ruskin, in the English Men of Letters series, is by F. Harrison. Among the critical commentaries may be mentioned " The Work of John Ruskin," by C. Waldstein (Harpers) and "John Ruskin, Social Reformer," by J. A. Hobson.

CHAPTER XV

THE NINETEENTH-CENTURY NOVEL

I. INTRODUCTION

THE novel of the nineteenth century is broader and more complex than that of the eighteenth, by virtue of the greater breadth and complexity of the life with which it has to deal. The world of fiction in the eighteenth century is a small one; its characters are, with a few notable exceptions, drawn from the leisure class and its dependents; they have usually no business in life beyond carrying on the action of the story. But in the nineteenth century we have novels which deal with the life of the sea, the army, crime, sport, commerce, labor, politics, and the church, and with the special difficulties, dangers, and temptations which each career involves. Again, the increase in knowledge of the past, and of remote parts of the world, which the century has brought, has thrown open to the romancer two great new fields. Finally, the deeper thought of the century, bearing fruit in rapid social changes, has given to the novel of purpose greater dignity and power. The attempt to reform government and institutions, the labor movement, the so-called conflict between science and faith, all have been reflected in novels, and have in turn been influenced by them. The nineteenth-century novel is therefore to be regarded not only as a vast and comprehensive picture of life, but as a powerful force acting upon society.

II. JANE AUSTEN (1775–1817)

Jane Austen's Life.—The earliest of nineteenth-century novelists, however, Jane Austen, is not representative of the wider scope of the novel in the new period, but is remarkable for her perfection in handling the limited interests of eighteenth-century fiction. Miss Austen was the daughter of a clergyman and, except for an occasional visit to a watering-place like Bath or Lyme, she spent her youth in a country parish. Her acquaintance included the families of country gentlemen, clergymen, and naval officers—for her brothers were in the navy. The chief business of these people, as Miss Austen saw them, was attention to social duties, and the chief subject of their thought was matrimony. This world, and the influences at work there, Miss Austen represents in her novels; outside of it she never steps.

Her Satiric Purpose.—Miss Austen, like Fielding, began her studies of real life with something of a satiric purpose. Two of her early stories, *Northanger Abbey* and *Sense and Sensibility*, were written in order to oppose to the impossible situations and strained emotions of the romanticists and sentimentalists a humorously sensible picture of life and love as they are. In the former she gives us a heroine who starts with a "thin awkward figure, a sallow skin, without color, dark lank hair, and strong features," and who wins an admirable husband, though "his affection originated in nothing better than a persuasion of her partiality for him." The keynote of *Sense and Sensibility* is expressed in the remark, "Sense is the foundation on which everything good may be based." In the novels which followed, "*Pride and Prejudice, Mansfield Park,* and *Emma,* Miss Austen carries farther her minute observation of life, sharpened by satirical comment. One suspects that she shared thoroughly in the view of life put forth by Mr. Bennet in *Pride and Prejudice,* "For what do we live but to make sport for our neighbors and to laugh at them in our turn?"

"Pride and Prejudice."—*Pride and Prejudice* is Miss Austen's masterpiece. There she shows her skill in constructing a plot. There also she is at her best in creating a background of minor characters drawn from the world of provincial folk which she knew—cynical Mr. Bennet and his fatuous wife; Mary Bennet the pedant, and Lydia the flirt; Mr. Collins, the type of pretentious conceit, and Sir William Lucas, of feeble dulness. These "humors" Miss Austen develops chiefly in speech, by her wonderful faculty of saying the thing that belongs to the character at the moment. Not only is the proper sentiment caught, but the turn of phrase, the manner, almost the modulation of the voice. And not only is this true of the limited characters who act always in the same way; in the sustained scenes between the more developed persons, where the dialogue is more highly charged with meaning, Miss Austen shows dramatic power of the highest order.

Miss Austen's stories are the most perfect examples of the eighteenth-century novel of manners, though by virtue of their technical skill they seem to belong almost to our own day. In striking contrast to the petty, provincial world which she mastered so thoroughly, is the great field of history and romance brought before us in the novels of her contemporary, Sir Walter Scott.

III. SIR WALTER SCOTT (1771–1832)

Scott's Early Life. — Scott was born in Edinburgh, August 15, 1771, of a family famous in the border wars, and in the long struggle of the Stuarts for the throne. His father, however, had forsaken the venturesome life of his ancestors and had become an attorney. He sought to bring up his son to the same profession, and did give to the latter's character that strong bent toward system and industry which he never lost. The young Walter, in spite of a slight lameness, the result of an illness in childhood, was distinguished for activity in bodily sports; and as a young man he found satisfaction for his roving disposition in journeys through the wilder parts of Scotland—the Cheviots and the Highlands. On these expeditions he learned to know types of Scotch character, as well as the legends and traditions of Scotch history of which he afterward made such brilliant use. As a youth Scott was much in the company of persons who stimulated and fed his interest in the past. The century before his birth had been one full of excitement. In Scotland the Puritans, under the name Covenanters, had fought their last battles against the restored Stuarts; and Scotland had been the scene of the romantic attempts of the princes of that exiled house to regain their throne in 1715 and 1745. To these things Scott was brought near by the companionship of his grandfather—whose father had been a famous adherent of the Stuarts, known as " Beardie " because of his refusal to cut his beard until that family should be restored—and by the conversation of his mother. Of her he wrote much later: "If I have been able to do anything in the way of painting the past times it is very much from the studies with which she presented me."

Scott at Abbotsford.—Scott was married in 1797 to the daughter of one of the French exiles from the Revolution. He lived first in a cottage at Lasswade, a few miles from Edinburgh. Then in 1804 he moved to Ashestiel, in Selkirkshire, of which county he had been made sheriff. The success of his poems, however, enabled him in 1812 to purchase the estate of Abbotsford, with which his name is forever connected. Scott at Abbotsford is charmingly described for us by Washington Irving, who visited him in 1817. " He was tall and of a large and powerful frame. His dress was simple, and almost rustic. An old green shooting coat with a dog-whistle at the button-hole, brown linen pantaloons, stout shoes that tied at the ankles, and a white hat that had seen service. He came limping up the gravel-walk, aiding himself by a stout walking-staff, but moving rapidly and with vigor. By his side jogged along a large, iron-gray stag-hound of most grave demeanor, who took no part in the clamor of the canine rabble, but seemed to consider himself bound for the dignity of the house to give me a courteous reception." An account of the life at Abbotsford in later years, when Scott had replaced his cottage by a baronial castle, and had developed his establishment to feudal magnificence, is given by Lockhart in his *Life of Scott.* It was Scott's custom to write conscientiously during the early morning, but, his task finished, he delighted to put himself at the head of a cavalcade of guests and retainers for a hunting expedition, or a ride to the Yarrow, or to Dryburgh Abbey.

To support this train of life, Scott relied on the profits of a secret partnership which he had formed with two brothers

SIR WALTER SCOTT
From a painting by C. R. Leslie, R.A.

named Ballantyne, in a printing and publishing business. The firm became considerably embarrassed about the time of the purchase of Abbotsford, and just then, too, Scott's popularity as a poet was on the wane. He retrieved his doubtful fortunes, however, when in 1814 he took up and finished a tale begun some nine years earlier, and published it under the title *Waverley.* This was the first of the great series of romances which fascinated the whole reading world. The name of Scott was not at first connected with them, but their authorship soon became an open secret. With the control of the Waverley novels in their hands the Ballantynes prospered, but in the end the mismanagement of the active partners and Scott's own etravaxgance resulted in the failure of the firm for £117,000, all of which Scott assumed. The last years of his life were a splendid struggle to pay this debt. In fact he did earn more than half of the needed sum, and the rest was discharged by the sale of his earlier copyrights. But the effort broke him physically and mentally, and hastened his death, which came in 1832. Carlyle, who saw him in these last years on the Edinburgh streets, made a sketch of him which must stand beside Irving's. "Alas, his fine Scotch face with its shaggy honesty, sagacity, and goodness was all worn with care, the joy all fled from it;—ploughed deep with labor and sorrow. We shall never forget it; we shall never see it again. Adieu, Sir Walter, pride of all Scotchmen, take our proud and sad farewell."

Scott's Character.—Scott's life was a blending of the old and the new. He tried to be both a feudal lord and a modern business man, and both attempts are curiously connected with his literary career. He wrote partly for the pleasure of creating in fiction the feudal ideal that he sought to realize at Abbotsford, partly for the money with which to sustain that experiment. In this almost mercantile aspect of his literary life there is something essentially unromantic, and indeed in many traits of character Scott has little likeness to his romantic contemporaries. We find in him nothing of the spiritual experience, nothing of the revolt against the conventions of the political and social world, that mark Coleridge and Shelley. But Scott had, on the other hand, a love of Scotland, of her scenery, of her history, of her people, which may be called the romantic passion of his life.

The Scotch Novels.—It is worthy of note that in his first novel Scott recognized his chief strength to be in his knowledge of his native land and its people. After some hesitation at the outset, he starts his hero for Scotland and plunges him into a society composed of quaint Scotch types,—Baron Bradwardine, the type of old-fashioned feudal prejudice, Laird Balmawhapple, Baillie MacWheeble, with David Gellatley and his mother, old Janet, for dependents. Waverley becomes involved in the attempt of the Young Pretender to win the throne in 1745, and Scott takes the opportunity to reinforce his story by the introduction of historical characters and events,—a device of which he thus early showed his mastery.

In the novels which immediately followed *Waverley*, Scott dealt with the material which he had most successfully at command—Scotch life in the eighteenth century, which he knew at first-hand or from recent tradition. These books are *Guy Mannering* (1815) and *The Antiquary* (1816), both of which may be called novels of private life. In later works he went into the more remote past, and relied more upon historical sources. In *Old Mortality* (1816) he treated the revolt of the Covenanters in the reign of Charles II., and in *The Abbot* (1820) and *The Monastery* (1820) the tragic events surrounding the life of Mary Queen of Scots. In *Redgauntlet* (1824) he returned to the eighteenth century, and to the last plots of the Jacobites to bring the Pretender to the throne.

Scotch Characters.—In this series of novels we find some of Scott's best characters, drawn from the humble life of both Highlands and Lowlands. In such characters Scott worked with his eye upon the object; many of them have been recognized as life-like portraits of persons whom he met in his wanderings, or of dependents like Tom Purdie, his huntsman. These local types show us the humor and the pathos of humanity warped by circumstances into a hundred fantastic forms, but capable of sometimes throwing itself into an attitude of noble disinterestedness, of dignified endurance, or of tragic despair.   When in *Waverley* the historic drama of the rising of 1745 has played itself out, and the love-story has been tamely concluded, the figure that remains with us as we close the book, is that of Evan Dhu, the humble follower of the Highland chief Vich Ian Vohr, standing at the condemnation of his master, and pledging himself and six of the clan to die in his stead.   "If the Saxon gentlemen are laughing," he said, "because a poor man, such as me, thinks my life or the life of six of my degree is worth that of Vich Ian Vohr, it's like enough they may be very right; but if they laugh because they think I would not keep my word, and come back to redeem him, they ken neither the heart of a Hielandman, nor the honour of a gentleman."   Among such types as these we look for Scott's greatest characters: Edie Ochiltree in *The Antiquary*, Baillie Jarvie in *Rob Roy*, Peter Peebles in *Redgauntlet*, and many more who stand out from the novels as complete and substantial figures in which the race of Scotchmen has expressed itself forever.   Only once, however, did Scott trust entirely to this element of native strength. In *The Heart of Midlothian* (1818), he puts aside all conventional plot, and gives us instead the story of Jeanie Deans the peasant girl, who goes to London to beg her sister's life.

Among these local Scotch types there is a group of characters whom Scott used especially to appeal to the romantic sense of his readers.   The fantastic figures which stand out of the background, Madge Wildfire in *The Heart of Midlothian*, Meg Merrilies in *Guy Mannering*, and Norna of the Fitful Head in *The Pirate* are far more terrible and mysterious in their reality than the imagined horrors of many of Scott's rivals.

Description and Incident.—In the Scotch novels, also, we find Scott's descriptive power at its best.   He himself lamented that he had not "the eye of a painter to dissect the various parts of the scene, to comprehend how one bore upon the other, to estimate the effect which various features of the view had in producing its leading and general effect." But," he adds, "show me an old castle, and I was at home at once, filled it with its combatants in their proper costume, and overwhelmed my readers by the enthusiasm of my description." And he goes on to tell how in crossing Magus Moor he gave such an account of the assassination of the Bishop of St. Andrews that one of his fellow-travellers complained that his night's sleep was frightened away. Scott loved scenery as a background for picturesque action. As Stevenson remarks, some places seem actually to cry out for an appropriate occurrence; and Scott's minute acquaintance with Scotch history suggested to him the incidents by which he gives to his scenes their final reality, and makes them an essential part in the dramatic action of his story. A noteworthy instance of this faculty occurs in *Old Mortality*, where Morton visits Balfour of Burley in the cave reached by a single tree-trunk bridging the chasm of a waterfall. As Morton approaches he hears the shouts and screams of the old Covenanter, in whom religious fury has become insanity; and at length he sees the fearful figure of Burley in strife with the fiends which beset him. The effect of threatening scenery and of the terror of madness is brought to a focus, as it were, at the instant when Burley sends the tree crashing into the abyss, leaving Morton to jump for his life.

Scott's Use of History.—In his later novels Scott went more and more outside of Scotland for material. In *Ivanhoe* (1820) he treated the return of Richard I. to his kingdom; in *Kenilworth* (1821), the intrigues of Leicester in seeking to marry Queen Elizabeth; in *The Fortunes of Nigel* (1822), the time of James I. In *Quentin Durward* (1823) he went to the continent, picturing the struggle of Louis XI. with Charles the Bold, and in *The Talisman* (1825) that of Richard I. with Saladin. In these English and continental novels it must be admitted that historical interest and study did not supply all that personal knowledge and enthusiasm gave to the Scotch. Yet in the former we find some of Scott's most brilliant portraits of historical characters, and his reconstructions of social and political conditions are among the triumphs of the historical imagination. And especially do these stories display Scott's mastery of the art of the historical novel—his power of making history live by virtue of its connection with fiction, and of giving interest and dignity to fiction by making it turn on the progress of great historical movements.

Scott's Example.—Since Scott's day many novelists—Dickens, Thackeray, Charles Kingsley, and George Eliot, have made attempts in the historical field. Bulwer Lytton's *Last Days of Pompeii* is the best known of his many volumes. In *The Cloister and the Hearth* by Charles Reade, we have the author's masterpiece, and one of the best historical novels since Scott. This vogue of the historical novel must be attributed in large part to Scott's example.

In general, however, the romantic temper, which first commended historical material to the novelist, gave place, after Scott's death, to a different mood. Scott's romantic pictures of the feudal past were flattering to a people struggling, as they thought, to preserve the relics of that past from the engulfing revolution. But after the immediate effect of the Napoleonic wars had passed away, new ideas began to make progress in England, broadening the current of English thought and life. The rapidity of social changes beginning with the Reform Bill of 1832, served to draw men's attention to the life of their own time. And while the taste for the new and the startling in literature still persisted, it was satisfied chiefly, as in Defoe's time, by the presentation of the exciting aspects of present-day society. Of these tendencies the best examples are to be found in the works of Edward Bulwer Lytton (1803–1873), Charles Reade (1814–1884), and Charles Dickens.

IV. CHARLES DICKENS (1812–1870)

Dickens's Life.—Charles Dickens was born at Portsea, where his father was a navy clerk in poor circumstances. The family moved to Chatham, and thence to London, where the elder Dickens was arrested for debt, his family accompanying him to the Marshalsea Prison. His son, a boy of ten years, was thought old enough to contribute his mite toward the parents' necessities, and was accordingly put at work in a blacking warehouse, sleeping beneath a counter, and spending his Sundays—his few hours of brightness in these wretched weeks—in the prison with his family. When matters improved a little, Charles Dickens was given a few years of school before he was obliged to take up again the part of bread-winner, first as a lawyer's clerk, and then as a reporter. His education remained deficient, but he brought from these years of desperate struggle with life a character of wonderful energy and resolution, a wide knowledge of the under world, and a deep sympathy with its inhabitants— all of which played a part in his subsequent career.

It was while Dickens, then about twenty, was a reporter that he began to write sketches of London life for the newspapers. These were collected in 1836 as *Sketches by Boz*, and from this time forth Dickens's fortune was changed. He became editor of magazines, and, for a time, of a great London newspaper; he travelled widely in Europe and America; he took up public questions and attacked social wrongs. And without any intermission he gave to the public that famous series of novels in which the humors of English life were displayed so abundantly, and the cause of the suffering pleaded so eloquently. Before he was thirty he was a great writer; and before he was forty, a notable public man. No writer in English ever gathered with a fuller hand the rewards of the literary calling. It is true, other writers have made more money, or have won peerages; but none has had in his lifetime so wide and intensely loyal a personal following; none has had, in addition to money, friends, and fame, the peculiar tribute which came to Dickens from vast audiences gathered together, not once or twice, but hundreds of times, in scores of cities, to testify by "roaring seas of applause" to his personal triumph. In middle life Dickens began to give semi-dramatic public readings from his works, and these grew to be his chief interest. The strain and excitement wore him out. It is a circumstance as tragic in its way as that which shadows the close of Scott's life, that this personal triumph was the direct cause of Dickens's death in 1870.

Dickens's Relation to the Public.—Dickens's peculiar success calls attention to the prime fact in his authorship, his nearness to his public. He began his career as a reporter, in the profession which is most immediately of the people. But though necessity made him a journalist, he wished to be an actor. As a young man he tried to get a position at Covent Garden Theatre. For years he was the leading spirit in a famous company of amateurs who played in various cities of England; and, as we have seen, his chief interest came to be his public readings. These two professional instincts account for much in Dickens's work. As reporter and as editor he studied his public; as actor, he taught himself to play upon it, through his writings and his dramatic readings from them, with incomparable skill.

Dickens's Characters.—From Dickens's success in *Sketches by Boz* came, in 1836, an engagement to write the letterpress for a series of cartoons representing the humors of sporting life. For this purpose he invented the "Pickwick Club," which at once made a popular hit. The death of the artist who was engaged upon the drawings left Dickens free to widen the scope of the adventures of the club, and to add other characters without stint. The complete result was a great book, formless as to plot, crowded with humorous figures. These figures are given with broadly exaggerated traits, as if Dickens had always in mind the cartoon which was to accompany the text. The characters talk freely, not to say inexhaustibly, and all differently. But the author's chief resource is his faculty for bringing his caricatures into contact with the actual world, in situations that expose their oddities in high relief. Mr. Tupman as a lover, Mr. Winkle as a duellist or a sportsman, Mr. Pickwick in a breach-of-promise suit with the Widow Bardell, the Pickwick Club contending with a recalcitrant horse, the Reverend Mr. Stiggins drunk at a temperance meeting—these incongruities are narrated in a style always copious, but often rapid and piquant.

In his later novels Dickens improved on his first attempts. He continued to be a caricaturist, to rely on distortions and exaggerations of feature or of manner, but his pencil became more subtle and his figures more significant. Micawber "waiting for something to turn up," Sairy Gamp haunted by the mythical Mrs. Harris, 'umble Uriah Heep, sanctimonious Pecksniff, cheerful Mark Tapley, all have distinct individ-

CHARLES DICKENS

uality, yet all label so conveniently common attitudes and habits of mind that we use their names freely to describe whole classes of mankind.

In *Pickwick* Dickens is purely a humorist; in the novels which followed he created figures of a different sort, to excite not laughter, but loathing and terror. In the portrayal of these types also he gained subtlety with practice. Fagin and Sykes in *Oliver Twist* (1838), Quilp, the dwarf, in *Old Curiosity Shop* (1841), monstrous as they are, do not haunt the reader with the terrible suggestion of inhumanity that lurks behind the placid, smiling face of Mme. Defarge in *A Tale of Two Cities* (1859), as she sits in front of the guillotine, knitting, and counting the heads as they fall. In the stories just mentioned Dickens showed again his fertility in inventing situations for his characters, using his dramatic power as freely in melodrama as in farce. The part of Fagin at his trial and in prison is worked out as if for the stage, by an actor careful to make every gesture, every expression, tell on his audience.

His Purpose.—A third type of character which Dickens developed, and which in his time made immensely for his popularity, was the victim of society—usually a child. In his second novel, Dickens made his story centre about a child, Oliver Twist, and from that time forth children were expected and necessary characters in his novels. Little Nell, Florence Dombey, David Copperfield, represent in most telling form the case of the individual against society. For with Dickens the private cruelty which his malign characters inflict, is almost always connected with social wrong. Bumble's savage blow at Oliver Twist asking for more food, Little Dorrit's life in the Marshalsea, are carried back and laid at the door of a society which permitted the poor-house and the debtor's prison to exist. The championship of the individual against institutions, which had been a leading motive in later eighteenth-century fiction, had been checked by the reaction against the French Revolution; but in Dickens's day the "redress of wrongs" had become again a great public movement. The workings of later romanticism had begun to be reflected in a kind of sentimental hatred of organized authority, a feeling to which Dickens constantly appealed. Undoubtedly there was something theatrical in Dickens's adoption of social wrong as a motive in fiction, but there was great sincerity also. He had himself known the lot of the persecuted; at the root of his zeal for reform was the memory of his own bitter childhood.

Dickens's Plots.—The types of character already discussed were sufficient to sustain the movement of Dickens's earlier books, which were usually simple in structure. In most of them we begin with the hero in childhood, and follow his personal adventures into the thick of a plot involving the popular romantic material of the day, kidnapping, murder, mob-justice, and other incidents of criminal life. In his later books, however, Dickens gained the power of constructing elaborate plots, and of creating characters of heroic dignity and tragic intensity, such as Sidney Carton in *The Tale of Two Cities* and Lady Dedlock in *Bleak House* (1853). These are the most enduringly powerful of his novels, but they are not those upon which his fame rests. Dickens is remembered not as a dramatic artist in the novel form, but as a showman of wonderful resources. He is master of a vast and fascinating stage, crowded with farcical characters, with grotesque and terrible creatures, more devils than men, and with the touching forms of little children. The action is sometimes merry, sometimes exciting, sometimes pathetic. We have laughter, and horror, and tears; but the prevailing atmosphere is one of cheerfulness, as befits a great Christmas pantomime.

Dickens dealt in the main with the world of his own day, but his spirit was not that of a realist bent on representing things as they are. On the contrary, his humor lies largely in exaggeration, and the interest of his stories generally in their use of the unusual and romantic elements in life. A further step in bringing the novel down to the world as it exists for the average man was taken by Thackeray.

V. WILLIAM MAKEPEACE THACKERAY (1811–1863)

Thackeray's Life.—Thackeray was born in Calcutta, India, in 1811. He was educated at the Charter-House School and at Cambridge. He gave some time to art study on the Continent, and after losing his small patrimony in a journalistic venture he tried to make a living as an artist. He applied, indeed, for the position as illustrator of Dickens's *Pickwick Papers*. Unsuccessful in this, he turned to literature, and became a contributor to *Punch* and to *Fraser's Magazine*. His first work consisted of light essays, sketches of travel, and burlesques in which the weaknesses of the romantic school are cleverly hit off in imitations of Scott, Bulwer and others. His intention to write of the world as it is is rather broadly proclaimed in his first considerable tale, *Catherine* (1839), of which the heroine is a female rogue, drawn with unsympathetic realism as a rebuke to the sentimental treatment of criminals exemplified by Dickens's Nancy, in *Oliver Twist*.

Thackeray gave his realistic theories larger scope in *Barry Lyndon* (1844), a spirited account of the exploits of an eighteenth-century adventurer, and in *Vanity Fair*, which was published in parts between 1846 and 1848. This at length gave Thackeray an assured position in English literature, but with a singular distrust in his future he made various attempts, fortunately unsuccessful, to escape into the civil or the diplomatic service. Thrown back upon his real vocation, he produced his other masterpieces, *Pendennis* (1848–50), *Henry Esmond* (1852), *The Newcomes* (1853–55), and *The Virginians* (1857–59). Meanwhile he delivered his lectures on *The English Humourists of the Eighteenth Century* and *The Four Georges*, in England and in America. In 1860 he became editor of the *Cornhill Magazine*, which position he resigned shortly before his death.

Thackeray's Temperament.—Thackeray was not happy either in circumstances or altogether in temperament. His long period of unsuccess, his wife's insanity, which came upon her soon after their marriage, and his own ill-health,

WILLIAM MAKEPEACE THACKERAY
From a drawing by George T. Tobin

spoiled much of his life, and a singular quality of distrust and indecision subtracted heavily from the joy of what was left. He lived much in the world of London clubs and society, a world of which he saw and pictured the pettiness and the insincerity in his books, but in which he, like Charles Lamb, found a necessary stimulus and distraction. Like Lamb also, he hid his melancholy behind an aspect of mirth, occasionally a little boisterous and hollow, but usually gentle and almost whimsically honest in confessing itself to be but a mask. Thackeray bore his own burdens with brave patience, and took those of others generously. He was far from being, as some have thought, either a sentimentalist or a cynic; he was in all ways a kind and gallant gentleman.

These facts are important, since, more than most writers of fiction, Thackeray wrote himself into his books. The form of his novels was determined in a way by his shortcomings. All his works except *Esmond* were published in parts, and, with natural indolence which he could never overcome, he seldom began his fresh instalment until it was actually called for, and had to be done in a hurry. Naturally, his novels are not models of construction; but it is to be said that this loose method of working suited not only Thackeray's temperament, but also his artistic problem. For Thackeray is primarily an observer, not an analyst. He saw life with the wide view of a man of the world. To have confined his multitude of characters within the narrow limits of what is technically called a plot would have introduced an element of unreality into his books. Again, the pressure under which he worked accounts for the many pages of comment which he gives us in his own person—comment that filled out his number nicely when invention halted and the story lagged. As a result Thackeray is, as someone has said, himself the chief figure in his novels. In the preface to *Vanity Fair* he speaks of his characters as a set of puppets whom he can make dance at will. He is the showman, and hence the most important, indeed the only real, person in the show.

"Vanity Fair."—As a showman Thackeray is incomparable. In *Vanity Fair* he has arranged his stage so perfectly that, but for his reminder, we should forget that it is a stage, and

English humurios

should think of it as a peopled world. The action of the book revolves about the heroines, Becky Sharp and Amelia Sedley—"the famous little Becky puppet,—pronounced to be uncommonly flexible in the joints and lively on the wire: the Amelia Doll,—carved and dressed with the greatest care by the artist." Both represent permanent types, Amelia, mild and incapable—a parasite, the author calls her—living on the chivalrous protection of Dobbin; Becky, keen and competent, making her world for herself, levying tribute on every man who crosses her path. The two stories begin together, and Thackeray supplies a link between them later in Jos Sedley; but in the end he gives over the attempt to unite them, and lets the two sets of characters diverge in his novel as they must have done in life.

The satire with which Thackeray treats his characters indicates his attitude toward the world which he pictures. In the metaphor of the puppets lurks a gleam of the irony which Swift showed in his sketch of society as Lilliput. The title too, *Vanity Fair*—Bunyan's fair, "where is sold all sorts of vanity, and where is to be seen juggling, cheats, games, plays, fools, apes, knaves, rogues, and that of every kind,"—suggests something of contempt if not of bitterness. The roguishness and weakness of Thackeray's puppets has long been a ground for calling their showman a cynic; but Thackeray's satire is strongly tempered with tolerance and with pity. Dickens draws his pathos from the spectacle of ideal innocence exposed to the evils of the world; but Thackeray makes no less pitiful the sorrows of men and women who are themselves sinful, weak, and stupid. Becky's husband, Rawdon Crawley, is not an admirable figure, yet we are sorry for him. George and Amelia Osborne are both in their way contemptible, yet the scene of their parting is full of tenderness. And in the great book which came later, *The Newcomes*, Thackeray has given a picture of human imperfection so inexpressibly real and touching, that every reader believes the story of the novelist's coming from his work-room one day, sobbing, "I have killed Colonel Newcome." Thackeray was merciful toward the feeble, flawed souls that he portrayed, because gentleness was a part of his nature. Without faith in most of the pretentious virtues of the world, he still believed in kindness, in the instinctive goodness of one being toward another, and he exemplified this belief in his books as in his life.

Thackeray's Use of History.—The vogue of historical fiction after Scott is shown by the fact that even the petty world of *Vanity Fair* is disturbed by a great national crisis; but Thackeray, instead of using Waterloo to impose dignity and splendor upon his story, characteristically gives us a "back-stairs" view of war. We follow the battle, not in the thought of Napoleon or the Duke, but chiefly as it is reflected in the fears of the wretched Jos Sedley, in the hopes of his servant Isidore, and in the calculations of Becky Sharp; chiefly, but not wholly, for there is poor, almost abandoned Amelia "praying for George, who was lying on his face, dead, with a bullet through his heart." Thackeray is interested in famous events and persons because of the light which they throw upon the common affairs of men. In *Henry Esmond*, however, as in *Vanity Fair*, Thackeray's own temperament is to be reckoned with. His sympathy with the preceding century gives to his treatment of it a warmth and brilliancy which make the most realistic of historical novels also the most poetic.

"Henry Esmond."—In *Henry Esmond* we follow the hero's childhood at Castlewood, in the mysterious atmosphere of plotting Papists, and his youth in the London of Queen Anne, where the persons and names of Addison, Steele, Swift, and Fielding meet us as casually as those of modern celebrities to-day. We see him take part in the wonderful victories of Marlborough, and in the daring game which the Pretender played for his crown. The vanished world lives for us in character and in episode, lives with a dignity and richness of conception and style that show Thackeray to have been, when he chose, the greatest artist among the English novelists. In his masterpiece he is writing, not as a careless, rather lazy master of a puppet-show, but in the person of the chivalrous Esmond. Every incident and description, then, must reflect his hero's character in some touch of nobility or of charm. In Esmond's repulsion from

Marlborough, in his devotion to Castlewood and his son, in his passion for Beatrix, and in his love for Lady Castlewood, there is the constant revelation of an honorable and loyal man. When he is telling us of the quarrel between Marlborough and Webb, there is something in the account which reminds us that it is a gentleman's story. When he surrenders his birthright, property, and name, he bears himself with a simplicity and a modesty which are in keeping with a great renunciation. The style itself, marvellous in its likeness to the manner of the eighteenth century, is yet more wonderful in its reflection of Esmond's personality. When he leaves Castlewood, or stands at his mother's grave, when he bends beside the body of his dear lord, killed by the villain Mohun, always his utterance is perfect in its intimacy, its simplicity, its distant, haunting rhythm. Even in a detail of the picture of Lady Castlewood vanishing from Esmond's sight in anger, Thackeray's distinction is evident. "He saw her retreating, the taper lighting up her marble face, her scarlet lip quivering, and her shining golden hair." Had Thackeray written only this scene, he might have been called a master. As it is he is the greatest writer who has used English in fiction.

VI. CHARLOTTE BRONTË AND CHARLES KINGSLEY

Charlotte Brontë.—The example of Thackeray, both as a realist and as a moralist, had a powerful influence upon a writer who, by force of circumstances and the impulse of her own temperament, was a romanticist. Charlotte Brontë (1816–1855) grew up in the Yorkshire parsonage of her father, with such experience of the world as came from country boarding-schools, a year in Brussels, and her own family life, with its terrible succession of tragedies—the death of her mother and three sisters, the blindness of her father, and the ruin of her brother through dissipation. She and her sisters wrote at first for their own amusement, inventing scenes and characters to supplement the scanty interests of the life that they knew. One of these stories, *Wuth-*

ering Heights, by Emily Brontë (1847) is still among the most strangely powerful of all novels.

"Jane Eyre."—Charlotte Brontë's masterpiece, *Jane Eyre*, appeared the next year. In this story Miss Brontë undertook to portray a real woman without the personal attractions of the ordinary heroine. Jane Eyre is modest, plain, insignificant in appearance. Her early life is merely a reproduction of Miss Brontë's own uneventful days at school. She soon passes beyond the world of the author's experience into the romantic realm of her imagination and longing, but though many of the incidents of her story are improbable, she remains a genuine woman. It was this honesty of purpose that attracted the attention of critics, and under their friendly advice Miss Brontë undertook in her later books, *Shirley* (1849), and *Villette* (1853), to confine herself to representing the life and the characters that she knew in Yorkshire and in Brussels. In this conscious attempt, however, she lost something of the freshness and fervor which make *Jane Eyre* a book of winning power and charm.

Her Feeling for Nature.—In one direction Miss Brontë's experience was adequate, namely, in her contact with nature. From her books we know how largely in her life the clouds, the ragged hills, the wide spaces of the Yorkshire moors under sunset or moonlight, made up for the inadequacy of human society and interests. She makes nature enter into the warp and woof of her stories through the part which it plays in the most essential element in them, the inner life of her heroines.

Kingsley.—Charles Kingsley (1819–1875) was a man of many interests, and only incidentally a writer of novels. He was a clergyman, Professor of Modern History at Cambridge, a leader in the "Broad Church" movement, the friend of Tennyson, and somewhat later of Carlyle, of whose strenuous philosophy of life he was a sort of popular exponent. His novels fall into two divisions. In the earlier ones, *Yeast* (1848) and *Alton Locke* (1850), Kingsley gives a view of the problems which perplexed men's minds in the middle years of the century, and tries to point out a middle course between Catholicism and scepticism in religion, between Toryism and revolution in politics. In the second division he works out his purpose through the historical novel. *Hypatia* (1853) is a study of the struggle between Christianity and Paganism, in Alexandria during the fourth century, and its sub-title, "New Foes With an Old Face," indicates its bearing upon the religious questions of his own time. His masterpiece, *Westward Ho* (1855), is a vigorous story of the times of Elizabeth, depicting the contest of England with Spain by sea and in America. In these later novels Kingsley shows many of the qualities of the artist. His scenes have the vividness of painting, and his incident is at times superbly dramatic. And in both, Kingsley is chiefly concerned with the presentation of types of character and ideals of life which made for national greatness and social health in the England of his own day.

VII. GEORGE ELIOT (1819–1880)

George Eliot's Life.—A still more significant illustration of the connection between fiction and the intellectual and moral development of England is the work of George Eliot. The author who so signed herself, Mary Ann Evans, was born in Warwickshire in 1819. Her father was of peasant stock, the agent for the estates of a number of gentlemen of the county, a man of strong and worthy character, instinctively religious and conservative. Mary Ann spent her earliest years in the country, except for some terms at boarding-school. When she was twenty-one, however, her mother having died, her father removed to Coventry. There she came into close contact with a group of people who were much interested in religious questions, and disposed to treat them in a spirit of rationalism. Under their influence Miss Evans gave up the formal Christianity of her childhood. Intensely serious and conscientious, she felt at first bound to mark her change of belief by a refusal to attend church. Later, however, she came to feel it right to express in every way her sympathy with all forms of moral beauty and earnest living, which were always more to her than differences of faith. On her father's death in 1849, Miss Evans spent some time at Geneva, returning to London to accept a position as sub-editor of the *Westminster Review*. This magazine was the organ of free thought, and her connection with it brought her into relation with John Stuart Mill, Herbert Spencer, George Henry Lewes, and other liberals. With Mr. Lewes she contracted, in 1854, a union which, on account of a legal impediment, could not become marriage in the eyes of the law. Her association with Mr. Lewes, while a great source of happiness and inspiration, constituted a kind of moral responsibility, which deepened the serious purpose of her life. In 1857 she wrote: "If I live five years longer the positive result of my existence on the side of truth and goodness will far outweigh the small negative good that would have consisted in my not doing anything to shock others." We may consider that it was in part as a fulfillment of this pledge that her novels were written.

George Eliot's Novels.—The name George Eliot first appeared in 1856, signed to a story in *Blackwood's Magazine*, called "The Sad Fortunes of the Rev. Amos Barton." This was followed by two other tales of moderate length, and all these were republished in 1858, as *S enes of Clerica Life.* The secret of the authorship was well kept. Not until after the publication of *Adam Bede* in 1859 were the names of Mr. Lewes and George Eliot connected, and by that time it was evident that another great writer had appeared. *Adam Bede* was followed by *The Mill on the Floss* (1860), and *Silas Marner* (1861). In her next books George Elliot broadened her scope to take in great movements and causes. *Romola* (1863) is a carefully wrought picture of life in Florence in the days of Lorenzo di Medici; *Felix Holt* (1866) is a study of social reform as it appeared in 1832. *Middlemarch* (1872) is an elaborate study of English provincial life, her longest and one of her best stories. In her last novel, *Daniel Deronda* (1876), she again tried to associate her ideas of individual righteousness with the claims of a great movement, in this case the re-establishment of the Jews in Palestine.

George Eliot as a Realist.—When George Eliot was making her first ventures in fiction she records that Lewes, ever her most sympathetic critic, applauded her wit, description, and philosophy, but doubted her dramatic power. Most of her

GEORGE ELIOT
From a drawing by F. W. Burton

readers since that time have agreed that dramatic power was the least of her great gifts. It was most constant when she dealt as a realist with life that she knew thoroughly; it waned when she was forced to rely on her imagination. For example, *Adam Bede*, one of the most successful of her novels, takes its starting-point from an incident in the life of George Eliot's aunt, who once accompanied to the scaffold a poor girl condemned for child-murder. This aunt was the original of Dinah Morris, the woman preacher who rides in the hangman's cart with Hetty Sorrel. Hetty's aunt, Mrs. Poyser, is said to show some traits of George Eliot's mother; and Adam Bede was drawn from her father. Indeed, in her realism she was in large measure dependent on the material of her own early life in Warwickshire and Derbyshire. Her earlier books abound in local studies of charming humor. The elder Tullivers, the Gleggs and the Pullets, and Bob Jakin, in *The Mill on the Floss*, are as definite as Scott's or Miss Austen's minor characters. The chief sign of decline in George Eliot's last novel, *Daniel Deronda*, is the attempt to replace these vigorous living beings with creatures of invention. She had used up the material of her youth, and found nothing in her life of culture and travel to take its place.

As a Psychologist.—*Adam Bede* is the most natural of George Eliot's books, simple in problem, direct in action, with the freshness and strength of the Derbyshire landscape and character and speech in its pages. Its successor, *The Mill on the Floss*, shows signs of a growing perplexity on the part of the author, of a hesitation between her art and her message. For George Eliot was more than an observer; she was also a scientist and a moralist. She was not content to picture human life as it appears. She tried to pierce behind the shows of things, and to reveal the forces by which they are controlled. Accordingly she analyzes her characters. In the case of the simple types this analysis takes the form of comment, rapid and suggestive. She tells us, for example, that Mrs. Tulliver was like the gold-fish who continues to butt its head against the encircling globe, and at once the type of cheerful incapacity to learn by experience is fixed before us. In the case of the more conscious, developed characters, her analysis is more elaborate and more sustained. For her heroines George Eliot drew largely upon her own inner experience, and this she supplemented by wide reading, especially of the literature of confessions. In this way she gained an extraordinary vividness in portraying the inner life. Her most significant passages are those in which she follows the ebb and flow of decision in a character's mind, dwelling on the triumph or defeat of a personality in a drama where there is but one actor. Such a drama is that which Maggie Tulliver plays out in her heart, torn between the impulse to take her joy as it offers itself, and the unconquerable conviction that she cannot seek her own happiness by sacrificing others.

As a Moralist.—Further, it is to be noted that George Eliot never lets her case drop with the individual analysis. She always strives to make her case typical, to show that the personal result is in accordance with a general law. Dorothea's defeat and Lydgate's failure in *Middlemarch*, Tito's degeneration in *Romola*, Gwendolen's humiliation and recovery in *Daniel Deronda*, are all represented as occurring in obedience to laws of the ethical world, as unchanging as those of the physical. This is George Eliot's chief object as a writer: to show how, in obedience to law, character grows or decays; how a single fault or flaw brings suffering and death, and throws a world into ruin; how, on the other hand, there is a making perfect through suffering, a regeneration through sin itself, a hope for the world through the renunciation and self-sacrifice of the individual. "It is a blind self-seeking," she tells us through Dinah Morris, "which wants to be freed from the sorrow wherewith the whole creation groaneth and travaileth," for, as she says again, "those who live and suffer may sometimes have the blessedness of being a salvation." It is this possibility of blessedness which in George Eliot's view is the compensation for evil; that we may

> "Be to other souls
> The cup of strength in some great agony"

in part makes up for the presence of that agony in the world.

REVIEW OUTLINE.—State some differences between the novel of the eighteenth and that of the nineteenth century. To which division does Miss Austen properly belong? Why? Give some instances of her turn for satire. For what qualities is " Pride and Prejudice" remarkable?

Narrate Scott's early life. How did his experience and surroundings equip him for his later work? What circumstances led him to attempt prose fiction? Relate the events of his later years. What qualities of romantic character did Scott possess? What elements appear in " Waverley "? Mention several of the Scotch stories which followed. For what types of character are they noteworthy? Is there any element of " realism " in these characters? What did Scott think of his descriptive powers? What use does he make of scenery? Mention some of Scott's attempts in English and European history. Wherein does his mastery of the art of historical fiction consist? Point out some effects of Scott's influence. What forces made against the continued supremacy of the historical novel?

Compare the early life of Scott with that of Dickens. Trace the effect of Dickens's training in his later work. Compare the later careers of the two novelists. What is " Pickwick Papers "? Wherein does its humor consist? On what types of character does Dickens chiefly rely? What connection had his novels with social reform? What advance do his later novels show in construction?

Compare Dickens and Thackeray in their presentation of real life. What was Thackeray's attitude toward " romantic realism " as shown in his earliest stories? What other realists began with burlesque? Mention Thackeray's later works. Describe his character. How did this influence his books? Why is his loose structure an advantage? On what ground is the amount of the author's comment in his books to be justified? What is Thackeray's view of the world implied in the title, " Vanity Fair "? What is his view of his function as author? Contrast his treatment of good and evil characters with that of Dickens. What use did Thackeray make of history in " Vanity Fair "? What is the subject-matter of " Esmond "? Discuss its style.

Under what influence did Charlotte Brontë become a writer? Explain the presence of romantic material in her novels. Contrast " Jane Eyre " with her later books. For what is her treatment of scene notable? Into what divisions does Kingsley's fiction fall? What element appears in all his novels?

Describe George Eliot's early life, and its effect on her novels. In what respect is " Adam Bede " superior to " Daniel Deronda " ? What is George Eliot's purpose as a moralist ?

READING GUIDE.—A few of the novels treated in this chapter are included in lists for college entrance—Scott's "Ivanhoe" and "Woodstock," Thackeray's "Henry Esmond," and George Eliot's "Silas Marner." These may be studied for plot and character development, with the general idea of bringing home to pupils the qualities of the novel as a literary form, and the difference between the opportunities open to the novelist and those of the dramatist. For the rest, the pupil should be encouraged to read widely, as interest prompts, in the other work of these authors. It is unnecessary to suggest any definite order, but there are a few novels which no one should omit. Scott's "Waverley," "Old Mortality," "Heart of Midlothian," "Kenilworth," "Quentin Durward," and perhaps "Redgauntlet" and "The Talisman"; Dickens's "Pickwick Papers," "David Copperfield," "Tale of Two Cities," and "Bleak House"; Thackeray's "Vanity Fair" and "The Newcomes"; George Eliot's "Adam Bede," "The Mill on the Floss," and "Middlemarch"; Charlotte Brontë's "Jane Eyre," Reade's "Cloister and the Hearth," and Kingsley's " Westward Ho," will be generally accepted as belonging in such a list.

TABULAR VIEW: 1800–1837

HISTORICAL EVENTS	POETS	ESSAYISTS, ETC.	NOVELISTS
GEORGE III., 1760–1820 (*continued*), Nelson defeats Napoleonic invasion of England at Trafalgar.........1805 Peninsular war against Napoleon ....1808–1814 First steamboat in Great Britain.....1812 Second American war.1812 Battle of Waterloo....1815 First Atlantic steamship..............1819 GEORGE IV.....1820–1830 Society for Prevention of Cruelty to Animals founded.....1824 First temperance society..............1826 Catholic emancipation..............1829 WILLIAM IV.....1830–1837 Reform Bill......1832 Emancipation of slaves in British colonies...1833 First Factory Act (in favor of women and children).........1833	WILLIAM WORDSWORTH, 1770–1850. Descriptive Sketches, 1793; Lyrical Ballads, 1798; Prelude, written 1805; Poems, 1807; Excursion, 1814; White Doe of Rylstone, 1815; Duddon Sonnets, 1819; Ecclesiastical Sonnets, 1822; Poems, 1836. SAMUEL TAYLOR COLERIDGE, 1772–1834. Kubla Khan, Ancient Mariner, Christabel (first part), 1797–1798; Christabel (second part), 1800; Ode to Dejection, 1802. ROBERT SOUTHEY, 1774–1843. Curse of Kehama, 1810. WALTER SAVAGE LANDOR, 1775–1864. Gebir, 1798; Count Julian, 1812; Hellenics, 1847; Heroic Idylls, 1863. WALTER SCOTT, 1771–1832. Lay of the Last Minstrel, 1805; Marmion, 1808; Lady of the Lake, 1810. THOMAS MOORE, 1779–1852.	CHARLES LAMB, 1775–1834. Tales from Shakespeare, 1807; Specimens of English Dramatic Poets, 1808; Essays of Elia, first series, 1823; second series, 1833. ROBERT SOUTHEY. Life of Nelson, 1813. SAMUEL TAYLOR COLERIDGE. Biographia Litteraria, 1817. WILLIAM HAZLITT, 1778–1830. Essays on the English Poets, 1818; English Comic Writers, 1819; Dramatic Literature of the Age of Elizabeth, 1821; Life of Napoleon, 1830. LEIGH HUNT, 1784–1859. Men, Women, and Books; A Jar of Honey from Mt. Hybla; Wit and Humor; Imagination and Fancy; Autobiography. THOMAS MOORE. Life of Byron, 1830. THOMAS DE QUINCEY, 1785–1859. Opium-Eater, 1821–1822; Murder as One of the Fine Arts, 1827; Re-	MARIA EDGEWORTH, 1767–1849. Castle Rackrent, 1800; Belinda, 1803; The Absentee; Patronage. JANE AUSTEN, 1775–1817. Northanger Abbey, written before 1797; Sense and Sensibility, 1811; Pride and Prejudice, 1813; Mansfield Park, 1814; Emma, 1816. WALTER SCOTT. Waverley, 1814; Guy Mannering, 1815; Old Mortality, The Antiquary, 1816; Rob Roy, 1817; Heart of Midlothian 1818; Ivanhoe, 1819; Kenilworth, 1821; Fortunes of Nigel, 1822; Quentin Durward, 1823; The Talisman, 1826; Woodstock, 1827; Anne of Geierstein, 1829.

TABULAR VIEW: 1800-1837 (*Continued*)

HISTORICAL EVENTS	POETS	ESSAYISTS, ETC.	NOVELISTS
	Irish Melodies, 1807; Lalla Rookh, 1817. THOMAS CAMPBELL, 1777–1844. Hohenlinden; Battle of the Baltic; Ye Mariners of England; Lochiel. GEORGE GORDON, LORD BYRON, 1788–1824. Hours of Idleness, 1807; English Bards and Scotch Reviewers, 1809; Childe Harold, 1812–1818; Eastern Tales, 1813–1816; Manfred, 1817; Cain, 1821; Don Juan, 1819 –1824. PERCY BYSSHE SHELLEY, 1792–1822. Queen Mab, 1813; Alastor, 1815; Revolt of Islam, 1817; Prometheus Unbound, and The Cenci, 1819; Witch of Atlas, 1820; Adonais and Epipsychidion, 1821; Triumph of Life, 1822. JOHN KEATS, 1795–1821. First volume, 1817; Endymion, 1818; Lamia, Isabella, Hyperion, Eve of St. Agnes, and Odes, 1820.	volt of the Tartars, 1837; Suspiria, 1845; Joan of Arc, 1847; English Mail Coach, 1849. WALTER SAVAGE LANDOR. Imaginary Conversations, 1821–1853; Pericles and Aspasia, 1836; Pentameron, 1837.	

TABULAR VIEW: 1837–1901

THE AGE OF VICTORIA

HISTORICAL EVENTS	POETS	ESSAYISTS, ETC.	NOVELISTS
QUEEN VICTORIA..1837–1901 Reform of Criminal Laws...1837 Electric telegraph in England ......1837 Penny postage established 1840 Act forbidding employment of children as chimney sweeps ....1842 Repeal of Corn Laws; beginning of Free Trade....1846 Chartist Agitation......1848 Public libraries established.1850 First "World's Fair" ......1851 Crimean War	ALFRED TENNYSON, 1809–1892. Poems, 1830–1832; Poems, chiefly lyrical, 1842; Princess, 1847; In Memoriam, 1850; Maud, 1855; Enoch Arden, 1864; Idylls of the King, 1842–1872; Ballads, 1880; Tiresias, 1885; Locksley Hall Sixty Years After, 1887; Demeter, 1889. ROBERT BROWNING, 1812–1889. Pauline, 1833; Paracelsus, 1835; Sordello, 1840; Pippa Passes, 1841; Dramatic Lyrics, 1842; Blot in the, 'Scutcheon, 1843; Colombe's Birthday, 1844; Dramatic Romances, 1845 Christmas Eve and Easter Day, 1850; Men and Women, 1855; Dramatis Personæ, 1864; The Ring and the Book, 1869; thirteen later volumes, ending with Asolando, 1889.	THOMAS BABINGTON MACAULAY, 1800–1859. Essays, 1825 – 1844; History of England, 1849–1857. THOMAS CARLYLE, 1795–1881. Sartor Resartus, 1833; French Revolution 1837; Chartism, 1839; Heroes and Hero-Worship, 1841; Past and Present 1843; Cromwell 1845; Life, of Sterling, 1851; Frederick the Great, 1858–1865. MATTHEW ARNOLD, 1888. Essays in Criticism, 1865; Celtic Literature, 1867; Culture and	BENJAMIN DISRAELI, 1804–1881. Vivian Grey, 1826; Henrietta Temple, 1837; Coningsby, 1844; Sybil, 1845; Tancred, 1847. EDWARD BULWER-LYTTON, 1803–1873. Pelham, 1828; Last Days of Pompeii, 1834; Harold, 1848; Zanoni, 1842; The Caxtons, 1850; My Novel, 1853. WILLIAM MAKEPEACE THACKERAY, 1811–1863. Barry Lyndon, 1844; Vanity Fair, 1848; Pendennis, 1849–1850; Henry Esmond, 1852; The Newcomes, 1853–1855; Essays: English Humourists, 1851; The Four Georges, 1855. CHARLES DICKENS, 1812–1870. Pickwick Papers, 1837; Oliver Twist, 1838; Nicholas Nickleby, 1839; Old Curiosity Shop, 1841; Barnaby Rudge, 1841; Martin Chuzzlewit, 1844; Dombey and Son, 1848; David Copperfield, 1850; Bleak House, 1853; Hard Times, 1854; Little Dorrit, 1857; Tale of Two Cities, 1859; Great Expectations, 1861; Our Mutual Friend, 1865. ANTHONY TROLLOPE, 1815–1882. The Warden, 1855; Barchester Towers, 1857; Framley Parsonage, 1861; Last Chronicle of Barset, 1867.

TABULAR VIEW: 1837-1901

THE AGE OF VICTORIA (*Continued*)

HISTORICAL EVENTS	POETS	ESSAYISTS, ETC.	NOVELISTS
("Charge of the Light Brigade") ....1854 Rise of cheap newspapers.1855 First Atlantic cable ....1858 (Darwin's Origin of Species).1859 Imprisonment for debt abolished .....1861 (Spencer's First Principles, setting forth the philosophy of evolution) .1862 Reform act extends franchise ....1867 Victoria becomes Empress of India ......1877 Electric light	ELIZABETH BARRETT BROWNING, 1806-1861. The Seraphim, 1838; Poems, 1844; Sonnets from the Portuguese, 1847 ; Casa Guidi Windows, 1851; Aurora Leigh, 1857; Poems before Congress, 1860; Last Poems (posthumous). EDWARD FITZGERALD, 1809-1883. Rubaiyat of Omar Khayyam, 1859. MATTHEW ARNOLD, 1822-1888. The Strayed Reveller, 1849; Empedocles on Ætna, 1852; Poems, 1853; Merope, 1858; New Poems, 1867. DANTE GABRIEL ROSSETTI, 1828-1882. Poems, 1870; Ballads and Sonnets, 1881. CHRISTINA ROSSETTI, 1830-1894. Goblin Market, 1861; The Prince's Progress, 1866; A Pageant and other Poems, 1881.	Anarchy, 1869; Literature and Dogma, 1871; Mixed Essays, 1879; Discourses in America, 1885. JOHN RUSKIN, 1819-1899. Modern Painters, 1843-1860; Seven Lamps of Architecture, 1849; Stones of Venice, 1851-1853; Unto This Last, 1862; Sesame and Lilies, 1865; Ethics of the Dust, Crown of Wild Olive, 1866; Queen of the Air, 1869; Fors Clavigera, 1871-1884. WALTER PATER, 1839-1894. The Renaissance, 1873;	CHARLES READE, 1814-1884. Peg Woffington, 1852; Cloister and the Hearth, 1861; Never Too Late to Mend, 1856; Put Yourself in His Place, 1870. CHARLOTTE BRONTË, 1816-1855. Jane Eyre, 1847; Shirley, 1849; Villette, 1853. CHARLES KINGSLEY, 1819-1875. Yeast, 1848; Alton Locke, 1850; Hypatia, 1853; Westward Ho, 1855; Water Babies, 1863; Hereward the Wake, 1866. ELIZABETH GASKELL, 1810-1865. Mary Barton, 1848; Cranford, 1853; North and South, 1855. GEORGE ELIOT, 1819-1880. Scenes of Clerical Life, 1858; Adam Bede, 1859; Mill on the Floss, 1860; Silas Marner, 1861; Romola, 1863; Middlemarch, 1872; Daniel Deronda, 1876. Poems: The Spanish Gypsy, etc., 1868-1874. GEORGE MEREDITH, 1828– . Richard Feverel, 1859; Beauchamp's Career, 1875; The Egoist, 1879; Diana of the Crossways, 1885; One of Our Conquerors, 1891. THOMAS HARDY, 1840– . Desperate Remedies, 1869; Under the Greenwood Tree, 1872;

TABULAR VIEW: 1837–1901

The Age of Victoria (*Concluded*)

HISTORICAL EVENTS	POETS	ESSAYISTS, ETC.	NOVELISTS
and telephone introduced in-to England. 1878 Acts extending suffrage: first "People's Parliament" 1884–1886 Queen's Jubilee 1887 Accession of Ed-ward VII. .1901	WILLIAM MORRIS, 1834–1896. Defence of Guinevere, 1858; Jason, 1867; Earthly Paradise, 1870; Poems by the Way, 1891. Poetic prose: House of the Wolf-ings, 1889; Roots of the Mountains, 1890. ALGERNON CHARLES SWIN-BURNE, 1837– . Ata-lanta in Calydon, 1865; Poems and Ballads, 1866.	Marius the Epicu-rean, 1885; Appre-ciations, 1889; Imaginary Por-traits, 1887; Plato and Platonism, 1893. ROBERT LOUIS STE-VENSON, 1850–1894. An Inland Voyage, 1878; Travels with a Donkey, 1879; Vir-ginibus Puerisque, 1881; Familiar Studies of Men and Books, 1881.	A Pair of Blue Eyes, 1873; Far From the Madding Crowd, 1874; The Return of the Native, 1878; Tess of the D'Urbervilles, 1892; Jude the Obscure, 1896. ROBERT LOUIS STEVENSON, 1850–1894. New Arabian Nights, 1882; Treasure Island, 1883; Prince Otto, 1885; Kidnapped, 1886; Master of Ballantrae, 1889; David Balfour, 1893; Weir of Hermiston (posthumous). Poetry: A Child's Garden of Verses, 1885; Under-woods, 1887; Ballads, 1891.

CHAPTER XVI

A GLANCE IN REVIEW

Introduction.—We have now followed the history of English literature from the prehistoric twilight of the race to our own day, a period of nearly fifteen hundred years. Let us take a hasty glance backward, and try to see the story of English letters in its broad features, as it unfolds itself with the centuries.

The Making of the Race and of the Language.—The English are a mixed race, and English literature owes its remarkable scope to the fact that many different peoples and different branches of peoples have been mingled together to form the national character to which literature gives expression. The history of English literature is, during its early period, largely the history of the mingling together of these different peoples and tongues, to form a single nation and language, in which many diverse elements are held in solution. This period of preparation begins, perhaps as early as the fourth century, with the songs chanted by pagan Saxons in their early home upon the German Sea, and ends with Chaucer, the first great writer in whom we feel the modern spirit, and whose language is near enough to our own to be read by modern men with only a small amount of preparatory training. If we neglect the earliest scraps of song which scholars have ventured to assign to a remoter antiquity, and date the true beginning of Anglo-Saxon poetry from the middle or end of the sixth century, when the great epic of *Beowulf* probably arose, we still have a period of nearly eight centuries during which the nation and the language were being formed.

The earliest historic inhabitants of Britain were of the Celtic race; but the basis of the English race and language was furnished, not by the Celts, but by the Anglo-Saxons, who invaded and possessed Britain during the fifth and sixth centuries. They mingled, to some degree, with the conquered Celts, and absorbed a small portion of the Celtic tongue, together with some words left behind by the Roman occupation. Toward the end of the eighth century, and during the ninth, England was overrun by the Danes and the Northmen, men of allied race to the Anglo-Saxons, but sufficiently different to contribute some new ingredients to the national character. In 1066, the country was conquered by the Norman-French, who had originally been Teutonic, like the Anglo-Saxons and Danes, but who had become by intermarriage half French in blood, and were wholly so in civilization. Thus a second and far greater infusion of Celtic characteristics was made in the already blended English character. For a period of three hundred years the process of amalgamating the natives and the conquerors went on; by the time of Chaucer it was virtually completed.

Old and Middle English Literature.—The literature of these eight centuries divides itself into two parts; first, that produced before the Norman Conquest, and written in Anglo-Saxon, or Old English; second, that which began to be produced at the beginning of the thirteenth century, in Middle English a tongue recognizably like our own, and becoming gradually more so as it absorbed French ingredients. Old English literature, in turn, divides itself into two parts; first, the early pagan poetry of which *Beowulf* is the chief monument; second, the Christianized literature of Northumbria and Wessex, of which Cædmon, Cynewulf, and King Alfred are the chief figures. Middle English literature, likewise, includes two periods; first, the pre-Chaucerian period, during which the metrical romance was the great staple of production; second, the period of Chaucer and his followers. During this latter period literature was greatly widened, both in form and matter. The verse tale was the most vital form which it took; but the lyric (especially the elaborate French lyric) was cultivated, the popular ballad flourished, and the miracle play took its rise.

The Renaissance and the Reformation.—During the fifteenth century the wave of creative impulse which had risen so high in Chaucer, ebbed away, chiefly because of the disturbed state of the country. But in the sixteenth century the life of England began again to be stirred by two great impulses. One of these was a literary and artistic influence, which came from Italy, and which we call the Renaissance. The other was a moral and religious influence, which came from Germany, and which we know as the Reformation. Under this double stimulus, aided later by the excitement of great geographical discoveries, the growth of commerce, and the national enthusiasm aroused by England's struggle with Spain, literature was again quickened. During the first quarter of the sixteenth century the wave of creative literature began to rise; and it continued to rise more and more rapidly until it reached its climax in the latter part of the reign of Elizabeth and in the reign of James I. It then ebbed rapidly away; but the great Puritan writers, Milton and Bunyan, continued on into a later age the double impulse of the Renaissance and of the Reformation.

Three Stages of the Renaissance Period.—We may profitably consider this period as divided into three stages. The first stage is represented by Sir Thomas More, by the translators of the second great English version of the Bible,* Tyndale and Coverdale, and by the courtly figures of Wyatt and Surrey, who brought the Renaissance influence into English poetry. This first stage of the new era also saw the rise of early English comedy and tragedy, developed out of the miracle plays and moralities, and given definite form by the influence of the Latin drama.

The second stage represents the high tide of Elizabethan literature. Its greatest figures are Sidney, Spenser, Marlowe, Shakespeare, Ben Jonson, and Bacon; and grouped around them we find a great crowd of poets, romancers, and playwrights. A wonderful efflorescence of the human mind, a wonderful energy and gayety in human life, mark the last years of Elizabeth and the first years of James I.

The third stage is marked by the over-ripeness and decline of the drama, and the growing sternness of the Puri-

* The first was Wyclif, whose age was marked by a movement somewhat similar to that of the Reformation.

tan temper.   To this stage belong Beaumont and Fletcher,
Webster, and the later dramatists; it saw the rise of a great
pulpit literature and a fervid religious poetry; the earlier
work of Milton, in which he shows himself half-Elizabethan
and half-Puritan, falls in it.   It ends amid the confusion of
the great Civil War, and the military despotism of Cromwell.
By this time the great wave of imaginative energy which had
begun to rise in the reign of Henry VIII. was exhausted;
and with the restoration of Charles II. to the English throne
a new epoch opened, an epoch of reaction and criticism.
But as we have said before, there are two great survivals of
the spirit of the Renaissance and the Reformation into the
age of the Restoration; for it was under Charles II. that
Paradise Lost and *The Pilgrim's Progress* were written.

The Era of Classicism.—The epoch of English literary history which opened with the return of Charles II. was pre-
eminently an epoch of prose, as the previous one had been
pre-eminently an epoch of poetry.   It is called the era of
classicism, because it believed that it had found in the
older classic literatures the kind of moderation and polish
which formed its own literary ideal.   As the previous age
had drawn its inspiration from Italy, the age which we have
now reached found its example in France, where the classical fashion in literature, long since firmly established there,
exerted its influence first upon the men of letters who were
exiled with Charles II., and afterward upon the English
nation as a whole.

Three Stages of the Classical Era.—The domination of
this "classical" ideal in English letters divides itself into
three parts.   The first is the age of Dryden, dating from
the Restoration to the end of the seventeenth century.   It
saw the heroic couplet take the place of all other forms of
verse (with trifling exceptions); it saw a flippant society
comedy in prose, and a bombastic rhymed tragedy, take the
place of the Elizabethan blank verse drama; it saw the development of a systematic literary criticism, and the development of a useful prose style.

The second epoch of the classical era is signalized by the
final perfecting of the heroic couplet, and of the "rational" type

of poetry, in the masterly hands of Pope; it also witnessed the development of a magnificent prose satire at the hands of Swift, and the creation of a new type of literature in the essays of Addison and Steele, which deal directly with the social life of the time, in a light and graceful way. Finally, it saw in the work of Defoe, the beginnings of the modern novel, the greatest literary discovery of the eighteenth century.

The third stage of the reign of "classicism" is represented by Johnson, Goldsmith, and Burke. In Johnson culminated eighteenth-century scholarship. In Goldsmith and Burke, along with a pronounced classical bias, we discover the workings of a more ardent, sympathetic, and ideal temper; in other words, we note in them the signs of a new feeling toward life and art, a feeling destined soon to grow strong enough to overthrow the classical standards and usher in a freer and more impassioned literature. This age of Burke and Goldsmith is also the age of the great eighteenth-century novelists who followed Defoe—Richardson, Fielding, Smollett, and Sterne. The work of the novelists, though thoroughly realistic, tended, by its intimate truth to life and its keen human sympathy, to contribute toward the triumph of the new spirit.

The Romantic Movement.—Finally, this latter half of the eighteenth century witnessed the beginnings and progress of a movement to regain for poetry the romantic freedom and wayward beauty of which the classical school had deprived it. This movement, known as the Romantic Movement, began with Thomson, was continued by Gray, Cowper, and Blake, and came to a more or less complete realization in Burns. Burns died four years before the end of the century; and two years after his death the publication of *Lyrical Ballads*, by Coleridge and Wordsworth, marked the decisive triumph of the new romantic poetry.

The Nineteenth Century: First Period.—The nineteenth century divides itself naturally into two parts, the first extending, roughly, to the accession of Queen Victoria in 1837; the second covering her long reign, 1837–1901. Throughout both the romantic tone prevails, but it is more conspicuous in the earlier period, which, like the romantic age of Elizabeth, is pre-eminently an epoch of poetry. During this epoch English literature felt strongly the influence of the French Revolution, which was itself the outcome of a vast "romantic movement" of a social and political kind. This influence is especially marked in Wordsworth, who first embraced and later repudiated the principles of the revolution. Revolutionary doctrine is deeply ingrained in the poetry of Byron and of Shelley. It is, however, conspicuously absent from the work of Keats, who stands apart as the poet of pure beauty in an age disturbed by social and political trouble. Wordsworth marks the entrance into poetry of a new sympathy with external nature, and a new understanding of the spiritual meaning of the universe in its relation to man. In Coleridge we meet a new power of making credible and real the world of dreams and of supernatural happenings. Byron stands chiefly for the revolt against social convention and hypocrisy; Shelley for the search after a more ideal existence, in which truth, justice, and beauty shall prevail. Scott, both in his poetry and in his prose romances, represents a new interest in the storied past. In the prose essays of Lamb and De Quincey we see the romantic spirit applied to the criticism of literature, to the description of various phases of social and personal life.

The Nineteenth Century: Second Period.—The literature of the Victorian age is especially marked by its interest in social problems, and in the problem of man's personal existence, the first being due to the spread of democracy and its resultant disturbances, the second to far-reaching discoveries in the realm of biology and psychology, which have given man a new conception of his place in the scheme of creation, and a new understanding of his own nature. The social interest is conspicuous in the work of Macaulay, Carlyle, Tennyson, Arnold, and Ruskin. The psychological interest also deeply colors the work of Carlyle and Tennyson; and in the work of Browning it is predominant. The novel, which is the most popular and widely cultivated form of literature in this age, reflects both these interests. In Dickens the desire to reform abuses and champion the oppressed, holds the chief place; Thackeray's interest is also chiefly a social one, but he cares to study and portray society rather than to reform it; in George Eliot as in Browning, the interest is mainly psychological and moral, dealing with the intimate personal life of men and women as it is affected by the life about them.

AMERICAN LITERATURE

CHAPTER I

AMERICAN LITERATURE BEFORE 1800

I. INTRODUCTORY STATEMENT

The Lack of Primitive Beginnings.—As an expression of national life, American literature is different from any other in its lack of primitive beginnings. It does not, like the early English, progress as civilization progresses, gradually passing from the ruggedness of orally transmitted song to the intricacies of Elizabethan verse, the polished felicities of the early eighteenth century, and the studious and deliberate variety of the Victorian era. Nor does it take all the successive steps which lead up to, through, and out of feudalism. The effect of chivalry is not to be traced in its mediæval life, for it had no mediæval life. As a consequence, therefore, American literature does not in its beginnings directly feel the world-awakening influences of the Renaissance and the Reformation. These influences are, of course, traceable in American life, but it is only because their effects were brought over ready-made into America, just as certainly as clothes and tools and furniture and books. In the Colonial period one can study the process of transplanting a hardy flower from a sunny and protected place around the corner into the shade and the wind. Its roots are disturbed, but not at first wholly torn away from the original soil. Will the plant survive, blossom, and come to fruitage under the new conditions? Is it its previous self or something new? Or is it both, as the old stem drinks in new sap?

American Literature Defined.—It has been the practice of a number of historians of American letters to declare that nothing worthy of the name of literature was produced in the country before 1800. In order to differ intelligently with critics of this type it is well to start with a definition. What is meant by literature, and what by American literature? The first requisite of literature is that it have some vital interest. If we can feel that an essay, a play, a song, or a story was the product of some living, energetic individual vitally interested in what he was doing, we can hardly maintain that we have not been reading literature. Yet it is necessary to go farther than this. It is not enough that a man show such enthusiasm or energy that " he tears a passion to tatters "; for with this element of vitality in any work of literature must also be combined a certain formal quality. The definition must be carried a step farther, moreover, to the other term, "American." What is it for literature to be national? Any national literature should be so distinct in its character that we could not conceive of its having been produced in any other country than that in which it was given birth. In this connection it appears that two main qualities are to be sought. First, literature may establish its claim to nationality by portraying or criticising the life in the midst of which it was written. The whole course of English letters is marked by works of this sort. The value of the Prologue to Chaucer's *Canterbury Tales*, with its fine series of portraits of the Knight and the Squire, of the Nun, the Priest, of the Merchant and the Shipman, the Clerk and the Wife of Bath, is that they make a composite study of English life in the fourteenth century, which is as useful to the historian as it is charming to the lover of literature. The comedies of Ben Jonson two centuries later, again help to expound the life of the subjects of Elizabeth. One hundred years after this, the satires of Joseph Addison on the subjects of Queen Anne are inevitably English. Then there follow a whole series of story-tellers from Richardson and Fielding to Dickens and Thackeray and on down to writers of the present day who have been respectively English and American because they have portrayed society in its different aspects, and perhaps passed criticisms upon it.

Yet to stop here with the definition of nationalism would be to omit some of the very greatest literature. Turn to Chaucer again. Thus far only the Prologue and connecting links to the *Canterbury Tales* have been cited. What are the stories themselves? They have, in the majority of cases, little to do with the England of Chaucer's day. They are based on originals in Greek, Latin, Italian, and French. Yet they are distinctly English in reflecting the taste of the England of Chaucer's day, an England which was so full of stories of romantic adventure that the love of them was one of the characteristics of the age. These points should be kept in mind in a survey of the literature of America between 1600 and 1800. Do we find anything written in this long period which is full of life and therefore is literature? Do we discover anything which possesses artistic form and thus lays claim to the title? Can we admit that any of the material portrays and criticises American life in its earliest stages? Does any reflect the taste of the times?

II. COLONIAL LITERATURE FROM 1600 TO 1700

Seventeenth-Century Life in America.—The significance of the century marks in the Colonial period has been well indicated. In 1600 none of the settlements which developed into the original thirteen colonies had been established. In 1700 all but one of the colonies, Georgia, were flourishing. By 1800 the Revolution had taken place, and they had become an independent nation.

A glance over the period between 1600 and 1700 shows that whatever literature there was at the outset had to be of a very elementary type. For, though it was the record of a highly educated group of men, these men had left one of the great centres of seventeenth-century life and settled under primitive conditions from which they were trying to free themselves as soon as possible. Their lives were given over to the work of ploughing, building, fishing, and hunting, and of carrying on an active commerce with the Old World. There was, of course, plenty of material for romance in this experience. They encountered resistance on every side. In the north they forced the reluctant soil to yield them the bare necessities of life. Their suffering brought them intimately together, and their nobler emotions and baser passions offered much material for literary treatment. In fact, they had everything necessary except leisure. But engrossed as they were in the material problems of getting for themselves food and fuel, shelter and clothing, what they did write, although sometimes not of the briefest, was of the simplest nature.

Early Motives for Authorship.—Their motives for authorship during the early days were few. They wrote to keep in personal contact with England, to inform their families and their friends, to keep in touch with their financial backers and with the state authorities. Aside from this personal sort of production they wrote to remove prevailing misconceptions about America, and in so doing to stimulate colonization. At rare intervals, even in these early days, a third motive appeared in the case of a few colonists who wrote for their own edification and pleasure. Yet during most of this century it is significant that little printing was done in America, and that comparatively few utterances were addressed through the press to American readers. In the main, English-born men were supplying to London printers material for the English public.

First Writings in the South.—Captain John Smith, the most picturesque of the early settlers, has appropriately the honor of being first writer, by virtue of his *True Relation of Virginia*, published in London, 1608. It is a spirited work, heavy in spots where he piles up rather dry accumulations of facts about plants and animals, but full of lively interest when he comes to his own experiences with the colonists and the Indians, and freshened by " tall " stories which, through his genial disregard for the facts, cast a good deal of light upon his own character. The same jaunty animation appears in the so-called *Burwell Papers*, an incomplete account of Bacon's Rebellion in 1676; and both of these works, which may be taken as the most interesting early products from the South, show the same evident attention to the rather intricate prose style of the later Elizabethans.

Religious Feeling in the North.—In the North, for evident reasons, the output was much greater. In 1620, and again in 1630, companies of Englishmen in Plymouth and in Boston had settled communities where they meant to worship as they chose. Almost at once, however, it became evident at both places that they had no more intention of allowing general liberty of worship than had William Laud and Charles I. of granting universal toleration in England. As a result, although the direct historical chronicles of such men as William Bradford, Nathaniel Morton, and John Winthrop may not be overlooked, we naturally turn with more interest to the writings which show the struggles of the orthodox old guard against the encroachments of the ungodly.

The Decline of Intolerance.—The best fighter against the sin of toleration was Nathaniel Ward, whose *Simple Cobbler of Agawam* (1646) was a bitter protest against the very kind of non-conformity of which he had previously been guilty in England. His protest came none too soon, however, for already Thomas Morton, a somewhat irresponsible adventurer, had, in *The New English Canaan*, written some galling satire on certain discrepancies between Puritan faith and Puritan practice. Sober and religious men entered the arena. Roger Williams suffered banishment rather than submit to the tyranny of the churchman, and Franklin's grandfather, Peter Folger, in his *Looking Glass for the Times*, explained that God was punishing New England for " the persecuting trade " by inspiring the Indians to the horrors of King Philip's War. Finally, with the last decade of the century, the Salem witchcraft tragedies were followed by an almost immediate change in public feeling toward religious fanaticism. Of the lack of true scientific knowledge among the New Englanders, and of their consequent openness to superstition, we find enough evidence in the *Remarkable Providences* of Increase Mather, a book of prodigious anecdotes about " things preternatural," " demons and possessed persons," " apparitions," and various remarkable deliverances, destructions, and judgments. A work of this author's great son, Cotton Mather, *The Wonders of the Invisible World*, is similar in content. Both made attempts at scientific handling of their subject, but both seem to have fanned the sparks which burst into flame with the Salem inquisition, causing the death within three months of nineteen alleged

witches. A closing chapter in this controversy was Robert
Calef's *More Wonders of the Invisible World*, a biting reply
to the unscientific credulity of all those who had been led so
far from the truth.

A Period of Change.—With the close of the century it is
thus very evident that a genuine period of change had arrived. The old domination of the church fathers had begun
to wane; they no longer controlled both church and state
without challenge; their point of view was no longer accepted without question by all respectable persons. They
had actually been tried and found guilty of grievous error.
Three New Englanders all living and writing at the end of
the century represent the conservative, liberal, and radical
attitudes.

Cotton Mather's " Magnalia."—Cotton Mather, already
mentioned, to the end keeps his eye upon the past. Appropriately, his greatest work in bulk and significance is *Magnalia Christi Americana, or The Ecclesiastical History of
New England*. The motive of the immense tome is made
clear by the concluding words of the introduction: "Grant
me thy gracious assistance, Oh my God, that . . . I may
find my labors acceptable and profitable unto thy churches,
and serviceable unto the interests of thy gospel." He
deals in some detail with the famous individuals and institutions of early New England, and concludes with " A Faithful Record of Many Illustrious Wonderful Providences "
and " The Wars of the Lord, being the Afflictions and Disturbances of the Church in New England." The whole
work is ecclesiastical, and based on the general assumption
that the salvation of New England rested upon her upholding
the traditions of the past.

Samuel Sewall and His Diary.—A more liberal attitude is
that of Samuel Sewall. He was an almost exact contemporary of Cotton Mather, and almost equally prominent in the
same town. After graduation from Harvard, he passed into
law by way of the church, being a preacher before he became
a barrister. Magistrate in 1692, and hence a representative
of temporal authority; deacon, and therefore deputy of the
Most High, he served in this double capacity as one of the

witchcraft judges. But five years later, conscience-stricken at his part in the spilling of innocent blood, he arose in church and made public acknowledgment of his sin and his contrition. Three years after, in his tract on *The Selling of Joseph*, he wrote the first real arraignment of the practice of slave-holding in America. His greatest work was his diary, a running comment on his life in Boston from 1674 to 1729. He appears in it as a fine example of the sturdy Puritan whose chief characteristic was a grave severity. He was opposed almost as staunchly as Nathaniel Ward to the encroachments of frivolity, " tricks," frolics, dancing, and the pagan celebrations of such festivals as Christmas, Easter, and May-day; but there is nevertheless a certain humane broadness of view in his comments on life which contrasts him with the " Mather dynasty." He is a touch more worldly and much less pompous, doing in the long diary the same service for his community that his two English contemporaries, Pepys and Evelyn, did for the courts of Charles II. and James II.

Mrs. Knight's Journal.—Quite different and far less austere than either of these dignitaries was Mrs. Sarah Kemble Knight, when, in 1704, she wrote her now famous *Journal of a Journey from Boston to New York*. Whether she would have written just as she did if she had known that her work was ever to be published, is an open question. As it stands, it is by all odds the most uniformly genial bit of writing that survives from her generation. Here and there in earlier productions appear situations and phrases which amuse the reader. These, however, were not always so intended, and they were at best mainly brief, interpolated quips. Mrs. Knight, in contrast, was irrepressibly jolly. Sometimes she lapses into vulgarity; frequently she is worldly wise; scattered along through the little book are refreshing signs of a very mild irreligiousness, especially in her use of biblical allusion; and in the fashion of many of the Puritans of her day, though not with Puritan gravity, she drops from time to time into verse. Withal, however, she was a devout, decent, orderly person.

Seventeenth-Century Verse.—Some reference is due the

Colonial verse before complete leave is taken of the seventeenth century. Much of the earliest verse was used merely for the sake of variety in the handling of commonplace themes. Thus R. Rich, writing his *Newes from Virginia* in 1610, offers a half apology when he says: " If thou ask me why I put it in verse, I prithee knowe it was only to feede mine owne humour." In New England this inclination to lapse into rhyme showed itself among explorers, historians, and preachers alike. Thus, when Governor William Bradford, of Plymouth, courted the muse, he wrote a set of verses on *Providence and the Pilgrim*, the stiffness of which can be gathered from the opening couplet:

> "From my years young in days of youth,
> God did make known to me His truth."

With equally awkward sobriety, William Morrell, resident in Plymouth 1623–1624, wrote in heroic couplets *A Recommendation of New England*, his title well indicating the prosy content of the work. Thus, again, Morton interspersed into his *New English Canaan* rhymes which were irritatingly superior to those of his Puritan adversaries. Bradford had a literary as well as an ethical grievance to inspire him when he recorded that " Morton likewise (to show his poetry) composed sundry rhymes and verses, some tending to lasciviousness, and others to the detraction and scandal of some persons, which he affixed to this idle or idol Maypole."

Two Literary Curiosities.—The most curious effusion in seventeenth-century American verse has also the distinction of being the first volume actually published in this country— *The Bay Psalm Book*, Cambridge, Mass., 1640. The original title was *The Whole Book of Psalms faithfully done into English Metre*, the task being a work of collaboration by many. It is a pathetic fact that the book has long been considered a mere curio, that the basis of choosing excerpts has been to select examples of the most ludicrous verse, and that dozens of historians have regarded it only as a fit target for critical epigram. Michael Wigglesworth, author of *The Day of Doom*, was probably edified by the beauties of the

Bay Psalm Book, for he seems to have adopted it for his poetic standard. He was a theologian of the sternly Calvinistic type who put into verse all the sense of present helplessness and future horror which belonged to the solemn creed of predestination. His masterpiece was *The Day of Doom, A poetical description of the great and last judgment.* Incredible as it may seem, though his poetry is almost as bad as that in the luckless *Psalm Book,* it was enormously popular in his day; but it was a perverted poem fed to an abnormal appetite.

Mrs. Anne Bradstreet.—The only genuine poet of this first century was Anne Bradstreet. She endured all the toils of a farmer's wife and the responsibilities of a mother of eight children; yet in spite of these burdens she wrote a considerable body of verse, much of which, contrary to the custom of the Puritans, " deviated into downright poetry." The nature of her work can in part be understood from the long title to her publication of 1850: *The Tenth Muse lately sprung up in America; or Several Poems, compiled with great wit and learning, full of delight; wherein especially is contained a complete discourse and description of the four elements, constitutions, ages of man, seasons of the year; together with an exact epitome of the four monarchies, viz., the Assyrian, Persian, Grecian, Roman; also a dialogue between Old England and New concerning the late troubles; with divers other pleasant and serious poems, by a gentlewoman in those parts.* It is sufficiently evident that there is little lightness of touch to be expected in such a production. It does possess, however, a fluent and rather dignified verse scheme, a richness of imagination, coupled with an over-eagerness to emulate the fantastic ingenuities of the English Jacobean poets. The work is better than anything else done in her generation in America. Her most effective poem, " Contemplation," a placid meditation on the delights of nature, written late in her life, is far superior to many of the laborious productions of her English contemporaries.

III. JONATHAN EDWARDS (1703–1755) AND BENJAMIN FRANKLIN (1706–1790)

The Spirit of the Eighteenth Century.—The division of the whole Colonial period into halves calls attention to the changing conditions at the beginning of the eighteenth century. If this century itself be cut in two, a further change in the nature of the problems to which thinking people were giving their attention becomes evident about 1750. From 1600 to 1700 practically all the literature had been intensely individual. From John Smith to Sarah Kemble Knight the authors presented their own impressions and personal experiences, whether these had to do with this life or the prospects of a world to come. By the middle of the century, however, communities were firmly established and things intellectual began more generally to get their due. English customs of thought were coming to be much more influential in America than they had been a century before, when the pick of the inhabitants had been voluntary exiles or even refugees from the mother country. The fashion of the day in England was the fashion of the worldly wise man. It was an age given over to the study of social life as it could be seen on the streets, at the club, in the coffee-house, in the church, and at the court. It was a rationalizing period from which all mystery was absent. Religion was a reputable practice for respectable people; patriotism was something to be observed without personal sacrifice; love of home was less devout than in the age to come. The worldly wisdom of Pope and Addison was a high ideal for the generation.

English Influence on America.—In searching for the effect of all this upon America, one would expect to find in the colonies, too, an application of common-sense, the cardinal quality of England. With reference to the life of the community just this is to be found. The same general problems are treated in a new way. In the first hundred years of the colonies the demands of material life had been in the ascendency. In the eighteenth century it was possible to turn the attention from the necessities to certain of the conveniences of life, and invention began to take the place of the ruder forms of manual labor. In the first hundred years with tears and sighs and lamentations the Puritan had prostrated himself before the Lord and examined his own heart to see if it was good. Now heresy began to spread. The age was moral rather than religious, and the study of ethics in its application to man's civic duties took in some measure the place of the faith of the Puritan. In the first hundred years schools had been established in order that children, by learning the Scriptures, might " foil the old deluder, Satan." Now the spirit of education became universal, and its aim was to put men in possession of all good books, and to acquaint them with their duty as members of the state. Two men stand out preëminent at this mid-period, both born at the very opening of the century, and both enormously active minded and progressive—Jonathan Edwards and Benjamin Franklin.

Jonathan Edwards's Life.—Edwards, born in 1703, developed into the greatest American divine since Cotton Mather. Like Mather, he was precocious as a youth, and as a man wonderfully diversified in his interests and activities, " fructuosus " in his good works, merciless in his discipline of self, and, consequently, insatiable in his demands upon others. He was born in East Windsor, Conn., graduated from Yale in 1720, a tutor in the college 1724–1726, and then pastor in the Northampton church till 1750. In this significant year, on account of the unrelenting rigor of his demands upon his parishioners, he was dismissed from the church. For seven years he acted as missionary to the Indians near Stockbridge. Then, in 1758, he became president of the College of New Jersey, at Princeton, and a month later came to an untimely death as the result of inoculation against the small-pox.

Edwards as an Original Thinker.—The first half of his life is by far the more remarkable. As a boy he was uncommonly precocious in his command of the most abstruse philosophy. At the same time he was an extraordinarily promising student of natural science. The catalogue of his achievements in astronomy, geology, biology, and physics is wellnigh incredible. As might be expected, his first attitude toward religion was one of free inquiry. " From my childhood up my mind had been full of objections against the doctrine of God's sovereignty in choosing whom He would to eternal life and rejecting whom He pleased. . . . It used to appear like a horrible doctrine to me." But he " convinced and fully satisfied " himself of the truth of this doctrine, and finally turned all his wonderful powers of mind to expounding its horrors to awe-stricken congregations. To-day Jonathan Edwards is remembered for two things. One is the great promise of his youth, as with his eyes to the future he searched the heart of nature and arrived at conclusion after conclusion which was far in advance of his time; the other is the work of his maturity, as he turned toward the past and devoted all his sermonic skill to reaffirming the savage doctrines of the Calvinistic faith.

Franklin's Life.—Benjamin Franklin, the other great mid-century man of letters, furnishes interesting points of comparison and contrast with Edwards. Their youthful promise, their powers of intense application, their scientific spirit, and their desire to share in and contribute to the life of the community, are evident at a glance. Yet in many phases of character and experience they were as different as two men of the same generation could well be. Franklin was born in Boston in 1706, the fifteenth in a family of seventeen children. Naturally, his father, a tallow chandler, was unable to give his youngest son many advantages in the way of formal education. The boy's experiences, first in his father's business and then as apprentice in the print-shop of his brother, his departure from Boston at the age of seventeen, his first residence in Philadelphia, the two years in England, the return to the land of Penn, and his subsequent career until he came to be the most remarkable American of his time—these are all commonplaces of political and literary history.

Franklin's Pursuit of Efficiency.—The one dominant feature which appears consistently at every phase of his life is his study of the problem of personal efficiency. His persistent and successful course of self-education, including his

BENJAMIN FRANKLIN

From a portrait by Duplessis in Boston Public Library

deliberate study of Addison for the acquisition of a prose style and his exercise in the use of the Socratic method to develop skill in debate, his systematic tabulation of the moral virtues, his adoption of a vegetarian diet, were all part of his general scheme to make of himself as powerful and smooth-running a human machine as nature and Ben Franklin could coöperate to upbuild. Of his two best-known works, the earlier, *Poor Richard's Almanac,* owed its popularity for the quarter century from 1732 to 1757 to the skill with which he preached these doctrines to an attentive public, filling all the odd spaces, as he records, with original epigrams, " chiefly such as inculcated industry and frugality, as the means of procuring wealth, and thereby securing virtue."

Franklin's " Autobiography."—His greatest book was, of course, his *Autobiography,* a piece of writing done at odd times between 1770 and 1783 at the urgent request of friends and relatives. The story is carried only up to 1757, in the thirty-three years after which most of his finest achievements took place. Its perfect frankness and simplicity, abounding energy, good sense, and humor must be experienced at first hand to be appreciated. The only excuse for lavishing critical praise upon it is that thereby some new readers may perhaps be converted to it.

Franklin's Doctrine of Common-Sense.—Franklin is the one American who, in the midst of the eighteenth century, most completely embodied the spirit of his age. Edwards had promised to rival him, but as he grew older he looked backward. Franklin's eye, to the day of his death, was turned toward the future of America. Edwards was passionately concerned with the affairs of the Kingdom of Heaven; Franklin was a tremendous citizen of this world. In religion he was, alas, on the verge of scepticism. He listened to the sermons of Whitefield, the evangelist, but while others were being stirred to their hearts' depths, he became lost in admiration of the preacher's voice and in mental computation of the number of individuals by whom he could be heard in the open air. Yet his doctrine of common-sense and clean morality made his sayings of *Richard* a sort of Bible which edified and influenced unnumbered thousands. In education, again, his efforts were ultimately for the good of the state. As an apostle of the arts and sciences, his work as printer, publisher, and founder of a library, a journal, and a college would alone place him among the foremost men of his day. All this appears in his own simple, personal story; but even here his community interest stands out in contrast to what one finds in the diaries and journals of the preceding century. For Franklin, unlike most of his predecessors, not only portrayed life, but also criticised it repeatedly and effectively, and while he was telling his own story, was telling very consciously the story of the entire group among whom his circumstances placed him.

IV. THE LITERATURE OF THE AMERICAN REVOLUTION

The Rights of the Governed.—As the century progressed, the interest of the Americans in themselves and their welfare came rapidly to a climax in their increasing jealousness for their own rights. This development offers one more evidence of the closeness of America to the influences which were actively working in England and on the Continent. Throughout the century in letters and philosophy the subject of the rights of the commoner was becoming more important. Gray, in his famous *Elegy in a Country Churchyard*, upheld the doctrine that the noble poor deserved their monuments no less than the noble rich. Goldsmith, in *The Deserted Village*, sang the praises of the upright peasant class, and Cowper and Crabbe in England, like Burns in Scotland, wrote for increasing bodies of readers always on the doctrine that all men were created free and equal. In the meantime, while this theme was steadily gaining ground in England, historians agree that in America the rights of the governed was a subject of accumulating importance for years and decades before the actual outbreak.

" Letters of an American Farmer."—Throughout most of these years, however, there was no talk of separation from the mother country. The question was rather whether King and Parliament might not be convinced that they were pursuing the wrong policy; and the discussion was based on the assumption that conditions as they existed in America were almost ideal. The best presentation of this point of view was made in the *Letters of an American Farmer*, a book of thirteen essays by a French Huguenot, John Hector St. John de Crèvecœur, who had come to America as a young man about the middle of the century. He settled in Pennsylvania, acquired and cultivated farm lands, brought up a family, and enjoyed to the full the contrast between the privileges of his later years and the hardships of his youth. The essays fall into three groups: those resulting from his travels up and down the Atlantic coast; the nature essays, the most heartfelt of which is on " The Pleasures of an American Farmer"; and his enthusiastic exposition of life in the New World as contained in the five successive chapters on " What is an American? " All that is desirable in life seemed to him to come from civic liberty and the ownership of land. A new society, uncrowded, free from cramping traditions, and offering to every man who desired it the chance to wrest a living from the soil, was in his eyes all that mortal could wish for. He looked, moreover, far ahead of his own generation, and saw in prospect that process going on which has made America the " melting-pot " of the nations. His genuine insight into the developing conditions of his adopted country was fortunately coupled with a simple, unaffected, spontaneous literary style. The combination makes Crèvecœur's *Letters of an American Farmer* one of the few real classics of Colonial times.

The War a Stimulus to Writing.—It was not until after Lexington and Concord that the Colonies as a whole were ready to admit that war was unavoidable; but when it came, instead of putting a stop to authorship, it actually furnished a new impulse for literary activity. In ordinary times of war there is little inclination and little ability shown for letters. But the present conflict was largely an intellectual revolt. Americans had not been down-trodden and oppressed; they were prosperous and, in a certain measure, content. Their struggle was against the possible loss of freedom rather than a fight to regain it. They felt that the Stamp Act, had they not forced its repeal, would have led to further encroachments on their freedom. They resented the tax on tea because they thought that the principle was wrong. So the uprising in America was as different from the Revolution in France as could be imagined. Naturally, as it grew out of a difference of opinion between two bodies of educated men, the use of force, postponed until the latest possible moment, was accompanied by a running fusillade of state papers, orations and addresses, political essays, satires, songs, and ballads. Throughout the war what was said from the provincial point of view was met by an almost equal volume of reply from the loyal supporters of the King in America. As time went on the Tories found it harder and harder to get their work printed and distributed, and they became the objects of increasingly rabid hatred and abuse; but the records, the best of which are their own writings, show that they were sincerely devoted to their principles and deserving of respectful admiration for the courage with which they defended a losing cause.

Thomas Paine.—The prose-writer whose works stand out from the great mass most clearly at this distance is Thomas Paine. Paine was a strange meteor in the political sky. He came to America in 1774, after half a lifetime of failures, armed with a letter from Benjamin Franklin. Going to Philadelphia, he " got into such company as would converse with him," as a disapproving Tory said quite truly, " and ran about picking up what information he could about our affairs." His first conclusions were strongly in favor of attempting that reconciliation which Burke advocated in Parliament as late as March, 1775; but by January of 1776 he had swung so strongly to the other side that he came out in print with his *Common Sense* as the first out-and-out advocate of separation between the mother country and the Colonies. The effect of this work by a " pilgrim and a stranger " was astounding. Within three months 120,000 copies had been sold, and whereas public opinion had up to this time been all against a final and complete rupture, by July 4th the turning of the tide was irrevocably recorded in the Declaration of Independence. Paine's later works, *The Crisis* during the war, and *The Rights of Man* and *The Age* *of Reason* after it, all show consummate journalistic skill in the handling of really abstruse themes in such concrete and reasonable style that his writings convinced even those whom they shocked. However, it is interesting to know that, though his name has come down to modern times as that of a pagan and heretic, most of his dangerous views have been absorbed into the orthodoxy of to-day.

John Trumbull.—Among the Revolutionary satirists two stood preëminent. First is John Trumbull, the leader of the " Hartford Wits." Fascinated by the eighteenth-century writers as a young man, he followed in the footsteps, first of Addison in the light essay, and then of Pope in verse satire. His best-known work is *M'Fingal,* named after the Tory leader in a New England town which is divided between Royalists and Provincials. The first part, which includes cantos one and two of the complete poem, turns him to ridicule in a town meeting where he is overthrown in argument and then roughly handled. The remaining two cantos, written six years after, picture him later in the same day mobbed, tarred, feathered, and left sticking to the liberty pole. He manages to release himself, but when, in the evening, he attempts to hold a meeting of his allies in his cellar, he is again routed and is fortunate, under cover of darkness, to escape with a whole skin to Boston. The subject-matter and the spirit of the satire is American, and full of the bitterness of partisan feeling. In form it shows Trumbull's debt to Butler's *Hudibras* and the satires of Churchill, as well as to the works of the leading English poets from Milton onward.

Philip Freneau.—Philip Freneau, Trumbull's companion satirist on the Colonial side, was a Princeton graduate of 1771. His verses, inspired by the war, were distributed along from 1775 to 1781 and roughly indicate the course of events. A group of poems were written and published in the autumn of 1775; two of them, *The Conquerors of America Shut Up in Boston* and *The Midnight Consultation,* were exultant outbursts after the Concord fight in April and the battle of Bunker Hill in June; the third, *Libera Nos, Domine,* an earnest prayer for escape from the horrors of a long trial at arms. Toward the middle of the war Freneau's confidence in ultimate victory for America found expression in *America Independent* (1778) and *George the Third, His Soliloquy for* 1779, in which the King is described as being pathetically despondent. The poet's cruel experience as a prisoner in a British ship impelled him to write his furious *British Prison Ship* before he was fully recovered from his experience there. Later, in 1780 or early in 1781, he contributed his last memorable satire in a mocking set of verses on *The Political Balance, or the Fates of Britain and America Compared.*

Aside from these purely occasional poems, Freneau wrote a considerable body of verse both before and after the war, in which his native ability is evident. His many experiences on the sea as traveller and ship's captain, and his observations of nature in the north and in the tropics, share honors with his short ballad poems of American history and tradition. Probably too much has been made of the fact that Scott and Campbell seem each to have borrowed one line from Freneau; it is much easier to show that the American was clearly dependent on the English eighteenth-century poets for the structure and versification of most of his works than to demonstrate that any of them were greatly in debt to him. A more evident claim for prestige may be based on the indisputable facts that Freneau, with the single exception of Anne Bradstreet, was the first American to write for its own sake poetry that will bear reading still, and that as between these two, both in quality and quantity of work, the New Jerseyan surpasses the New Englander.

Charles Brockden Brown.—There is still one man who belongs in a discussion of American letters of the eighteenth century—Charles Brockden Brown. He is a lonely figure, for his character and career separate him from all of the foregoing authors, without grouping him with the great New York pioneers who immediately follow. He was born before the Revolution, in 1771, and did his chief work just on the century border-line, but for the most part actually after 1800. Yet no trace of the great struggle of his boyhood days appears in his work, which is done in the spirit of cer-

tain minor English novelists. As the first American novelist
(as well as the first professional man of letters) he naturally
was open to English influence. The peculiar quality of the
man determined, moreover, the kind of English models
which were bound to influence him. He was a lover of
nature, and given to solitary meditations amidst romantically
gloomy surroundings. At the same time, while he was full
of pride in his country, he had a keen sense of the abuses in
human institutions which emphasized the difference between
what they were and what they were designed to be. In view
of this double liability to a somewhat sentimental treatment
of man and nature, he was a natural admirer of the " Gothic
romance " as developed by Horace Walpole, Mrs. Rad-
cliffe, " Monk " Lewis, and, most notably for him, William
Godwin. Of Godwin and his *Caleb Williams* Brown became an ardent admirer. To the modern sophisticated novel
reader it is hard to see just why. Godwin's political views
are better presented in his essays than in his fiction, and the
strongest features of his story are surpassed in Smollett's
Roderick Random. Caleb Williams was, however, popular
and timely, and congenial to Brown's taste; how congenial is
shown by the striking resemblances to it in his own work.
All his novels portray guiltless—depressingly guiltless—
heroes or heroines subjected to the hostilities of diabolically
powerful foes. The whole narrative is regularly enshrouded
in an atmosphere of mystery which is at last dissipated in
orthodox fashion by a scientific explanation. All have
deeds of darkness, sudden reactions, shiveringly prolonged
passages of suspense. The characters are all vague, the conversations unreal, the plots involved; but the descriptions of
nature, of mysteriously effective backgrounds, and of American life are very vivid, and the development of emotional
narrative is at times of the highest order. Brown precedes
Cooper in the use of American subject-matter, and Poe and
Hawthorne in his use of the mysterious and grotesque. Even
though none of them was consciously or appreciably affected
by his work, he still holds a well-earned place of preëminence
in this intermediate period in the history of American
literature.

most work after 1800

Concluding Summary.—To go back to the tests as to whether or no there was such a thing as American literature between 1600 and 1800, certain general conclusions can be drawn. There was a great mass of writing which portrayed the Colonial life and at times passed criticism upon it. As a result, the books of the period possess real vital quality, though, of course, in varied degrees. As there was not, in the modern sense, either a great reading public or a class of professional authors, there was not a general literary demand. This decreased the conscious attention of writers to the formal quality of their work, and when this did exist it was in evident reflection of the literary fashions of England. It must be remembered, however, that all these Colonial writings correspond in general to the primitive beginnings of other literatures. Considered in this light, they surely lose little by comparison.

REVIEW OUTLINE.—What is the reason for the striking points of contrast between the primitive beginnings of American literature and the early history of the English, French, or German literatures? In using the term "American Literature" for products preceding 1800, what tests may be applied to determine whether the writing is literature and what tests to establish its genuine American quality?

Certain broad statements may be made concerning the state of civic affairs in America in connection with the century marks. What are these? What material fit for literary treatment was presented during the early days of settlement? What three general motives of authorship, even in those days of distraction, can be enumerated? Mention two writings from the South and the chief characteristics in content and form. What fundamental difference existed in the character of the Northern settlers and the Southern? How does this account for the difference of their literary utterances? What general line of interest is shown in the writings of Ward, Morton, Williams, and the Mathers up to the time of the Salem witchcraft disturbance?

With the end of the century, what contrasting points of view are illustrated by Cotton Mather's "Magnalia," by Samuel Sewall in his Diary covering a half century, and the brief Journal of Mrs. Knight? Make a broad generalization as to the character of the seventeenth-century verse, keeping in mind the general tests laid down for the determination of American literature. Can you justify the introduction of " The Bay Psalm Book " and " The Day of Doom " in a literary history? What can be said of Mrs. Anne Bradstreet's poetry as to content, and as to poetic form?

What were the general habits of thought of the eighteenth century? In what respects do these become apparent in the difference between eighteenth- and seventeenth-century Colonial ideas? What were the chief facts of Jonathan Edwards's life? What was the promise of his youth and young manhood? What was the achievement of his later years? On the basis of Franklin's experience up to coming of age, why would one expect a different kind of literary output from that of Edwards? How does his worldliness show itself in his pursuit of personal efficiency? In his contributions to the life of his community as a literary man, educator, and statesman? What are his chief works? What are their qualities?

Does the approach of the Revolutionary War in America correspond to any intellectual development in the mother country during the years preceding 1775? What is the value of the " Letters of an American Farmer? What is the attitude of their writer toward the coming conflict? Is this representative of the Colonies as a whole? It is a remarkable fact that during the struggle the literary output should have been increased. Is there a reasonable explanation for this? What was the influence of Thomas Paine upon the public opinion of 1776 to 1783? How does his experience in this country illustrate the youth and impressionableness of the country? In what respects is the work of John Trumbull American and in what respects English? Is there an essential difference between the work of Freneau as a satirist of the Revolution and as a more spontaneous poet? For what does Charles Brockden Brown defy classification either with Revolutionary writers or with his immediate successors? By what minor influences in the history of English fiction was he influenced? Is there any comparison between him and the great American writers of romance who followed him?

Recall the tests applied to American literature at the beginning of the chapter and generalize on the basis of them concerning the nature of the writings during these two hundred years.

READING GUIDE.—The most useful general history of this entire period has been written by Moses Coit Tyler in two parts: a "History of American Literature During the Colonial Times" (Putnam), and the "Literary History of the American Revolution" (Putnam). The former of these is especially valuable, as it contains selections made from many authors who are difficult for modern readers to reach. The best collection of material for the whole range of American literature, but particularly for these first years, is Stedman and Hutchinson's "Library of American Literature," eleven volumes, the first three being devoted to this early period. A few good selections are contained in "American Prose," by G. R. Carpenter (Macmillan). Valuable historical background can be secured through the reading of selections about this period as presented in "Poems of American History," edited by B. E. Stevenson (Houghton, Mifflin). Valuable prose histories are numerous, but among the most readable are Alice Morse Earle's "The Sabbath in Puritan New England," "Home Life in Colonial Days," and "Customs and Manners in Puritan New England"; John Fiske's "Beginnings of New England" and "New France and New England"; Edward Eggleston's "The Beginners of a Nation" and "The Transit of Civilization"; Chamberlain's "Samuel Sewall, and the World He Lived In." Reprints are easy to obtain of Franklin's "Autobiography," and the "Letters of an American Farmer" have recently been republished.

Illustrative prose literature corresponding to the poems in American history includes Hawthorne's "The Scarlet Letter," Mary Johnson's "To Have and to Hold," Cooper's "The Spy" and "The Pilot," Mitchell's "Hugh Wynne," Ford's "Janice Meredith," and Churchill's "Richard Carvel."

CHAPTER II

NEW YORK AND THE KNICKERBOCKERS

I. INTRODUCTION

New York a New Literary Centre.—The two centuries from 1600 to 1800 completed a period of preparation without which the pioneers of the nineteenth century could not have done their work. As Irving and Cooper were growing up, a new nation was also first becoming aware of itself. All the scattered experiences of the separate colonies were being gathered into a general fund of tradition, and rival interests were slowly giving way to the impulse of a common national pride.

One result of this unifying process was that it was possible to develop a literary centre from which something representatively national could emanate. During the Revolutionary period and immediately thereafter Philadelphia served as such a centre. Under normal circumstances the national capital attracts to itself the authors and publishers; but Washington in the District of Columbia differs from London, Paris, or Berlin in being a compromise selection. The tide of life flows by it, and as a result other cities have enjoyed what might have been its privilege of being the chief home of American letters. The first town to do this was New York, birth-place of Irving and adopted city of Cooper and Bryant. On account of the changed conditions, the work of these men was destined to be of a different stamp from that of their predecessors. Before their day, American literature was characterized by a certain degree of vigor and given almost entirely to reproducing the life of the country in rough-and-ready fashion. In the pages of these early nineteenth-century writers the pictures of life are more complete;

the artistic finish of their work is far higher in degree. All of them felt a great patriotic pride in their country, now flourishing in independence, and all of them enjoyed what is quite necessary to a full and just appreciation of the home land—varied, repeated, and long-continued travel in foreign countries.

II. WASHINGTON IRVING (1783–1859)

Irving's Youth.—Washington Irving was born in New York, of Scotch and English parents, in 1783. With his ten brothers and sisters he was brought up in the narrow paths of strict Presbyterianism, and by a natural reaction grew up with an abnormally developed taste for frivolity. At sixteen his formal education, at which he had but faintly applied himself, was over, and his failure to make any head-way in law during the next five years enrolled him in the distinguished company who have developed by this route into eminent men of letters. At twenty-one, threatened with consumption, he was sent abroad by his family. He jaunted about through France and Italy, seeing people and enjoying them with boyish eagerness, and carefully abstaining from conscientious sightseeing. He had more than one adventure that was moderately exciting, and barely escaped from more than one promising romance. A journal which he kept in Paris for three weeks credits him with attendance on one lecture in botany and scores up seventeen theatrical performances. After nearly two years he returned to New York, a complete dandy and an accomplished idler.

But his training for twenty-three years had been by no means useless. He had seen many peoples and had attended perhaps more freely than he was aware to their manners and their morals. In a fashion more or less similar to that of his closest model, Oliver Goldsmith, he had knocked about the world most profitably. Now he was ready to produce something worth while, as he gave evidence in the *Salmagundi Papers* of 1806.

" Salmagundi Papers."—These were written in the main by Irving and J. K. Paulding, and enjoyed high popularity

WASHINGTON IRVING
From a painting by Charles Loring Elliott

for the year in which they ran. The young satirists blandly announced it as their purpose " to instruct the young, reform the old, correct the town, and castigate the age." They discoursed on the American political system from election methods to the proceedings of Congress. They touched up society for many of its short-comings, and even jovially burlesqued some of the prevailing literary fashions. The whole series was done in a mood of boyishly exuberant good-humor, and it was brought to a conclusion only by the whim of its irresponsible authors. Three years later the *Knickerbocker History of New York* appeared in the same general vein, but from 1809 on there was an increasing element of sober dignity in Irving's work.

" The Sketch Book."—It was during a seventeen years' absence from America that *The Sketch Book* appeared in London in 1819, after a long and unproductive period in which Irving had been dabbling more or less in business. This, his best-known work, though written and published in England, and for the most part on English subject-matter, was very evidently from the American point of view. As a visitor from a new country, he was fascinated by the dignity and stability of English life and by the stalwart healthiness of English traditions. But at the same time he realized the virtues of his own people keenly enough to write with honest indignation of those " British Writers on America," whom he accused of deliberately and short-sightedly provoking hostility between the two peoples. Moreover, two of his three short stories, epoch-making in their way—" Rip Van Winkle," " Sleepy Hollow," and " The Spectre Bridegroom "—are interesting not only in themselves, but because they put upon American soil foreign traditions that endured the transplanting and have flourished marvellously ever since.

Irving's Later Works.—His career was now marked out except for the work that he was to do as a writer of history. The early period of boyish exuberance was over; *The Sketch Book* was to be followed by *Bracebridge Hall*, *Wolfert's Roost*, *Tales of a Traveller*, and *The Alhambra*, all collections of the same general type; and besides these and several lesser books, he was to write three notable works as a historical biographer—the lives of Columbus, Goldsmith, and Washington. With his list of productions thus finely rounded out, he passed through an old age filled with honors, and died in 1859.

Irving's Point of View.—Throughout his work, from beginning to end, Irving's knowledge of the external world and his enjoyment of its oddities appear in his writings. He does not delve very deeply into life. In literary sympathy he belongs with certain English men of letters who lived from one to three generations before. In his earliest and most imitative work he is clearly indebted to Addison and Goldsmith for his style, and even for certain obvious devices in essay structure. And their point of view was his. Of the great spiritual problems which were absorbing men as Irving's life progressed, he showed no deep consciousness. It is perhaps enough to define him in this negative fashion. We might call him superficial; but later we should regret the word. In his way, which was the way of Hazlitt and Lamb and Goldsmith and Gay and Prior, and of many another man from the days of Addison to the days of Thackeray, Irving was doing what it fell naturally to his lot to do, in interpreting the externals of social life as they caught and held his attention.

III. JAMES FENIMORE COOPER (1789–1851)

Cooper's Early Life.—James Fenimore Cooper, who was born six years after Irving and died eight years before him, shared the honors with his contemporary, succeeding as eminently with the novel as Irving did with the essay. Like Irving, too, he passed through a long period of quite unconscious preparation for the life-work which was to make him famous, and like Irving he shows in his books not only his training at home but as well his experiences abroad. He was brought up at Cooperstown, N. Y., a town which, though only a few miles from Albany, was, in his boyhood, a simple frontier settlement. After some tutoring with a ne'er-do-well English clergyman in Albany, and two years in Yale, he left college with more abruptness than grace and undertook life on the sea, first on a merchantman and later in the American navy. When just of age, he resigned his commission to marry the daughter of a loyal supporter of George III. in the War of the Revolution.

Cooper's Best Romances.—It was not until he was past thirty years of age, a settled proprietor of the family estates at Cooperstown, and father of five daughters, that he turned his hand to writing. The story goes that his first novel, *Precaution*, a tale of English society life, was written as an expression of his discontent with a similar work of English authorship. It was of little value except to prove his ability. But when he wrote a war-story, *The Spy*, based on recent history and using much that his wife's family had lived through, his success was greater. Better still was his achievement in *The Pilot*, a tale which employed his own sea experiences placed against an historical background. And he worked the richest vein of all when he wrote *The Pioneers*, which was a development of his own frontier life that ultimately was expanded into the whole Leatherstocking series, *The Deerslayer*, *The Last of the Mohicans*, *The Pathfinder*, *The Pioneers*, and *The Prairie*.

Cooper's Social Satires.—If Cooper's productions were limited to the list here mentioned, the loss of all the others would not greatly affect his fame. Unfortunately for his own future peace of mind, however, he took a journey abroad of more than seven years which influenced his whole subsequent career as a literary man, and led him to the commission of two serious literary errors. The first of these was to write in essay style comments and criticisms on the ways of Americans, Englishmen, and Europeans. His judgments were many of them sound, but his manner of expressing them was offensive, for he did not have Irving's gift of serving up unpalatable truths with the piquant sauce of good-humor. As a result, though he wrote as a loyal American, he made many enemies and failed to accomplish his purpose.

A mistake which was yet more serious took place when he later attempted to show his disapproval of his countrymen's shortcomings in such novels " with a purpose " as *The Monikins*, *Homeward Bound*, and *Home as Found*. He had neither the natural ability nor the training to write fiction of this type. The consequence was—more enemies. Then, when he went a step farther to suggest how Old-World civilization might be improved by the adoption of certain New-World standards of thought and action, the reading public poured "contempt on all (his) pride."

General Estimate of Cooper.—Throughout his later career, nevertheless, he wrote from time to time the two sorts of romance on which his fame is rightly based: the sailor yarns and the tales of pioneer life. In these numerous stories of exciting bodily adventure Cooper committed the faults which are common to authors who write fast and abundantly. These have been most aggressively set forth by Mark Twain in an essay on Cooper's literary offences, in which he indicts the unfortunate novelist on twenty-eight different counts. Lowell, in his invaluable *Fable for Critics*, is rather more charitable. By all except the most enthusiastic it is agreed that Cooper was often careless in diction, in sentence management, and in the employment of the narrative machinery of plot structure and development. Most of his men, whatever their nation or race, are conventional, though no more conventional than the reader learns to expect in stories which are based on event rather than character. His women, it must be admitted, are "all sappy as maples and flat as a prairie." Yet, in spite of these defects, he shows fine creative power.

> "Don't suppose I would underrate Cooper's abilities.
> If I thought you'd do that I should feel very ill at ease;
> The men who have given to *one* character life
> And objective existence are not very rife;
> You may number them all, both prose writers and singers,
> Without overrunning the bounds of your fingers.
> And Natty won't go to oblivion quicker
> Than Adams the Parson, or Primrose the Vicar."

Cooper's leading male character, moreover, with his fine combination of shrewd sense and native poetry, whether he be Harvey Birch of war-times, Long Tom Coffin at sea, or Natty Bumppo on the frontier, is placed before a vivid background of nature and plunged into an exciting rapidity of action that well repays a great deal of wading through tedious introductions and unconvincing dialogues.

IV. WILLIAM CULLEN BRYANT (1794-1878)

Bryant's Boyhood.—William Cullen Bryant occupies the same position with reference to American poetry as Irving did with relation to the essay and Cooper to the novel. His long life, like theirs, was begun before 1800, and did not end till after the mid-century. In poetry he was the first to win a wide audience in America, and to secure recognition from abroad. He was born in a Massachusetts village in 1794. His father, a country doctor, was a public-spirited man, active in politics, adept in his profession, and among his friends known, furthermore, as a scholar. Bryant's boyhood is interesting because in the Berkshire hills he came to his first love of nature, and because while still in school he wrote and published his first verses. When his college experience came to an abrupt close through lack of funds, he went on with his reading, and pored eagerly over such of the English poets as he found in his father's library. Southey and Cowper were the greatest whom he first came to know, Wordsworth not falling into his hands until he was twenty. In 1811 he wrote his "Thanatopsis," though it was not till six years later that it was published in the *North American Review*.

Law and Journalism.—Until he was thirty-one years of age he gave himself up to the study and practice of law, swayed all the while by his feeling for pure poetry in contention with his desire to do contributive work as a citizen. It was a struggle between the "Hellenic" and the "Hebraic" elements in his nature, as Arnold has defined them. Finally, in 1825, he abandoned the law, went to New York, and by a fortunate turn of events found himself four years later editor of the New York *Evening Post*, a position which he held until his death. During the fifty-two years of his connection with this journal the character of his editorial writings gave it increasing dignity. He was alive to the problems of the day, and eager to do his part toward the moulding of public opinion. He was active in organization of the Republican party, a zealous supporter of Lincoln in the campaign of 1860, and as time went on an ardent advocate of emancipation. In his closing years, by his conspicuous and popular participation in public meetings of various sorts, he earned the title of "the old man eloquent." It was immediately after the delivery of an oration at the unveiling of a statue of Mazzini in Central Park that he fell, sustaining an injury which resulted in his death in June, 1878.

Bryant Not an " Occasional " Poet.—Seldom is there so emphatic a line between a man's daily life and his literary product as was drawn during the last half century of Bryant's career. His work as a journalist and his output as a poet were each admirable, yet they were almost totally separated. With Poe, Bryant held that poetry should be devoted to the pursuit of beauty. His conscious work as an intellectual leader he did from his editorial chair, even while in his capacity as an artist he cried out against "the vain low strife that makes men mad." In order to build for beauty alone by touching the emotional side of man, he avoided, except in rare instances, writing "occasional" poetry and devoted his pen to nature themes, whether in the broader aspects, as in "Thanatopsis," "A Winter Piece," "Autumn Woods," "A Forest Hymn," or on the more specific subjects—"The Yellow Violet," "To a Fringed Gentian," and "Robert of Lincoln."

The Puritan Survival in Bryant's Poetry.—Frequent though the comparisons are between Bryant and Wordsworth, the two poets stand in marked contrast in their attitudes toward God and nature. Wordsworth regarding the external world "in a wise passiveness" is uplifted in spirit, for nature to him is a symbol of the Creator—a vaguely abstract power. Bryant, starting from the same point, comes back to a personal God who rules His creatures by a series of conscious volitions, and to whom each individual is responsible. In his conception of death this same "Hebraic" point of view appears. Just as Bryant's nature is not complete in the power to uplift the soul to a height of spiritual calm, so death is not simply a profound abyss of despair. It is rather a symbol of the Divine Judge who has always inexorably ruled mankind.

Thus the old Puritanic conceptions "creep and intrude and climb" into a verse from which the poet theoretically banishes them. As he stands in bereavement by his father's grave, for example, he recognizes the wide chasm between his own stricken faith and the dogma to which he has given utterance in his "Hymn to Death," where he extols death as God's instrument for striking down the tyrant, the atheist, and the reveller. With difficulty he refrains from blotting out the verses of his inexperience. Again and again recurs the conflict between his inclination toward the worship of beauty and his inherited deference to traditional laws of conduct imposed from without.

"Thanatopsis."—The whole bulk of Bryant's work is slight, a fact which may account for its unusual evenness. Though "Thanatopsis" was composed at seventeen, it may be fairly chosen as representative. Richard H. Dana asserted on hearing it read: "No one on this side of the Atlantic is capable of writing such verse." It is a meditation on the transitoriness of human affairs as revealed by the "still voice" of nature. In the midst of eternity the poet stands for a brief moment on the shore of time and tries to look beyond. "Under the open sky" he makes a resolve. It is sublimely worded and conceived in poetic exaltation. He will so rule his life that when the end draws near he can approach his grave

> "Like one who wraps the drapery of his couch
> About him, and lies down to pleasant dreams."

Milton recorded the same determination upon coming to the age of twenty-three, Cotton Mather and Jonathan Edwards on each day of their lives. For it is the resolution of a Puritan poet.

The Form of Bryant's Verse.—In the form of his verse Bryant is more Wordsworthian than in his subject-matter. He employs various simple metrical schemes with uniform fluency and effectiveness. He abandons the heroic couplet and uses blank verse in almost all his more sustained and elevated poems. This, too, he handles freely, avoiding the end-stopped lines, and distributing his pauses at will. His wording is simple and, like Wordsworth's, free from the tiresome circumlocutions of the old-time "poetic diction." He takes adroit advantage of alliteration without allowing his effects to be offensively obvious. Seldom are his lines harsh or rough, almost invariably his phrases are discriminating, and as a rule his work shows the fine sense of a classical scholar whose closing diversion was found in the monumental labor of translating the Homeric stories.

The Decline of the Supremacy of New York.—Before the work of these three pioneers was completed, the literary supremacy of New York began to wane. The poetry of Bryant was cool, quiet, and dignified, and lacking "the one merit of kindling enthusiasm." No set of younger men undertook to write in the same vein. In the meanwhile Cooper was keeping alive a kind of story which but for him would have declined in popularity much earlier than it did; for the novel of adventure was giving way to the novel of character. Irving was the only one of the three who served in any degree as a leader for his literary generation. The *Knickerbocker Magazine*, founded in 1833, and the so-called "Knickerbocker School" of authors owe both their names and something of their spirit to Irving's famous character, Diedrich Knickerbocker.

Irving was a tempting but dangerous model for a group of nineteenth-century men to adopt. In the first place, he wrote in the spirit of a by-gone age; and, if this were not a sufficient obstacle, his success lay in a certain personal grace and charm of character which is seductive but almost impossible to imitate with success. Of those who tried it, some fell into sentimentalism and some into cheap affectation. The fruits of this school—or the worst of them—were collected into a variety of illustrated annual publications. For a few years there were scores of them with names as fantastic as those of the collections of Elizabethan lyrics— Love's Tokens, Friendship's Offerings, Gems, Garlands, Amulets. "Those steel-engraved beauties . . . that Highland Chieftain, that Young Buccaneer, that Bandit's Child . . . what kind of a world did they masquerade in? It was a needlework world, a world in which there was always moonlight on the lake, and twilight in the vale; where drooped the willow and bloomed the eglantine, and jessamine embowered the cot of the village maid; where the lark warbled in the heavens and the nightingale chaunted in the grove 'neath the mouldering ivy-mantled towers; . . . a world in which there were fairy isles, enchanted grottoes, peris, gondolas, and gazelles. All its pleasantly *rococo* landscape has vanished, brushed rudely away by realism and a 'sincere' art and an 'earnest' literature." With the gentle decline of New York, New England reassumed the literary supremacy.

REVIEW OUTLINE.—For what reason does it happen that the national capital of America is not a literary centre? As New York assumes preëminence, what characteristics are found in the writers of the nineteenth century who settled there? What sort of training for authorship did Irving secure up to the writing of his first satirical papers? What was the nature of these? By what broadly humorous work were they followed? Into what two chief classes can the contents of "The Sketch Book" be grouped? What subsequent works of the same sort followed? What were his contributions to the writing of history? To what English essayists who preceded and followed him may Irving be justly compared?

What preparation up to the time that Cooper was thirty years of age did he gain for writing stories of English social life, of the American Revolution, of life on the sea, of life on the frontier? Why did he depart from his successful romantic writing of fiction? What two attempts did he make in other lines? What are the most conspicuous defects in his stories of adventure, and what are the qualities which still make them read by readers of romance to-day?

What are the chief events in the life of William Cullen Bryant? How close a relationship can be established between his work as a journalist and his work as a poet after 1825? Cite the chief point of contrast between Bryant and Wordsworth in their attitude toward nature and the Creator. In what sense is Bryant a Puritan? What points in common does he share with Wordsworth in the form into which he threw his work?

Give reasons for the failure of these three New Yorkers to exert a lasting and significant influence on American literature during the middle of the nineteenth century.

READING GUIDE.—Selections from Irving should come first of all from "The Sketch Book," and include "The Author's Account of Himself," "Rip Van Winkle," "English Writers on America," "The Spectre Bridegroom," and "The Legend of Sleepy Hollow." A second group should include "The Boar's Head Tavern," "Westminster Abbey," and the five Christmas Sketches. The best specimens of his earlier and later styles are "The Salmagundi Papers" and the "Life of Goldsmith." Good one-volume biographies are C. D. Warner's (American Men of Letters series) and H. W. Boynton's (Riverside Biographical series).

The reading from Cooper must be limited in such a course. Before reading all the Leatherstocking series, it is highly advisable to read "The Spy" and "The Pilot" in order to see Cooper at his best in stories of military and nautical life. T. R. Lounsbury's life of Cooper (American Men of Letters series) has no close competitor. It is brief, readable, and complete.

The selections from Bryant's poetry should include "Thanatopsis," "To a Waterfowl," "Hymn to Death," "Monument Mountain," "The Poet." A further group should include "Green River," "To the Fringed Gentian," "Song of Marion's Men," "The Planting of the Apple-Tree," "Robert of Lincoln." Two good one-volume biographies are John Bigelow's (in American Men of Letters series) and W. A. Bradley's (in English Men of Letters series). Among the best critical essays are those by Churton Collins, in "The Poetry and Poets of America"; E. C. Stedman, in "Poets of America"; and Walt Whitman, in "Specimen Days," April 16, 1881.

CHAPTER III

A GROUP OF SPIRITUAL LEADERS

I. TRANSCENDENTALISM IN NEW ENGLAND

Definition of Transcendentalism.—During the second quarter of the nineteenth century there developed in New England a group of thinkers and writers the quality of whose work was wholly different from that of the leaders in American letters who preceded them. The passing of the influence of the great New York pioneers in essay, novel, and poetry has been accounted for in the last chapter. The time was therefore ripe for the rise of new and vigorous leaders in American life; and the men who were to assert themselves were being bred along the Massachusetts seaboard during those years in which Irving, Cooper, and Bryant were at their height. They are known as Transcendentalists because of their belief in "A system of philosophy founded on the assumption that there are certain great truths, not based on experience, not susceptible of proof, which transcend human life, and are perceived directly and intuitively by the human mind." They were, it is evident, a group of reactionaries against the hard common-sense which had dominated eighteenth-century philosophy and literature before the triumph of the Romantic Movement.

New England Hospitable to New Ideas.—New England was fertile ground for such a system of thinking as this. It had flourished in Germany during the later years of the eighteenth century and the opening of the nineteenth. Through constructive English thinkers it had been imported to England, such leaders as Wordsworth, Coleridge, and Carlyle performing the work of transmission. In part through their influence, though in part from other causes, it had taken root on this side of the Atlantic. Yet only in Massachusetts did it so far affect a considerable body of people and so far shape their conduct of life as to earn the title of "Transcendentalism" as a school of philosophy definitely located in time and place. There was a natural reason for this. Society in the New World was in a plastic state, free as no Old-World society was from the trammels of tradition. The country had passed recently through the wars of the Revolution and of 1812. It was no time for the smug adoption of self-satisfied orthodoxy in creed and conduct. Little was maintained simply because of its age. Religious theory in America had experienced great modifications; statehood was still much more of a possibility than an achieved fact. The condition of affairs was at once full of promise and full of danger; it was a period of delight for the mercurial temperament. In the most serious thinkers, however, was aroused the feeling of mingled distress, irritation, and alarm at the flightiness of the community mind. Sometimes they commented upon the situation in seriousness, but more often with a touch of humor. Says Emerson in one mood: "The reforms whose fame now fills the land with Temperance, Anti-slavery, Non-resistance, New-government, Equal-labor, fair and generous as each appears, are poor, bitter things prosecuted for themselves as an end." In another he writes whimsically to Carlyle: "Not a reading man but has a draft of a new community in his waistcoat pocket. I am gently mad myself."

The Inspiration to Self-Perfection.—In such a soil and in such an atmosphere Transcendentalism took root and flourished. What were the great truths which transcended human experience upon which the new school laid its foundations of belief? They believed, as one can see perhaps most easily in Emerson and Thoreau, in the creation as a great unity of which God is the centre, Man the noblest achievement, and Nature the physical symbol. In this great scheme the individual soul was to them the chief fact, and the chief duty was proper nurture of this soul. Each man, they believed, included within himself a spark of the divine. His task in life was therefore to do justice to his own nature by perfecting himself to discharge as best he could his duties in an earthly life. The escape from one kind of hereafter was an affair of little interest to him, the enjoyment of another kind a matter which could take care of itself. The greatest problem of man was how best to comport himself as a God-created individual in the community in which God had placed him. For guidance he looked into his own heart, and to nature, which was to him a symbol of the Most High.

II. RALPH WALDO EMERSON (1803–1882)

Emerson's Youth and Education.—Ralph Waldo Emerson, the high-priest of Transcendentalism, was born in Boston in 1803. He came of good blood, boasting among his ancestors on both sides a surprising number of the intellectual aristocrats of New England, the members of the professional class. As was to be expected, he went to the Boston Latin School and from there to Harvard. At college he was not a leader in social or intellectual activities. His acquaintances, even while they respected him, greatly deplored his apparent lack of masculine qualities. "He was so universally amiable and complying," wrote one of them, "that my evil spirit would sometimes instigate me to take advantage of his gentleness and forbearance; but nothing could disturb his equanimity." Between the time when he was graduated and the year in which he began studying for the ministry, he is remembered as a school-teacher by certain youths who regarded him with an almost awful respect. Unattracted by the possibilities of pedagogy, he resorted to the church, studying in the Harvard Divinity School and finally receiving his degree without examination by virtue of the fact that trouble with his eyes had prevented him from taking regular lecture notes.

Emerson as a Clergyman.—At the age of twenty-nine he unexpectedly found himself pastor of the leading church in Boston, and here, if he had chosen to remain in the rather easy path of orthodoxy marked out by the most liberal of churches, he might have continued in possession of a very comfortable ecclesiastical berth as long as he lived. But he was destined to "belong" to no church; he was moving toward a condition of absolute freedom of thought; and it

was therefore probably just an accident that the issue which
became a vital one happened to be the necessity for his ad-
ministering the sacrament of the Holy Communion to his
congregation. He believed that the formal rite was being
observed by a generation which did not feel its original
significance, and with this belief in mind preached a sermon
which concluded with these words: "I have no hostility to
this institution; I am only stating my want of sympathy with
it.   That is the end of my opposition to it, that I am not interested in it.   I am content to let it stand to the end of the
world if it please man and if it please Heaven.   And I shall
rejoice in all the good it produces."

Emerson's English Friends.—Soon after, as a natural consequence, his duties with the Second Church of Boston came
to an end, and he began his career anew.   His first step was
to go abroad, visiting in the course of his trip those centres
of European life which travellers all "do" on their first journey, but coming also into contact—and this was far more
important—with certain of the great English men of letters.
Landor and De Quincey he enjoyed; Wordsworth he revered;
and with Carlyle he entered into an acquaintance which developed into a life-long friendship.   Two years after his
resignation he moved to Concord, where he lived for nearly
all the half century which remained to him.

" Nature."—During his early years in the town appeared
in annual succession the most significant trio of essays he was
to write.   In 1836 was published a tiny volume under the
title *Nature*.   It was Emerson's second public appeal for
vigorous, thoughtful, individual independence.   The keynote is in the first paragraph: "Our age is reduced to the
sepulchre of the fathers; it writes biographies, histories, and
criticisms.   The foregoing generations beheld God and Nature face to face; we, through their eyes.   Why should not
we also enjoy an original relation to the Universe?"   He
tells of the delight he feels in the presence of God's creation,
and sees in it a source not merely of physical pleasure, but of
creative inspiration, and a motive for righteous living.   The
reception of the booklet was not promising, only a few copies
being sold in a considerable time.   Most of the American

From a Photograph, Copyright, by Elliott and Fry

RALPH WALDO EMERSON.

critics, moreover, were hostile. In contrast, Carlyle was emphatic in his commendation, and he lent it about to all his friends "that had a sense for such things," always receiving a similar verdict.

"**The American Scholar.**"—The matter of applause was of no great moment to Emerson, however, and he went on in 1837 to preach his gospel of independence to *The American Scholar*. This essay, perhaps the most completely organized of his productions, was read to the honorary scholarship society at Harvard. At the outset, as in the opening lines of *Nature*, he sounds the cry of freedom: "Our day of dependence, our long apprenticeship to the learning of other lands, draws to a close." Then he writes of the three great influences which surround the scholar—that of nature, that of the past, that of life. All of them demand that he have confidence in himself. "Let him not quit his belief that a pop-gun is a pop-gun, though the anointed and honorable of the earth affirm it to be the crack of doom."

The "Divinity School Address."—So inspiring was this appeal to his auditors that a year later he was reinvited to Cambridge, this time to speak to the students of the Divinity School. As in his address to the Phi Beta Kappa Society, he made a demand for honest freedom of opinion; but when he applied his principles to religion the conservatism which always jealously stands guard over it was shocked and horrified. It was indeed a new thing for a distinguished official speaker to bid a group of divinity students to cast behind them all conformity. Yet it was no more than Emerson had done with respect to every great problem that he had faced. His feeling was that he could trust his conclusions only when he had worked them out for himself, and this process he asked of all to whom he gave advice. Unconformity did not, therefore, mean to him disagreement with others, but rather freedom to agree or to differ with them as his honest judgment might dictate.

Emerson's work for the remainder of his life followed the lines marked out in these early essays. Whatever the subject on which he wrote, he was dealing with great fundamental ideas. He was seeking and finding his inspiration in nature, in books, and in the life about him. He was always conscious of his own noble duty as a subject of God, and was practising what he preached, the fullest development of his own powers. And he was perfecting himself as far as he might in order best to serve his fellows. No single passage better sums up Emerson's philosophy of life than this:

"Solitude is impracticable and society fatal. We must keep our head in one and our hands in the other. The conditions are met, if we keep our independence, yet do not lose our sympathy."

Emerson and the New England Lyceum.—The result of Emerson's withdrawal from the pulpit of the Second Church of Boston was simply that he continued to preach under secular auspices, exchanging the pulpit for lecture platform. The old New England Lyceum was a rare institution of which we can get only a partial conception to-day. With a perfect development of journalism, the enormous circulation of cheap and more or less improving magazines, the great number of low-priced books, the rise of the public-library system, and the social and literary extension of the school in the community, with the adoption of the summer assembly and the correspondence course by the best of our colleges and universities, we of the twentieth century enjoy opportunities which in Emerson's day were hardly dreamed of. Yet to-day there is no single medium for general culture which could rival the excellence of the old Lyceum. The speakers of the stamp of Emerson, Hawthorne, and Thoreau, of Theodore Parker and Holmes and Whittier, of Sumner, Webster, Phillips, are hard to be found except under extraordinary circumstances and before high-priced audiences. But men such as these members of the academic tribe were speaking all over New England to little audiences in little towns and for little pay, on the great subjects of the hour. The field was therefore ready for such a man as Emerson, and attentive or even devout audiences gathered for nearly a generation wherever he was announced to speak. It is to be anticipated that he sometimes must have spoken over their heads, and that from every lecture some must have gone away more edified than instructed. Yet even when the plain New England folk left his presence with a wistful desire that he had spoken more simply, the testimony of thousands remains that the sound of his voice was an inspiration, and his presence a benediction.

Emerson's Influence.—Lowell writes an essay in grateful tribute to Emerson's work as a lecturer, dwelling for the most part upon his personal effect on each hearer, in spite of a certain obscurity in his style. "To some of us that long past experience remains as the most marvellous and fruitful we have ever had. . . . Did they say he was disconnected? So were the stars that seemed larger to our eyes, still keen with that excitement, as we walked homeward with prouder stride over the creaking snow. . . . Were we enthusiasts? I hope and believe we were, and am thankful to the man who made us worth something for once in our lives. If asked what was left? what we carried home? we should not have been careful for an answer. It would have been quite enough if we had said that something beautiful had passed that way. Or we might have asked in return what one brought away from a symphony of Beethoven?" It is such passages as this—and there are scores of them in the literature of American biography and reminiscence—which prove beyond doubt the width and depth of Emerson's influence on modern thought. The number of his readers to-day is comparatively limited, just as was the number of intelligent hearers in his own lifetime; but then as now thinking people possessed themselves of his ideas and passed them on to the multitude. It is impossible exactly to measure his contribution to the preachers and teachers and poets of the twentieth century. There is slight danger of over-estimating it.

HENRY D. THOREAU (1817–1862) AND THE LESSER TRANSCENDENTALISTS

Thoreau's Life.—Of all the men who came under Emerson's spell, none has written with more freshness or originality than his townsman, Henry D. Thoreau. He was born at Concord in 1817; he received his degree from Harvard with the class of 1837. Returning to Concord, where Emerson was now established, he spent here the quarter century remaining to him before his death in 1862. He lived with the greatest simplicity, earning what he needed from manual labor, now in his father's business of pencil-making, or, again, in surveying or carpentering. Through his ability to do without things, and the ease with which he could satisfy his simple desires, he secured for himself leisure and contentment beyond the power of gold to buy. Like that other American of French lineage, Crèvecœur, he prized civic freedom extravagantly, but in contrast with the author of *The American Farmer* he felt that the possession of property was more of a curse than a blessing. "I see young men, my townsmen, whose misfortune it is to have inherited farms, houses, barns, cattle, and farming tools; for these are more easily acquired than got rid of." The most notable experience of Thoreau's life was his residence at Walden, a pond some two miles out from Concord. Here he built a house for himself at a cost of a little over twenty-eight dollars, and here he lived for something over two years, earning enough from labor and the sale of garden produce to meet his expenses of about four dollars a month. He wrote regularly during this period and after it, publishing two books during his life and contributing to several magazines. After his death some eight more volumes were edited and published by his literary executor.

 "Walden."—*Walden,* his chief work, contains in essence all that is to be found in his complete writings. The impressions gained from it naturally fall into two groups. Especially in the earlier part of the book Thoreau is rather impudently self-confident and ostentatiously hostile to society. He asserts boldly, often peevishly, sometimes vindictively, a large number of negations about human institutions and mankind in general: "Thank God, I can sit and I can stand without the aid of a furniture warehouse." "Men say, a stitch in time saves nine, so they take a thousand stitches to-day to save nine to-morrow." "Wherever a man goes, men will pursue him and paw him with their dirty institutions, and, if they can, constrain him to belong to their desperate odd-fellow society." He is not merely destructive, however, for he goes on to tell how he has solved the problems of food, clothing, fire, and shelter—his four economic necessities; and having presented his case, he urges that no one follow him in any respect except that of finding and pursuing his own way. It is this advice which saves Thoreau from a seeming inconsistency when in conclusion he says: "I left the woods for as good a reason as I went there. Perhaps it seemed to me that I had several more lives to live, and could not spare any more time for that one."

Thoreau's Feeling for Nature.—Thoreau's love of nature is a corollary to his dislike of society. He feels an "intimate knowledge and delight" in all the changes of the seasons as they show themselves in plant and animal life. Walden Pond in both summer and winter is a sort of shrine to him. Nothing about it is too minute for his attention. There is a wholesomeness about his scientific interest in growing things which serves as an antidote to the gushing generalities of sentimental "nature lovers." He had the keen eye of a trained observer and a ready pen to transcribe what he saw. But he had also the eye and pen of a poet, as frequent passages attest. These may be mere glimpses, as when he describes the pond bottom seen below the ice, where "a perennial waveless serenity reigns as in the amber twilight sky"; or they may be in sustained descriptions or anecdotes such as are to be found in chapters on "The Bean Field," "The Ponds," "Brute Neighbors," "Winter Visitors," and "Spring."

Thoreau and Emerson.—The inevitable comparison with Emerson reveals two things. Thoreau knew far more about external nature, and as a result was able to transmit his love of it to many whom Emerson failed to touch. *Walden* is the first great contribution to the modern library of nature literature. No one but John Burroughs, a disciple of Thoreau, has yet rivalled it. In his attitude toward men and society, however, Emerson shows his wider outlook and his better balance. Thoreau is often saucy where Emerson is serene; Mercury at the court of Jove. The older man, confident in his own sincerity, felt "charity towards all"; the younger was often irritated and querulous. Emerson's brilliant epigrams are too frequently offset by Thoreau's conscious cleverness. Yet to the wider public, and particularly to the inexperienced, his obviousness and his impertinence—actual defects—are attractively refreshing, and a reading of his pages acts as a sort of literary tonic.

Alcott and the Transcendental Club.—These were but two men of a group so important that between 1835 and 1840 they were dignified as the "Transcendental Club." They met informally from time to time, and without programme held discussions in philosophy and religion. One of the most celebrated was Amos Bronson Alcott, a strange dreamer whose life, in terms of practical success, was a chapter of failures at peddling, school-teaching, and lecturing. His *Orphic Sayings* and *Concord Days* are little read. It is hard to recall more than the ridiculous anecdotes of which he is the butt. Yet among a distinguished circle he was held in such high regard that he must be remembered, like Dr. Johnson, more for his friends than his books.

George Ripley and Brook Farm.—The Reverend George Ripley was another Transcendentalist whose voluminous writings have gone the way of all the earth, though his chief work, as organizer of the Brook Farm Association, holds a place for him in literary history. This "Institute of Agriculture and Education," established on a Boston suburban farm in 1841, was designed to be a self-sufficient community in which all should share in the industrial and intellectual life. For six years Brook Farm was a centre of interest to New England thinking people whether they disapproved, endorsed, or actually promoted the enterprise; but when, in 1846, the new and still uncompleted main building—the "phalanstery"—burned down, a death-blow was dealt to the project, and not long after the Association was dissolved.

Margaret Fuller and " The Dial."—One more evidence of the strength of the Transcendentalists may be found in *The Dial*, their literary organ, established under the editorship of Margaret Fuller. For four years it appeared as a quarterly, filled with essays on philosophy, art, music, literature, translations from the Oriental scriptures and from the German, and much good verse. Yet in spite of the stalwart support of Emerson, Thoreau, Lowell, Ellery Channing, and many others, there was not enough demand to keep it alive after 1844. It was joked at by the outer world and more or less criticised by the inner circle, some of whom thought it too timid and others too bold. To-day we look on it as an interesting monument to the enthusiasm of Emerson and his associates.

III. NATHANIEL HAWTHORNE (1804–1864)

Hawthorne's Boyhood and College Days.—Nathaniel Hawthorne represents in many ways the same current of thought expounded by Emerson and Thoreau. He was born in 1804 in Salem, Mass., and after the death of his father at sea while the son was still a little boy, lived among sober surroundings that must have affected his whole later life. His mother belonged to a generation which made it a practice to surrender to prolonged and ostentatious mourning at the loss of any loved one. The house in which he lived was thus overshadowed by grief, and he grew up in the midst of a domestic gloom from which he did not escape at all until he was fourteen. For a year he lived the normal life of a boy, out of doors in the country town of Raymond, Me. Then followed three more years in Salem before he went to Bowdoin College.

In Bowdoin he was a classmate of Henry Wadsworth Longfellow and an acquaintance of Franklin Pierce, later a President of the United States. His friendships were cordial, and he seems to have indulged in frivolities now and then, distinct enough even to incur college censure. It is significant that he lost his commencement appointment on the ground of his refusal to appear on the public platform. Yet on the whole, he appears to have been a normal, moderately industrious, wide-awake college boy.

The Period of Waiting.—His return to Salem, however, brought him back to the sombre surroundings of his boyhood, and in the midst of these he stayed for the next fourteen years, from 1825 to 1839. During all this time he was a lonely figure in the midst of his home town, seldom seeing his

NATHANIEL HAWTHORNE

neighbors and holding little intercourse even with members of his own family. The records show that he was writing diligently and persistently, and his journal and some of his shorter published stories and sketches give evidence, not only that he had the artistic gift at the time, but, further, that he was very definitely, almost systematically, gathering his strength for the great work still before him. Roughly, he may be described as writing anonymously or under various noms de plume for Peter Parley's *Tokens*, a kind of annual publication which was popular in his day, and for certain other periodicals, which paid little enough in the cases where they did not become bankrupt before his claims were settled. The best of this work appeared in the volume *Twice Told Tales* in 1837. His emotions and his non-success are elaborated in 1838 in "The Devil in Manuscript," and in a notable letter written to Longfellow, in both of which he shows clearly how hard he had been striving to get away from himself and into the world, and how almost impossible his long habits of solitude had made this.

Hawthorne in the Community.—Nevertheless, there are three attempts recorded, each one of which emphasizes the character of the man as he appears in his later works. The first was when, for two years, he held a position faithfully and well in the Boston Custom-House. At the outset he was overjoyed to become a real member of the community, but as the months went on his comments of discontent increased until he hailed with positive joy the political upheaval which caused him to lose his position. His next attempt to get into the world was as a member of the Brook Farm Association, of which he was one of the original stockholders. The experience of a few months showed that, at least for him, this attempted combination of the intellectual and material problems of life was not a success, and again he withdrew. The third was when, now married and the father of two children, he was given another Federal appointment, this time as head of the Custom-House in Salem, a task which proved as irksome to him as the earlier one in Boston.

Hawthorne's Final Success.—When, however, political intriguing resulted in his dismissal from this post, he became so embittered that it might have gone hard with him if now, at the age of forty-six, his real literary career had not begun. When he went home one day in the fall of 1849 to tell his wife that he had "left his official head behind him," she hailed the occasion as an opportunity for him to write "his book," and the book appeared as a result of her coöperation and the kindly encouragement of James T. Fields, under the title of *The Scarlet Letter*. His fame was now achieved. In the next year appeared *The House of the Seven Gables*. In 1852 *The Blithedale Romance*, and finally, after seven years abroad in the consular service—the third appointment which he owed to his college acquaintanceships—he published his last great work, *The Marble Faun*.

The Central Theme.—In all four of his great romances Hawthorne definitely dealt with that conflict between the individual and the group which his own experience had illustrated. One the one hand stands the individual, sensitive, full of emotion, keenly alive to the possible joys of life, instinctively independent. Whether it be the Hester of *The Scarlet Letter*, the Hepzibah and Clifford of *The House of the Seven Gables*, the Zenobia of *The Blithedale Romance*, the Donatello or the Hilda of *The Marble Faun*, this character persists in all of the stories, and in all of them recalls to mind something of Hawthorne's own experience. In opposition to this individual stands the great outer world embodied in the person of one rough, harsh, unsympathetic man.

"The Scarlet Letter."—In *The Scarlet Letter* the opposing forces are Hester, with her secret lover, Arthur Dimmesdale, and Roger Chillingworth, who in some measure stands for the world at large. The punishment to the two who have sinned is imposed on them by the machinery of the law, brutal in process and ineffective in results. Man's social way of dealing with sin, Hawthorne seems to say, fails because it does not touch the soul; and Hester, rising above the persecution of her neighbors, transforms the Scarlet Letter, intended as a symbol of her disgrace, "into a message of mercy to all who suffer."

"The House of the Seven Gables."—In *The House of the Seven Gables* the two branches of the Pyncheon family carry on the conflict. Hepzibah is a piece of faded gentility nursing a passionate love in the solitude of her thwarted life. Clifford, unattractive though he be in his weak sentimentality, is nevertheless a touching victim of society whom the law has mistaken and outraged and left ruined. Jaffrey Pyncheon, on the other hand, is the incarnation of that sort of unscrupulous shrewdness which is able to make its way through life under the guise of complacent respectability. There is no doubt about Hawthorne's sympathy with the weaker characters, or his indignant contempt for the opulent judge.

"The Blithedale Romance."—In *The Blithedale Romance*, again, these same two elements appear. The sensitive character in this case is Zenobia, who is set apart by her secret history and physical nature; and the embodiment of the outside world, the reformer Hollingsworth, who, in an apparently good cause (the elimination of certain evils in society), is as harsh and unsympathetic as the villains in *The Scarlet Letter* or *The House of the Seven Gables*. He is selfish, faithless to his associates, and willing to wreck them and their enterprise because it stands in his way and does not elicit his sympathy. *The Blithedale Romance* is an Emersonian protest against that type of man who loses sight of the good of society in his misdirected enthusiasm for some particular and often petty reform.

"The Marble Faun."—After *The Blithedale Romance* Hawthorne's first great burst of industry seems to have worn itself away. The man who, for forty-six years, had achieved only two small volumes of sketches and stories had in barely more than two years, encouraged by the late but sincere applause of the outer world, put out three times as much as in all his previous career and written in this number three of his greatest works. At this point, when in all probability his first vein was worked out, his old classmate, now President Franklin Pierce, was able to make him consul, first at Liverpool and later at Rome. More than seven years of literary inactivity followed, in all of which time Hawthorne was doing a dignified work thoroughly, well, and with no small degree of satisfaction to himself. Daily intercourse with foreigners and Americans abroad gave him a better acquaintance with that outer world which he had long and vainly yearned to know. In 1860 came out his final great book. If one were to theorize in advance about it the chances would be all in favor of its being closer to life, more intimately familiar with the ways of the world, and more genial and cosmopolitan in tone than his earlier writings. But the strange fact is that *The Marble Faun*, which developed out of his experience at Rome, while different in many ways from his first two romances, and while in one sense his most complete expression of life, is, nevertheless, more vague, mysterious, and remote than any of his previous works. It is the same old study of the individual and the community. But where he had "formerly set forth the history of sin in the heart, taking the evil for granted, and reflecting upon it as a thing given; he now looked backward and is engaged with the genesis of sin in a natural man, the coming of sin into the world of nature." Donatello plays the rôle occupied in the earlier stories by Zenobia and Hepzibah and Hester. Innocent and guileless at the start of the book, he is relentlessly drawn into the current of human affairs, until finally, stained and besmirched through his intercourse with other men, he becomes guilty of sin and aware of its consequences. Hawthorne attempted to account for the presence of evil in human life, and his conclusion is embodied in the experience of Donatello, who is made into a living soul as the result of his crime.

Hawthorne as a Spiritual Leader.—Throughout his works Hawthorne thus developed a philosophy which is quite his own, yet quite in harmony with the prevailing ideas of his day. He showed a high and abounding respect for the dignity of the individual man, and a conviction that each member of the community should be permitted to think his own thoughts and live his own life. In contrast to his contemporaries in the field of fiction, Dickens or Reade or Kingsley or even Trollope, Hawthorne displayed little interest in the handling of concrete social problems. The Present of Hawthorne is a picturesque background; the church, even in depraved form, furnishes him simply with an occasion for a suggestive revery. The approach of the

Civil War does not overshadow the pages of his fiction. With the concrete social reformer Hawthorne had nothing in common. Moreover, he is almost equally far away, although in a different fashion, from Thackeray and George Eliot and Meredith. Read his pages as you will, you will find little in the way of definite advice to individuals as to how to act under any given set of conditions. Hawthorne was a spiritual leader; to provoke action was not his task; but deeply conscious that the majority of people fail to think for themselves and fail to sympathize with those who do, Hawthorne attempted to lead people into a wider and more satisfied spiritual life. So, like Thoreau, Hawthorne looked upon society from his own point of view, and pleaded for individual freedom and individual courage. So, like Emerson, he recognized the double problem of living true to himself and performing his part in the midst of the social group. But to a greater extent than either of them, he had the artistic gift which made it possible for him to put into almost perfect literary form the essays, sketches, and stories which were the expressions of his deepest life.

REVIEW OUTLINE.—Summarize the reasons for the failure of any permanent schools of literature founded on the work of Irving, Cooper, and Bryant.

Define Transcendentalism. In what way was this philosophy evidently a reaction against the eighteenth-century habits of thought as developed by Benjamin Franklin in America? To what Englishman did Franklin correspond in his point of view? Give reasons for the fertility of New England soil for the sowing of such philosophy. What are the three fundamental elements in life in which the Transcendentalists believed? What is the relation between the three?

Give the chief facts in Emerson's career up to his return from his trip abroad. What were his three notable essays in 1836–1837 and 1838 and what was the common element in them all? Cite the passage in which Emerson reconciles his desire for solitude and his need of society. In what respect was the New England Lyceum through which Emerson addressed the public a notable institution in his day? In what lay his chief influence as a lecturer?

Thoreau was a disciple and follower of Emerson and yet was too individual to be a copy. In what respect did he differ in his attitude toward the life of the community? In what respect did he surpass Emerson in his feeling for and knowledge of nature?

What were some of the organized ways in which the Transcendental group gave evidence of their earnestness? Mention the relation of Amos Bronson Alcott to one of them, of George Ripley to another, and of Margaret Fuller to a third.

Mention the experiences of Hawthorne's boyhood, college days, and subsequent years after his return to Salem. What negative fact in his life did he first record and then struggle against? Mention his three successive attempts to overcome what he felt to be a defect in himself as a citizen. What fundamental fact in his previous experience appears in his great romances? Mention the first three of these in turn with brief analyses. What in general was the effect throughout his life of certain of the friendships which he made in college? What was the effect of these upon his life abroad from 1853 to 1860? What is there notable in the fact that his last great romance was not markedly different in fact and experience from those written before his years in Liverpool and Rome? In what respect is Hawthorne comparable with Emerson and Thoreau in their attitude toward individual freedom, and in their attitude toward organized reform?

READING GUIDE.—Readings from Emerson should include first of all "Nature," "The American Scholar," "The Divinity School Address," and "Society and Solitude." These may be supplemented by "Compensation," "Self-Reliance," "Friendship," and "Character," and by the following poems: "The River," "Written at Naples," "Written at Rome," "The Problem," "Fable," "Hamatreya," "Brahma." The best short biographies are E. W. Emerson's "Emerson in Concord" and George E. Woodberry's (English Men of Letters series). Among the good critical passages are C. F. Richardson's "American Literature," I, IX and II, V; E. C. Stedman's "Poets of America"; Whitman's "Specimen Days," April 16, 1881.

Readings from Thoreau should include the first fourth of "Walden," together with a few of the essays which make up the rest of the book.

Readings from Hawthorne should include from "Twice Told Tales," "The Great Carbuncle," "The Snow Image," "The Great Stone

Face "; from the four long romances, "The House of the Seven Gables." The best short biography is by George E. Woodberry (American Men of Letters series). Other good studies from his life are Rose Hawthorne Lathrop's "Memories of Hawthorne" and Bridge's "Recollections of Hawthorne."

For a study of the Concord group in general, the best books are O. B. Frothingham's "Transcendentalism in New England," H. C. Goddard's "Studies in New England Transcendentalism," and Lindsey Swift's "Brook Farm." Lowell's essays on "Thoreau" and on "Emerson the Lecturer" are sympathetic and interesting.

CHAPTER IV

THE POPULAR SPOKESMEN OF THE MID-CENTURY

I. INTRODUCTION

The Prophet versus The Spokesman.—As between the poet philosophers, often called the Concord group, and the popular spokesmen who centred more about Boston and Cambridge, there are certain points of clear contrast. The former concerned themselves almost exclusively with the nature and improvement of the individual; the latter were laboring with the nation as a whole, and attempting to uplift or reform its institutions. The New England prophets cried down existing evils and pointed to their certain consequences; the spokesmen looked for causes and did their best to remove them. A further distinction can be made with reference to the contrasted form of their messages. It is not the function of the prophet to please: his message is disturbing and almost certain to be unpopular. His cause is desperate, and his audience, if they listen at all, will listen only under protest. The prophet, therefore, speaks with high seriousness, and embellishes his discourse with parable and suggestive allusion. He challenges attention; he stimulates thought, and leaves his readers or his hearers to their own best devices, not applying the moral of what he has said or written. But the spokesman has a different task. He is attempting to move men to immediate action. He must be heard, he must be understood, and that at once. His work, therefore, has certain characteristics that appeal to the popular mind. In form it is symmetrical and familiar; in content easy to understand at a glance; the narrative scheme is frequently used, and in most cases the moral is definitely applied.

II. JOHN GREENLEAF WHITTIER (1807–1892)

Whittier a Practical Man.—The life of Whittier, like that of several others of the New England group, practically spanned the century. He was as near to the war of the Revolution in childhood as are the present generation of college students to the war of the Rebellion. He died while this same group of college students were in their kindergarten days. The briefest study of Whittier's life to one hitherto unacquainted with him is usually attended with a distinct experience of surprise. His picture, as it is commonly published, is that of a genial, gray-haired, elderly man, with a far-away expression and an almost deprecating poise of the head and turn of the lip. If he had been the poet simply of "Snow-Bound" and "The Barefoot Boy," we should feel that his look expounded his life, and satisfy ourselves by summing him up as a complacently contemplative Quaker, whose whole career was passed in placid rumination. But this was a part and only a lesser part of Whittier's activity. For he was a most eminently practical man.

Whittier's Education.—He was born of parents who lived respectably but perforce with such economy that they were not able to give their son a liberal schooling. Hence, in addition to his farm work, he learned to make shoes, and with his extra earnings gathered together a sum sufficient to carry him through six months at Haverhill Academy. The money for further education he earned by dispensing in district-school teaching the scanty knowledge that he had already gathered. From this he drifted into a kind of journalism, writing for *The Boston Philanthropist* and *The Haverhill Gazette*, and actually doing editorial work on *The New England Review* of Hartford. Thus early, by knocking about among people in town and country, and acquainting himself with men of all sorts of professions and prejudices, he prepared himself for a life of intellectual activity.

Whittier and the Abolition Movement.—In the course of his youthful experience he had become acquainted with William Lloyd Garrison, and largely through his influence he became more and more closely connected with the anti-slavery movement. He believed that the way to achieve reform was through legislation, and that political pressure could best be exerted through swaying public opinion. His convictions were strong; they were not unusual; but he was better able to express them than the majority, and through all the long years which preceded the war, and until its conclusion in 1865, he wrote from time to time spirited popular verses which carried thousands of readers with them. Five of these bits of verse may be cited to show the history of his relation to the abolition movement. First, "Expostulation," written in 1834; then "Massachusetts to Virginia," a clear protest against the enforcement of the fugitive slave law with reference to the case of Anthony Burns. Next, in "Ichabod," Whittier was the voice of the North speaking with hasty indignation at Webster's famous Seventh of March speech (1851), in which he seemed to have sold his loyalty to the North for the sake of strengthening his political future. Next, "Barbara Frietchie," a typical war-ballad, no better and no worse than many others. Last, that fine outburst of reverent praise, "Laus Deo," at the close of the war.

Whittier's Poems of New England.—At the same time that Whittier was writing in this vein, he was using his poetical powers even more ably in terms of many poems about New England life. They may roughly be classified as verses on the early history of New England, and poems on his own times. He loved to look back to the lives and achievements of his ancestors, and when he found incidents in history which combined picturesqueness of quality with that sturdiness of moral character with which the old settlers were blessed, he delighted, in such poems as "Abraham Davenport," "Cassandra Southwick," "The Wreck of Rivermouth," "The Garrison of Cape Ann," and "Skipper Ireson's Ride," to pay his tribute to them. In all these appear the sources of poetic popularity always to be found in favorite poems. These are short, clear stories couched in simple language and in more or less conventional verse, and capped with a moral which would be evident enough even if it were not printed in black on white.

Whittier's greatest poem, "Snow-Bound," falls in the remaining group—his poems of contemporary New England. It could stand alone out of all his poems as earning for the poet a permanent place in letters. With satisfaction and sympathy it upholds the noble and simple life of the peasant class. It is hardly too much to say that it deserves to be ranked with Gray's "Elegy," Goldsmith's "Deserted Village," and Burns's "Cotter's Saturday Night."

Whittier's " Puritan Pluck."—It has become a habit for the present generation, as it moves daily farther from the fixed traditions of early New England days, to think and speak of the old-time Puritans in a rather patronizing tone. It is the fashion to refer with impatience to what we term their antipathy to art, to speak superciliously of their austere manners and customs, and to flout as Puritan relics the survival of any traditions which are more than ordinarily conservative. It is well to remember that the "Puritan principle," though perhaps confined in its course to a path which to-day seems narrow, was coupled with indomitable "Puritan pluck." It is this combination which demands respect in the person of the Quaker-Puritan John Greenleaf Whittier. We recognize the truth of his self-criticism. He could not emulate

> "the old melodious lays—
> The songs of Spenser's golden days."

There does often appear in his verses

> "The rigor of a frozen clime.
> .   .   .   .
> The jarring words of one whose rhyme
> Beat often Labor's hurried time,
> Or Duty's rugged march through storm and strife."

But in the support of that noble and long unpopular cause to which he devoted himself, we recognize a courageous consecration as great as that of the martyrs of Lexington and Concord. Overcome with bodily weakness which compelled him to withdraw from the swift currents of active life, in his own way he accomplished more than many who were in the thick of that conflict. Rightly he cried out in his agony that God should "make the balance good."

> Oh power to do! Oh baffled will!
> Oh prayer and action! Ye are one.
> Who may not strive may yet fulfil
> The harder task of standing still
> And good but wished with God is done.

Then when it was given him to rejoice at the end of the conflict, and to live on to a noble old age, he was able in his "simple lays of homely toil" to show, as only a few poets have done, "The unsung beauty hid life's common things below." Whittier, in his best work, was a frankly "provincial" poet, and in this fact is the source of his strength. He loved the past and the present of his own people and the country that they lived in, no less than did Burns and Wordsworth.

III. JAMES RUSSELL LOWELL (1819–1891)

Lowell's Early Surroundings.—In James Russell Lowell the student finds the same practical qualities which belong to Whittier, the same inclination to think about the problems of the day, and the same ability to express himself on questions of the hour. Lowell seems, however, to have been drawn into active life in spite of his expressed and strongly recurring desire to devote himself to art. No one could have been brought up among more genuinely literary circumstances than was he. His early home was in a dignified old mansion in Cambridge, within sight of the Charles, surrounded by magnificent trees, the visible reminders of those rich memories which clustered about the estate. Born of cultured parents, accustomed from youth to their conversation and that of their friends, and given almost from babyhood to priceless hours in the large and well-appointed family library, he enjoyed an education which was calculated to endow him with a love for letters.

Lowell's Early Manhood.—In college he took his own time and picked his own path, achieving results hardly more notable than those of Emerson, and so conducting himself during the later months of his course that the university authorities were compelled to "rusticate" him for some weeks. During the years that immediately followed graduation, Lowell was uneasily seeking his as yet not chosen field. He enrolled himself in the distinguished army of literary men who signally failed at law. He restlessly surveyed the motley procession whom he passed in his daily walks. It was fortunate at this time that he fell in with a group of eager, congenial, and thoughtful companions of his own generation, who centred about him and drew out the best that was in him. One of these, Maria White, subsequently became his wife.

For a short while they endured the hardship of early matrimonial rigid economy until her father left them money and his provided them with a roof. Then in the years that immediately followed, culminating when Lowell was only twenty-six, he established himself as one of the popular spokesmen of America. He had passed through that period in which his main attempt was to dedicate himself to the expression of beauty. Aroused by the restlessness of the age, he looked about him in the social world, and in the stirring lines of the "Present Crisis" showed the vigorous moral sense which was to find utterance in a succession of poems extending over more than twenty years.

By 1848 he had come to his most productive year, publishing some two-score articles and poems in magazines and papers, and four volumes. In these volumes are expressed all sides of the character of Lowell that men remember. In the "Vision of Sir Launfal" he showed his literary upbringing, his love of beauty, and at the same time his strong moral bent. Verses which share honors with this poem, the "Biglow Papers," show his effort to influence public opinion by any effective legitimate means. The first of the two series came out in protest against the Mexican War, at the time when President Polk called for 50,000 volunteers, asking Massachusetts for 777 men. The papers were written in the Yankee dialect, a homely dress well calculated to set off their whimsical seriousness. They were the pretended product of Hosea Biglow, whose father, in the introduction (written in the same style), comments on him as follows: "Hosy he cum down stares full chizzle, hare on eend and cote tales flyin, and sot rite of to go reed his varses to Parson Wilbur bein he haint aney grate shows o' book larnin himself, bimeby he cum back and sed the parson wuz dreffle tickled with 'em as i hoop you will Be, and said they wuz True grit." So successful were these papers that a dozen years later, upon the outbreak of the war, a second series connected with the stirring events from 1860 to 1865 met with renewed and even increased popularity.

Lowell as Teacher and Diplomat.—To return, however, to 1848, the struggle in his nature was still going on, for soon after he writes to a friend: "Now I am going to try more wholly after beauty herself. Next, if I live, I shall try representing life as I find it. I find that reform cannot take up the whole of me." Yet in 1854 a new and dominant activity for a while took up the whole of him. For in that year he was called to Harvard to become the Smith Professor of modern languages and literature, occupying that distinguished chair which had been held before him by George Ticknor and Henry Wadsworth Longfellow, and which, after his death in 1891, remained empty until almost the present day.

Now are the three sides of his life developed—the apostle of the beautiful, the reformer, the teacher. To the end of his life he continued his activity in all three directions. And yet, long before the end of it, he was drawn out of the seclusion of the college yards and classrooms into the active service of his country, this time as a diplomat. In 1877 he was appointed as Minister to Spain, and was welcomed cordially there by those who could still remember the residence of Washington Irving in similar capacity many years earlier. In 1880 he was transferred to England, the most important of all our foreign posts. Here he did his work vigorously and effectively, and yet with such self-control and tact that he was described as "the most invited and the most inviting man in London," and credited as having found the Englishmen strangers but having "left them all cousins."

Lowell's Versatility.—In the roster of American men of letters, Lowell has earned the distinction of being the most talented and the most completely rounded of them all. His work in education and in the representation of his country abroad must, in such a history as this, be considered secondary to his achievements in literature; yet in letters alone his work is varied and variously successful. His poems of affairs seldom failed to meet a genuine response among the great body of American readers. His lyric poems were simple, sincere, and affecting, and in prose his letters, as edited by his friend and colleague, Charles Eliot Norton, are abounding in interest, while his literary essays are as substantial and discriminating as anything of their kind yet produced in this country.

IV. OLIVER WENDELL HOLMES (1809–1894)

Holmes's Uneventful Career.—Oliver Wendell Holmes may be said to be the last of the foremost New England writers who wielded a contemporary influence, or even wished to wield one. Like the great majority of the men of letters with whom we instinctively associate him, he was born almost within the shadow of the Massachusetts State House and was launched on the world a Harvard graduate. The story of his career is remarkably uneventful. After some study of medicine abroad and a short period of medical practice in Boston, he occupied a chair at Dartmouth College for a year, after which he returned to "the Hub" for the rest of his life, holding incidentally the Parkman Professorship of Anatomy at Harvard from 1847 to 1888. This long tenure of office was a natural expression of Mr. Holmes's character, which notably combined vigor and stability. His loyalty did not impel him during the war to go to the front, and yet he was a sincere patriot. His interest in men and things did not draw him into long sojourns in Europe in search of recreation or learning. His zeal for reform did not bring him into the movement which made it necessary for him to run up and down the land. Yet in the midst of one of our greatest and oldest cities and in a circle of distinguished friends, the like of whom America will not see again for generations, he not only held his own, but more often than not he made himself the central figure.

Holmes's Lighter Satires.—The reason for this lies in his combination of fine common-sense and spontaneous humor, the one leading him to seek the best in the circumstances among which he was placed, and the other helping him to interpret what he saw in a new and fresh and vivid way. Throughout his career his rationalism was evident in all he wrote and said. He was, on the whole, too keen to be sentimental, too observant to be deluded by meaningless doctrines, too individual to accede to any habitual line of conduct which did not commend itself to his judgment, and, withal, as a moral agent he was gifted with a genuine power of satire which made much of what he said widely influential as well as very amusing. Thus in his "Ballad of the Oysterman" he not only wrote an exceedingly silly bit of verse, but by writing it in the fashion of much popular verse of his day he turned it all to ridicule. So in the "Lines to His Aunt," his "dear, unmarried aunt," he was expressing the keenest of criticism upon the still popular, although improved, finishing school. Again, in "Contentment," he made, from the point of view of the luxury lover, a statement on the simple life which has as much truth in it from the metropolitan point of view as Thoreau's *Walden* has from that of the nature lover.

Holmes's "Occasional" Verse.—As a writer of occasional verse he was the indefatigable poet-laureate of the neighborhood. It was more the fashion forty years ago in Boston than it is in our own hurried day to celebrate events of minor interest. So year after year, when his own class reunited at the Harvard commencement, he versified for them. For the annual meetings of the Harvard Phi Beta Kappa Society he wrote more verses. When his friends left for Europe he sped the parting guests and in happy verse he welcomed them on their return. No poet of any celebrity could pass a birthday in his region without running the risk of a commemorative tribute from Holmes.

The Prose Essays.—If it were only for his verse, however, the place of Holmes in our literature would be but a slight one. He had the rather remarkable experience of turning, at the age of forty-eight, to a new form of expression and of continuing to use it successfully for over thirty years of the remainder of his long life. In 1857, when the *Atlantic Monthly* was founded, James Russell Lowell, upon assuming the editorship, stipulated as one of his conditions that Mr. Holmes should be secured as a regular contributor. Through the columns of the *Atlantic* there followed as a result the oracular utterances first of *The Autocrat of the Breakfast-Table*, then, two years later, of *The Professor at the Breakfast-Table*, then, in 1873, of *The Poet at the Breakfast-Table*, and finally, in 1890, of the old philosopher as he talked charmingly and genially *Over the Tea-Cups*. If these four books had been produced among people who had less to read, their popularity would have been even greater than it is now. We may compare them with *The Spectator*, with Goldsmith's *Citizen of the World*, with Johnson's *Rambler*, with Irving's *Salmagundi Papers*, and find in them the same critical sense and the same pleasant humor. They touch less than these other papers upon all sorts of subjects in connection with the externals of human life. They deal with real matters of conduct, but avoid subjects so profound as to confuse the ordinary reader. As a consequence, for thirty-three years they made their author at different times the public mentor of the community, counselling, warning, rebuking, deprecating, or even ridiculing, as the situation demanded. Holmes was not, as he is sometimes said to be, a merely accomplished dabbler in letters. Like the men about him, he felt the impulse to search for the truth and report it, and much of what the Autocrat and the Professor and the Poet said at the breakfast-table or over the tea-cups was distinctly in advance of his time.

V. HENRY WADSWORTH LONGFELLOW (1807–1882)

The Popularity of Longfellow.—Though Longfellow was an almost exact contemporary of the popular spokesmen just discussed, his interests were not identical with theirs, nor may he be classified with Emerson and the Concord group. Yet if he does not deserve the title "Spokesman," there is no American poet who has so widely earned the right to be called popular. Examination of the catalogues of the British Museum shows that in numbers of titles of works, editions, and articles by and about Longfellow he stands in the whole roster of nineteenth-century poets second only to Tennyson, and far in advance of his next rival. His works, in more than a hundred editions, have been translated into eighteen languages. They can be found in the book-stores of almost any English-speaking city, so constant is the demand for them; and in books of selections his poems are printed in such numbers as to indicate that editors and the reading public alike recognize the demand for his best-known verses.

Longfellow's Education.—He was born on February 27, 1807, of distinguished New England parentage, in Portland, Me. As his father was a trustee of Bowdoin College, Longfellow was sent there rather than to Harvard. Entering the class of 1825, as a sophomore, he became a classmate of Hawthorne. His career as a student was a little more promising than that of the novelist, for he was graduated third in his class, showing an ability to subject himself to routine work in spite of his appetite for miscellaneous reading. Before he had left the college campus the two chief features of his subsequent work as a poet had both been foreshadowed. One of these came in the shape of his commencement oration, which was upon the subject "Our Native Writers." For himself, he declares his purpose to speak as an American for America, and the utterance is interesting as compared with similar early declarations by Trumbull, Freneau, Bryant, and Whittier. The other promise for the future came in his skill as a student of the languages, which was so great that at the age of nineteen, when the trustees of Bowdoin had decided to establish a chair of modern languages, Longfellow was offered the position.

Longfellow's Two Lines of Interest.—To the acquisition of scholarship, then, and to training for authorship he set himself, grateful for the intervention of Providence which saved him from the irksome experience of going into the law. In

From a Photograph, Copyright, by London Stereoscopic Company

HENRY WADSWORTH LONGFELLOW

1826 he went abroad for three years of study, equipping himself before his return with a thorough knowledge of three languages and a reading acquaintance with several more. He was ultimately more or less a master of fourteen modern tongues. With all of this study, nevertheless, he had not lost sight of his original desire to be distinctly an American man of letters, and soon after his return he gave evidence of this in a vigorous essay on the "Function of the American Poet." The time for echoing foreign literatures was past; foreign subject-matter should no longer usurp the attention of the American writer. "To this effect it is not necessary that the warwhoop should ring in every line, and every page be rife with scalps, tomahawks and wampum. Shade of Tecumseh forbid! The whole secret lies in Sidney's maxim —'Look in thy heart and write'!"

His work as a teacher was far different from that of his successors to-day. The only other man of his kind was Professor George Ticknor, whom he was later to succeed at Harvard. There was no machinery for teaching, so that he had actually to prepare and publish his own text-books. As a consequence, he was almost submerged with the petty details connected with his pioneer professorship. After seven years so well had he succeeded, that upon the resignation of Professor Ticknor, Longfellow was called to the Smith Professorship at Harvard, the invitation being accompanied with the practical request that he again go abroad "for a year or eighteen months" for the purpose of a more perfect attainment of German. Settling in Cambridge in 1836, he found his work more attractive and less burdensome than in his earlier position. He was confined to teaching only three days in the week, and began to write, publishing *The Voices of the Night* in 1839, *The Spanish Student* in 1842, and *The Belfry of Bruges and Other Poems* in 1846.

In these works the two lines of interest in Longfellow seem evidently to have converged. He was still eager, as he had been while in college, "after future eminence in literature." He was a thorough and successful student and teacher of the modern languages. He was consciously an American citizen. A glance at the poems of the period shows his academic enthusiasm, as it led him to translate foreign poems, to imitate and paraphrase them, and to use material drawn from continental sources. "The Return of Spring," "The Beleaguered City," "Excelsior," and "Nuremberg" serve by way of illustration. His American poems of the same period may be drawn from local American themes, as in the case of "The Village Blacksmith," "The Arsenal at Springfield," and "The Bridge," or written as the result of his adopting Sidney's maxim and looking into his own heart, as illustrated by "The Light of Stars," "Footsteps of Angels," "The Rainy Day," "Mezzo Cammin." In each of these groups of poems there appears a mingling of spontaneous simplicity and somewhat conventionalized romantic feeling.

Longfellow's Long Poems on American Themes.—By the end of 1845 Longfellow started on a period which was to end with an emancipation from his college duties and a more complete devotion to the writing of essentially American poems. He was reverting frequently to the monotony of his college work, and frequently questioning whether he could dare to continue in the harness. "I am too restless for this. What should I be at fifty? A fat mill-horse, grinding round with blinkers on—this will not do. It is too much for one's daily bread when one can live on so little." Thus he wrote not long after going to Cambridge; yet he was but three years short of fifty when, in 1854, he withdrew from his professorship. In the meanwhile *Evangeline* had appeared in 1847; *Hiawatha* was completed in the following year; the *New England Tragedies* were written in 1856–1857, although not published for some time; *The Courtship of Miles Standish* in 1858. This short period saw the production of his great group of long poems and his finest development of themes drawn from the life of his own country. Too little attention is given to the fine *New England Tragedies*, "Governor Endicott," a drama based on the persecution of the Quakers in Boston, and "Giles Corey," a Salem witchcraft episode in dramatic form.

In spite of this great output of American material, Longfellow still drew on the fund of European literature and tradition. His greatest remaining work in this field consisted in the translation of Dante's *Divine Comedy*. But at the very end of his published works there appears significantly a collection of twenty poems in six groups, from the Spanish, the Swedish and Danish, the German, the Anglo-Saxon, the French and the Italian.

The Range of Longfellow's Subject-Matter.—In a general estimate of Longfellow and his work it must be admitted first in connection with his subject-matter that "He was inspired chiefly . . . by noble and beautiful records of facts long since dead and gone." Even when dealing with native themes the inclination to draw upon memories and imagery derived from foreign literatures is apparent. The image in "The Bridge" of the goblet falling into the sea is not unfamiliar to students of German lyric poetry. "The Slave's Dream" is told in a romantic spirit quite out of keeping with the supposed subject of the poem. In his use of material he shows as broad a range as Tennyson, although, with the exception of "The Masque of Pandora," there is exceedingly little which harks back beyond the Middle Ages. Of the more modern subject-matter much is presented in ballad form, the briefly presented significant event full of objective interest; much, as in the "Tales of the Wayside Inn," is in the fashion of one or another of the longer mediæval narrative forms such as are found in *The Canterbury Tales;* and much, notably the drama *Michael Angelo*, shows the magic influence of Italy and all the wealth of Renaissance art. He feels the same spell which successively overcame before him Shelley, Keats and Byron, Landor, the Rossettis, the Brownings, and many another. The American subject-matter should not be dismissed without reference to the simple poems drawn from homely contemporary life, such as "The Day is Done," "The Old Clock," "Children's Hour," and "The Hanging of the Crane."

Form of Longfellow's Poems.—As to the form of his poetry, it was mostly in narrative discourse and characterized by skilful general structure. Most notably it was simple, not so much in diction, for Longfellow sometimes used recondite words and conventional phrases, but simple in sentence structure and easily understandable in its allusions. His

lines are either short or, if long, are broken by distinct
pauses; his scansion is regular; his rhymes frequent and
unequivocal. Further than this he has contributed to common speech many memorable lines, for he is distinctly
quotable. His "Silently blossom the stars," his "She
seemed to feel a thrill of life along her keel," his "Footprints
on the sands of time," his "He looked the whole world in the
face," show his aptitude for pat felicity.

Longfellow, the Man.—As a man, Longfellow is eminently
sound and sane. Like Tennyson, he seems always to have
written as though "a staid matron had just left the room."
In general he was a man in whom a sense of the proprieties
was very well developed. He loved children and birds; he
believed in the family and the uninterrupted monotone of
happy domesticity; he had an unimpassioned respect for
patriotism. But in a larger way he upheld his belief in the
essential goodness of man. From "The Village Blacksmith" to "Giles Corey," and from "Giles Corey" to
"Michael Angelo," he was consistently defending mankind to
itself. And, last of all, he performed what Matthew Arnold
declared to be the function of culture: the task of "justify(ing)
the ways of God to man." He was a consistent, healthy, en-
couraging optimist, who doubted not that "through the ages
one unceasing purpose runs."

REVIEW OUTLINE.—Contrast the essential characteristics of the
popular spokesmen of the mid-century with those of such men as Emerson, Thoreau, and their followers. Give an outline of Whittier's life,
as it shows his practical nature in his ability to support himself as a
youth and in his hard sense as applied to the influencing of public
opinion. Tell how his attitude to the Abolition movement can be
traced in his lyric poems from 1834 to 1865. How does he show his
affection for New England traditions, as well as for the New England
of his own day? Were his comments on his own poetical power and
his physical strength true to the facts?

State the main facts in the life of James Russell Lowell. Show how
his attempt to find himself resulted in the struggle between the love
of the beautiful and his strong moral sense. See how this was carried on
in terms of "The Present Crisis," "The Biglow Papers," and "The Vision

of Sir Launfal" in different ways. How was his versatility further developed by his relationship with Harvard University? In what respects is it fair to say of him that he was the Elizabethan of the New
England nineteenth-century poets?

Why is the uneventfulness of the life of Oliver Wendell Holmes worth
commenting on in view of his work as a man of letters? Contrast his
experience with that of Addison, of Goldsmith, and of Irving, all of
whom developed into satirists, who were comparable to himself. What
various kinds of society verse did Holmes write which show in different
ways his relation to his town and his college? Notice the shift in his
literary activity when at the age of forty-eight he turned toward the
four books of prose essays which he was originally stimulated to write
by Lowell for the " Atlantic Monthly." What justice is there in the
common assertion that Holmes was an echo of the eighteenth century
in the substance and in the form of his works?

What concrete evidence exists that Longfellow enjoyed greater popularity than any other American poet? Give the main facts in his
life, particularly as these show the development of his enthusiasm for
scholarship and his ambition to become a man of letters. Why should
his mastery of various languages and literatures affect him when he
attempted to write native American verse? What evidences of this
exist in the poetry which he wrote up to 1845? Give the names of his
chief poems, drawn directly from American material. Do these show
that he followed Sydney's precept to look into his own heart and write?
Was his interest in America directed toward the social facts of his day
in any such way as that of Whittier, Lowell, and Holmes? Select any
of his most popular poems and test them to see whether there are present in them the common sources of popularity: familiar and symmetrical form, clearness of content, the narrative thread, and an applied
moral.

READING GUIDE.—Readings from Whittier should include in
the first group "Snow-Bound," "In School Days," "The Trailing Ar-
butus," "Skipper Ireson's Ride," "Cassandra Southwick," "Abram
Davenport." The second group should include his war-poems mentioned in the text. Good short lives of Whittier are by T. W. Higginson (English Men of Letters series) and George R. Carpenter (American Men of Letters series).

Readings from Lowell should include in the first group "The Present

Crisis," selections from "A Fable for Critics," "The Vision of Sir Launfal," and selections from "The Biglow Papers" (second series). The second group should include "She Came and Went," "The First Snow-Fall," "After the Burial," "The Harvard Commemoration Ode." From his prose, his essays on "New England Two Centuries Ago," "Cambridge Thirty Years Ago," "Emerson the Lecturer," and "Thoreau" have a double value as Lowell's work and as literary history. Good biographies are by H. E. Scudder and by Ferris Greenslet.

Readings from Holmes should include, from his verse: "Old Ironsides," "The Last Leaf," "Latter-Day Warnings," "The Chambered Nautilus," "The Deacon's Masterpiece, or The Wonderful 'One Hoss Shay'"; from his prose, chapters either from "The Autocrat of the Breakfast-Table" or from "Over the Tea-Cups." The best short life is by S. M. Crothers (announced in American Men of Letters series).

Readings from Longfellow should include "The Courtship of Miles Standish," "The Song of Hiawatha," "Evangeline," "A Psalm of Life," "The Village Blacksmith," "Excelsior," "The Bridge," "The Arrow and the Song," "Curfew," "The Building of the Ship," "Paul Revere's Ride," and others as time affords the opportunity. Two good one-volume biographies are by George R. Carpenter (Beacon Biographies) and by T. W. Higginson (American Men of Letters series).

Note: "The Chief American Poets," edited by Curtis Hidden Page, is the most useful single book for study of the poets in this chapter. Recommendations for reading are limited to the selections included therein, from the poets above as well as from Bryant, Emerson, Poe, Whitman, and Lanier.

CHAPTER V

POE, WHITMAN, AND THE SOUTHERN POETS

I. INTRODUCTION

Two Isolated Poets.—In the Old World Edgar Allan Poe
and Walt Whitman are considered by most critics to be the
greatest men of letters whom America has yet produced. By
their own countrymen they are not so generally applauded.
A possible explanation for this is suggested by the fact that
both of these men in a measure defy the "historical" method
of criticism, for neither was involved in ordinary community
life of the country after the fashion of the normal man of
letters. They belonged to no groups and represented no
social movements. Both of them, moreover, were victims of
a certain degree of unbalance as measured by the standard
adopted by Emerson. Poe kept his head too much in solitude and lost sight of the world; Whitman plunged his hands
so deep in society that he forfeited to some extent his sense
of perspective. Out of this a curious paradox arises, for
Poe, who lived in point of sympathy almost wholly apart from
the people, is steadily gaining in popularity; while Whitman,
who was deep in the stream of life and elected himself to be
the poet of democracy, has always been more talked about
than read.

II. EDGAR ALLAN POE (1809–1849)

Poe's Early Opportunities.—The parents of Edgar Allan
Poe were actors known as the "Virginia Comedians." He
was born in Boston, January 19, 1809, and within two years
was an orphan. The three children (for he had an older

brother and a younger sister) were adopted into Southern families, Mr. John Allan, of Richmond, Va., a prosperous merchant, becoming the foster-father of Edgar. The boy had the best of educational advantages, first in an English school from the age of six to eleven, then in two Richmond academies, and later in the University of Virginia, which he entered at the age of seventeen. Here he was brilliant but irregular, his creditable work in Latin and French not offsetting the gambling debts which caused his first separation from Mr. Allan. Two years in the army were concluded by an honorable discharge in 1829 and a reconciliation with his father; but his West Point experience, which came next, ended so disastrously that Mr. Allan at his death, three years later, left nothing to his foster-son.

Poe's Later Life.—The remainder of his life was a pathetic struggle to adjust himself to the ways of the world. He married his cousin, Virginia Clemm, in 1834, and was faithfully devoted to her till her death, thirteen years later. He became the literary editor of various magazines: *The Southern Literary Messenger*, 1835–1837; *The Gentleman's Magazine*, 1839–1840; *Graham's Magazine*, 1841–1843; *The Evening Mirror* (New York), 1844; *The Broadway Journal*, 1845. It was in these periodicals that the majority of his poems and stories appeared, but his income from them never removed him from the verge of poverty. After the loss of his wife, in 1847, he wrote less frequently. The distressing circumstances of his death in October, 1849, have never been fully explained.

The Testimony of N. P. Willis.—So persistent is the tradition that Poe was given to unrestrained self-indulgence that the characterization by Nathaniel Parker Willis, of the *Evening Mirror*, cannot be quoted too often: "With the highest admiration for his genius, and a willingness to let it atone for more than ordinary irregularity, we were led by common report to expect a very capricious attention to his duties. . . . Time went on, however, and he was invariably punctual and industrious. With his pale, beautiful, and intellectual face as a reminder of what genius was in him, it was impossible, of course, not to treat him always with deferential courtesy. . . . (He was) a quiet, patient, industrious, and most gentlemanly person, commanding the utmost respect and good feeling by his unvarying deportment and ability."

Poe's Choice of Subject-Matter.—Poe is not alone among artists in having developed and clearly expounded his theory as to choice of subject-matter and method of workmanship. No student of his works can afford to ignore two of his essays, "The Philosophy of Composition," published in *Graham's Magazine* in 1846, and "The Poetic Principle," delivered as a lecture almost on the eve of his death. Although the larger part of his work is in the form of short prose stories, these all contain what he declared to be the essentials of poetry. He divided the whole world of mind into the realms of pure intellect, the moral sense, and the field of taste, and choosing for his own part to deal only with beauty which "is the sole legitimate province of the poem." As in his opinion no piece of literature could achieve its full effect if it could not be read at one sitting, he almost invariably chose to treat of brief and unified conceptions. These dealt with beauty—or its opposite—and were usually tinged with grief, so that even when humor appeared, there seemed still to be underlying it a "pleasurable melancholy." As a rule, the stories in their progress subordinate the actual events to the feeling which accompanies them, or, at the most, make what visibly happens an almost incidental conclusion to a long and exciting train of emotional experience.

The tales are of many degrees of credibility. Among his detective stories "The Murders of the Rue Morgue," "The Purloined Letter," and "Thou Art the Man" appeal, as he planned, to the reader's sense of logic. Every step is defined, every deduction demonstrated. These are the acme of clearness—if they were not, they would fail as detective stories. Again, in such accounts as "The Gold Bug," although deliberately an air of mystery is maintained for a considerable time, the elucidation is all so careful that the reader follows without hesitation to the end. Taking a step farther, to the tales of horror and death, the same convincing quality remains. You cannot interpret in ordinary terms; you cannot conceive as possible in human experience such events as are narrated under the titles of "The Fall of the House of

Usher," "The Cask of Amontillado," "The Black Cat," "The Pit and the Pendulum," "The Tell-Tale Heart," "Morella," "Berenice," and yet, as you read, it is only by the utmost exertion that you can resist their compelling detail. Even in the only remaining kind of story, the accounts of marvellously, incredible adventure, the episodes and situations in "Hans Pfaall," "The Narrative of Arthur Gordon Pym," and "The MS. Found in a Bottle" are at once beyond belief and beyond doubt.

"The Fall of the House of Usher."—"The Fall of the House of Usher" is representative. The teller of the story recounts the experiences of a few short weeks which he spends in the "melancholy house of Usher," in response to an importunate request from its owner. Roderick Usher is living in the midst of the "irredeemable gloom" of his mouldering castle, a victim to strange and awful fears. Ghostly servants attend him. His only companion has been his dying sister, the Lady Madeline. During the last days of her life the despairing man seeks to divert himself with the solace of wild music, rhapsodic verse, and the reading with his guest of ancient and mysterious books. Finally comes her death and then her entombment in a castle vault, for a fortnight before her last burial. A week passes, when, in the midst of a violent storm, under the most awe-inspiring circumstances, the Lady Madeline reappears. "There was blood upon her white robes and the evidence of some bitter struggle upon every portion of her emaciated frame. For a moment she remained trembling and reeling to and fro upon the threshold; then, with a low, moaning cry, fell heavily inward upon the person of her brother, and in her violent and now final death-agonies bore him to the floor a corpse, and a victim to the terror he had anticipated." Horrified by what has occurred, the friend flees in fear from the mansion, but has hardly left it when, with a roar of mighty walls, the building crashes to earth and thus completes the fall of the House of Usher.

Poe's Methods of Story-Telling.—No one reading this with sceptical disbelief could be deceived into thinking that the events narrated ever actually took place, and yet the story is uncannily thrilling. If this effect upon the reader does not arise from the nature of the subject-matter, it must be traced to the methods by which the story is told. If one seeks for an explanation in these, the reasons for the vividness of interest are not hard to find. In the first place, Poe "staged" his stories with great care, making the backgrounds harmonize perfectly with the dominant mood of the narratives. He found that he could best keep the attention concentrated by putting his episodes in a closely circumscribed space within which no detail was beneath his concern. To the suggestive value of draperies, for example, and especially of moving draperies, Poe was keenly alive; and illustrations of the subtle value of color or the absence of color can be found on almost every page. With the scenery thus provided for, he accumulated interest during the course of the story by a variety of means. He was adroit in throwing the attention forward by skilful opening paragraphs; he employed ingenious catch words and apparently random suggestions which disturb the reader's peace of mind; he was so convincing in his elaboration of the concrete detail that the very material progress of the story becomes a matter of engrossing interest; and finally, he so felt the emotions he described that he contrived to involve the reader also, and to make him re-live the stories as he turns the pages.

The Limitation of Poe's Art.—Such a limited kind of subject-matter as that in Poe's stories reflects the limitation in his own experience, and suggests the intensity of his life within its narrow confines. He does not attempt to instruct, for he regards the intellect in connection with his art as a mere channel for the emotions. He does not attempt to reform; it was not for him to appeal to the moral sense. Neither of human institutions nor of human nature in its social aspect has he anything to say. Even in the realm of the emotions— the domain of taste—he upholds no ideal but the ideal ecstasy. He presents each individual passion as an end in itself. In spite of his own beautiful self-abnegation for the sake of his wife, he omits in his stories the devotion of self-sacrifice, or worship, or patriotism. Working in this field and by the most extraordinary means, he catches and holds the reader's attention, dealing with passions of love, hatred, revenge, physical fear, and varying degrees of madness. His works, in the effect which they produce upon the reader, are like those scenes in Shakespeare which introduce the ghostly and supernatural. In life and in letters Poe was a meteoric character, swift-moving, saturnine, keen of intellect, a "melodramatic creature of genius" who suggests many another man of letters but can be closely compared with none. In his own age he was miserably unrewarded, but to-day we see in these fantastic and often horrible stories works of art which, of their kind, are hardly to be surpassed.

III. WALT WHITMAN (1819–1892)

Whitman in Contrast with Poe.—As an American of tremendously marked individuality, Walt Whitman is often mentioned in the same breath with Poe. Yet in the two men there is much more to contrast than to compare. Whitman was the son of a farmer artisan, and was given no particular education. His travels were those of a wanderer and almost a vagrant. Where Poe was filled with the love of the beautiful, and was a deliberate and painstaking master of conventional technique, Whitman was absorbed in the lively contemplation of a great social idea. He was tumultuously infatuated with the life which he could not too intimately know, and in his treatment of this was regardless of conventional form. Again, by way of contrast, he was able always to take care of himself, and though in part he was disabled as a result of his work as a soldier-nurse in war time, he survived to a ripe old age and achieved a wide reputation, dying finally full of years in the arms of his friends.

Whitman's Training.—Whitman was born at Huntington, Long Island, in May, 1819. Although the family moved to Brooklyn when he was four years old, he remained a country boy in spirit, haunting the shores of the island winters and summers. His education was gained partly like Franklin's, in the printing-shop, and partly like Whittier's, in country-school teaching. Between the ages of twenty and thirty he was in and about what is now Greater New York, a printer, reporter,

WALT WHITMAN

and editor on daily papers, and contributor to at least one important magazine. In 1849 he extended his intimate acquaintance with American people by taking a leisurely trip down the Ohio and Mississippi rivers to New Orleans, and thence, after working awhile on the *Daily Crescent,* back to New York by way of the Great Lakes and southern Canada. He was now ready to do the work which made him famous.

" **Leaves of Grass.**"—In 1855 appeared the first edition of his *Leaves of Grass,* a tall, thin book, not issued by any publisher, but actually set up in type and printed by Whitman's own hands or under his direction. Its first reception was similar to that of Emerson's *Nature;* and just as Carlyle had supplied the only real piece of encouragement to the Concord essayist, so Emerson was almost alone in his greeting to the printer-poet. "I find it the most extraordinary piece of wit and wisdom that America has yet contributed. . . . I greet you at the beginning of a great career, which must have had a long foreground somewhere for such a start." Naturally enough, the other great original mind in Concord was similarly impressed. Says Thoreau in 1856: "That Walt Whitman . . . is the most interesting fact to me at present. I have just read his second edition . . . and it has done me more good than any reading for a long time." The edition of 1856 was double the size of the first. In 1860 it appeared once more, with an added group of poems on the friendship of men, "Calamus." The 1867 edition included "Drum Taps," his poems of the war. Six times more, under the same general title, the book appeared during Whitman's life, the last issues being in 1888, with "November Boughs" as the added section, and in 1891, when he printed his valedictory, "Good-bye, My Fancy." His noble experiences as a hospital nurse in Washington from 1863 to 1865 left him weakened by poisoning from a wound he had helped to dress. In 1873 came a stroke of paralysis; for the next nineteen years, till his death in 1892, he was an invalid.

Whitman's Form a Stumbling-Block.—The single poem of most importance in all Whitman is naturally the "Song of Myself." It is a long series of discursive observations on life, presented in fifty-two sections or chapters. Some of them are philosophical expositions; some are vivid pictures briefly drawn and unaccompanied by any comments; some are stirring anecdotes; some are tender and sympathetic nature poems; but many, and far too many, are rambling lists of people or places presented without any apparent coherence or system. When one reads a passage like the following the fatigue of the long inventory soon oppresses him, and yet the quoted part is a very small fraction of the almost interminable sentence:

"By the city's quadrangular houses—in log huts, camping with lum-
     bermen,
  Along the ruts of the turnpike, along the dry gulch and rivulet bed,
  Weeding my onion-patch or hoeing rows of carrots and parsnips,
     crossing savannas, trailing in forests,
  Prospecting, gold-digging, girdling the trees of a new purchase,
  Scorched ankle-deep by the hot sand, hauling my boat down the
     shallow river,
  Where the panther walks to and fro on a limb overhead, where the
     buck turns furiously at the hunter,
  Where the rattlesnake suns his flabby length on a rock, where the otter
     is feeding on fish,"

No discussion of Whitman is complete which does not take some account of his literary form. Though the current criticisms of him are for the most part widely extravagant, they have, of course, evident basis. There is no dodging the fact that he shows so little inclination to select or arrange his material that the impatient reader is tempted to interpret his long and frequent inventories or catalogues as the vagaries of a wildly unregulated mind. Nor may his diction be justified when measured by commonly accepted standards. He is given to the wanton use of words that are no words at all, or words from foreign tongues used for no good reason, and certainly for no American reason, such as "Habitan of the Alleghenies," to "effuse," to "promulge," "imperturbe," "Americanos," "comerados," "translatress," "oratress"; he calls himself "no dainty, dolce affetuoso" in the same poem in which he hails "Ma femme" and speaks "with reference to ensemble." The critic is tempted to assent when Whitman says: "I sound my barbaric yawp over the roofs of the world." Yet it may be readily demonstrated by any who will take the time, that instead of being formless he wrote in a style of his own; that his earliest work, instead of being haphazard, was a result of frequent and painstaking revision. In *Specimen Days* he writes: "I had great trouble in leaving out the stock 'poetical touches,' but I succeeded at last"; and in his *Rules for Composition* he expressed his desire for "a perfectly transparent, plate-glassy style, artless, with no ornaments, nor attempts at ornaments, for their own sake." Whether the result is poetry or not has been discussed at somewhat unprofitable length. It is much more important to discover what his writings mean and what kind of man they show him to be.

Whitman's Democracy.—He considered himself to be the poet and prophet of the American people. He was frankly infatuated with them. Certain attributes of his country and his countrymen seemed to him essentially American and the birthright of his nation. Without discriminating and without first knowledge of other lands, he said confidently that the best sort of nation was a new nation and that all old nations were abominable. So he cried up an ideal democracy which was quite irrational and actually non-existent in either the Old World or the New. The weakest point in the philosophy of Whitman seems to have been his extravagant enthusiasm over this conception of democracy which appears to deny the superiority of any man to any other man, a theory which is rendered void on its first application to daily life.

Whitman a Transcendentalist.—This deep absorption in the moral problems of life shows, however, that though he did not possess the balance of Emerson, he was for the most part in surprisingly close accord with the Concord sage. His poems are filled with references to the dignity of the individual man, and the necessity of his living freely in the light of his own judgment. Against tradition and custom he makes the same protests as do the Transcendentalists, and like them he finds in nature not only objects of beauty for passive contemplation, but also the visible handiwork of the Creator. The wonder of the simplest growing things in field and forest stir his heart. He sees the same law in them and in himself. So, when he hears in the cool night the honk of the wild gander,

> "The pert may suppose it meaningless, but I, listening close,
>   Find its purpose and place up there toward the wintry sky."

Whitman's work, though it has its eminent admirers, lacks the cardinal features which belong to widely popular literature. It is not simple and familiar in its external dress; it is not easily intelligible in content; it does not take advantage of that narrative form which is dear to the reading public. The enthusiasm of a few champions strives in vain to offset the neglect of the people at large.

IV. A GROUP OF SOUTHERN WRITERS

Sidney Lanier.—Sidney Lanier was a Georgian, born in 1842, of courtly and artistic lineage. Descended as he was from cavalier stock, he inherited a love of the beautiful which was by no means universal among the Northern descendants of Puritan blood. As a boy he was able to play many musical instruments; in school and college he was a natural student. After four years' service in the Confederate army he came out with wrecked health. For a while he taught, for a while practised law. During his last nine years he was engaged in a continual struggle for life and a livelihood, making Baltimore his home, but for his health's sake often retiring to the uplands. He was first flute in the Peabody Symphony Orchestra; he was the editor of four boys' versions of English classics; and from 1879 to his death in 1881 he was Lecturer on English Literature in Johns Hopkins University. A passage from one of his letters leaves a touching record of his toilsome aspiration as an artist: "I find within myself such entire yet humble confidences of possessing every single element of power to carry (all my ideas of art) out, save the little paltry sum of money that would suffice to keep us clothed and fed in the meantime. I do not understand this." Naturally this tragic element in his life begot a high seriousness in his work. He was convinced that he had a mission to perform—to do what he might to retard certain evil tendencies of his generation, and, as an artist, to promote holiness and beauty. On the broad reaches of nature he loves to repose: the blackness of a summer night in "Columbus"; the silence just before dawn in "Sunrise"; the expanse in "The Marshes of Glynn" are to him full of infinite suggestion and infinite sympathy. Though he does not often write what would be called religious poetry, he is as one with all men to whom nature is "a living garment of God," a symbol of the Most High. Two characteristics are most prominent in Lanier and his work: the first is his view of art as a moral force, and the success with which he combines his love of beauty and his love of truth with little apparent loss of either; the second is his mastery of poetic form as a pure artist. His fine sense of the possibilities of the poetic line, his appreciation of the connection between meaning and sound, and his almost complete control of various metrical schemes are productive of many exquisite passages.

Timrod and Hayne.—Two Charleston contemporaries, towns-fellows, and friends through life, next to Sidney Lanier, have made the most genuine contribution to the poetry of the South—Henry Timrod (1829–1876) and Paul Hamilton Hayne (1830–1886). Timrod's experiences as a boy and young man were very similar in some ways to those of Lanier. When he went to the front during the Civil War and was rejected from the ranks as unfit, he served as nurse in the army. There is a rich sensitiveness of personality which pervades his work. His is the work of a Southerner in its point of view, in its courtliness, in its somewhat naïve self-satisfaction, and also in its wealth of imagery and allusion. Most characteristic of his own country are two poems, "Ethnogenesis," a poem celebrating the birth of that new nation which secession was to bring into being, and "The Cotton Boll," a poem of the peculiar product of the South as it is suggestive of far more than its commercial value. Timrod writes much, however, which is only tacitly local in its quality, part of which is in his lyric poems of love, and part in his nature poems, which are full of the South in warmth, glow, and color, and of delight in the changes of the year, and references to bird, plant, flower, and tree. At his best, Timrod is frequently suggestive of certain passages in Dante Gabriel Rossetti.

Paul Hamilton Hayne, born a year later than Timrod, came of better parentage and was more robust in person, his education was less interrupted, his war experience more fortunate. A comparison between the two men comes back always directly or indirectly to the physical strength in Hayne with which Timrod was not endowed. Assuming that both are essentially Southern in character, in poetic imagery and allusion, in choice of subject-matter, and in point of view, certain contrasts present themselves. Hayne with his more abundant vigor is at times strident where Timrod is simply passionate. Hayne has a tendency to declaim his feelings, and so strong an inclination to make them known, that at times he appears to lash himself into a state of frenzy in order, as it were, to have something to talk about. Timrod shrinks sometimes from self-expression, because a thought once uttered ceases to be his own. Hayne's pleasure in self-revelation and in gaining an audience is revealed by the great volume of his work compared with that of his friend. In subject-matter this superior masculine robustness determines further contrast between Hayne and his townsman. In the first place, he lived long enough to see the reconstruction and reconciliation for which Timrod prayed and hoped until the time of his death; Hayne consequently celebrated what Timrod could only invoke. However, as he was given to the enjoyment of self-expression, Hayne tried his hand at poetic construction other than lyric. He composed a variety of legends derived from classical, later continental, and contemporary sources, and wrote a large number of poems in memory of Northern, Southern, and foreign distinguished men.

REVIEW OUTLINE.—Recalling Emerson's attempt to compromise the charms of solitude with the call of society, note in what respects both Whitman and Poe fail to keep that perfect balance which Emerson advocated and succeeded in maintaining. Give the main facts in Poe's life. What was the tribute of Nathaniel Parker Willis in contrast to the common estimate of Poe's character? Into what three divisions did Poe separate the world of mind, and to which did he elect to devote himself? What were his convictions as to the legitimate length of a poem, its subject-matter, and its dominant mood? In what sense should his stories be read with the same kind of attention which is demanded by poetry? In terms of the credibility of his stories, what general classes can be made? How does Poe secure the vividness of interest in his narrative, (a) in the setting of his stories, (b) in the methods of introduction, and (c) in the lyric or emotional quality? In what degree do his stories reveal the limitation of Poe's own experience in the life of the world?

Contrast in its main events the career of Whitman with that of Poe. What were the circumstances attending the reception of the first edition of " Leaves of Grass " ? In spite of these facts, what was the history of the successive editions up to the time of his death? What concessions have to be made in connection with Whitman's style in point of structure and diction? What defence can be made of it in spite of these damaging admissions? Whitman, in a measure, was a Transcendentalist. How does this show itself in his attitude toward the individual, toward the democratic life of the community, and toward external nature? Is there a reasonable explanation for Whitman's failure to secure a wide reading in spite of the fact that he aspired to be a poet of the people?

Since early Colonial days almost all American literature up to Civil War time emanated from the North; now a group of Southern poets appear. What is significant in the parentage and descent of Sidney Lanier? Give the main facts in his life. Note his combined desire to do a work at once as an artist and as a moral agent. With what success does he make this attempt?

The two Charleston poets, Timrod and Hayne, are more limited in their outlook than Lanier. In what respects is their work definitely Southern in its quality? How may the two be compared in point of vigor of physique and character, and in what evident respect is this contrast between them discoverable in their manner of writing and in the nature and variety of their production?

READING GUIDE.—Readings from Poe should include from his verse, "Lenore," "The Coliseum," "The Raven," "Ulalume," "Annabel Lee"; from his prose, "The Fall of the House of Usher," "The Gold Bug," "The Purloined Letter," "The Cask of Amontillado."

Good one-volume biographies are by George E. Woodberry (American Men of Letters series) and W. P. Trent (announced for English Men of Letters series).

Readings from Whitman should include "There Was a Child Went Forth," "Crossing Brooklyn Ferry," "Out of the Cradle Endlessly Rocking," "I Hear It Was Charged Against Me," "Mannahatta," "Myself and Mine," "A Broadway Pageant," "The Wound-Dresser," "Give Me the Splendid Silent Sun," "O Captain! my Captain!" "Ethiopia Saluting the Colors," and others as time permits. The best one-volume biographies are by Bliss Perry (Houghton, Mifflin) and by George R. Carpenter (English Men of Letters series).

Readings from Lanier should include "The Symphony," "The Marshes of Glynn," "Marsh Song—At Sunset," "Sunrise." The American Men of Letters series includes a good life by Edwin Mims.

NOTE: As in the preceding chapter, recommended readings from the three poets are for convenience limited to selections from the contents of C. H. Page's useful volume, "The Chief American Poets."

CHAPTER VI

AMERICAN FICTION SINCE 1860

The Rise of Realism.—In the foregoing pages three American masters of fiction have been mentioned who wrote for wider audiences and did what will probably be a more lasting work than any three to be mentioned in this chapter. These men, James Fenimore Cooper, Edgar Allan Poe, and Nathaniel Hawthorne, were all writers of romance who laid down their pens before the Civil War. With the new generation a new kind of fiction has come into vogue. Neither in choice of subject-matter nor in method of narration could this earlier trio be confused or identified with the leading story-tellers of the present day. It is perhaps more easy to feel this distinction than to define it; it is the difference between romance and realism. The former term has been expounded at length in connection with the great English poets and novelists of the opening nineteenth century; the latter is that kind of fiction which "does not shrink from the commonplace (although art dreads the commonplace) or from the unpleasant (although the aim of art is to give pleasure) in its effort to depict things as they are, life as it is." If this be a fair definition, it follows that the essential feature of realism is not so much the subject-matter as the way in which the subject-matter is presented; and that the most complete realist is he who has become most intimately familiar with a limited section of society.

Howells's Chosen Field.—William Dean Howells (1837–) is doubtless the man who would be most generally selected as the leader of the realistic school, both in workmanship and in resultant popularity. As in the case of Dickens, his experience in journalism, even before he had become of age, trained him as an observer and critic. Several years in the con-

466

sular service in Italy were followed by his appointment to the assistant editorship of the *Atlantic Monthly*. Since then his life has been wholly spent in two strongholds of Eastern conservatism—Boston and New York. It is a natural result that his stories develop the point of view of the fortunate and cultured members of metropolitan society. In many of his books he is content to indulge in a pleasantly realistic portrayal of these people. In this special field the life that he deals with is a life of infinitely minute distinctions: the man who departs from the norm even a fraction of a degree becomes interesting under the microscopic lens of his keen observation.

Howells's Command of Detail.—Thus, in the opening pages of *Silas Lapham*, the attention is called to a whole catalogue of social peccadilloes. As Bartley Hubbard enters the paint-manufacturer's office, Silas, without rising, gives him "his left hand for welcome," seals a letter and pounds it "with his great heavy fist," pushes the door to with a huge foot, and intersperses his conversation with little touches which show not actual vulgarity, but simply a lack of complete refinement in speech and manners. By innumerable little touches Silas Lapham is set apart from the group of Bostonians among whom he is trying to rise. Only in the hands of the most skilful could such a character be made interesting; but in Mr. Howells's hands the triumph is achieved.

Howells's Theory as to Plot.—It is not, however, only in the raw material of his craft that such a realist limits himself. As he constructs his novels, he writes in the belief that life cannot be separated into a series of stories which are wholly isolated from the events which precede and follow them. The writer of romance, starting from the traditional "once upon a time," lures the attention from point to point until he concludes with a wholly satisfactory "and so they lived happily ever after." To the realist this is much more pleasant than lifelike. Mr. Howells gives the impression sometimes of having told as much as he chose, and sometimes implies that a sequel to the story just completed might be more interesting than what he has related so far. Thus, on the concluding page of *April Hopes*, the reader finds himself in a position hardly less baffling than that with which Stockton ends his famous story, *The Lady or the Tiger*. Throughout the book two young people have been progressing toward the wedding with which it ends. The lover has been irresolute at times, at times elusive and almost dishonest; the bride has not been without hours of jealousy and distrust. As they roll away to the station after the wedding-reception a brief dialogue for the last time reminds the reader of these sources of danger; and when Mr. Howells concludes with "This was the beginning of their married life," the reader is by no means as content with the prospects of the future as the "happy-ever-after" formula would leave him. The reason for his dissatisfaction is to be found at the very root of realism in the theory that no story ever comes to a complete stopping-point.

Howells's Interest in Socialism.—Mr. Howells has not been content merely with making pen-portraits of interesting individuals, for a group of his most important works are significant as increasingly definite criticisms of society. Long before there was any such thing as a Socialist party, or even a Socialist movement in America, *A Hazard of New Fortunes* and *The World of Chance* revealed a keen interest in the difference between democracy as it might be and democracy as it exists in America. The appearance of *The Traveller from Altruria* and *The Eye of a Needle* showed that this was no passing interest, but that Mr. Howells was deliberately using his story-telling skill to encourage clear thinking on one of the great problems of his time. To-day scores of other writers are doing, or attempting to do, the same thing.

Henry James.—Henry James (1843–), a man slightly younger than W. D. Howells, is so severely realistic in his method that he has been the subject of much lively discussion. Mr. Howells has declared him the most distinguished author now writing English, and, naturally, Robert Louis Stevenson, as a champion of romance, assailed him with a fervor which verged on bitterness. An idea of the nature of his subject-matter can be gained from almost any of his books, for he has been consistent from *Daisy Miller* to *The Golden*

Bowl. His backgrounds are almost always intercontinental or European; his characters belong to the leisure class. His episodes, when there are any, are adventures of the mind; his most abundant source of excitement, duels of repartee. His narrative method is unmistakably his own. In his plots there is an absence of finality, though this is sometimes wrongly adduced as demonstrating that his stories lack structure. To be sure, his way is "startling when contrasted with the usual methods of solution by rewards and punishments, by crowned love, by fortune, by a broken leg or a sudden death." The usual demand of mankind—to be set at rest—is never met by one of the James novels. They end as episodes in life end, with the sense of life still going on. In detail his analytical habits of mind lead him to a refinement of accumulated detail which is interesting or fatiguing according to the temperament of the reader. As for his attitude toward life, he pays attention to little but the *beau monde*. It is not to be desired that he should take a trip into the slums or indulge in one digression on the masses *versus* the classes in each book, but the fact is worth noting that he never does those things. On the whole, there is a distinct absence of "problems" or discussion of human institutions. He restricts himself to a treatment of human nature in the narrow field of polite society.

The Realism of the West.—From the realism of metropolitan society to the romantic realism of the Far West, there is a long step. Just after the war time, Mark Twain and Bret Harte were both of them citizens of the Pacific coast. The society in which they found themselves was as ungoverned as the society of the frontier must always be. It was made up of a composite group of members in whom the only common feature was their restlessness. They were for the most part men who had failed to "get on" at home or who rebelled at "getting on" in the manner of a conventional society which restricted their goings in and comings out and limited their language to the yea and nay of the Sermon on the Mount. So they chose to try their fortunes anew in a freer atmosphere. Here all was yet to be done, and here the capacity to do was at a higher premium than the capacity to conform. The popular idea, however, that San Francisco was full of thugs and bandits is as false as that early Virginia was populated only by the off-scourings of London society. In both communities there were men of sound character and high ideals, and in the Californian community the opportunity to write of both good and bad, and the range of really romantic possibilities which a keen observer could find in an account of actual conditions, made an opening for something which is true realism though as far from the work of Howells and James as the East is from the West.

Bret Harte (1839–1902).—It is interesting and amusing to read Bret Harte's introductory statement concerning his first success, " The Luck of Roaring Camp." While the San Franciscans and the Californians were not discontented with existing conditions which prevailed among them, they had a lingering sense of the proprieties of the conventional East, and a keen distaste for the inevitable amusement which a true account of themselves was sure to stimulate. The first opposition to his story which Harte encountered was from a decorous young woman on the *Overland Monthly*, of which she was proofreader at the time. She could not be a partner to the publication of a story which mentioned with perfect frankness characters and events which are not discussed in the drawing-rooms of Beacon Street and Fifth Avenue. From her the contagion spread to the proprietors of the *Monthly*, and when, by somewhat heroic means, Harte succeeded in overruling them both, the publication of an account of the native heroism and devotion of a Western mining-camp was pounced upon by illustrious defenders of California as an outrage. The significant fact is that the first genuine endorsement of this scandalous production came from the magazine of all magazines which stands for New England conservatism—the *Atlantic Monthly*. As quickly as the slow methods of communication of a half century ago could reach the West, came a congratulatory letter from its publishers, offering what was then almost magnificent pay for as many stories of the same outrageous sort as the author would supply.

To draw near really

The point is, that the literary East recognized the literary quality of the tale, which is true and vivid even though it is shocking to the pride of the people of whom it is told. And so Harte went on. His first success was the tale of the regeneration of a whole camp through the uplifting effect of common respectability which it felt in the presence of a little foundling thrown into its midst. The second was the story of "The Outcasts of Poker Flat," in which the evil off-scourings of a tough frontier boom town showed themselves capable of sacrifice and heroism in a desperate struggle for life with a mountain blizzard. Full of exciting adventures as the strong stories of Harte are, romantic in nature as are the episodes, they are as real as the subjective adventures of New York and Boston life in their effort to portray things as they were and life as it was. In this vein, which necessitated the introduction of the unpleasant to as great a degree as the tales of Howells demanded the introduction of the common-place, Bret Harte did his best work.

Mark Twain.—Samuel Langhorne Clemens (1835–) began as Bret Harte did and with equal success, but, all in all, has done a much broader and more varied work. He was born in Missouri and brought up in Hannibal, a river-town. While a boy he learned the printer's trade, but was lured away from this by the fascination of life on the Mississippi, and for five years followed the profession of river-pilot. It is from one of the familiar calls of the boat's crew when sounding the depth of the channel that his nom de plume was drawn. His next experience was in a trip to the West and an unsuccessful attempt at mining. Next he drifted into journalism on the Pacific coast, and at last, in 1867, established his reputation with a book of humorous stories of which "The Jumping Frog" was the chief. The joy of this foolish yarn is not in the frog but in the character of the man who is supposed to tell about it. A real Western character tells the story in living tones.

Mark Twain's Personal Observations.—From this point on, Mark Twain's work falls roughly into two classes, of which the more important contains the books filled with his rambling observations on men and manners. Their titles indicate the subject-matter: *Life on the Mississippi, Roughing It, A Tramp Abroad, Innocents Abroad, Following the Equator.* They are largely autobiography of a very free-and-easy sort. On a rather tenuous narrative thread are strung descriptions, amusing episodes, essays in satire suggested thereby, and occasionally serious commentaries on the ways of the world. These books are uneven in quality, and quite without structure, if by structure is meant a plot. Yet the reader is lured on by the intrinsic interest of passage after passage. When he has once really started, even if occasionally the narrative does seem to flag, he is reluctant to stop, for fear of missing something good on the next page.

The Short Stories and Novels.—The other group includes his stories, long and short. The best of these are simply modifications of the personal anecdotes just mentioned. *Tom Sawyer* and *Huckleberry Finn* are annals of the kind of boy life through which the author himself had passed. *Pudd'nhead Wilson* was a little more mature member of the same generation. *The Gilded Age* (written in collaboration with Charles Dudley Warner) was a series of observations, as far as Mark Twain's contribution goes, on the Middle West in which he had grown up. They all deal with the unpolished life of a new and growing country, not shrinking from the unpleasant as they introduce the corner-loafer, the cheap promoter, the risky financier, and the unscrupulous politician. So keen and biting is their satire, not only on fallible human nature in general, but also on definite American conditions and institutions, that one might carelessly assume that the novelist was in despair about his country. The most aggressive portions of *Martin Chuzzlewit,* with which Dickens offended his American friends, are no harsher than many pages to be found in *The Gilded Age.* Yet, in truth, *A Connecticut Yankee in King Arthur's Court* and *Prince and Pauper* show that if there be any failing of judgment it is to be found in the overzealousness with which Mark Twain upholds democratic theory and turns to ridicule the romantic traditions of court and castle.

Characteristics of Mark Twain.—The element which chiefly marks his writings is his own buoyant individuality.

He is one of the great comic story-tellers. Although he has written on "How to Tell a Story," his own gift as he exercises it is an incommunicable thing. His eye is keen for "copy" as he goes through the world. He has the journalistic sense developed to an extraordinary degree, and this journalistic sense involves not only seeing things from an external and superficial point of view, but also interpreting them with firm, sure touch, and finally presenting the results in a simple, effective, intelligible style. Mark Twain is a critic as well as a jester; his contribution to American fiction comes from an application of his twofold powers to the presentation of the Western life of the mid-century.

Two Kinds of Realism.—An evident difference exists between the realism of Howells and James as contrasted with that of Bret Harte and Mark Twain. In the one case the Eastern writers restricted themselves to a portion of life which was separated from the rest by social lines, dealing for the most part with the well-to-do members of a conservative society, and for the most part excluding the harsh and common types. The Western writers limited their field of vision as well; but since they were dealing with little towns instead of great cities, they succeeded in their endeavor to portray the life of the whole community. Both "schools" have developed many writers and many good stories, but of the two kinds that after the fashion of Bret Harte and Mark Twain has become far the more popular both among writers and readers. There is no part of the country, North, South, East, or West, which has not of late been plentifully expounded in fiction. Every kind of town and every kind of citizen has come in for the attention of a delighted book and magazine-reading American public.

Aspects of Contemporary Fiction.—Nor is this all. Of late the country has been passing through a period of national self-consciousness, during which it has been absorbed not only in the way it looked but also in the way it was behaving. Questions of social conduct as they affected business, politics, the bar, the school, and the church have been in everybody's mind. The problems of how to hold in check the baser human instincts of selfishness and insincerity, and how to promote the feeling for business integrity and civic righteousness, have attracted the novelists as well as the legislators and preachers and teachers. It is natural that this should be so. The present literature of affairs owes its being to the awakened interest of the people in the vital questions of their own community life; and it is very interesting while it lasts. But literary history shows beyond peradventure that the most permanent kind of national literature is that which "deals with what is national and local in a way that is natural and universal." Much of what is written to-day could be understood in a hundred years only with the aid of footnotes and historical introductions. That of American fiction which has most of human nature in it, must outlive the part which is for the most part interesting merely because of its relation to current events.

REVIEW OUTLINE.—Note the fact that the three great American fiction writers who did their work before the Civil War were all writing in a different vein from the most popular story-tellers of the present generation. Define realism. In what field does William Dean Howells chiefly find his characters? What is his habit and point of view in connection with the conclusions of his stories? What is the distinction between the realism of character portrayal and the realism of social reform? Mention several books of Mr. Howells which fall into each of these classes. In what respects is the work of Henry James comparable to that of Mr. Howells? In what way does he carry the process of realism even farther? In what respect is his outlook upon life rather more limited?

What was the general character of Californian society in the years following the Civil War, and what unjust generalization is frequently made? How does the nature of the life out there give rise to a new kind of realistic story? What were the circumstances of Bret Harte's first success? What is the significance of the respective attitudes of the West and the East to his first story immediately after its appearance? What variety of Western experiences did Samuel L. Clemens have up to the time of his first famous story? In what books does he recount directly his own personal experiences. What story-books are less informal in structure and less personal in quality but still full of the

West in which he grew up? What books develop the attitude of an American toward the traditions of the Old World? Is Mark Twain's attitude in this respect representative of Americans as a whole? In what different ways did the Eastern novelists and the Western novelists limit the field of life from which they drew their material? Can it be said that one of these pairs has had more followers than the other?

What has been a strong tendency in the fiction of the last few years? Why is this tendency a natural one? Is fiction which deals with local and contemporary problems likely to achieve permanency? What is the test?

READING GUIDE.—A useful book for the general problems raised in this chapter is "A Study of Prose Fiction" by Bliss Perry (Houghton, Mifflin). The field is too broad and the time for extensive reading in a school course too limited, to make a detailed reading list of immediate value. Good representative stories of the four men specifically mentioned are "The Rise of Silas Lapham," by Howells; "The American," by Henry James; "Tom Sawyer," by S. L. Clemens (Mark Twain), and "The Luck of Roaring Camp," by Bret Harte.

INDEX

Robert Grant

Henry Dyke

...ild Carlton

Ella Wilcox

William Hathorn

Brander Mathews

Jane ...

Clara Gray ...

Eliza Sturgis Bethel Ward

Edith Horton.

Thomas Nelson Page

Winson Churchel

Gilbert Parker.

John Fiske

Maurice Thompson.